D1388697

Knowledge Representation

PJ 12 +13
слор 4
слор 3
слор 2 слоёности

Knowledge Representation

Arthur B. Markman
University of Texas at Austin

LEA LAWRENCE ERLBAUM ASSOCIATES, PUBLISHERS
1999 Mahwah, New Jersey   London

Lawrence Erlbaum Associates, Inc., Publishers
10 Industrial Avenue
Mahwah, NJ 07430

Cover design by Kathryn Houghtaling Lacey

Cover artwork, "Reptiles," by M.C. Escher.
©1998 Cordon Art B.V. - Baarn - Holland. All rights reserved.

Library of Congress Cataloging-in-Publication Data

Markman, Arthur B.
Knowledge representation / Arthur B. Markman.
     p.   cm.
Includes bibliographical references and indexes.
ISBN 0-8058-2440-5 (hardcover : alk. paper). —
     ISBN 0-8058-2441-3 (pbk. : alk. paper).
1. Mental representation. 2. Intellect. 3. Thought and thinking. 4. Cognitive science. I. Title.
BF316.6.M37   1998
153—dc21
                                98-19006
                                CIP

Books published by Lawrence Erlbaum Associates are printed on acid-free paper, and their bindings are chosen for strength and durability.

Printed in the United States of America
10 9 8 7 6 5 4 3 2 1

To Betsy

Contents

Preface

At first glance, calling this book *Knowledge Representation* seems to remove all suspense as to what it is about, but actually I think it heightens the tension. Cognitive scientists have seldom agreed about what knowledge representation is (or even whether there really are representations). Furthermore, many people have their own favorite way to think about knowledge representation and regard anyone who thinks otherwise with guarded skepticism.

As I wrote it, I thought of this book as a Michelin guide to knowledge representation. (I would call it a Fodor's guide, but there seems to be a Fodor who has had a few things to say about knowledge representation and who has apparently written his own guide.) The typical travel guide presents an overview of a city, country, or region. It defines boundaries, describes languages and currencies, and mentions museums, monuments, and other sights. The descriptions are never as rich as the sights themselves (or people would never travel). Invariably, there are suggestions of things to see that you would not have considered, and sights your mother's best friend said not to miss that are not even in the guidebook.

I hope that this book serves as a good guide as well. In chapter 1, I define representation and discuss some foundational issues. Then, in chapters 2 to 7, I discuss kinds of representations (akin to regions of a country), ways that people have thought about representations in the context of psychological, computational, or linguistic models. By organizing the book around types of representations, I have tried to bring together things that I think are deeply similar, although investigators may traditionally not have considered them to be similar. Chapters 8 and 9 focus on the role of specific content in representation, and chapter 10 draws some general conclusions about the uses of representation in cognitive models.

By design, I have written this book to accommodate people just entering the field (like the advanced undergraduates and graduate students in my classes on knowledge representation). That means that some approaches have been sketched to give the flavor of the representational scheme. I have tried to provide enough references to other sources of information for people who want to learn more about the topics covered here. Like a traveler, if you see something interesting, go there.

Any travel guide has biases. The authors of the *Let's Go* series are college undergraduates who place a premium on inexpensive places to eat and drink. Other guides that cater to wealthier clientele include a different list of culinary delights. I also have my biases. My own research has focused on similarity, analogy, and categorization, and this research focus has had two effects on this book. First, I have drawn many examples from work on similarity and analogy. Second, the work on similarity and analogy assumes structured relational representations. I have tried to be evenhanded in my approach to representation in this book, but some biases seep through from my own research. My deepest bias about knowledge representation is that there is *no single right way* to think about the topic. Different problems require different representational decisions. For this reason, I think it is important to be conversant with many different techniques of representation and to know their strengths and weaknesses. Thus, this book is also a bit like a field artillery guide: It provides information about the weapons available to attack various problems in cognitive science.

In an effort to draw parallels between models with similar sets of representational assumptions, I have sometimes ignored familiar distinctions that are made in cognitive science. Perhaps the most obvious of these concerns connectionist models. Readers may expect an entire chapter on connectionist models in a book on knowledge representation, but a glance at the contents shows that there is none. I have included at least a chapter's worth of material on connectionism in the book, but I present specific connectionist techniques along with other models that make similar representational assumptions. I describe distributed connectionist models along with spatial models of representation, parallel constraint satisfaction networks following a discussion of spreading activation, and techniques for role–argument binding in connectionist models in the chapter on structured representations. Although this approach is nonstandard, I think it ultimately provides a good indication of how these connectionist tools work.

For the past few years, I have taught a course in knowledge representation in which we have read articles about different types of knowledge representation and have talked about their strengths and weaknesses. We have also focused on how different representational assumptions bias the way people think about different psychological processes. If you are interested in using this book as a class text, I would recommend a similar approach. To facilitate class discussion, I have numbered all the examples throughout the book. The chapters of the book must be supplemented with readings that provide more details than I can include here.

As I said, I wrote this book with graduate students seeking an introduction to knowledge representation in mind. Because knowledge representation is a crucial topic for anyone who has an interest in cognitive science, however, I recommend the book to psychologists in general (except perhaps those whose names already appear in more than three of the references). I think the book is particularly useful for people in the cognitive science community outside psychology (such as those working in philosophy of mind or cognitive anthropology) who want to know how psychologists have thought about representation.

Finally, the preface of every academic book has an obligatory paragraph that tells readers how to read it. My recommendation is to read it straight through. I have tried to provide pointers from one chapter to another for discussions of related material, but I think the book reads better front to back. Readers with an intense need to skip around may start with chapter 1; chapters 5 to 7 should be read as a group in that order; chapter 8 should probably be read after chapters 2 to 7; chapter 10 makes the most sense if it is read last.

Bon voyage.

ACKNOWLEDGMENTS

Since I started studying cognition, I have had the good fortune to be in contact with people who have had an abiding interest in knowledge representation. Foremost on the list is Dedre Gentner, who was once my graduate advisor and is now a colleague and friend. I based my knowledge representation course on hers, and the rest followed from there. Ken Forbus was also an important influence. His guidance in thinking about the computational aspects of analogy have been invaluable. Finally, I would be remiss to leave out Jim Anderson and Doug Medin, who were also role models in my formative years.

Over the past few years, I have also had the benefit of knowing many extremely bright colleagues, friends, and students who have been willing to talk about representation for hours, among them Larry Barsalou, Curt Burgess, Rob Goldstone, Tory Higgins, Robert Hoffman, Keith Holyoak, John Hummel, Mark Keane, Bob Krauss, Patricia Lindemann, Valerie Makin, Gary Marcus, Tomislav Pavlicic, Robert Remez, Brian Ross, Michael Schober, Colleen Seifert, Yung-Cheng Shen, Bobbie Spellman, Ed Wisniewski, Takashi Yamauchi, and Shi Zhang. Thanks also to the students in my knowledge representation classes, whose ideas have contributed to this book in ways known and unknown. Special thanks to Frank Riebli, who read drafts of some chapters in their early form.

I want to acknowledge the help of Eric Dietrich for many discussions about representation and for letting me steal from our joint paper for chapter 10. Thanks also to Terry Regier for answering some questions about prepositions. Philip Johnson-Laird provided thorough and thoroughly useful comments on the manuscript, and was also kind enough to supply me with a copy of a computer program that generates spatial mental models. Gregory Murphy also gave me extensive feedback and an ink-filled manuscript. His thoughts greatly improved the clarity of the arguments here. David Krantz was a great help, particularly in walking me through the intricacies of measurement theory. Thanks also to David Leake, who sent me a copy of microSWALE to play with.

I'd like to thank Judi Amsel for encouraging me to write this book after I mentioned the idea to her at Psychonomics in Los Angeles. Thanks also go to Barbara Wieghaus, who kept the process of book production moving along on schedule.

During the time that this book was being written, my research was generously supported by National Science Foundation CAREER Award SBR-95-10924.

Finally, I want to thank my wife Betsy for putting up with my work hours and for willingly sharing the life and times of an assistant professor without going crazy. Because she has been a constant source of support as well as a great mother to our son Lucas, this book is dedicated to her.

—Arthur B. Markman

Foundations

In the study of the mind, cognitive scientists seek explanations of mental life, which consists of perceptions, emotions, social interactions, and cognitive abilities. In many of these explanations, they refer to goals, beliefs, mental images, concepts, and other mental entities. They are also concerned with retrieval, analogy, inferencing, reasoning, categorization, and many other processes that create, combine, and use the information "in our heads." The aim of this book is to consider ways of thinking about goals, beliefs, mental images, concepts, and other mental entities to understand how different decisions about the way to characterize these entities affects what is easy to do with them and what is hard to do with them.

In particular, this book is concerned with the question of mental representation. That is, what formats are used for the information that makes up mental life (and how is the information used)? In this book, I explore a variety of options for representing information and focus mainly on the assumptions made by different representational formats and on the ways these assumptions affect what is easy or hard to do with them. Before the discussion can proceed, however, several preliminary issues must be dealt with. First, what is a representation? Second, why worry about the nature of mental representations? Finally, how do representations fit into the study of cognition? Chapter 1 addresses these topics.

AN EXAMPLE

The issue of mental representation may seem uninteresting. Perhaps there are not many options for representing a situation, or the choice of representation may be irrelevant to what a model of mental processing can explain. Even if there are differences between models, these differences may have no practical significance for the way psychology is carried out as a science. In this section, I present an example demonstrating that there are often many different ways that something can be represented, that differences in representations do affect the explanatory capability of a model, and that the choice of representations has important implications for how psychology is done.

My example comes from the study of people's ability to do logical reasoning. The prototypical version of the task was presented by Wason and Johnson-Laird (1972) and has become known as the Wason selection task. In this task, researchers show people four cards on a table and tell them that all the cards have a letter on one side and a number on the other. The four cards are laid out so that they face the subject as shown in Figure 1.1. Then, the subject is asked to point to the smallest number of cards necessary to test the truth of the rule "If there is a vowel on one side of the card, then there is an odd number on the other side of the card."

Countless researchers (Johnson-Laird, 1983; Rips, 1994) have examined variations of this task. When the problem is framed as presented in Figure 1.1, people often have difficulty getting the right answer. Most people will say that the card with the letter *A* must be turned over. Few people think that they have to turn over the card with the letter *J*. People are split on what to do with the numbers. Some think that both numbers can be ignored, some feel the *seven* must be turned over, some feel the *four* must be turned over, and some feel that both cards must be turned over. The correct answer is that the *A* and the *four* must be turned over: If there is an even number on the other side of the *A* card, the rule is invalid, and if there is a vowel on the other side of the *four* card, the rule is invalid. The *J* need not be turned over; the rule does not apply to it, and it does not matter what is on the other side. The *seven* need not be turned over;

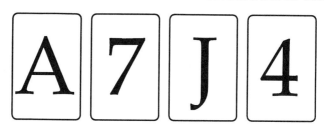

FIG. 1.1. Wason selection task.

if there is a vowel on the other side, the rule applies and is valid, but if there is a consonant on the other side, the rule simply does not apply. Thus, turning over the *seven* does not provide a way to invalidate the rule.

How can I explain subjects' difficulty with this task? Perhaps people represent the task as one of logical reasoning. Turning over the *A* card corresponds to the valid logical inference schema *modus ponens*:

$$\frac{\begin{array}{l} \text{IF } P, \text{ then } Q \\ P \end{array}}{Q.} \tag{1.1}$$

This schema reads "If some statement P is true, then some statement Q is true. Statement P is true. Therefore, Statement Q is true." For this schema, any statement that can be either true or false may play the roles of P and Q. Turning over the *four* card requires the logical schema *modus tollens*:

$$\frac{\begin{array}{l} \text{If } P, \text{ then } Q \\ \text{NOT } Q \end{array}}{\text{NOT } P.} \tag{1.2}$$

Not all schemas give rise to valid rules of inference. The valid rules are those for which if the premises (i.e., the statements above the line) are true, then the conclusion (i.e., the statement below the line) is guaranteed to be true. One example of an invalid schema is *affirming the consequent*:

$$\frac{\begin{array}{l} \text{IF } P, \text{ then } Q \\ Q \end{array}}{P.} \tag{1.3}$$

The problem with this schema is that it fails to take into account that the statement Q can be the case for some reason other than the rule "If P, then Q." This schema would be valid if the rule were "Q is true if *and only if P is true*" (sometimes written IFF P, then Q).

Taking logical rules seriously as a representation of people's ways of reasoning suggests that correct performance on the Wason selection task requires both *modus ponens* and *modus tollens*, but not incorrect schemas like *affirming the consequent*. Because most people turn over the *A* card and fewer people turn over the *four* card, *modus ponens* must be an easier rule to learn than is *modus tollens*. Accounts of logical reasoning of this type have been proposed by Rips (1994) and Braine, Reiser, and Rumain (1984). This account of reasoning assumes that people use general rules of reasoning across domains. By adopting this framework, a researcher makes certain questions particularly interesting to answer. For example, a researcher who assumes this representation may focus on the rules people tend to have, the factors that promote the acquisition of new rules, and the factors that control whether people recognize that a particular rule is relevant in a given context.

According to an alternative account of logical reasoning ability, however, people do not have logical rules that apply across domains. After all, logical rules do not care about the content of the statements *P* and *Q*. As long as a situation has the right form, the logical rules apply. According to one such account, people have a *mental model* of a situation about which they are going to reason (see chap. 9). Mental models are not general schemas of inference but instantiations of particular situations. This account suggests that problems framed in an abstract way (like the Wason selection task) are difficult, because it is difficult to construct models for abstract situations. Thus, a problem with the same structure (an isomorphic problem) may be easier to solve if it is in a domain for which it is easy to construct a model.

This view of representation suggests that the selection task should be tried with different problem contents. As an example, imagine you are working for the security patrol of a college on a Saturday night, and it is your job to make sure that campus bars serve alcohol only to people of the legal drinking age (21 years old in the United States). You enter a bar and see one person you know to be 18 years old, a second you know to be 22 years old, a third person, whom you do not know, holding a beer, and a fourth, unknown to you, drinking club soda. Which people must you check to ensure that the bar is satisfying the rule "If a person has a drink, then he or she is over 21"? College undergraduates given versions of the selection task in familiar domains like this performed quite well. Nearly all knew that only the 18-year-old and the person drinking beer need to be checked. This problem is isomorphic to the task with the cards, but people have much less difficulty with the concrete version (see Johnson-Laird, Legrenzi, & Legrenzi, 1972).

Mental models are not exactly the same as logical rules. Although mental models can be described as having rules, the scope of these rules differs from that of logic. With a particular logical rule, anything with the proper form can be reasoned about. In contrast, the procedures for constructing mental models are domain specific. A person may have rules for reasoning about drinking in bars without having rules for reasoning about genetics or abstract logical forms. For those who have adopted a framework based on logical rules, the content effects discovered in the selection task are difficult to explain. Rips (1994) argued that content effects in this task may reflect people's remembering what happened in their own personal experience and that this personal experience augments but does not replace logical rules. For example, when given the selection task in the context of verifying the rule about the legal age for drinking, people may just recall a situation in which they were in a bar and remember who was asked for identification. In this case, no rules were used at all; the answer to the problem was just remembered. Assuming that reasoning uses logical rules of inference makes it easy to explain logical reasoning abilities at the expense of making content effects more difficult to explain.

People's performance on a psychological task may often be explained in many ways, each of which has a different approach to mental representation. Each way may provide a good account of the phenomenon being studied, but the approaches may differ in their predictions for subsequent studies that should be designed and carried out. Indeed, as I discuss next, adopting particular representational assumptions affects which new questions are most interesting to answer.

WHAT IS A REPRESENTATION?

Mental representation is a critical part of psychological explanation, but it has also been a source of great confusion. Different researchers have used the word *representation* in different ways. Psychologists have used representation in somewhat different ways from other cognitive scientists, such as philosophers and computer scientists, who are interested in representation. To avoid confusion, I offer a broad definition of representation, one that includes all things that cognitive scientists have considered representations, although it may admit some things that people may feel uncomfortable calling representations, or at least uncomfortable thinking of as psychological representations. My definition of representation has four components. The first two components of representation are:

1. **A represented world:** the domain that the representations are about. The represented world may be the world outside the cognitive system or some other set of representations inside the system. That is, one set of representations can be about another set of representations.

2. **A representing world:** the domain that contains the representations. (The terms *represented world* and *representing world* come from a classic paper by Palmer [1978a].)

As an example, consider various representations of the items pictured in the top row of Figure 1.2. These items are the represented world for this example. In this world, there are three objects of interest, an ice cube, a glass of water, and a pot of water on a fire. I can choose to represent many aspects of this world, but for now, I focus on the temperature of the water. This representational decision has consequences. If I represent only

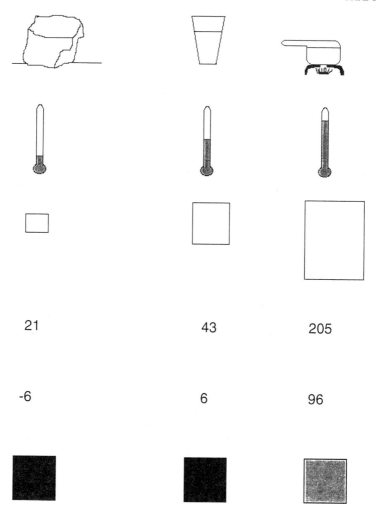

FIG. 1.2. Various ways of representing temperature. The top row depicts water that is frozen, at room temperature, and boiling. The next two rows depict possible analog representations. The two following rows show numerical temperature notations. Finally, the last row depicts temperature with the darkness of the square.

the temperature of the water, all the rest of the information about the situation is lost, including the shape of the ice cube, the size of the glass of water, and the degree of curvature of the handle of the pot. This point is not trivial: In all known representational systems, the representing world loses information about the represented world.

In modern culture, the representation of temperature, as in the second row of Figure 1.2, often appears as the height of mercury in a thermometer.

That is, I can use the height of mercury as a representing world, in which the higher the line of mercury, the greater the temperature. In this representation, however, a few important issues lie buried. First, the height of mercury in a thermometer works as a representation of temperature, because there is a set of rules that determine how the representing world corresponds to the represented world. Thus, the third component of my definition of representation is:

3. **Representing rules:** The representing world is related to the represented world through a set of rules that map elements of the represented world to elements in the representing world. If every element in the represented world is represented by a unique element in the representing world, there is an *isomorphism* between the represented and representing worlds. If two or more elements in the represented world are represented by one element in the representing world, there is a *homomorphism* between the represented and the representing worlds.[1]

As an illustration of this component of the definition, when temperature is represented as the height of mercury in a thermometer, each temperature is reflected by a unique height of mercury. The specific height that the mercury reaches is determined by the circumference of the thermometer as well as by the physical laws that govern the expansion of mercury with changes in temperature. Because each temperature has its own unique height, there is an isomorphism between the temperature in the represented world and the height of mercury in the representing world, but not all representations of temperature need to be isomorphisms. If a digital thermometer that gave readings on the Fahrenheit temperature scale (as in the second row of Figure 1.2) gave readings accurate to only 1 degree, any temperature between, say, 20.5 degrees and 21.4 degrees would be represented as 21 degrees. In this case, the relation between the represented and representing worlds is a homomorphism. When there is a homomorphism between the representing and represented worlds, the representation has lost information about what it is representing.

Another issue that arises with this example is that nothing inherent in a mercury thermometer alone makes it a representation. Since the dawn of time (or soon thereafter), mercury has had the property of expanding and contracting with changes in temperature, but mercury was not always a representation of temperature. For something to be a representation,

---

[1]There is much debate in philosophy about how physical systems (like minds) have the power to represent things in the external world, but in this book, I am not concerned with solving this problem. Instead, I assume that cognitive systems have the capacity for representation, and I focus on proposals in cognitive science for the nature of these representations.

some process must use the representation for some purpose. In this culture, having been schooled in the use of a thermometer, people can use the column of mercury as a representation of temperature. A vervet monkey who lacks the mathematical skills and cultural upbringing (among other things) to read a thermometer cannot use the column of mercury as a representation of temperature. More broadly, something is a representation only if a process can be used to interpret that representation. In this case, the combination of the thermometer and the person who can read it makes the thermometer a representation. More generally, the fourth component of a representation is:

4. **A process that uses the representation:** It makes no sense to talk about representations in the absence of processes. The combination of the first three components (a represented world, a representing world, and a set of representing rules) creates merely the potential for representation. Only when there is also a process that uses the representation does the system actually represent, and the capabilities of a system are defined only when there is both a representation and a process.

The importance of processes when thinking about representations cannot be underestimated (J. R. Anderson, 1978; Palmer, 1978a). In the temperature example, there is no representation until someone can use the thermometer to read off the temperature. In general, it may seem obvious that certain cognitive processes can be explained by a representation, but in many instances two very different kinds of representations can make exactly the same predictions when the right set of processes acts over them.

To demonstrate how the four components of representation interact to create a representation, we return to the temperature example. The rectangles in the third row of Figure 1.2 can also be representations of temperature. For example, the area of each rectangle could be used as a representation of a particular temperature. In this case, comparing two temperatures may involve laying one rectangle on top of another to see which is larger: A larger rectangle corresponds to a higher temperature. Of course, a different set of representing rules and processes completely changes the interpretation of this representation: If the heights of the rectangles are used to represent temperature, pairs of temperatures can be compared by laying the rectangles next to each other. It is easy to generate other possibilities: For example, smaller rectangles can represent higher temperatures. For each possibility, the representing rules and associated processes for interpreting the representation must be configured accordingly.

The representations in the second and third rows of Figure 1.2 depict a continuous quantity with another continuous quantity. Once the length of the line is linked by a representing rule with the temperature of the object, a change in the length of the line can be interpreted as a change in temperature. Using one dimensional quantity to represent another seems to provide some information for free. These representations are often called *analog*, because the representing world has an inherent structure that governs how it operates and the relations between aspects in the representing world are not arbitrary. For example, it is a fact about spaces that if line *A* is longer than line *B* and line *B* is longer than line *C*, line *A* is also longer than line *C*. Length is an appropriate representation for temperature, because temperature has the same transitive structure as length. If temperature did not have a transitive structure, length would not be an appropriate representing world to use for temperature.

Not all representations are analog. The fourth row of Figure 1.2 shows such a representation. In modern culture, people use numerical representations of quantities such as temperature all the time. This representation is very different from those in the second and third rows: Making the numbers taller or shorter does not signal changing the temperature of the objects; only changes in the digits change the representation. Nothing inherent in the scratches of ink requires the number 21 to be larger than the number 20 or smaller than the number 22. Rather, a system of representing rules links the written numerals to the represented world of abstract mathematical quantities. These representations are often called *symbolic* because a convention is established to link all the elements in the representing world. The relation among elements in the representing world is arbitrary and could have occurred in some other way had the representing rules been differently constructed. (The arbitrary, conventionally established use of symbols in mental representation is similar to the use that, for example, allows the symbol Σ to play one role in Greek writing and a different role in mathematical equations.)

For a symbol system like Arabic numerals to be used as the basis of a representation of the represented world of temperature, a set of representing rules must be established between symbols and temperature. First, there must be rules that map the numerals onto numbers, but even after this mapping has been established, there are many possible ways to map the numbers onto temperatures. For example, with the Fahrenheit temperature scale as representing rules, there is a set of correspondences between the represented and representing worlds different from that with the Celsius scale. An infinite number of sets of representing rules can be constructed to map numbers onto temperatures. The same point is true for analog representations (such as using lines to represent temperatures): Different lengths of a line can represent the same degree of temperature change. The particular correspondence between temperature and line length is established by the representing rules.

A particular representation makes some information obvious and other information difficult to extract (Marr, 1982). The length of a column of mercury as a representation of temperature makes it easy to make direct comparisons between pairs of temperatures. A simple procedure of laying two lines next to each other and seeing which extends further accomplishes this task. To compare two numbers, in contrast, extensive knowledge of the system of symbols underlying numbers and an understanding of numerical relationships, must be brought to bear. Not all things are easier to do with the length representation of temperature, though. If a specific value for temperature is required to make a complex calculation, say for understanding a chemical reaction, the length representation is poorly suited as a representation of temperature; for this purpose, the numerical representation may be better.

To summarize, representations have four components. At the heart of a representation is a representing world that is used to represent information in the represented world. The particular representations in this world are bound to the represented world by representing rules that relate aspects of the representing world to aspects of the represented world. The process of representing some world typically produces a loss of information, because information can be used only when there is a procedure for extracting it. I have made a distinction between *analog* representations, for which the relations among elements in the represented world are fixed by the structure of the representational system, and *symbolic* representations, for which the relations among elements in the represented world are arbitrary and must be fixed by convention. Finally, any representational choice makes some information easy to find but may make other information very difficult to determine.

Representations and Cognitive Representations

My working definition of representation is quite broad. For example, according to this definition, a thermostat has representations although a thermostat is not a cognitive system. What exactly constitutes a cognitive system or cognitive representation is a difficult question that has occupied researchers in cognitive science for some time. No satisfactory definition exists that includes all and only things that all researchers are happy calling representations, but I hope to demonstrate the range of things that are good candidates for psychological representations. In this way, I can triangulate on a good definition for cognitive representation.

Before we examine the notion of cognitive representations in more detail, however, there is one danger with defining a cognitive system that we must discuss explicitly. There is a strong intuition that a thermostat is not a cognitive system. After all, a thermostat is not that interesting a device. The bimetallic plate changes its shape with the temperature in the room, and at some point the change causes a switch to close and to turn on the heat (or perhaps the air conditioning). Later, the change in temperature in the opposite direction causes the switch to open, and the heat (or air conditioning) stops. Why is this not cognitive?

J. A. Fodor (1986) gave an answer to this question. He argued that the behavior of systems like thermostats is well described, perhaps even best described, by using the principles of physics and chemistry. A bimetallic plate changes its shape because the two metals expand at different rates (a change predicted by laws of physics and chemistry). Thus, although a thermostat has a representation, it is a representation that needs no principles of psychology to be understood, and thus it is not a cognitive representation.[2] This way of distinguishing between cognitive and noncognitive representations seems reasonable. Although the behavior of any representational system can be described by the laws of physics at some level, no interesting generalizations from physics or chemistry can explain how a cognitive system (like a brain or a suitably programmed computer) represents information, and so it is necessary to appeal to other sciences.

An inappropriate answer (in my view) to the question of what makes something a cognitive representation is that a thermostat is a deterministic device. The physics of thermostats is well enough understood to predict their behavior with striking accuracy. A complete psychology may allow predictions of the behavior of humans and other animals with alarming effectiveness as well. I raise this point here, however, because implicit in many discussions of representation is the notion that a cognitive system has an element of free will in it. I do not choose a definition of cognitive system in a way that assumes that there is (or is not) free will.

The Meaning in a Representation

In a cognitive representation, the representation is an internal state; that is, in humans, mental representations are in the head. The nature of the represented world is controversial. Is the represented world in the head, outside the head, or some combination of the two? Cognitive scientists have often assumed that some represented worlds are outside the head and others are inside. In order to look more at what it means for a representation to be about something, we must explore some work in the philosophy of mind.

---

[2]Actually, Fodor argued that thermostats do not have representations at all and that what makes something a representation is having properties that cannot be explained by the laws of basic sciences (what he called *non-nomic* properties). This position does not explain how a thermostat makes contact with its environment to do something interesting in a way that a rock heating in the sun does not. See Markman and Dietrich (1998) for a more complete discussion of Fodor's view and problems with it.

Philosophers have been concerned with the notion of *intentionality* (Dennett, 1987; Dietrich, 1994; Searle, 1992). Rather than referring to the familiar idea that something may be done with intent or on purpose, the philosophical concept of intentionality refers to what a representation is about. For example, my representation of the computer screen I am looking at is about this computer screen. My belief that chocolate ice cream is good is about chocolate ice cream. My belief that unicorns do not exist is about unicorns. Defining *aboutness*, however, is not straightforward. For my belief about the computer screen, it is enough that there is a computer screen in front of me (barring a very convincing hallucination). Likewise, my belief about chocolate ice cream can refer to instances of chocolate ice cream in the world, particularly those instances I have experienced in the past (that were good). Unicorns are more problematic: There are none, and never were. Thus, it is not enough to assume that representations are about things in the world because not everything represented is in the world (or ever was). Some things may be abstract concepts without good visualizable forms. Finally, even when a representation *is* about something in the outside world, there may be a mismatch between what is in the world and the way I represent it. On a dark foggy night, I may represent something as a black cat, only to find out too late that it is a skunk. A theory of representation must allow such mistakes to occur.

A complete catalog of theories of intentionality in philosophy would take up more room than I have in this chapter (or in this book; see J. A. Fodor, 1981; J. A. Fodor & Lepore, 1992; Stich & Warfield, 1994). To understand representation, it is important to think about how the elements in a representation can mean something. One solution to this problem (discussed again in later chapters) is conceptual role semantics, in which the meaning of a representational element is fixed by its relations to other representational elements. This situation is analogous to a dictionary, in which a word is defined in terms of other words. For example, the glossary of an introductory psychology textbook may define the term *olfaction* as "the sense of smell." This definition is helpful only if there already is a meaning for the phrase "the sense of smell" (and you know what that definition is).

A conceptual role semantics has two problems: First, the meanings of at least some elements in the representation must be known, or none of the elements means anything. The representational elements with known meanings are the *grounded* elements. Without knowing the meanings of any words, it is not helpful to look up words in a dictionary: Everything is gibberish in this case. In the chapters that follow, it is worth thinking about which elements in the representing world may be grounded, and how may the grounding take place?

The second problem with conceptual role semantics is holism (J. A. Fodor & Lepore, 1992). If representational elements are given meaning by their relations to other representational elements, the meaning of any one element depends on every other representational element. According to this view, two people's concepts of *dog* differ because each knows different things about dogs, and also about the 1986 New York Giants. If the meaning of any concept depends on the meaning of every other concept, then how can people function without accessing all information at all times? If each person's concepts differ from every other person's concepts, because of differences in past experience, communication is impossible: One person's meanings of the concepts used in a discourse must differ radically from another person's concepts on the basis of differences in past experience. The holism problem requires that cognitive systems be able to do some processing without having to make use of every piece of their knowledge for every process. Again, in the chapters that follow, it is worth thinking about how particular representations avoid having to access and use every piece of known information to function.

A final problem that philosophers have often raised in conjunction with discussions about representation concerns how representations are interpreted. If I have a picture of the Grand Canyon, I believe the picture represents the Grand Canyon because of particular color saturation patterns that map onto color saturations that were at the Grand Canyon at the time the picture was taken. When I look at it, because I have the right kind of visual system, I can interpret the picture and extract information from the representation. The problem comes with thinking about cognitive representations. The representing world in a cognitive representation is assumed to be internal to the organism. Who looks at the representation to interpret it? There cannot be another person in my head (a *homunculus*) who looks at my representations, because then who would interpret the representations in the homunculus's head?

Cognitive scientists have generally avoided this conundrum by assuming that the cognitive system is a computational device. That is, the cognitive system has representations, and it also has processes that manipulate the information in these representations, just as a familiar digital computer can have data structures, which can be manipulated by procedures in computer programs. Digital computers are able to carry out algorithms, because they have instructions encoded in them to allow them to follow a program in the same way that a cook follows a recipe.[3]

---

[3]The ability to follow a program is based on the theoretical concept of a Turing machine. A description of Turing machines is beyond the scope of this chapter; interested readers should consult the description of Turing machines by Johnson-Laird (1988). A clever introduction to Turing machines appeared in Barwise and Etchemendy's work (1993b); they provided a computer program that allows readers to construct Turing machines to solve a variety of problems.

In this section, I have raised two important philosophical issues about representation. The first is intentionality (i.e., what a representation is about): How is the representing world connected to the represented world? The second is computation: There is a danger when positing psychological theories of requiring an intelligent agent to interpret the representations in it. According to the concept of computability derived from Turing machines, a process designed to make use of a representation can be carried out without needing such an intelligent agent.

THREE DIMENSIONS OF VARIATION
IN REPRESENTATIONS

How does one representational format differ from another? Are the differences merely a matter of notation, or do actual substantive issues separate the types of representations? Proposals for representations can vary along many dimensions (see also Markman & Dietrich, 1998).[4] As a demonstration that these dimensions of variation are substantive, I consider three: the duration of representational states, the presence of discrete symbols, and the abstractness of representations. In the following section, I discuss some general criteria for deciding that one proposal for representation is better than another.

The first dimension of variation is in the duration of representational states. The definition of representation given here does not require that representational states exist for any particular time. In the case of a mercury thermometer, representational states are instantaneous; the height of the mercury in the thermometer represents the temperature at the moment. Any changes in temperature change the height of the mercury and leave the system without any memory of past states. Representations may also endure for long periods. I can remember the day that my parents and I moved from an apartment to a house when I was about 3 years old (some 28 years before I am writing this). The fact that I have a mental image of the moving truck behind our car means that some representation of this event has endured in my cognitive system for a long time (although my current mental image of this state may reflect only a transient activation of neurons in my brain). Thus, different representational systems may focus on transient or enduring representational states.

A second important dimension of variation is the presence of discrete symbols. Many representational formats assume that discrete elements in the representing world bear some relation to elements in the represented

---

[4]Markman and Dietrich (1988) actually discussed five dimensions of variation, but three are most central for this discussion.

world. When the relation between these discrete elements and the things they represent in the represented world is arbitrary, these discrete elements are called symbols. Although symbols are common in representational systems (see chaps. 3–9), they are not obligatory. For example, as I discuss in chapter 2, many systems use space as a representation. Space is continuous and hence does not divide the representing world into discrete parts. Thus, symbols are commonly used in representations but are not required.

The issues of duration and symbol use are not trivial and have been the source of some controversy in cognitive science. Indeed, theorists who have focused on representations that exist for only short periods and do not require explicit symbols have considered the possibility that cognitive systems have no representations at all. One example presented by van Gelder (1992; see also Thelen & Smith, 1994) involves Watt's apparatus used as the governor for a steam engine. The mechanism, shown in Figure 1.3, spins around; the faster it spins, the higher the balls on the outside rise. As the balls rise, they close a valve that lets steam flow through the engine; this process reduces the pressure and causes the mechanism to spin more slowly. The decrease in the rate of spin lowers the balls, which causes the valve to open more, thereby increasing the pressure, and so on. This elegant machine keeps steam engines from exploding by keeping pressure in the engine from rising too high.

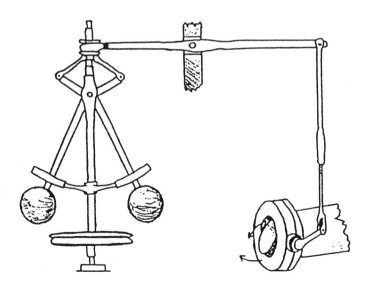

FIG. 1.3.   Diagram of Watt's steam engine governor. From *Dynamic Systems Approach*, by E. Thelen and L. B. Smith (1994). Copyright © 1994 by MIT Press. Reprinted with permission.

Van Gelder suggested that this mechanism requires no representation. The function of the governor is clearly not carried out in the way that it would be if one programmed a digital computer to reason qualitatively about a system (see chap. 9). There is no mental model of the inside of the steam engine, and nothing in the system allows the governor to reason about aspects of the engine in case of a problem. Furthermore, there is no explicit symbolic representation of pressure that a problem-solving program can use to reason about the optimal level of pressure needed to run the engine at peak efficiency. Indeed, if the valve jammed in its open state, the governor would continue to spin faster as the steam built up until the engine exploded despite the governor's best efforts.

Although the governor has no symbolic representation of the pressure inside the steam engine, it does represent the pressure through the speed at which the governor spins. This speed, which is a stable representation of pressure, is a function of the weight of the balls on the sides of the apparatus. There is also a process that extracts information from the representation, namely the lever connecting the arms of the governor to the valve. This representation is an excellent example of how a particular representation may make some information obvious at the expense of other information. The system can react only to current pressure; it cannot reason about the information in any other way.

This representation is also not enduring: At any moment, all that is available is a measure of the current pressure inside the engine. There is no way to compare the current pressure to the pressure at any previous time, because this information is not stored. The advantage of this representational choice is that it provides a simple, elegant method that allows the governor to carry out its function. If it was important for the governor to make comparisons with past states, however, this representation would be insufficient: The system would need a representational format that was more enduring. Thus, the governor uses simple, nonenduring representations to carry out its task. Like the thermostat described earlier, however, the representations in the governor are well described by physical laws, and so they are not good candidates to be cognitive representations.

Finally, consider the issue of abstractness. Since Aristotle, human thought has been prized for its logical facility. Unlike any other species, people can reason in ways that are independent of the content of a domain and can see similarities across items that appear to be wildly dissimilar on the surface. The recognition that human cognition is privileged in its ability to reason abstractly has led to the supposition that cognitive representations seek abstractness. As a result, many proposals for mental representations have focused on how to represent cases that are abstracted across surface details.

More recently, as exemplified by the content effects in logical reasoning problems discussed earlier, psychologists have begun to study the ways in which reasoning is embedded in the content of domains. The move away from abstract representations does not remove representations from the picture in cognitive science but simply stresses that in models of psychological processing more abstract does not necessarily mean better. This abstraction process has also taken place at the level of theory. Studies of higher cognitive processing have often assumed that mental representations used by higher cognitive processes are independent of the representations used by perceptual systems that take in information from the world and independent of the representations used by motor systems to act on the world. This assumption may be unjustified. (I discuss the importance of domain-specific information in cognitive processing in chaps. 8 and 9.)

A similar argument can be made about the temporal duration of representational states. When cognition is viewed as a process that aspires to a logical ideal, creating enduring representations that exist across the life of an organism is the ideal state. Indeed, cultural systems may be one way that humans try to build lasting representational structures in different individuals over time. There is, however, much flexibility in cognitive processing. The Necker cube (Figure 1.4) is one simple example. If a person stares at the cube long enough, perception flips back and forth between two stable states that place two different sides at the front of a three-dimensional cube. Because the two interpretations of the cube are incompatible, people do not consciously perceive both interpretations at the same time. In this case, the representation of the cube changes from one state to another every few seconds. These changes in the psychological construal of different situations can probably occur for conceptual situations as well as for perceptual ones like this example. This may occur when people go back and forth while making a decision, first favoring one option, and then the other. Repre-

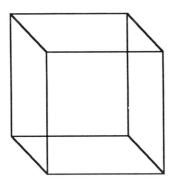

FIG. 1.4. Necker cube.

sentational structures, however, are not constructed once to remain un-changed in a psychological system. Rather, some psychological processes require representations that change rapidly over time.

The view that human beings aspire to a logical ideal carries with it an assumption that the optimal form of psychological representation is con-tent free and enduring. Many proposals about psychological repre-sentations carry these assumptions by default, but they are not obligatory. Demonstrations that psychological representations contain information about specific domains or that representations change dynamically during the course of processing are simply more data points that constrain the way people think about representation. In this book, I have made an effort to construe representation broadly, because there is little hope of under-standing the effects of content and temporal change in psychology without thinking carefully about representation.

EVALUATING PROPOSALS FOR REPRESENTATION

I explore different proposals for mental representation in this book. These proposals differ along a number of lines including the three just described (i.e., the enduringness of the representation, the presence of symbols, and the abstractness of the representation). In view of these proposals, which representation is best for explaining a given cognitive process?

One important criterion for selecting a representation is its power. Not all representations are powerful enough to represent all represented worlds. For example, in chapter 5, I discuss representations that permit *quantification* (i.e., representations that allow people to say things like "Some dogs are small"). Some representations cannot represent quantified assertions (i.e., they can talk about dogs and even small dogs, but they cannot represent that *some* dogs are small). Thus, if a particular model requires the ability to handle quantified statements, then a representational system that is not powerful enough to represent quantified statements is not appropriate. A repre-sentation may be rejected as a candidate for a particular process because it is not expressive enough to represent the information needed for that domain.

A person faced with two or more representations that are powerful enough for the domain can find the problem of deciding between them quite difficult. As I have discussed, processes that use representations are an important part of the concept of representation. J. R. Anderson (1978) demonstrated that if two different representing worlds are both sufficient to represent the information in a represented world, it is often possible to find in each domain a set of processing assumptions that allow systems using either representation to explain the same set of data. Thus, it is generally impossible to argue decisively against a particular form of mental representation on the basis of data from a set of studies.

Because of this difficulty, there may seem to be no point in trying to determine which model of representation is best; the question is not answerable. There are, however, other criteria for favoring one model of representation over another. One critical use of representation is in generating further research questions. As one example, consider behavior that is rule governed. Traditional symbolic accounts of phenomena in developmental psychology have led researchers to focus on stages of development: Piaget constructed a theory about the levels of cognitive competence that children achieve and the ages at which they achieve these levels of performance. He then described general mechanisms that allow children to process complex and abstract information. Because all children are assumed to acquire the same capacities to process rules in about the same order, the appropriate way to test this view involves looking at the average performance of children in different age groups. The average performance is assumed to reflect the underlying mechanism, and individual variations are assumed to be uninteresting.

According to an alternative way of thinking about development, representations have a smaller grain size and only nonenduring states (Thelen, 1995; Thelen & Smith, 1994). On this view, what children learn at some new point depends critically on their previous knowledge. Because children differ in their experience and knowledge, their developmental patterns differ as well. This *dynamic systems* view focuses not on stages of development, but rather on longitudinal data in which the patterns of changes that individual children go through are important. The variability in a single child's performance becomes interesting data to be explained in addition to the stable patterns observed by averaging the performance of many children on a given task. In this way, people adopting symbolic and dynamic systems views of development are led not only to different explanations of behavior but also to different kinds of experiments.

Another case in which assumptions about representations affect the way a psychological process is studied comes from models of the acquisition of past tense forms of English verbs. A key finding to be explained is that early in development, children use both regular and irregular past tense forms properly but then go through a stage of overregularization of the rule, in which they sometimes use the regular past tense form even for irregular verbs (e.g., *goed* instead of *went*). Finally, children learn when to use the regular past tense ending and when not to use it. This pattern of use is reflected in a U-shaped accuracy function in which children start out using irregular past tense forms accurately, get less accurate, and then use the irregular past tense forms properly again. Many models of this process have assumed that past tense learning takes place by learning a set of rules. Because these models are concerned with the formation of rules, the relevant experimental questions are those about the information underlying rule formation, the way that new rules are added, and the way that people learn exceptions to these rules.

An alternative theory was developed by Rumelhart and McClelland (1986), who argued that a representational system sensitive to the statistical structure of the input the child received could explain the observed use of past tense forms. Specifically, they developed a connectionist model of past tense learning (see chap. 2 for more on connectionism). This model also exhibited a pattern of overgeneralization like that observed in children, even though it contained no rules. Rather, the model assumed that children first learned a small number of verbs, most of which were irregular, followed by a larger number of verbs, most of which were regular. At the point at which the large number of regular verbs was added, the model showed some overgeneralization. The learning procedure that the model used was sensitive to these changes in relative frequency of regular and irregular verbs. Subsequent analyses of this model have suggested that it does not capture the fine details of the data (Pinker & Prince, 1988), but the adequacy of this model as an explanation of the development of past tense forms in English is not an issue here. The point is that testing these models experimentally requires examining the statistical structure of the linguistic input that a child receives rather than focusing on the rules that characterize the child's behavior. Thus, the choice of representation embedded in a model (in this case, a distributed connectionist model) leads to a change in the evidence collected. Representational choices affect not only the way cognitive scientists think psychological systems work, but also the way they think about psychology.

This discussion suggests that an important criterion for the adequacy of a proposal about representation is whether it leads to new and interesting experimental questions. I might favor a particular model of mental representation on pragmatic grounds, not on empirical grounds. Ultimately, pragmatic factors of this type have had an important influence on many debates about representation. Eventually, information about how the brain implements cognition will also influence decisions about representations. To think about how the implementation of a process affects the way people think about representation, I first address the general idea of levels of description of cognitive systems.

LEVELS OF DESCRIPTION

Although I posit mental representations in the process of creating descriptions of psychological processes, there are many ways to describe a system. Both Marr (1982) and Pylyshyn (1980) have explored the idea of levels of description at some length. (In the following discussion, I adopt Marr's terminology, because it is used most often in discussions of representation.) Marr distinguished among *computational*-level descriptions, *algorithmic*-level descriptions, and *implementational*-level descriptions. Each of these describes the same system, but the goal of the description is different in each case.

Imagine a machine that took as input two positive integers and gave as output a third quantity that was the sum of the first two. In what ways can I describe it? At the computational level, a system is characterized simply by the inputs it takes, the output it gives, and the relation between them. In the case of this machine, if I am familiar with arithmetic, I can characterize the machine as taking inputs *a* and *b*, both of which are positive integers, and providing output *c* such that $c = a + b$. For many purposes, this is a perfectly good description of the system. I now know the range of allowable inputs to the machine, and I can make accurate predictions of its behavior with those inputs.

Still, there are a number of things I do not know about the system with only a computational-level description. For example, I do not know how the system has chosen to represent these quantities or how it combines these quantities to form the sum. These issues of representation and process are the central aspects of an algorithmic-level description.[5] For example, the machine may use binary notation as a representation. When told that the value of its first input is 8, it first translates the decimal notation given as input into the internal binary representation 100. When told that its second input is 4, it translates this quantity into the internal representation 010. Knowing the way quantities are represented is only half of the battle, though. I must also describe how the represented quantities are combined to form the sum. There may be many ways that the information represented in a particular fashion can be combined to form the sum. The builder of the machine must decide how the representations are combined.

In the case of this machine, it might first contain instructions to look at the right-most digit of each representation. If both digits are 0 or 1, then the right-most digit should be 0; otherwise, it should be 1. If both digits are 1, then a *carry* digit must be set: The machine should look at the next digit to the left in each input quantity, as well as at the carry. The machine may have a table like the one in Table 1.1, which tells it how to set the output digit and carry digit with different patterns of input. For example, with the input $a = 1$, $b = 0$, carry = 0 shown in the fifth row

---

[5]The term *algorithmic level* is a bit misleading from my point of view. Formally, an algorithm is a particular computational procedure frequently associated with digital computers. Specifically, it is the kind of procedure that, when run on a generalized computational device (a Turing machine), is guaranteed to complete its processing in a finite amount of time. The term *algorithm* can also refer to any effective procedure. Only this latter type of algorithm (one that may not halt in a finite amount of time) is central to algorithmic-level descriptions.

TABLE 1.1
Sample Lookup Table for Adding Machine

Input			Output	
a	*b*	*Carry*	*c*	*Carry*
0	0	0	0	0
0	0	1	1	0
0	1	0	1	0
0	1	1	0	1
1	0	0	1	0
1	0	1	0	1
1	1	0	0	1
1	1	1	1	1

of the table, the output digit would be set to 1, and the carry digit would be set to 0. The machine then continues by moving to the next input digit to the left in both input quantities until it reaches the left-most digit of the larger quantity.

Choosing this process has many implications. For example, one can predict how long the machine should take to finish combining two numbers. As the numbers to be added get larger, the machine should take longer to add them. In fact, it adds one time step for each new binary digit that it adds to the numbers. Other choices of algorithms make different predictions about timing. For example, the arithmetic and logic units in modern computers add a number of binary digits in parallel. As long as the two inputs do not exceed some value, the addition takes place in a constant time.

For many purposes, the algorithmic level of description is also adequate, but things are still missing from this description. How is the machine constructed? Is it made from silicon chips, pipes filled with water, gears and levers, or animals systematically making marks in the sand? Nothing in either the computational-level description or the algorithmic-level description provides this information. Rather, the physical stuff that makes the system work is the province of implementational-level descriptions. An implementational-level description specifies what the machine is made of. If the machine was constructed from integrated circuit chips, the description would specify the configuration of logic gates. It would state that the binary digit 1 corresponded to a particular voltage in a logic circuit and the binary digit 0 corresponded to another voltage level. It would further specify a mechanism for carrying out the procedure, for allowing the machine to focus its "attention" on the right-most digit and then sequentially to each digit to the left of that one. The implementational-level description is not complete until a working machine could be constructed that would carry out the computation described at the computational and algorithmic levels.

The same computation can be implemented in many ways, although there may be particular time, space, energy, or stability benefits to particular designs. For example, both the old stereo that was in my bedroom when I was growing up and the stereo that is now in my house play vinyl records and produce music. The stereo in my childhood bedroom had vacuum tubes that took a while to warm up. The first album played on any day always sounded a bit worse than the rest of the records, because the system had not reached peak performance. With the advent of solid-state technology, the same function is carried out in silicon chips that do not have to warm up; now even the first record sounds good.[6]

In sum, there are three different levels for describing a mental system. Each level offers a different description of the same system. The computational level specifies the input taken by the system and the output it produces. This input and output need not be symbolic as in addition; they can be a set of forces acting on a limb, with the output being the movement of the limb. The algorithmic level specifies the representations adopted by the system and the processes that extract and use the information from these representations to carry out the function described in the computational-level explanation. The procedure need not be an algorithm that a digital computer can run but simply a process that acts on the representations used by the system. Finally, at the implementational level, the mechanism that is used by the system is actually described.

Use of Levels of Description in Psychology

In psychology, descriptions of psychological process often move from a computational level to an algorithmic level down to an implementational level. In Kosslyn's (1994) description of the role of mental imagery in the visual system, he began with computational-level descriptions of the components of the system. In fleshing out this description, he presented algorithmic descriptions of the components and, where possible, evidence of how these computations are actually carried out in the brain. Presumably, psychologists would be satisfied with an explanation of the visual and imagery systems if they understood the relation between brain functioning and the representations and processes used.

---

[6]Of course, in the interim, modes of representation of music have changed to compact discs (CDs), which use different processes to extract information from the representation as well. Indeed, the entire algorithmic level of description has changed, as we have gone from the analog representation embodied in grooves on a record to the digital representation used by compact discs.

The usual order of development is computational-level descriptions followed by lower level descriptions. However, descriptions of algorithms can suggest that a system is too computationally intensive to be feasible. In this case, other potential algorithms that are viable may change the computational-level description of a system. Likewise, evidence about how a process is implemented in the brain may influence both the algorithmic and computational descriptions of the system. The potential of new brain-imaging techniques for the study of psychology is the opportunity to get information about the implementational level of mental processing that can be used to constrain explanations at the computational and algorithmic levels.

The algorithmic level is most central in this book. This level is concerned with descriptions of systems at the level of representations and processes that act over the representations. Thus, when trying to characterize a psychological process and positing potential representations that are used by this process, people think at an algorithmic level.

The boundaries between the levels of description are not always sharp, and the way people think about representations affects psychological descriptions even when working at the computational or implementational level. An example may help make this point clear.

A significant amount of research, particularly in cognitive psychology, adopts the computational level of description. Much of this work aims at developing mathematical models of cognitive processes that characterize the variables that influence a process and uses the mathematical models to specify how these variables affect the process of interest. Nosofsky's (1986) influential generalized context model of classification (see chap. 8), for example, proposed that when learning to place objects into categories, people store representations of the individual category members they come in contact with. When they encounter a new object, they compare it with the specific exemplars stored in memory and classify the new item based on its similarity to the stored exemplars. A description of the entire model is beyond the scope of this chapter, but the model includes parameters for different aspects of categorization, including weights given to attributes that describe the exemplars and weights given to similar and dissimilar values of the attributes.

To make it possible to fit the mathematical model to data, it is assumed that the attributes of the exemplars (e.g., color, size, and shape) can be treated as independent of each other. In particular, it is assumed that each attribute can be compared to a corresponding attribute of other objects: The color of one object can easily be compared to the color of another object without regard to any other attributes of the objects. The model is meant as a description of the kinds of information that are important to the ability to form categories, even though it does not provide specific processes for making comparisons between new objects and previously stored exemplars or for storing old exemplars.

This model does, however, make some assumptions about the nature of mental representations, for instance, that the attributes describing objects are well characterized as being independent features (see chap. 3). This assumption is not only implicit in the mathematical model but is also carried through to the materials used in empirical studies of categorization. These studies often use simple materials with a small number of easily separable and conceptually independent dimensions. Thus, even though this work is ostensibly directed at forming a computational-level description, it also influences the representations deemed most appropriate for understanding the behavior.

A computational-level description need not place strong constraints on the representations posited at the algorithmic level. Often, many different representations and processes are consistent with a computational-level description (e.g., Barsalou, 1990). In practice, however, the computational-level description does seem to place constraints on how people think about the representations relevant to the process and in turn about what evidence is collected to test the descriptions of the process.

This link among levels of description, representation, and collecting and interpreting psychological evidence is the main motivation for this book. Every decision about how to describe a psychological process carries with it some assumptions about mental representation. Ideas about representation and processing carry with them suggestions about how to collect evidence for this process, and it is important to think carefully about the representations assumed by a description of a psychological process. It is crucial to be aware of making a set of representational assumptions. Better still is making choices about representations because of the particular things that a representation makes easy or hard to do.

ORGANIZATION OF THIS BOOK

What is the best way to think about mental representation? Researchers have extensively studied the types of representations related to particular tasks. Debates about how people carry out logical reasoning tasks have focused on assumptions about whether people's representations are more sentence-like (e.g., Rips, 1994) or more model-like (Johnson-Laird, 1983; Johnson-Laird & Byrne, 1991). Debates over people's ability to use mental imagery have focused on whether people's visual perception and imagery ability use analog or propositional representations (Cooper, 1975; Kosslyn, 1994; Pylyshyn, 1981). It is tempting to look at particular tasks and to examine the representations used to represent the content in these tasks. I have decided, however, to take a different tack.

Very similar sets of representations have been proposed across many areas of cognitive science. Some of these similarities are well-known, as in the assumption that sentence-like representations are useful for understanding both logical reasoning and mental imagery ability. Other similarities may be less obvious, as those between distributed connectionist models and multidimensional semantic space models of similarity. In an effort to make some of these similarities more apparent, I have organized this book around types of representations.

The book begins with simple representations and moves to representations of greater complexity. To illustrate the uses of many of the models, I describe implemented computer programs in which the representational assumptions have been made explicit. The link between serious thought about representation and computational modeling is important: Computational work can confirm specific predictions of a theory. Indeed, constructing a working model of a process can provide an existence proof that the theory can actually account for a set of phenomena (Kosslyn, 1994). Furthermore, when developing a computational model, both the representation and the process must be fully spelled out. This specificity may enable researchers to make new predictions about the nature of the cognitive process under study.

Chapters 2 to 4 deal with unstructured representations, which contain no explicit bindings or ownership between elements in the representations. Chapter 2 examines spatial representations, chapter 3 featural representations, and chapter 4 associative networks. These representations are simple and have the advantage of carrying with them simple processes that act over them. Despite this apparent simplicity, they are very powerful, and many aspects of cognitive processing may be well modeled using these representations.

Chapters 5 to 7 focus on structured representations. Chapter 5 introduces the notion of binding and presents some general structured representations. Chapter 6 examines how structured representations may be used in perception and how this use may extend to conceptual thought. Chapter 7 looks at scripts and schemas, which are perhaps the most common structured representation incorporated into psychological models.

Chapters 8 and 9 deal with general issues. Many examples in chapters 2 through 7 involve abstractions, like a typical bird or a typical visit to the doctor. Chapter 8 examines how people incorporate information about specific episodes (e.g., a particular doctor's office visit), or specific items (e.g., a particular doctor) into representations. Chapter 9 looks at mental models and tries to clarify the way the term *mental model* has been used in psychology. Finally, in chapter 10, I return to some general issues addressed in chapter 1 and discuss them in light of the representations presented in the book.

Spatial Representations:
What Do We Mean by Space?

WHAT DO WE MEAN BY SPACE?

In this chapter, the tour of types of psychological representations begins with a focus on spatial representations. A spatial representation has a representing world that incorporates a notion of space in it. Although the representing world is a space, the represented world need not be a space. Indeed, in many of the examples in this chapter, the represented world is not space, but rather concepts or word meanings. In addition to thinking about how space can be used as a representation, I also examine the processes that can be applied to a spatial representation.

What is meant by spatial representation? First, think about the notion of a space. From where I sit now, I see my computer and keyboard. To the left is a telephone and in front of that a coffee mug. The coffee mug is closer to the telephone and farther away from the computer. All these objects have a set of spatial relations to each other, with a distance and direction to each other object. What I perceive as real space has three dimensions. From my current vantage point, if I fix an origin directly between my eyes, I can think of the locations of objects in the world in terms of their coordinates in three dimensions: One is vertical and passes directly between my eyes; the second is horizontal and passes through each eye; and the third is depth, which is perpendicular (or *orthogonal*) to the other two dimensions and meets the other dimensions at the origin. I fix this origin arbitrarily. It could easily be fixed at the door to my office, in the ceiling or even on the George Washington Bridge, a good 5 miles from where I am now. Likewise, the three dimensions, which all pass through the origin, are arbitrarily oriented with respect to the origin. As long as the dimensions are independent (that is, *orthogonal*), I can select three dimensions to describe space in any way I want. In real space, a pair of orthogonal dimensions is a 90-degree angle with respect to each other. When the origin changes, the coordinates used to fix the locations of the objects in space are different, but the relations among the objects themselves do not change. In each space, the objects have the same relative locations with the same distances between them. For now, I focus on three key aspects of a space: (1) points that fix locations in a space, (2) distances between points in a space, and (3) a set of orthogonal dimensions that specify important reference directions in a space.

Space is commonly used as a representation in diagrams. For example, a football coach may draw *X*s and *O*s on a diagram like the one in Figure 2.1. In this diagram, the two-dimensional space correponds to the two dimensions on the ground of a football field. An origin can be fixed in this space at the point where the ball would be located, and two orthogonal dimensions (shown in Figure 2.1 as dotted lines) can be drawn. In this diagram, the *X*s and *O*s represent players (*X*s are defensive players, and *O*s are offensive players). The distance between points corresponds to the distance between players. In general, points in a space can correspond to some entities in the represented world, and distances between points can be used to represent some relation between the entities in the represented

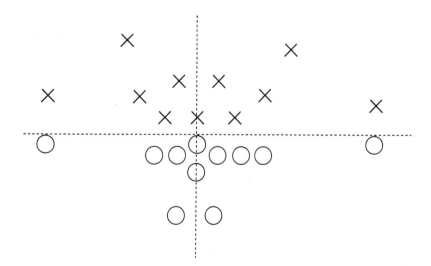

FIG. 2.1. Diagram illustrating positions of players on a football field. The spatial relations between players in the represented world is represented by the spatial relations between circles and *X*s in the representing world.

world. In Figure 2.1, the representing space represents a real spatial configuration, and distance in the representing space corresponds to distance in the represented world.

The represented world need not be a space; the points in a space can represent objects, and the distances between them can represent similarities between objects (as in Figure 2.4). In this case, points close in the space represent objects that are similar to each other. Points that are far away represent objects that are dissimilar. This use of distance fits with the commonsense notion that similar things are mentally "nearer" to each other than are dissimilar things. The distance need not be construed as similarity, however. It is also possible to think of the space as a preference space, with the distance between points corresponding to differences in preference between them. Any quantity that can be construed as changing with the distance between points in this mental space can be represented by distance. Finally, the dimensions of the space can be conceptual features. For example, the dimensions in a space representing a set of animals may reflect size and predacity.

A space is a mathematical concept (I give a formal definition of a space later). This concept is useful for explaining how to measure distance between points in physical space, but I can abstract the definition of a space to more than three dimensions. Of course, the physical world appears as a three dimensional space and most people cannot imagine a space with more than three dimensions. Nonetheless, high-dimensional spaces have been used as representations in many psychological models.

MULTIDIMENSIONAL SCALING

Mental distance models have been very popular in psychology because they are supported by a sophisticated mathematical technique for deriving a map of a space from the distances between points. This technique, called *multidimensional scaling* or MDS, takes as input the distances between points. Using some algorithm (often a gradient descent algorithm that moves the points in the space in directions that improve the fit between the positions of the points and the actual distances), an MDS program develops a map that locates all the points in space (Kruskal & Wish, 1978; Shepard, 1962). Imagine giving an MDS program the lower diagonal matrix in Table 2.1. Each number in the table represents the flying distance between the city in the row and the city in the column. For example, the flying distance between Atlanta and Chicago is 587 miles. The MDS program needs only the lower diagonal matrix, because distances are symmetric, and the upper diagonal matrix would be redundant.

TABLE 2.1
Flying Distances Between 10 Cities in the United States

	Atlanta	Chicago	Denver	Houston	Los Angeles	Miami	New York	San Francisco	Seattle	Washington, DC
Atlanta										
Chicago	587									
Denver	1,212	920								
Houston	701	940	879							
Los Angeles	1,936	1,745	831	1,374						
Miami	604	1,188	1,726	968	2,339					
New York	748	713	1,631	1,420	2,451	1,092				
San Francisco	2,139	1,858	949	1,645	347	2,594	2,571			
Seattle	2,182	1,737	1,021	1,891	959	2,734	2,408	678		
Washington, DC	543	597	1,494	1,220	2,300	923	205	2,442	2,329	

Figure 2.2 shows the best two-dimensional solution for the distances in Table 2.1. The MDS analysis reconstructs a spatial map for these cities in which the cities appear in the same relative locations as on an ordinary map of the United States. The dimensions generated by MDS are arbitrary. In this solution, the east-west dimension is similar to that seen in maps, but the north-south dimension is inverted. Because the dimensions are arbitrary, I can rotate the dimensions to any position desired, as long as the dimensions are orthogonal. Thus, I can easily invert this dimension to get the configuration typically seen on a map.

For cities in the United States, it seems strange to take all this trouble to develop a map, particularly because I can get the same information from an atlas. The power of MDS comes from mapping uncharted mental spaces. Imagine that instead of entering distances between U.S. cities, people were asked to listen to pairs of letters in Morse code and to press one button when the letters were the same and another button when the letters were different. Morse code was developed for telegraphy, and consists of letters made up of combinations of long and short tones. People unfamiliar with Morse code will make some errors in this task. The errors can be placed into a lower diagonal matrix, like the distances between U.S. cities, and a space can be developed. Rothkopf (1957) did such a study and fed the confusion data into an MDS program, which generated the two-dimensional solution shown in Figure 2.3. For reference, the Morse code signals for the 26 letters of the English alphabet are shown in Table 2.2.

The data from this study were simply confusions between Morse code signals. The two-dimensional solution generated is only a spatial description of the data in the lower diagonal matrix. Yet, the MDS solution is a candidate for the representation underlying people's perception of Morse code signals, and the space seems to divide the signals in a way that seems

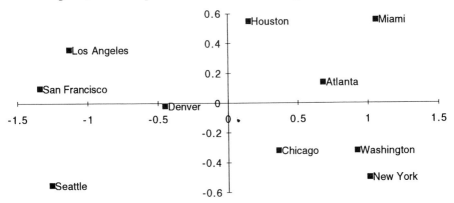

FIG. 2.2. Configuration generated by a multidimensional scaling program with the distances given in Table 2.1. This configuration reconstructs the relative positions of U.S. cities, although the north-south axis is reversed.

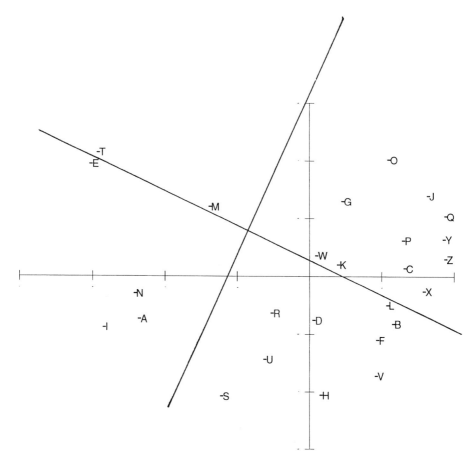

FIG. 2.3. MDS solution obtained from the data from Rothkopf's (1957) study of the similarity of Morse code characters. Two interpretable dimensions are shown as dotted lines on the figure. The more horizontal dimension corresponds to the number of tones in a character; the more vertical dimension corresponds to the relative number of short and long tones in the character.

psychologically plausible. The shortest signals (*E* and *T*, which correspond to the Morse code strings /./ and /-/, respectively) are together in the upper left corner of the space. Following these to the right is a band of four other letters (*I*, *A*, *N*, and *M*), which correspond to Morse code strings with two tones each. In this band, the *I* and *M* are farthest apart, a sensible arrangement because *I* corresponds to the string with two short tones /. ./, and *M* corresponds to the string with two long tones /- -/. The letters *A* (/.-/) and *N* (/-./), which have one short tone and one long tone, are between them. This band of two-tone letters is followed by a band of

TABLE 2.2
The 26 Letters of the English Alphabet and
Their Corresponding Morse Code Signals

Letter	Signal	Letter	Signal
A	. -	N	- .
B	- . . .	O	- - -
C	- . - .	P	. - - .
D	- . .	Q	- - . -
E	.	R	. - .
F	. . - .	S	. . .
G	- - .	T	-
H	. . . .	U	. . -
I	. .	V	. . . -
J	. - - -	W	. - -
K	- . -	X	- . . -
L	. - . .	Y	- . - -
M	- -	Z	- - . .

three-tone letters (*S, U, R, D, W, K, G,* and *O*); again, the letters farthest apart (*S* and *O*), consist of all short tones /.../ and all long tones /- - -/, respectively. Finally, there is a band of four-tone letters at the farthest right (*H, V, F, B, L, C, X, P, Z, Y, J,* and *Q*). In this case, *H*, the letter consisting of all short tones /..../ is farthest to the bottom. There is no Morse code string with four long tones, but the three letters with three long tones (*J, Q,* and *Y*) are all at the opposite end of the four-tone band from *H*. Thus, the dimensions of the space seem to be the length of the Morse code strings and the long and short tones in the character string. The actual dimensions derived from an MDS program are arbitrary: Rotating the dimensions and drawing a pair of orthogonal dimensions make the character length and long- versus short-tone dimensions clearer. These dimensions are also drawn in Figure 2.3.[1]

In many situations, the experimenter determines the dimensions underlying the space by looking at the configuration of points. In the case of the Morse code data, it is straightfoward to look at this configuration and pull out length and tone type as dimensions. Another technique that can produce interpretations of the dimensions derived from MDS requires people to give ratings of the objects forming the points in space on dimensions expected to form the basis of the space. These data can be entered into a multiple regression equation in which the scale rating for each point is predicted by the coordinates of the point in some arbitrary

---

[1]To see what the configuration looks like with the other axes drawn, rotate the page so that the other axes are vertical and horizontal. This may seem obvious, but a configuration can look different when rotated to a different orientation.

space. If the multiple regression equation predicts significant variance in the rating, the best fitting regression line may be interpreted as a dimension underlying the space.

MDS provides a powerful tool for describing psychological data. From responses by participants in studies (in this case, judgments of "same" and "different"), it is possible to derive a description that seems like a plausible candidate for the information people extract from the stimuli presented. Regardless of whether mental space representations are a good idea for developing an account of a particular psychological process, MDS remains an important tool for describing proximity data of this type. Although I am not concerned here with the many MDS algorithms that have been developed for data analysis, a number of excellent sources have reviewed these techniques (Arabie, Carroll, & Desarbo, 1987; Kruskal & Wish, 1978).

USING SPACE TO REPRESENT SPACE

If mental spaces are used as representations, it seems straightforward to use mental space as a representation of physical space and particularly of the visual experience of physical space. Researchers have offered many proposals that have implicitly or explicitly assumed that key spatial properties of images are preserved in mental representations of visual images (Glenberg, Kruley, & Langston, 1994; Shepard & Cooper, 1982; Tye, 1991). According to these models, representations of mental images are like real images: The format of the mental representation of visual images preserves spatial relations among elements. In this representation, points near each other in the represented space are represented by points near each other in the representing world, and operations performed on the representing world treat it as a space. For example, to move from one point in a representation to another requires traversing the intermediate points.

A number of classic studies were performed to support this view. For example, Kosslyn, Ball, and Reiser (1978) asked people to learn the locations of objects on the map of an island. After this learning phase, the researchers asked the subjects to form an image of the whole map and to focus on an object on the map named by an experimenter. Then, a second object was named. If the new object was also on the map, people were to scan their mental image of the map from one location to the next and to press a button when they reached the location of the second object. As expected if mental images preserved spatial relations, it took longer to mentally scan between objects distant on the map than to scan between objects close together on the map. Expanding the image of the map uniformly increased the scanning times, as expected if the image representation was spatial.

A second classic phenomenon that bears on visual representation is that of mental rotation (Shepard & Cooper, 1982). In the typical study of this phenomenon, researchers showed people nonsense figures or letters. For the nonsense figures, pairs of figures oriented in slightly different ways were shown. On each trial, participants were to press one button if the figures were identical (except for the difference in orientation) and a second button if they were mirror images of each other. For letters, a single letter was presented with some degree of rotation from its canonical position, and participants were asked to press one button if the letter was presented as it is normally written (except for the difference in orientation) and a second button if the letter was a mirror image of the way it is normally written. For both studies, the time to respond was essentially a linear function of the angle of rotation, with figures at higher degrees of rotation requiring more time for response than figures at low degrees of rotation.

Both of these studies were motivated by the assumption that representations of visual information have a spatial component. That is, the mental image itself has a two- or three-dimensional form, and operating on an image involves processes like "scanning" from one point in the image to another or "rotating" the image. Early critics of these models (e.g., Pylyshyn, 1981) described flaws in this approach to mental representation. Pylyshyn pointed out that going from one point to another in an image requires knowing the relative locations of the points. Otherwise, a person is likely to take a mental journey in the wrong direction. Similarly, to rotate one figure into another through the shortest distance requires some knowledge of what the figure depicts. To know the relative location of pairs of points or to know what a figure depicts, a person must have some way of looking at the entire space. If the mental image was really a "picture" in the head, though, looking at the entire space would require someone who could look at the image and interpret it. This is the homunculus problem discussed in chapter 1.

The homunculus problem is avoided here by assuming that all mental representations are acted on by computational processes. These computations can be carried out without benefit of an intelligent agent (e.g., Kosslyn, 1994; Tye, 1991). This process, however, does not obviate the fact that going from point A to point B requires knowing the direction in which the journey takes place. To solve problems of this type, most models of mental imagery assume that there are both spatial representing worlds for mental images and also other representing worlds that explicitly represent relations. The mental representation of a space may have a relation telling it that point A is north of point B. This qualitative relation is hard to represent in a space; because distance is a continuous quantity, it is better to use discrete symbols to represent such relations (see chaps. 3

and 5). Thus, mental imagery is likely to require both a spatial representing world and a representing world with discrete symbols in it (see also Kosslyn, 1994).

USING SPACE TO REPRESENT CONCEPTS

As already discussed, mental spaces can be used to represent actual spaces. How can a mental space be used in a psychological model of conceptual processing? In the example of Rothkopf's study of Morse code, I used a matrix of confusion data to develop a spatial representation, then decided that the space looked psychologically plausible. I did not specify a process that may act on such a representation or embed this representation in a model of a psychological task. Fortunately, there are examples of spatial representations that have been used in models of psychological processes. This section describes a few such models.

One simple and elegant model was developed by Rips, Shoben, and Smith (1973) to account for the ease with which people can verify simple class-inclusion statements like "A robin is an animal" and "A robin is a bird." The typical measure of ease for verifying these statements is a person's response time to say True or False when presented with a statement of the form "An *X* is a *Y*." People generally need less time to verify that an object is a member of its immediate superordinate category than to verify that it is a member of a more distant superordinate category. For example, people are faster to respond True to the sentence "A robin is a bird" than they are to respond to the sentence "A robin is an animal." This finding is not surprising, as *bird* is a more specific category than is *animal*. The opposite pattern of results, however, also occurs: People are *slower* to respond to the sentence "A bear is a mammal" than to the sentence "A bear is an animal," even though *mammal* is a more specific category than is *animal*. People also respond faster to the sentence "A bear is an animal" than to the sentence "A robin is an animal," even though both sentences require examining a common superordinate category.

To explain patterns of data like this, Rips et al. (1973) derived a spatial representation of animals and a representation of birds by collecting ratings of pairwise relatedness for all pairs in a set of mammals and in a set of birds. These relatedness ratings were then submitted to an MDS program. The configurations generated by the MDS program are shown in Figure 2.4. The researchers assumed that people verified one category as a subset of another by traversing the distance from one to another. If the points were near to each other, that would be evidence that the categories were related. Rips et al. did not specify how the subset–superset relation is determined; nothing inherent in distance discloses the relation between

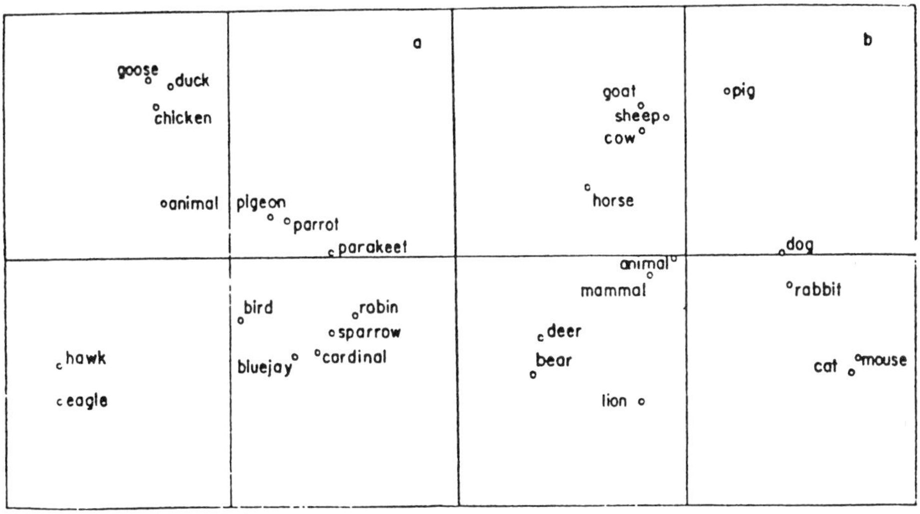

FIG. 2.4. MDS solution obtained from judgments of relatedness among a set of birds and a set of animals. These spatial solutions were used in a model of people's ability to verify sentences of the form "An *X* is a *Y*." From L. J. Rips, E. J. Shoben, and E. E. Smith (1973). Copyright © 1973 by Academic Press. Reprinted with permission.

objects, and distance measures only the relatedness of the concepts. Nonetheless, according to this model, people would be faster to respond to sentences involving points that are near to each other than to respond to sentences involving points that are far apart. To test this hypothesis, the distances from the derived space were compared to the response times in the verification task. The distances between the object and its superordinate category in the mental space were correlated with the statement verification times, a finding suggesting that the more similar the object was to its superordinate, the faster that a statement of the form "An *X* is a *Y*" could be verified.

A more elaborate use of spatial representations was developed by Rumelhart and Abrahamson (1973), who used such a representation to model people's performance on four-term analogy problems (see also Rips et al., 1973; Tourangeau & Sternberg, 1981). Four-term analogy problems are the *A* is to *B* as *C* is to *D* problems typically seen on achievement tests; a person must extract some relation between the *A* and the *B* terms and then find *C* and *D* terms with the same relation between them. In a spatial representation, an analogy can be thought of as a correspondence between one dimensional structure and another. Rumelhart and Abrahamson (1973) suggested that analogies can be solved by a parallelogram method in which the relation between the *A* and *B* terms is found by drawing a line from the A term to the B term. Next, a line is drawn from the A term to the prospective C term. The analogy is a good one to the extent that the line drawn from the C term to the D term is of the same distance and direction as the line from the A term to the B term. For example, Figure 2.4 shows the two-dimensional space for birds developed by Rips et al. (1973). A simple analogy such as Robin is to Sparrow as Duck is to ? is processed by first drawing a line between Robin and Sparrow and then drawing a line from Robin to Duck. Finally, a line of the length and direction between Robin and Sparrow can be drawn. This procedure suggests that Chicken is an appropriate completion to this analogy.

In a variety of studies, Rumelhart and Abrahamson (1973) and Rips et al. (1973) gave people four-term analogies in which they had to select the most appropriate D term from a set of choices. The results suggested that people were indeed selecting a D term that differed from the C term by about the same distance and direction as the B term differed from the A term. Rumelhart and Abrahamson found that people could learn new animals by analogy to old ones. In one study, they arbitrarily placed new points in a space of animals and labeled the points with nonsense words. During the study, the nonsense words sometimes appeared in the four-term analogies. By the end of the study, people appeared to place the nonsense words in approximately the right point in space.

Although this kind of representation provides an interesting account of analogies, there are problems with this approach, in particular, the analogies used to test it seem rather strange. For example, in the absence of a set of choice alternatives, it is not clear that people can generate the correct solution to an analogy like Pigeon is to Parrot as Goose is to ? even though the spatial representations in Figure 2.3 suggest that Duck provides a reasonable response to this analogy. In contrast, in many analogies that people think are good ones, they can generate responses on their own. For example, Cat is to Kitten as Dog is to ? can be solved fairly easily. One reason that the first analogy seems strange whereas the second seems natural is that people apparently prefer relations between A and B terms which they can name explicitly; the relation between Pigeon and Parrot seems hard to name. The model of analogy based on spatial representations requires only a distance and a direction and needs no more explicit labeled relations between things; hence it seems to lack something as a model of analogy.

Indeed, there is evidence that subjects found the analogies used in studies testing this spatial model to be odd. Sadler and Shoben (1993) demonstrated that people in these studies were probably not using the parallelogram model suggested by Rumelhart and Abrahamson (1973). Instead, participants tended to select the answer from the set of choices closest to the C term in space. This result suggests that participants could not find the relation between the *A* and *B* terms and so used a simple heuristic to select a *D* term for the analogy on the basis of a *C* term and choices of possible *D* terms. This solution strategy contrasts with people's behavior with analogies like the Cat is to Kitten analogy, for which the relation between the *A* and *B* terms is readily apparent and easily extended to other objects.

Despite these problems with the model of analogy, these examples offer some lessons on the use of spatial models. First, it is straightforward to use spatial representations in models of psychological processing. In the case of sentence verification, the key aspect was a correlation between distance in a mental space and response time. Of course, many details would have to be filled in to make an algorithmic-level description of sentence verification. In the case of analogy, the process was somewhat more complex and required a mapping between two spaces. In the examples discussed here, the points were both in the same space, and so this mapping was not required. With more complex analogies in which birds were mapped to animals or characters in a play, the dimensions of two distinct spaces would have to be aligned. Indeed, Tourangeau and Sternberg (1981) suggested that metaphors become more apt not only as the distance and direction between the *A* and *B* terms match the distance and direction between the *C* and *D* terms, but also as the distance between the domain encompassing the *A* and *B* terms and the domain encompassing the *C* and *D* terms increases. Thus, a metaphor comparing one person's eyes to another person's is less apt than a metaphor comparing one person's eyes to the sun.

These examples also demonstrate the limits of the power of a spatial representation. The processes that operate on a spatial representation are sensitive to the distance between points. Thus, spatial models do not employ ways of describing points which do not use distances. A psychologist looking at an MDS solution like the one in Figure 2.4 may infer that people were sensitive to the size of birds, because small birds lie on one side of the space and large birds on the other. A model that operates over this space, however, does not use these dimension interpretations explicitly and thus does not explicitly use information about size.

Using the Definition of Space

Earlier, I pointed out that space is a mathematical notion with a formal mathematical definition. In this section, I discuss some main axioms that must hold for something to be a space. The formal properties of a space make spatial representations easy to test. If a domain that needs to be represented does not obey the axioms that define a space, a spatial model may be a poor choice as a representing world for that domain. The axioms help determine the power of spatial representations.

A. Tversky (1977) discussed three metric axioms that define the concept of a space: *minimality, symmetry,* and the *triangle inequality.* Minimality is captured by the mathematical regularity:

$$d(x,\ x) = d(y,\ y) = 0, \tag{2.1}$$

where $d\ (x,\ y)$ is the function that returns the distance between two points (here x and itself). This axiom states that the distance between any point and itself in a space a minimum (that is, 0). This minimum distance is the same for any point and itself. That is, I am as close to myself as I can get, and you are as close to yourself as you can get.

The symmetry axioms can be cast as:

$$d(x,\ y) = d(y,\ x). \tag{2.2}$$

That is, the distance between any two points (here x and y) is the same regardless of whether measured starting with point x or with point y. For example, a person travels the same distance from New York to Boston whether the departure is from New York or Boston (otherwise, a host of junior high school algebra problems would not work at all).

Finally, the triangle inequality states:

$$d(x,\ y) \leq d(x,\ z) + d(y,\ z). \tag{2.3}$$

That is, the distance between any two points is always less than or equal to the sum of the distances between those points and a third point. If the third point lies on the line between x and y, the distance is equal. Otherwise, the sum is always greater than the distance between x and y. This axiom simply says that it cannot be shorter to travel from point A to point B by going through point C than it is to go directly from point A to point B.

Another aspect of the mathematical concept of space is that it is not always necessary to calculate distance as it is calculated in the world. In daily life, people calculate distance "as the crow flies": They draw a straight line from point x to point y, and the length of the line is the distance between points. This is the standard Euclidean notion of distance. Mathematically, I can write this distance calculation as:

$$d(x, y) = \left[\sum_{i=1}^{N} (x_i - y_i)^2 \right]^{\frac{1}{2}}, \tag{2.4}$$

where N is the number of dimensions, and x_i and y_i are the values for points x and y along dimension i. In two dimensions, this is the familiar Pythagorean formula for the length of the hypotenuse of a right triangle, but this equation can be generalized to consider noneuclidean distances. The generalization of this formula is simply:

$$d(x, y) = \left[\sum_{i=1}^{N} (x_i - y_i)^r \right]^{\frac{1}{r}}. \tag{2.5}$$

The exponent r in this formula is called the Minkowski metric. When $r =$ 2, distance is Euclidean. Another frequently used metric is the *city block* distance metric, which is obtained with an exponent of 1. In the city block metric, distance is not measured "as the crow flies," but rather as if a person was walking on the sidewalks of a city. For each unit of distance on each dimension, the person must walk along the perimeter of the triangle rather than cutting across. For example, in New York, getting from 120th Street and Broadway to 119th Street and Amsterdam requires walking one block east (from Broadway to Amsterdam) and one block south (from 120th St. to 119th St.) It would be convenient to cut the corner and walk straight, but Columbia University is in the way.

The importance of this variety of distance metrics is that people can choose to measure distance in a representing space in different ways depending on what they are representing with it. If the represented world is a real space, they may calculate distance in the representation by using a euclidean distance metric. If the represented world is something that comes in discrete steps, they may use a city block metric. I can use a space to represent bags of Halloween candy collected by children; here, each dimension corresponds to a type of candy. The distance between points can represent the perceived similarity of the load of candy collected by each child. Because candy bars are discrete units, however, it probably makes more sense to calculate the distance between points by using a city block metric rather than a euclidean distance.

One nice thing about having a strict formal definition for a space is that, for any given application of spatial representations, it is possible to test whether a representation is appropriate for the task. A. Tversky (1977) examined whether metric axioms held for similarity judgments to test whether spatial representations were appropriate for models of similarity. He found systematic violations of all three metric axioms. As a violation of the minimality axiom, Tversky pointed to studies like the one by Roth-kopf described previously. In that study, the probability that people made a correct same–different judgment was not the same for all items. This result can be interpreted as an indication that people consider some pairs of identical objects more similar to each other than to other pairs (at least in this task context).

Tversky also found violations of the symmetry axiom, most typically from embedding objects in different sentence contexts. People (at least in the United States) prefer to say "Mexico is like the United States" rather than "The United States is like Mexico." This example suggests that comparison statements do not necessarily mean the same thing when the order of the terms is reversed. As another example, the metaphorical statement "That butcher is a surgeon" is a compliment, but the statement "That surgeon is a butcher" is not.

Finally, researchers have pointed out violations of the triangle inequality. Typically, these violations result from different comparisons that use different aspects of an object. William James (1892/1989) noted that the moon is similar to a ball, because both are round; that the moon is similar to a lamp, because both are bright; but that a ball and a lamp are not at all similar. A. Tversky and Gati (1982) obtained a similar result with a variety of materials.

These findings do not mean that mental space representations are incorrect for all applications in psychology, but they may have limitations on their effectiveness. When cases lead to violations of the metric axioms, it is possible that some other kind of representation is more appropriate as the basis of a psychological account of these phenomena. Of course, faced with data like these, it is important to remember that explanations of psychological processes require both representations and statements of processes that use these representations. Changing the way that representations are processed can also help explain violations of the metric axioms.

To save mental space models, Nosofsky (1986) proposed that the weights on dimensions be adjusted dynamically. For example, dimensions along which there are close matches may be given greater weight than dimensions along which two items have very different values. Thus, in the William James example earlier mentioned, "roundness" may have greater weight when comparing the moon to a ball than when comparing the moon to a lamp. Similarly, "brightness" may have greater weight when comparing the moon to a lamp than when comparing the moon to a ball. The comparison of a ball to a lamp has no close matches, and so no dimensions are weighted heavily. Processing principles like this one may explain violations of the metric axioms.

Krumhansl (1978) gave a comprehensive suggestion for dealing with violations of the metric axioms. She proposed that the density of points in a neighborhood can be factored into calculations of similarity in a mental space representation. As one test of this hypothesis, Krumhansl examined asymmetries in Rothkopf's Morse code data. In all, she found 39 cases with large asymmetries in correct responding (in which presenting the pair with one of the letters appearing first led to more incorrect responses than did presenting the pair with the other letter first). Consistent with her hypothesis, in 26 cases, there were more errors when the first letter presented in the pair had more neighbors in semantic space than did the second letter (i.e., the space around the first letter was more dense). In contrast, for only 5 cases did the asymmetry show more errors when the first letter presented had fewer neighbors in semantic space than did the second letter presented (there were eight ties). Thus, by assuming that mental distance can be sensitive to the density of points in a space, data that appear to violate the metric axioms can be accommodated.

A final objection against MDS models as techniques for uncovering latent psychological dimensions arises from studies examining the relation between MDS solutions and ratings of other psychological dimensions (Gerrig, Maloney, & Tversky, 1991). As discussed previously, ratings on scales can be used to label the dimensions of a space derived from MDS. Gerrig, Maloney, and Tversky asked subjects to state the degree of relatedness of personality traits by filling in the proportion of people likely to have one trait if they were known to have another. This relatedness task was done with a set of positive traits, a set of negative traits, or a mixed set of positive and negative traits. Subjects also rated the traits on dimensions like agreeableness and potency. Gerrig et al. reasoned that if the resulting MDS solutions reflect the underlying psychological dimensions, then the relation of the rated dimensions to the personality traits should be the same in all three data sets (i.e., positive, negative, and mixed). In contrast to this prediction, the relation between the ratings and the coordinates of the traits in space was very different for each set, a finding suggesting that, although MDS provided a reasonable description of the relatedness data, it did not extract a set of fundamental psychological dimensions that form people's representations of personality traits.

To summarize, mental distance models have assumed that objects are represented as points in a multidimensional space. The examples discussed so far consist of fairly low-dimensional spaces. Indeed, MDS techniques rarely yield more than five dimensions and generally give only three dimensions for which there is a clear interpretation. Some work (like Tversky's) has suggested that the rigid geometric definition of spaces limits the applicability of mental space models to psychology, but with sufficiently rich processing assumptions, spatial models can account for violations of the metric axioms. In the next section, I discuss representational systems using high-dimensionality mental spaces.

HIGH-DIMENSIONAL SEMANTIC SPACES

As just mentioned, many applications of mental space models in psychology have used low-dimensional spaces because spaces derived from MDS models tend to have no more than five good dimensions and typically have only three usable dimensions. Dimensions above the third tend to be unusable for two reasons. First, it is often difficult to figure out what the dimensions mean psychologically, and it is unsatisfying to use dimensions that seem nonsensical. More important, MDS techniques build spaces by minimizing the difference between the distances obtained from data and the fitted distances in the space derived from the model. As the number of dimensions increases, there is less distance that is not fit well. Furthermore, in most applications of MDS, fewer than 30 points are placed in the space because a lower diagonal matrix has:

$$\frac{N(N-1)}{2} \qquad\qquad (2.6)$$

entries in it, where N is the number of points in the space. Obtaining the distances between the 26 letters of the alphabet (and the 10 numerals) as Rothkopf did requires 630 distances. If these distances are obtained by having people do pairwise comparisons, 630 experimental trials would be required. At a rate of one trial every 10 seconds, this experiment would require an hour and 45 minutes. It is difficult to get people to sit through so many trials for that long a period without getting frustrated, and so psychological experiments often use many fewer points. For example, getting the pairwise distances between 16 points requires 120 observations to fill the lower diagonal matrix. At 10 seconds per trial, this study can be done in 20 minutes.

There are, however, other techniques for developing higher dimensional spaces. Increases in the speed of computers have allowed brute-force techniques that develop representations of words in the lexicon by analyzing large corpora of text (Burgess & Lund, 1997; Landauer & Dumais, 1996, 1997). For example, Landauer and Dumais developed a model of the lexicon through the analysis of a large corpus of text. Their interest was in the practical problem of retrieving articles from a large database on the basis of a query in the form of a set of keywords. One way to solve this problem, used in many database retrieval systems, is to index each entry by a set of keywords determined in advance. With this technique, however, new keywords cannot be added, and if a user enters a synonym to a keyword, the system finds nothing. In traditional systems, getting around this problem requires a thesaurus of index terms so that people can look up the proper word to enter for their query.

It would be convenient to have a system developed on the basis of articles entered into the database, rather than on the basis of pre-established keywords. Unfortunately, devising a system like this requires creating a method for dynamically establishing the meaning of keywords used for a search. Landauer and Dumais's solution to this problem was to use a mathematical technique called singular value decomposition (related to factor analysis) to analyze statistical relationships among words in a corpus. In this way, they obtained some notion of the "meaning" of the words in the articles being indexed.

In this technique, a large number of documents are put into a matrix in which words that are part of the system are placed in the rows of the matrix; documents in the corpus make up the columns. This matrix is then factored, and many factors that account for only small amounts of variance in the original matrix are discarded. Thus, the matrix may start with 50,000 rows (corresponding to 50,000 words); after dimensions are discarded, it may be reduced to between 150 and 300 dimensions. This reduced matrix contains much information about the higher order correlational structure between the words in the input.

Imagine that a new query is entered into a system that has been reduced to 200 dimensions. This query is translated into a 200-dimensional vector. It may be hard to visualize 200 dimensions, but things work just as if there were only 2 or 3 dimensions. Just as a 2-dimensional vector is a ray in 2-dimensional space, a 200-dimensional vector shoots out in a particular direction in a higher dimensional space. By using the trigonometric function cosine, it is possible to find other vectors in space that are similar to the vector formed by the query. In a space, cosine is a measure of similarity. Two vectors that go in exactly the same direction have a cosine of one, and two vectors that are orthogonal have a cosine of zero. Vectors that go in approximately the same direction have cosines near one. Those vectors in the system with a high vector cosine with the query are likely to be semantically similar to the query. In practice, this system has eased retreival of journal articles from a database.

This method was also tested on the synonyms test from the Test of English as a Foreign Language (TOEFL). First, a singular value decomposition was obtained for segments of text from over 30,000 articles in an encyclopedia. The initial matrix had entries for over 60,000 words, and optimum performance was obtained with a decomposition that reduced this structure to between 300 and 325 dimensions. The system was given the vector corresponding to a word from the test, and the cosine between the vector corresponding to the test word and the vectors corresponding to the forced choice options were determined. The choice option with the highest cosine to the test vector was selected as the right answer. This system was able to get about 65% of the responses correct, approximately the level obtained by the average student from a non-English speaking country who takes the test.

This test demonstrates both the strengths and weaknesses of this high-dimensional space approach. On the positive side, a simple brute-force mechanism was able to capture semantic similarities between words. Although the system must process a lot of text to work, it is unclear that the amount of text is much greater than is the experience of a child learning language. Furthermore, the calculations are very simple: There is no need for an extensive decomposition of the text entered. The system does not analyze words and does not even remove morphological endings (like the -ed past tense ending on verbs). Rather, the system must discover the similarities between the same word stem with different morphological endings. Nonetheless, with very little tweaking, it performs a synonyms test at the level of non-native speakers of English who also take the same test.

Despite this success, there are weaknesses with this kind of spatial representation. In particular, it is fortunate that the model was tested with the synonyms test and not the antonyms test. The commonsense view is that antonyms are dissimilar from each other, but from another viewpoint, antonyms are very similar. *Depressed* may be an antonym for *elated*, but it is far more similar to *elated* than it is to *rhinoceros*. Indeed, a good pair of antonyms is as similar as possible to each other except for a very different value along a salient dimension. If a language processor cannot decompose a representation into a dimensional or featural structure, it cannot tell the difference between synonyms and antonyms. Thus, although techniques like singular value decomposition are very powerful, they cannot provide a complete basis for understanding word meaning, because they can determine only the proximity of two words in a semantic space. The representations do not contain all the information about the meanings of words that people seem to be able to use when processing language.

CONNECTIONIST MODELS: HOW THEY WORK

High-dimensional spaces like those developed using singular value decomposition can be quite powerful. In the example just described, the vectors were processed in only a simple way: Pairs of vectors were compared to find the vector cosine between them. Researchers have developed, however, a powerful set of techniques that allow pairs of vectors to become associated in much the same way that people can learn associations between concepts. The technique used to develop these associations involves a form of *connectionist modeling*. In this section, I discuss connectionist models that learn associations, and I examine their use of high-dimensional spaces (see J. A. Anderson, 1995; McClelland & Rumelhart, 1986).

Connectionism is a blanket term for a computational model described by analogy to the way the brain may function. Although the brain has an enormous number of neurons, each individual neuron does not do much. It can "fire" or send an electrical signal from the cell body to the end of the cell. When this signal (called an *action potential*) reaches the end of the cell, it sends chemicals (called *neurotransmitters*) into the space between cells (called a *synaptic cleft*). These chemicals influence neighboring cells. If the influence makes a neighboring cell more likely to fire, the relation between cells is *excitatory*. If the influence makes a neighboring cell less likely to fire, the relation between cells is *inhibitory*. No single cell seems to serve a vital function in the brain. Rather, the collective activity of groups of neurons leads to interesting behavior.

These basic facts about the brain are at the core of connectionist models. A simple connectionist model is illustrated in Figure 2.5. The models consist of *units* (analogous to individual neurons) and *connections* (analogous to *synapses*). In Figure 2.5A, four units, depicted as circles, are labeled input units (for reasons that will become clear), and four units labeled as output units. The connections are illustrated as lines connecting an input unit to an output unit. The connectionist models I discuss in this section

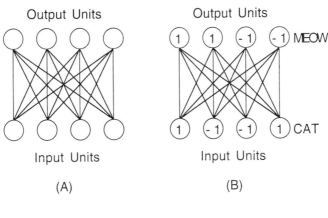

Input Patterns

| 1 | -1 | -1 | 1 | CAT |
| -1 | 1 | -1 | 1 | DOG |

Output Patterns

| 1 | 1 | -1 | -1 | MEOW |
| -1 | -1 | 1 | 1 | BOW WOW |

(C)

FIG. 2.5. A: An illustration of a simple connectionist model. B: The same model with a pattern of activity on its input units giving rise to a second pattern of activity on its output units. C: A set of input and output patterns used in the example of how connectionist models use spatial representations.

are not identical to neurons: Instead of discrete signals that influence neighboring units, each unit has a level of *activation*, which is a value that measures the current influence of a given unit. Activation may be analogous to the rate of firing of a neuron (i.e., how many pulses the neuron sends in a given time). The connections between units determine how the activation of one unit affects the activation of a second unit. If high levels of activation in one unit promote high levels of activation in a second unit, the connection is *excitatory*. If high levels of activation in one unit promote low levels of activation in a second unit, the connection is *inhibitory*. Connections also vary in their *weight*, which determines the degree to which the activation on one unit affects another. Finally, as in the brain, no single unit in a connectionist model represents a concept; the *pattern* of activation across a set of units is used to represent a concept. For example, in Figure 2.5B, the network has activation levels of 1, −1, −1, and 1 across its four units. For the moment, assume that this pattern of activation represents the concept *cat.*

In a simple connectionist model like the one shown in Figure 2.5A, the activation of the input units influences the activation of the output units. For example, I want the network to learn to produce a pattern of activation representing the concept *meow* when the pattern of activation representing the concept *cat* occurs. For this example, I assume that the concept *meow* is represented by the pattern of activity −1, −1, 1, 1 on the four output units. How may this association be learned?

Understanding how connectionist models do what they do, requires thinking about the spatial properties of the distributed representation. (This discussion draws heavily on concepts from linear algebra, and I present vectors and matrices with the text that follows. Readers not familiar with the concepts of linear algebra can read this section without spending too much time on the mathematics and still get the general flavor of what a distributed connectionist model does.) To think of a distributed representation as a spatial representation, first notice that the values of the input units can be written as a vector. For example, the activations of the units representing *cat* in Figure 2.5B can be written:

$$\mathbf{f}_{cat} = \begin{bmatrix} 1 \\ -1 \\ -1 \\ 1 \end{bmatrix}. \tag{2.6}$$

This vector points from an origin in a four dimensional space to the point $(1, -1, -1, 1)$. What is needed is some way of having this pattern of activation on the input units pass through the connections and give rise to the vector:

$$\mathbf{g}_{\text{meow}} = \begin{bmatrix} 1 \\ 1 \\ -1 \\ -1 \end{bmatrix} \tag{2.7}$$

on the output units. In the discussion that follows, I refer to whole vectors and matrices using bold type (e.g., **f**) and individual elements of a vector or matrix using regular type (e.g., f). Following established conventions, I refer to input vectors as **f**, with a subscript that states what the vector represents. I refer to output vectors as **g**, also with a subscript that states what it represents. Sometimes it is convenient to write a vector as a row rather than a column. In this case, I refer to the *transpose* of a vector **f**, as **f′** or:

$$\mathbf{f}'_{\text{cat}} = [\ 1 \ -1 \ -1 \ 1\ ]. \tag{2.8}$$

The connections between the input and output units can be written as a matrix (typically called **A**), in which a given element A_{ij} represents the connection between input unit i and output unit j.

Simple connectionist models assume that the activation of a unit in the output is just the sum of the activations of the input units connected to that output unit multiplied by the weight of the connection. That is, the activation of some output unit g_j is just:

$$g_j = \sum_{i=1}^{N} A_{ij} f_i, \tag{2.9}$$

where A_{ij} is the connection between input unit i and output unit j, and f_i is the activation of input unit i. More generally, with a matrix of connection weights **A** and an input vector **f**, the operation:

$$\mathbf{g} = \mathbf{A}\,\mathbf{f} \tag{2.10}$$

determines the entire output vector (where each element g_j of the output vector is determined by equation 2.9).

There is a way of getting just the right pattern of connections between the input and output units through the linear algebraic operation called the *outer product*. The outer product is the operation **g f′**, which with two N-dimensional vectors yields an $N \times N$ matrix. The change in each element of the matrix **A**, which I denote $\Delta \mathbf{A}_{ij}$, is:

$$\Delta \mathbf{A}_{ij} = g_j\, f_i. \tag{2.11}$$

If this formula is applied to the vectors corresponding to *cat* and *meow* in Figure 2.5C, the resulting weight matrix is:

$$\mathbf{A}_{\text{cat meow}} = \begin{bmatrix} 1 & -1 & -1 & 1 \\ 1 & -1 & -1 & 1 \\ -1 & 1 & 1 & -1 \\ -1 & 1 & 1 & -1 \end{bmatrix}. \tag{2.12}$$

To see that this connection matrix really does create the output vector for *meow* (vector 2.7) with the input *cat* (vector 2.6), apply equation 2.9 to this matrix of connection weights. The outer product operation allows the weights on the connections between the input and output units to be created in a way that produces a given output with the corresponding input. In this way, the input is associated with the output. Thus, like a toddler learning to make animal sounds, this matrix is learning the association between the animal name and the sound (if there really is a way of attaching these representing vectors to some represented world).

If connectionist models learned only a single association, they would not be very interesting. Connectionist models have generated excitement in the cognitive science community because the same set of units can be used to store a variety of distinct associations. For example, Figure 2.5C shows activation patterns for CAT, DOG, MEOW, and BOW WOW. If I have already taught a connectionist model the association between *cat* and *meow* by using the procedure just described, I can now teach it the association between *dog* and *bow wow* in the same way. I take the outer product of the vectors for *dog* and *bow wow* and generate their outer product by using equation 2.10 yielding:

$$\mathbf{A}_{\text{dog bow wow}} = \begin{bmatrix} 1 & -1 & 1 & -1 \\ 1 & -1 & 1 & -1 \\ -1 & 1 & -1 & 1 \\ -1 & 1 & -1 & 1 \end{bmatrix}. \tag{2.13}$$

Then, I add the connection matrix with the weights that yield MEOW with CAT (matrix 2.12) to the connection matrix that yields BOW WOW with DOG (matrix 2.13). Adding two matrices involves adding together all the corresponding elements in a pair of matrices. This operation yields:

$$\mathbf{A}_{\text{combined}} = \begin{bmatrix} 2 & -2 & 0 & 0 \\ 2 & -2 & 0 & 0 \\ -2 & 2 & 0 & 0 \\ -2 & 2 & 0 & 0 \end{bmatrix}. \tag{2.14}$$

First, I can demonstrate that the two associations entered into the system were learned by multiplying the connection matrix and the input vector as in equation 2.9. Carrying out this multiplication for the *cat* association yields:

$$A_{combined} * f_{cat} = \begin{bmatrix} 2 & -2 & 0 & 0 \\ 2 & -2 & 0 & 0 \\ -2 & 2 & 0 & 0 \\ -2 & 2 & 0 & 0 \end{bmatrix} * \begin{bmatrix} 1 \\ -1 \\ -1 \\ 1 \end{bmatrix} = \begin{bmatrix} 4 \\ 4 \\ -4 \\ -4 \end{bmatrix}. \tag{2.15}$$

Notice that the elements in the resulting array have the value 4, whereas the initial association for MEOW shown in Figure 2.4C had the value 1. This vector, however, does go in the same direction. Indeed, the obtained vector is simply the vector for MEOW with each entry multiplied by 4. Such a scalar multiplication preserves the direction of the initial vector. In connectionist models, it is the direction of vectors that matters. If I was worried about vector length, I could have arbitrarily set the values of the elements in the input and output vectors so that the vectors would have a length of 1, and then the values in the input vector would have matched the values in the output vector exactly, but this procedure would have made the example harder to follow. Finally, for completeness, we can also retrieve the association for DOG by:

$$A_{combined} * f_{dog} = \begin{bmatrix} 2 & -2 & 0 & 0 \\ 2 & -2 & 0 & 0 \\ -2 & 2 & 0 & 0 \\ -2 & 2 & 0 & 0 \end{bmatrix} * \begin{bmatrix} -1 \\ 1 \\ -1 \\ 1 \end{bmatrix} = \begin{bmatrix} -4 \\ -4 \\ 4 \\ 4 \end{bmatrix}. \tag{2.16}$$

The output vector associated with *dog* is in the same direction as the *bow wow* vector, but it is longer.

This example demonstrates that one can superimpose multiple patterns and still retrieve information from the system. How is all this related to the notion of a space? The ability to overlay one pattern of connection weights on another is made possible by the geometric (i.e., spatial) properties of vectors. In the section on high-dimensional semantic spaces, I introduced the idea that the similarity of a pair of vectors can be determined by finding the cosine between them. The cosine of a pair of vectors can be determined by taking the *dot product* of those vectors as follows:

$$\text{Dot Product} = \sum_{i=1}^{N} f_i g_i \tag{2.17}$$

and then dividing the dot product by the lengths of the vectors being compared (the length of a vector is simply the sum of values of each unit squared). Taking the dot product of the DOG and CAT vectors yields a value of 0; thus there is no similarity between these vectors (they are orthogonal). No part of the DOG vector goes in the direction of the CAT vector. This result is important, because the output of the multiplication of the weight matrix and a new input vector in a system like this is proportional to the amount of the input vector in the same direction as (i.e., the amount that *projects on*) input vectors that the system has already seen. Because the DOG and CAT vectors go in orthogonal directions, the DOG → BOW WOW association and the CAT → MEOW association can be stored in the same connection matrix.

This geometry is evident in two additional examples. First, imagine a new vector for the input pattern *pig*, which the system has not learned. *Pig* is represented by:

$$\mathbf{f}_{pig} = \begin{bmatrix} 1 \\ 1 \\ -1 \\ -1 \end{bmatrix}. \tag{2.18}$$

Calculating the dot product of this vector with both the *dog* and *cat* vectors shows that both are 0. That is, this vector is in a new direction from the *cat* and *dog* vectors. Associated with *pig* in the current weight matrix is:

$$\mathbf{A}_{combined} * \mathbf{f}_{pig} = \begin{bmatrix} 2 & -2 & 0 & 0 \\ 2 & -2 & 0 & 0 \\ -2 & 2 & 0 & 0 \\ -2 & 2 & 0 & 0 \end{bmatrix} * \begin{bmatrix} 1 \\ 1 \\ -1 \\ -1 \end{bmatrix} = \begin{bmatrix} 0 \\ 0 \\ 0 \\ 0 \end{bmatrix}. \tag{2.19}$$

Thus, there is no already learned association for *pig*. The network gives no output.

What happens if I ask the network about an animal that was like a *cat*? To make a vector for an animal similar to a *cat*, just add a bit of "noise" to the vector by adding and subtracting a bit from each of its values:

$$\mathbf{f}_{like\ a\ cat} = \begin{bmatrix} 1.3 \\ -1.0 \\ -0.7 \\ 1.2 \end{bmatrix}. \tag{2.20}$$

This vector is not in quite the same direction as the *cat* vector. In fact, it has a vector cosine of 0.93 with the *cat* vector. Obviously, it is still similar to *cat*, but it is no longer in an identical direction. The output obtained when this vector is presented to the system is:

$$
\mathbf{A}_{\text{combined}} * \mathbf{f}_{\text{like a cat}} =
\begin{bmatrix}
2 & -2 & 0 & 0 \\
2 & -2 & 0 & 0 \\
-2 & 2 & 0 & 0 \\
-2 & 2 & 0 & 0
\end{bmatrix}
*
\begin{bmatrix}
1.3 \\
-1.0 \\
-0.7 \\
1.2
\end{bmatrix}
=
\begin{bmatrix}
4.6 \\
4.6 \\
-4.6 \\
-4.6
\end{bmatrix}.
\qquad (2.21)
$$

The output pattern is still in the same direction as the vector for *meow*. That is, the network was able to "generalize" to another input that was geometrically similar but not identical to the one that the model learned.

This geometry holds the power of distributed connectionist models. The input vectors exist in a space defined by the weight matrix, and new vectors that have never been seen can still generate an output to the extent that some portion of the vector falls in a direction for which the network already has an association. In connectionist models, there are generally more than four input and output units. For a two-layer network (one with only an input and an output layer), a maximum of N distinct associations can be learned perfectly, where N is the number of dimensions because only N orthogonal vectors fit into an N-dimensional space. In practice, because the input vectors used in applications of connectionist models are not crafted to ensure that they are all orthogonal, the number of vectors that can be stored before there is too much interference between them to properly learn all the desired associations is often only about 10 to 20% of the number of dimensions. Thus, it is not uncommon for a connectionist model to have hundreds of units that form a high-dimensional space similar to those described in the previous section.

AN EXAMPLE OF A CONNECTIONIST MODEL

As an example of connectionist models in action, I examine a model of prototype formation developed by Knapp and Anderson (1984). The basic psychological phenomenon follows from Posner and Keele's (1970) classic work on classification. They presented participants in a study with dot patterns in a two-dimensional array and asked them to classify the dot patterns into one of two groups. As shown in Figure 2.6, each class of dot patterns was developed from a prototype pattern. Although the prototype was never shown to people, participants saw various distortions of the prototypical pattern. After learning to classify the patterns reliably, people saw various distortions of the prototype as well as the prototype itself (which had not been seen before), and they were asked to classify them. Participants classified the prototype correctly even though it was not seen during learning. Indeed, participants classified the prototype correctly more often than they did examples presented during learning, examples that were extreme distortions of the prototypical pattern.

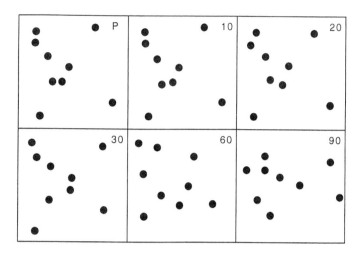

FIG. 2.6. Configurations of points modeled in the simulation by Knapp and Anderson.

To create a connectionist model that exhibits this pattern of behavior, Knapp and Anderson assumed that dots were represented as a pattern of activity in a two-dimensional grid. As shown in Figure 2.7, the pattern of activity was greatest at the center of the dot and fell off gradually as the dot moved farther away. This distributed representation corresponded to a vector of activation values in an input layer. Such input patterns can be associated with output responses. Because the input represents dots as patterns of activity, new patterns that are similar to those seen during learning have vector representations in a direction similar to patterns used to form associations during learning. The prototype of a category, which is similar to many different learned patterns (all of which are distortions of that prototype) is categorized easily by this system. In contrast, patterns that are large distortions of the prototype pattern are not categorized as well, because few patterns stored in the network are similar to the distorted pattern. Thus, the geometric similarity between different input vectors allows this simple connectionist model to account for prototype formation.

This model also highlights the distinction between two uses of space. At one level, this model uses a spatial representation of space: As shown in Figure 2.6, each point in perceptual space is represented by a point in a grid, and nearby points in perceptual space are represented by points near to each other in representational space. At another level, the grid representation is a vector in a high-dimensional space, and similar perceptual patterns give rise to vectors with high vector cosines. Knapp and Anderson were careful to point out that both types of representation are critical for understanding the behavior of the system. It is crucial to the

RESPONSE TO A DOT

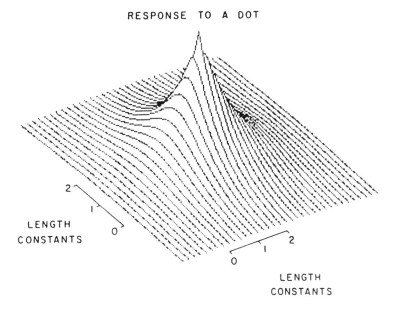

FIG. 2.7. Distributed representation of a dot in space. Units representing points at the center of a dot are most strongly activated. Units representing points farther from the center of a dot are less strongly activated. From A. G. Knapp and J. A. Anderson (1984). Copyright © 1984 by American Psychological Association. Reprinted with permission.

functioning of the model that points are represented as widely distributed patterns of activity in a two-dimensional grid. If each dot is represented as activity in only a single unit in a two-dimensional grid, there is no generalization. Similarly, if activity is spread too widely across the grid for each dot, all patterns tend to interfere with each other. If a spatial grid is not used, the network cannot recognize which points are near to each other in space. The use of an intermediate level of distributed activity combined with the geometric properties of vector representations allows the network to account for the observed pattern of results.

HOW SHOULD WE THINK ABOUT CONNECTIONIST MODELS?

There is often some confusion about how to think of representations in connectionist systems. Because units do not have meaning by themselves, it is tempting to think of them as implementing an alternative representation that is not like the symbols often seen in computer programs and in many psychological models. Indeed, Smolensky (1988) suggested that connectionist models operate at a subsymbolic level, inspired by the fact that each individual unit can best be thought of as representing a very fine-grained feature active in many concepts. People may be unable to interpret what a given unit means, but because the collected activity of a set of units does a reasonable job of representing a concept, a fine-grained set of features must be there somewhere.

In this chapter, I have suggested that the behavior of a simple distributed connectionist model is probably best conceptualized as a high-dimensional space. Thinking about the role of individual units is confusing, but seeing the patterns of activity as vectors makes it clear how the connectionist model is doing what it does. In this way, the representing world in a connectionist model is a lot like the representing worlds in other spatial models described in this chapter.

STRENGTHS AND WEAKNESSES

Some of the same limitations of spatial models discussed previously also apply to connectionist models. I pointed out earlier that the models perform well as long as the major operation is one of finding neighbors in space. For example, the space created by singular value decomposition performed quite well on a test of synonyms, although it would have performed poorly on a test of antonyms. Likewise, simple associative connectionist models gave an output based on the spatial similarity between an input vector and previously seen input vectors. The process of multiplying a weight matrix by an input vector does not allow the vector to be analyzed in any way needed for searching for antonyms rather than synonyms.

Still, connectionist models of this type are very powerful. The example presented previously is J. A. Anderson's (1972) simple linear associator. There are more powerful learning mechanisms, even for simple two-layer networks (Widrow & Hoff, 1960). In addition, researchers have developed algorithms for creating connectionist models with additional layers of units (called *hidden units*) between the input and output units. These hidden units perform a function similar to that of the singular value decomposition described earlier: They find a way of reducing the dimensionality needed to represent information. This dimension reduction finds higher order statistical relations in the activation patterns of units in the network. The networks maintain the basic geometry but are capable of learning more complex associations between input units and output units.

BRINGING THIS ALL TOGETHER

This chapter has been quite a tour. I started with low-dimensional spaces that were used to represent a few points in a common frame. These spaces were supported by multidimensional scaling programs illuminating the information that people used to make judgments. Then, I examined high-dimensional space representations formed by finding statistical relationships among words in large corpora of text. Finally, I discussed connectionist models, which also operate in high-dimensional spaces. In these systems, the geometric similarity of input vectors to vectors learned in previous associations determines the new output.

The great strength of spatial representations is power in simplicity. Spaces have a rigid formal definition that gives modelers a few well-controlled aspects to use in developing the representing world. Several dimensions can be created for the space. Points or vectors can be located in that space, in which the distance between points or vectors becomes an important quantity. In many of the examples I discussed, distances represented psychological similarity, but distance can represent other constructs like perceived distance or preference as well. Other factors have been considered for spatial models, such as variable attention weights for dimensions in space and density of points in neighborhoods in the space, although most models have focused selectively on distance between points or vectors.

Mental spaces are often associated with rather simple processing assumptions. The model of sentence verification was concerned with only a measurement of distance between points. Similarly, the analogy model of Rumelhart and Abrahamson (1973) involved drawing only a few lines between points in a space. High-dimensional space and connectionist models derive most of their power from simple calculations in linear algebra. As discussed in subsequent chapters, when proposals for the nature of mental representations grow more complex, the processes needed to extract and use information from representations also become more complex. Thus, it is a virtue of mental space models that elaborate processing assumptions are not needed.

Despite this simplicity, mental space models have formed the basis of various psychological models. In this chapter alone, I described models of sentence verification, analogy, category formation, and word meaning. Although there are problems with all these models, it is important to point out that they are very successful. Indeed, the problems with models that use mental space representations almost all boil down to a single issue: the need to make use of specific parts of the representations. In all applications of mental space models, the interaction of two points or vectors yields only a quantity, a measure of proximity in the space. When proximity is all that is needed, these models are quite powerful, but many complex processes involve not only the sense of conceptual proximity but also an understanding of what makes two points near to each other or far apart. In these situations, it seems important to have access to the elements that make up the representations. For example, to determine that *corrupt* is the opposite of *virtuous*, it is necessary to go beyond simply determining that both terms are part of the same conceptual field. I must also determine in what way *virtuous* and *corrupt* are related. After all, *virtuous* and *chaste* are also in the same conceptual field, but they are not antonyms. In cases like this, mental space models falter.

Chapter 3

Featural Representations

WHAT IS A FEATURE?

In the discussion of spatial representations in chapter 2, I pointed out that spatial representations are continuous. Points can lie arbitrarily close to each other in a representational space, and a distance between points can be calculated. That distance is then used to represent a psychological quantity like similarity or preference. A different approach to representation assumes that the elements in mental representations have discrete components often called features.

Features are a form of symbolic representation. Semiotic theorists (going back to Peirce; Buchler, 1940) have distinguished among iconic, indexical, and symbolic representations. Icons are signs (or representations) that bear a perceptual resemblance to the thing they represent. A painting of George Washington is an iconic representation of him. Indices are items that derive their meanings from direct (generally physical) connections to the object they denote. A plumb bob indexes verticality because it is pulled down by gravity. Clouds index a storm because they are causally related to the storm. Finally, a symbol denotes its referent because of an established convention. Words in language are symbolic because the connection between a pattern of sounds and a concept is determined by the convention of the linguistic community. Features are symbolic because the cognitive system arbitrarily associates a feature with the thing it represents.

To get an intuitive sense of what is meant by features, think of all possible properties of dogs. At a crude level, properties like "four legs," "barks," "has fur," "eats dog food" can be considered features of dogs.

These features specify properties of dogs, that are shared to a greater or lesser degree with other objects in the world.

In this chapter, I discuss featural representations in some detail. I begin by discussing independent features and the notions of additive and substitutive dimensions. Then, I examine information that may become associated with features. Next, I address the issue of primitives in featural representations, look at some processes that may act over featural representations, and discuss some uses of featural models in psychology. Along the way, I discuss the strengths and weaknesses of featural representations.

FEATURES

Features are symbols that correspond to particular aspects of the represented world. A feature is an entity or object in the representing world. Analogous to a real object, a feature is a discrete unit that can be manipulated. A feature may also have sharp boundaries like a real object so that there is often a clear dividing line between what is and is not represented by a particular feature. These properties are guidelines; in some instances, features have fuzzy boundaries.

An early use of features in psychology was to represent the set of phonemes in human languages. Phonemes are the speech sounds of language. For example, the /g/ in gate or gone is a phoneme. A phoneme (like /g/) can be described by a set of *articulatory features*, which are organized into a set of *dimensions*. Dimensions are qualities along which a speech sound can vary. For example, articulatory features have dimensions including voicing (whether the vocal cords are engaged), place of articulation (where the air in the vocal cavity is blocked), and manner of articulation (how the air in the vocal cavity is blocked). To represent a particular speech sound, each dimension must be given a *value*. The phoneme /g/ is *voiced* (the vocal cords are engaged early in the production of this sound). The place of articulation of /g/ is *velar* because the tongue meets the roof of the mouth at the soft palate (velum). Finally, the manner of articulation of /g/ is a *stop* consonant; producing the sound /g/ requires stopping the flow of air for some period. The important values of articulatory features can be determined by looking at *minimal pairs*, which are pairs of words that differ in meaning, but whose phonetic form differs in only a single phonetic feature such as *gap* (/gæp/) and *cap* (/kæp/). In this case, the initial phonemes /g/ and /k/ differ only in that the vocal cords are engaged early for the first and late for the second—that is, they differ in

TABLE 3.1
Some Articulatory Features of English Consonants

Consonant	Voicing	Place of Articulation	Manner of Articulation	Note
k	Unvoiced	Velar	Stop	as in coat
g	Voiced	Velar	Stop	as in goat
t	Unvoiced	Alveolar	Stop	as in tote
d	Voiced	Alveolar	Stop	as in dote
p	Unvoiced	Bilabial	Stop	as in pit
b	Voiced	Bilabial	Stop	as in bit
f	Unvoiced	Labiodental	Fricative	as in fine
v	Voiced	Labiodental	Fricative	as in vine
th	Unvoiced	Interdental	Fricative	as in thin
TH	Voiced	Interdental	Fricative	as in the
s	Unvoiced	Alveolar	Fricative	as in sip
z	Voiced	Alveolar	Fricative	as in zip
sh	Unvoiced	Palatal	Fricative	as in ash
zh	Voiced	Palatal	Fricative	as in azure
ch	Unvoiced	Palatal	Affricate	as in chill
j	Voiced	Palatal	Affricate	as in Jill
l	Voiced	Alveolar	Liquid	as in lip
r	Voiced	Velar	Liquid	as in rip
m	Voiced	Bilabial	Nasal	as in mine
n	Voiced	Alveolar	Nasal	as in nap
ng	Voiced	Velar	Nasal	final sound in ring
y	Voiced	Palatal	Glide	as in yap
w	Voiced	Labiovelar	Glide	as in wit
h	Voiced	Glottal	Glide	as in hit

voicing. Table 3.1 presents the articulatory features of a number of English phonemes.[1]

Articulatory features are thought to be discrete, with sharp boundaries between phonemes. This claim is supported by evidence of categorical perception of speech sounds. In one classic study of categorical perception, investigators repeatedly played a simple syllable to infants (e.g., /ba/) and measured the rate at which the infants sucked a nipple (Eimas, 1971). After a short time, the infants habituated to the speech sound being played, and their sucking rate decreased. At this point, the speech sound was changed by altering an aspect of its sound. For example, the voice onset time could be varied by changing the amount of time from the onset of the syllable during which a spectrum of energy corresponding to the engagement of the

---

[1]English phonemes can also be described by a set of phonetic features, which are a set of mutually exclusive features that are also discrete and binary.

vocal cords was added to the speech signal. Infants dishabituated to the change (as evidenced by a sharp increase in sucking rate) only when the speech sound changed the phoneme from voiced to unvoiced (or vice versa). Thus, when the change in voice onset time changed the syllable from a /ba/ to a /pa/, infants' sucking rate increased. Changes in a phoneme (e.g., two different versions perceived as /ba/) did not change infants' sucking rate. This pattern of data suggests that the boundaries of features deciding between phonemes are sharp.[2] A further property of discreteness is that a phoneme either possesses a given feature or it does not. For example, in an articulatory representation of English phonemes, a given consonant is either a velar or it is not. It cannot be partially velar.

Because articulatory features are organized into dimensions, groups of features all describe the same aspect of a phoneme. The voicing dimension can take on the values *voiced* and *unvoiced*. Likewise, the place of articulation dimension can take on values like velar, alveolar, labial, or dental, which each describe a place where the tongue meets a portion of the mouth. The dimensions of phonetic features are *substitutive* because having one value along a particular dimension, like voicing or manner, precludes having any other values at the same time (Gati & Tversky, 1982). That is, a consonant cannot be both voiced and unvoiced, both a labial and a velar or both a stop and a fricative. (I come back to the issue of substitutive dimensions later.)

Another important property of articulatory features is that they are *primitive*. Primitive features are those that cannot be decomposed into more basic units. The articulatory feature theory of speech assumes that no representational elements are more basic than the features that can be combined to form an equivalent representation. (I discuss primitives later.)

Buried in the concept of primitives is the assumption that features can vary in their level of specificity. Psychologists have often assumed that features of objects have a particular grain size reflecting the degree of a feature's specificity. Specific features can represent only a narrow range of things in the represented world. General features have a broad range of things that they represent. A feature representing a particular shade of red, say brick red, is a highly specific feature, applicable to an object only

---

[2]Of course, as in every other aspect of psychology, the picture is substantially more complex than this. Although there are clear demonstrations of categorical perception in adults and children (and even in chinchillas), there are also situations in which people integrate speech information and visual information. The classic phenomenon of this type is the McGurk effect (McGurk & MacDonald, 1976) in which the subject hears the phoneme /ba/, sees a face mouthing the phoneme /ga/, and actually reports hearing the phoneme /da/. These effects do not argue against the use of features as a representation of phonemes, but they do argue that the connection between speech sounds and the perception of phonemes is not direct.

if the object is brick red. At the other end of the spectrum, evaluative features like *good* or *rugged* are very general. Exactly what is meant by a feature like *good* or *rugged* varies depending on what is being described by those features. A good boy is not the same as a good horse, which is not the same as a good movie. At heart, though, all of these features imply some type of positive evaluation.

FEATURES AND FEATURE DETECTORS

The featural view of representation has received some support from work in neuroscience on the feline and monkey visual systems (believed to be good models for the human visual system). The pioneering work of Hubel and Wiesel (e.g., Hubel & Wiesel, 1965; Hubel, Wiesel, & LeVay, 1975) produced results consistent with the presence of "feature detectors" in the visual cortex. Hubel and Wiesel found neurons that were sensitive to lines of particular orientations in particular areas of visual space in the visual cortex. When a neuron is sensitive to a line in a particular orientation, it fires more often for lines in this orientation than for lines in other orientations. Cells near each other in the visual cortex are sensitive to lines of similar orientations. Other cells, called *hypercomplex* cells, seem to fire selectively to more complex environmental features like line segments of a particular length or corners. Although this work is exciting in that it suggests that the brain may actually code some aspects of the perceptual environment as features, researchers must take care in interpreting these data. They do not specify any process that uses the representation: If the selective firing of neurons in the visual cortex does correspond to the encoding of visual features, it is not clear how these features are used to turn the featural information into a perception of the visual world. Thus, before knowing what sort of representation the visual system is constructing, we must know more about how the information is being processed (see also Uttal, 1971).

It is interesting that to the extent that neurons encode visual features, the features are not discrete. When a neuron is said to fire selectively for lines of a particular orientation, it means that the firing rate of the neuron[3]

---

[3]For those who are unfamiliar with neuroscience, here is a brief and terribly oversimplified description of the neuron. A neuron collects electrical charge in its cell body (*soma*) until a threshold is reached, at which time an *action potential* is sent down its axon to the end of the neuron. This action potential causes chemicals called *neurotransmitters* to be released, and these can then affect the firing of other cells. Because neurons fire in an all or none fashion (via action potentials), it is assumed that the firing rate of the neurons carries information. Thus, the action potential itself is always the same strength, but the number of action potentials per unit time can vary.

is highest for a line of that orientation. Lines with an orientation *similar* to that of the optimal rate yield somewhat lower firing rates. The overall rate of neural firing is like that depicted in the schematic graph in Figure 3.1. Thus, the features that these detectors are sensitive to have fuzzy rather than discrete boundaries. These fuzzy boundaries confer several advantages on neural systems. First, because there are many cells with similar preferred orientations, the loss of any individual cell is not catastrophic. Second, the activity of neurons with similar preferred orientations can be combined to yield more accurate assessments of the orientation of the line than can be determined from the firing of any single cell. In sum, an analysis of feature detectors in the visual system suggests that there is a high degree of redundancy in feature representation and also that the features themselves have fuzzy boundaries.

TYPES OF FEATURE DIMENSIONS

Featural models have two types feature dimensions: *additive* and *substitutive* dimensions (Gati & Tversky, 1982). Additive dimensions are features that can be added to the representation of an object regardless of what other features it has. For example, imagine the head of a novel animal. This head may have ears, but whether it has ears is not dependent on other features that the head is imagined to have.[4] In contrast, substitutive dimensions are collections of features for which any given object can have only one value. True psychological dimensions have this substitutive structure. For example, a simple object cannot be both large and small because having the feature *large* precludes the object from also having the feature *small*.[5] Shape, color, and texture are other examples of substitutive dimensions, as are the articulatory features discussed in the previous section.

---

[4]This is not to say, of course, that people do not have theories about organisms suggesting what features they should and should not have. Rather, having ears does not preclude the object from having a range of other features as well.

[5]One can object to this statement by suggesting that sentences like "Even a large mouse is small, and even a small elephant is large" are interpretable, but it is necessary to distinguish between what can be stated in a sentence and what a representation permits. Presumably, a feature dimension like size represents values on some absolute scale in mental representations. According to this view, a sentence like "That is a small elephant" uses knowledge of elephants to give it a size representation that is still large, but perhaps not as large as a large elephant. There are, of course, other ways to represent size, for example, in a relative way. On this view, representing an elephant as small would actually mean "small relative to other elephants." Although this view of representation is appealing, it requires the ability to represent relations between objects. (I discuss representational systems capable of representing relations in chaps. 5 to 7.)

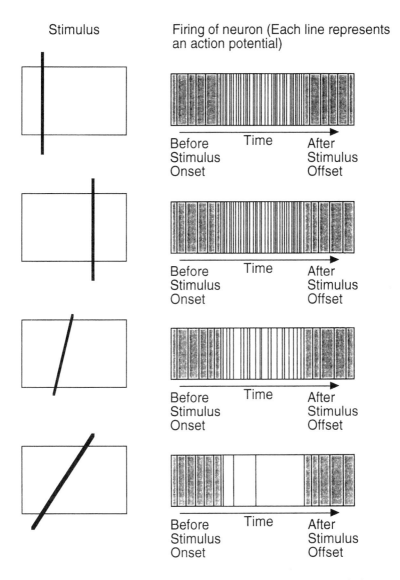

FIG. 3.1. Demonstrations of firing frequencies to lines of particular orientations in a receptive field. The receptive field is tuned to vertical lines. Vertical lines appearing anywhere on the receptive field give rise to a high rate of firing relative to a background. Lines at orientations near vertical give rise to somewhat lower rates of firing. Lines at orientations far from vertical give rise to very low firing rates.

FEATURE INDEPENDENCE

Objects are described by collections of features. To facilitate the creation of processes that act over the features of an object, it is handy to assume that the features are independent of each other. The assumption of feature independence takes a few different forms, and so it is worth discussing in more detail. One possibility is that, across the features of represented objects, there is no correlation between features possessed by objects. On this view of independence, the probability that an object has some feature c_1 given that it has some other feature c_2 is simply the base-rate probability that any object has feature c_1. This view of feature independence is unlikely to be correct. For natural kinds (e.g., animals and plants), there are correlated sets of features in the world. Objects with leaves tend not to have legs and fur, although objects with legs often have fur. Indeed, Rosch and Mervis (1975) suggested that a fundamental aspect of natural kind categories is that they reflect correlations between features that exist in the world (see also Malt, 1995). Likewise, substitutive dimensions consist of features that are decidedly not independent; any object can have at most one value along a substitutive dimension.

A second possibility is that the presence of features may be correlated, but features are treated as being independent by the processes that act over them. For example, A. Tversky's (1977) contrast model assumed that features representing objects are grouped into sets (in a formal set-theoretic sense). This situation is depicted in Figure 3.2. Each circle stands for a set of features representing an item in the represented world. The advantage to treating objects as sets is that elementary set operations can be used to compare pairs of objects. In Figure 3.2, the overlapping region of the circles is the intersection of the feature sets. The nonoverlapping regions of the circles are the set differences. According to the contrast model, the similarity of two objects a and b represented by feature sets A and B is determined by

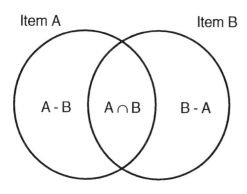

FIG. 3.2. Feature sets that are compared. The overlap of the feature sets is the commonalities of the pair, and the nonoverlapping regions are the differences.

$$s(a, b) = \theta f(A \cap B) - \alpha f(A - B) - \beta f(B - A), \tag{3.1}$$

where θ, α, and β are weighting factors. In this model, each feature is treated independently of every other feature. The independence allows the determination of whether any particular feature is a common feature (i.e., a member of the set intersection $\{A \cap B\}$) or a distinctive feature (i.e., a member of either of the set differences $\{A - B\}$, or $\{B - A\}$) to be done separately for each feature.

In this model, the perceived similarity of a pair increases with the size of the set of commonalities and decreases with the size of the set of differences. The weighting factors (i.e., θ, α, and β) allow the contrast model to account for changes in emphasis on commonalities or differences in different contexts. One reason that these weighting factors can be used is that the set of common features and the sets of distinctive features (called the *components of similarity*) are independent of each other. Because of this independence, the weighting factors can be set individually. In some circumstances, it may be beneficial to give high weight to the commonalities (if the focus is on what a pair of objects have in common). In this case, the parameter θ can be large and can allow the perceived similarity of a pair to be strongly dependent on the set of common features. Similarly, it may be important to weight one or both sets of distinctive features heavily (i.e., to use large values of α or β). Only when the components of similarity are independent can the value of each parameter be set independently of the values of the other parameters.

Treating features as independent allows models to avoid a variant of the *holism* problem described in chapter 1. In philosophy, holism has been identified as the problem that the meaning of any particular representational element (in this case, features) may depend on the meaning of every other representational element that an individual knows. If every feature is independent, understanding the meaning of a concept described by a set of features requires only looking at the set of features used to describe that object. Because the processing capacity of any cognitive agent is finite, it is important to have a way to constrain the features that must be considered when processing a representation.

To provide evidence for the contrast model of similarity, A. Tversky (1977) asked subjects to list the features of a number of objects and asked a second group of subjects to rate the similarity of several pairs of these objects. Tversky determined the common and distinctive features for each pair in the ratings task by matching the features from the feature listing task. He weighted features by the number of subjects that listed each feature and found a positive correlation between the number of common features and rated similarity and a negative correlation between the number of distinctive features and rated similarity. This study provides clear evidence supporting the contrast model and also demonstrates that assumptions about knowledge representation can affect the way psychological data are collected. The contrast model assumes that objects are represented as collections of features, and so it is reasonable to ask subjects to list features of objects to confirm the predictions of the model. Testing a model of similarity that made other assumptions about knowledge representation would require a different methodology (see Markman & Gentner, 1993a, 1996; chap. 5).

By treating features as independent, featural models can use straightforward processes like elementary set operations to determine the commonalities and differences of a pair. The components of similarity are also independent, and the weights given to the commonalities and differences can be set independently. Unlike the continuous mental space models discussed in chapter 2, featural models provide an explicit indication of how a pair of objects is similar and how it is different, whereas mental space models gave only a distance between points. Featural models have a set of commonalities whose features can be examined to see what makes a pair similar. This property is important, because the presence of discrete objects in the representing world allows featural models to determine in what way a pair is similar. Likewise, a featural model has sets of differences whose features can be examined to see what makes a pair dissimilar.

USING FEATURES TO REPRESENT CONCEPTS

How can a list of features represent a concept? Researchers have developed several feature-based models of concepts. Early workers on concepts searched for a set of features that were necessary and sufficient for an item in the world to be an instance of that concept. Necessary features are features that an item must have to be an instance of the concept (see Smith & Medin, 1981, for a discussion of this issue). A sufficient set of features is the minimal set of features such that if an item has this set, it is an instance of the concept, but removing any feature from the set keeps the item from being an instance of the concept. A bachelor can be defined as an unmarried male, where the features *unmarried* and *male* are necessary and jointly sufficient to specify instances of the concept *bachelor*. It has proved difficult, however, to specify necessary and sufficient features for most natural concepts (Wittgenstein, 1968), even for a straightforward concept like *bachelor*. An unmarried 10-year-old boy is not a bachelor. Would extending the set of features to include *adult* solve the problem? Aside from the ambiguity of a feature like *adult* (is an 18-year-old an adult?), there are other problems. A 30-year-old priest is an unmarried (adult) male, but he is not a very good instance of a bachelor. It is appropriate to say that a 30-year-old priest is *technically* a bachelor, but then an explanation is required for why the hedge *technically* is appropriate for 30-year-old priests, but not for 30-year-old unmarried male lawyers.

A featural model of concepts need not assume that concepts are defined by collections of necessary and sufficient features. Research on category representations in psychology has suggested other possible representations. According to one view, category representations consist of *prototypes* or average members of a category (Posner & Keele, 1970; Reed, 1972; Rosch, 1975; Rosch & Mervis, 1975). On this view, the category representation contains information about features that are typically associated with the category. The concept of *bird* may consist of features typically associated with birds, such as wings, feathers, small size, and chirping. Deciding whether a new instance is a bird involves comparing the features of the new instance with those of the prototype. If there is sufficient overlap, the new instance is categorized as a bird. Of course, some mistakes might be made, such as identifying a bat as a bird, but these mistakes often occur, and may require that exceptions to the prototype be stored specially.

Another important property of prototypes is that they can be considered the default values for a concept. Default features are properties of an item that one would guess to be true of the item without other information. If I say that something is a bird and say nothing else about it, then it is possible to make some assumptions about what properties it has. Default features can also be used to guess the values of features unknown about an object. If I say that I saw a small eagle at the zoo, it is known that the eagle is small, because I say so, but it is likely to be further assumed that it has wings and feathers, because they are default properties of birds.[6]

Another proposal for the nature of category representations is that people store specific *exemplars* of categories that they have seen (Kruschke, 1992; Medin & Schaffer, 1978; Nosofsky, 1986, 1987; see chap. 8). Exemplar models assume that the features associated with individual category members (or exemplars) are stored in memory. Like prototype models, exemplar models also assume that new instances are categorized with respect to their similarity to the stored category representation, but the stored category representation consists of various stored exemplars. In both exemplar and prototype models, featural representations can be used to categorize items without requiring that the category representation consist of a set of necessary and sufficient features. Instead, these models propose

---

[6]The idea that something can have features by default goes beyond what can be done with some kinds of representations. For example, in chapter 5, I discuss first order predicate calculus (FOPC). In FOPC, a property is known to be true of an object only if it is explicitly stated about the object (or can be proven to be true of the object by the rules of logic). In this instance, there is no notion that some property can be true by default (with no other justification).

that a measure of featural similarity (i.e., the degree of feature match and mismatch between the new instance and the category representation as in A. Tversky's, 1977, contrast model) can be used to categorize the objects.

FEATURE PROCESSING AND INFORMATION BUNDLED WITH FEATURES

When objects are represented as points in a multidimensional space (as discussed in chap. 2), the dimensions of the space can be thought of as ordered substitutive dimensions whose particular values correspond to the feature values along them (see Gati & Tversky, 1982, for a similar discussion). In a spatial representation, however, the processing operations consist only of ways of measuring the distance between points by using some metric. In contrast, featural models permit a wider range of processes and by extension allow a broader range of information to be associated with features.

A simple process that can be carried out with featural models is comparison. The central example of a feature comparison model is A. Tversky's (1977) contrast model described in the previous section. Another simple comparison model can be used to illustrate how featural representations can be extended. In chapter 2, I discussed the model of sentence verification described by Rips et al. (1973). These researchers demonstrated that the time it took for subjects to verify sentences of the form "A robin is a bird" was related to the similarity between the nouns in the sentence, when similarity was defined as the inverse of distance in a multidimensional space.

E. E. Smith, Shoben, and Rips (1974) also presented a featural model of sentence verification. In this model, a key fact to be explained was the presence of fast *true* and fast *false* responses in the sentence verification task. Subjects can very quickly verify sentences like "A robin is a bird" and can very quickly determine to be false sentences like "An aardvark is a bird." In contrast, sentences like "An emu is a bird" require a long time to verify as true, and sentences like "A bat is a bird" require a long time to reject as false. Smith et al. suggested that objects are represented as sets of features and that the features of objects are further subclassified as *characteristic* or *core* features of an object. Characteristic features are those typically associated with the object, but that are not necessary for an object to be a member of a class. For the category *birds*, the feature *flies* is characteristic, because not all birds fly. Core features are necessary for inclusion in the category. All birds have feathers, and so *feathers* is a core feature of birds.

With objects represented as sets of core and characteristic features, Smith et al. assumed a two-stage process of sentence verification. The first stage involves a comparison of all features (both core and characteristic) of the nouns in the sentence. If the objects are very similar (i.e., they share many features), people quickly deem the sentence true. If the objects are very dissimilar (i.e., they share few features), they quickly deem the sentence false. Objects that fall in an intermediate range of similarity are passed to a second stage, in which only the core features are considered. At this stage, if the objects share core features, a true response is made (in this case, the response is slow, because two stages must be carried out). In contrast, if the objects do not share core features, a slow false response is made. Subjects can make mistakes when objects in a sentence share many characteristic features but few core features or have few characteristic features but share the core features that make them a member of a category.

This model has two key aspects. First, the use of core and characteristic features demonstrates that features can have other information associated with them in addition to the information they encode about an object. This information can affect subsequent processing of the object that the features describe. Second, this featural model demonstrates that cognitive processes can be based on information that is technically irrelevant to the task but that eases processing. Comparing objects using all their features is easier than segregating features by their status as core or characteristic and then comparing. In most cases, the comparison yields the correct results quickly and thus is used instead of a more thorough but more labor intensive process.

The use of overall similarity as a heuristic is common in many psychological processes (e.g., A. Tversky & Kahneman, 1974). Tversky and Kahneman described situations in which people who are making a judgment focus on an object's similarity to (or *representativeness* of) a general class rather than on other factors that may be more relevant to the judgment at hand. In one situation, the researchers told people that, from descriptions of 100 people, one description had been selected at random. They also told the subjects that 80% of the people in the group were lawyers and 20% were engineers. The description selected at random was designed to be highly similar to the stereotypical engineer (e.g., has good mathematics ability, dresses poorly, likes to read science fiction books for pleasure). People judged that the person described was highly likely to be an engineer, despite the fact that the base-rate probability of the person's actually being an engineer was only 20%. The judged likelihood that the person was an engineer did not change much if people were told that the description was drawn from a population of 80% engineers and 20% lawyers. Tversky and Kahneman suggested that people in this judgment task attended too much to the similarity of the object to the stereotypical engineer and did not focus enough on relevant statistical information like base rates.

DEGREE OF MEMBERSHIP AND DEGREE OF BELIEF

The core-characteristic distinction used by Smith et al. (1974) is actually an example of a general class of information that has often been associated with featural models encoding the degree of membership (or typicality) of a feature or the degree of belief in a feature along with the feature itself. In these models, features are not classified as exclusively core or exclusively characteristic; rather it is assumed that a dimension specifies to what extent a feature is criterial of a given category (Smith et al., 1974, also acknowledged the possibility that their core-characteristic distinction was graded).

The degree of membership of features in categories has been examined explicitly in prototype models of categorization. As discussed previously, a prototype is an average member of a category, and researchers have proposed them as a way that people structure concepts. The concept *bird* may be associated with an average bird that is probably more like a robin than a penguin (Posner & Keele, 1970; Reed, 1972; Rosch & Mervis, 1975). Prototypes may store only information about features typically associated with a category. Smith and Medin (1981) and Barsalou (1990) argued that prototypes (or more generally category abstractions) may store features associated with a category along with information about the frequency with which the feature appeared in the category. Table 3.2 shows a simple prototype for the category *bird*. The numbers at the right of the table are the number of instances of birds with the features at the left. This frequency can be thought of as the degree of membership or degree of typicality of the feature for a concept. Prototypes may contain information about sets of features whose membership is typically correlated. For example, animals with wings and feathers also tend to fly.

TABLE 3.2
Prototype of the Category *Bird*

Feature	Instances
Wings	100
Feathers	100
Sings	86
Flies	89
Small	62
Medium	36
Large	2
Beak	96
Legs	100
Brown	27
Red	14
Blue	9
Black	14
Gray	18

Once the membership of features in concepts is graded rather than all or none, more complex processing assumptions must be made. When the features are discrete, new instances of a category presumably have the features in the abstraction. When the features are graded, the degree of membership of a feature is an estimate of the likelihood that the feature is part of the new instance (or in the case of correlated features, the likelihood that the set of features is part of the instance). Some way of combining the information about degree of feature membership is needed.

Research in artificial intelligence (AI) on belief maintenance offers some insight into how the degree of belief in a feature is processed. One way of thinking about the graded membership of features in concepts is as the degree of belief that the feature describes a member of the category. Often, large AI reasoning systems have databases of knowledge called *knowledge bases*. The facts in these knowledge bases may not be known with certainty to be true or false. Modelers have handled statements not known to be true or false with *certainty factors*, which are typically numerical values associated with each fact in the knowledge base and which express the degree of belief in the statement.[7] Along with these values come procedures for combining certainty factors from more than one statement to allow reasoning about statements whose truth value is uncertain.

The certainty factor can be a statement of probability. In the prototypes described earlier, in which the number of instances with a given feature is tracked, the numbers can be converted into the proportion of instances of the concept (e.g., *birds*) with the feature. If the sample that generated the prototype reflects the population of items that one is likely to encounter in the future, the proportions can be thought of as probabilities that a new instance of a category has a given feature of the prototype. The probabilities can be combined to judge the probability that the new instance has conjunctions of features of the prototype by using standard laws of probability (Shafer, 1996). If the presence of two features in a category is independent, the probability that a new instance has both features is simply the product of the probabilities that it has either feature alone.

The certainty factors need not be interpretable as probabilities, however, and the rules of probability combination need not apply. Lenat and Guha (1990) discussed other ways of using certainty factors in knowledge bases. The facts in a knowledge base are the beliefs of an agent. Lenat and Guha argued that the best way to know how strongly a belief is held is to know *why* it is held (see J. L. Pollack, 1994). A belief can be strongly held because it is connected to many other beliefs that depend on it, or it can be strongly

---

[7]Few AI models use certainty factors any more. Instead, they use other techniques for reasoning about strength of belief like Bayesian statistical methods (Shafer, 1996). The basic idea behind certainty factors is intuitively appealing, however, and it is worth knowing about them and the potential pitfalls of using them.

held because there is a strong argument that the fact's being true (or a strong argument against a fact's being true [J. L. Pollack, 1994]). When one does not know exactly why a belief is true or false, certainty factors can be used.

These certainty factors can be numbers, such as numbers on a scale from 0 to 100, which, unlike probabilities, need not be interpreted as expected likelihoods. Lenat and Guha (1990) argued against this use of certainty factors, because it establishes a common currency of belief. Imagine that one believes that all birds have wings and holds the belief with certainty 96 (pretty sure, but leaving open the possibility that there is a wingless bird). Imagine one has another belief that bricks are made out of clay, and one holds the belief with certainty 95. These certainty factors may be excellent values for reasoning in the domain of birds or in the domain of bricks. These certainty factors are global numbers, however, and setting them allows one to assume that the belief in birds having wings is stronger than the belief that bricks are made out of clay. Such hairsplitting about beliefs across domains does not seem to be cognitively plausible.[8]

Lenat and Guha (1990) advocated a system of certainty with five states of belief: absolutely true, true, unknown, false, absolutely false. The true and absolutely true states differ only in that true leaves open the (small) possibility that the belief can turn out to be false, whereas absolutely true does not leave open even a glimmer of doubt. A similar difference holds between false and absolutely false. These five states allow combinations of certainty factors in a modified truth table, as shown in Table 3.3. With two arguments related to a belief, as shown in Table 3.3, if both arguments support the absolute truth of the belief, it is believed with a certainty of absolute truth. Likewise, pairs of arguments for absolute falseness yield beliefs with certainty absolutely false.

When there is a contradiction between true and false beliefs, the system assumes that the certainty of the belief is unknown. This is actually a reasonable course of action. In a situation in which two people give compelling arguments on opposite sides of an argument, if there is no good reason to favor one argument over another, then one may decide that the truth of the fact in contention is unknown pending a resolution to this debate.

The purpose of this section is not to provide a detailed review of work on belief maintenance but to emphasize two main aspects of belief maintenance. First, most information attached to features (or beliefs) is simply a

---

[8]When researchers ask people to give numerical probability estimates that particular facts are true, they give them, but there is reason to believe that these estimates are not readouts of internal certainty factors. For example, people tend to round their certainty factors to the nearest number ending in zero or perhaps five, a result suggesting that they think of the probability range in terms of a set of categories (see also Budescu & Wallsten, 1995).

TABLE 3.3
Truth Table for Certainty Factors

	Absolutely True	TRUE	Unknown	FALSE	Absolutely False
Absolutely True	Absolutely True	Absolutely True	Absolutely True	Absolutely True	*
TRUE	Absolutely True	TRUE	TRUE	Unknown	Absolutely False
Unknown	Absolutely True	TRUE	Unknown	FALSE	Absolutely False
FALSE	Absolutely True	Unknown	FALSE	FALSE	Absolutely False
Absolutely False	*	Absolutely False	Absolutely False	Absolutely False	Absolutely False

*When absolutely true and absolutely false statements collide, the difference must be resolved through reasoning.

a stand-in for other information not known more specifically. For example, a value of the "degree of core-ness" of a feature is a stand-in for knowledge about why the feature is a core or characteristic feature of a category. Likewise, a certainty factor is a stand-in for more detailed knowledge about why the belief is true or false. Such stand-ins are useful for two reasons. First, one may not always know the reason for holding a belief (or why a feature is a core feature). Second, actions must often be taken quickly, and reasoning from domain knowledge about beliefs (or typicality or core-ness) may take more time than is available; thus storing a shorthand notation for certainty (or typicality or core-ness) may make online processing more efficient.

A second important aspect of belief maintenance is that adding new information to features requires the addition of new processing assumptions that use the information. In the case of core and characteristic information, the new processes must filter out the characteristic features when making comparisons as in the second stage of the model of E. E. Smith et al. (1974). In the case of belief, the use of certainty factors requires positing a truth table that can combine these factors. The use of probabilistic information can require more complex combination schemes. Thus, adding complexity to the representation comes at the expense of requiring additional processing assumptions.

PRIMITIVE REPRESENTATIONAL ELEMENTS

What does a feature mean? As previously discussed, it is possible to label features like *voiced* for phonemes or *has wings* for birds, but these labels are there for our benefit. They allow us to look at a description of the knowledge possessed by the system and to know what it must mean. A computational system cannot directly interpret a feature label; what would the label be interpreted into? The system must operate the same way, even if features have labels that are uninterpretable by English speakers. For example, the prototype for the bird category shown in Table 3.2 can easily be rewritten with generic symbols. The cognitive model must be able to use these generic symbols, even if an outside observer does not know what they mean. A system must operate even if the feature *wings* is coded as GXB1, the feature *feathers* is coded as GQR4, and so on.

As discussed in chapter 1, part of a symbol's meaning involves *grounding*. At some point, the represented world for some symbols must be perceptual information coming from the outside world. Presumably, this perceptual information grounds the symbol in physical reality (or at least the part of reality to which sensory systems are attuned). Not all symbols need a represented world that involves perceptual information. Indeed, many proposals for mental representation suggest that symbols with complex meanings can be built up by having represented worlds that are other representational elements in the cognitive system. In such systems, complex symbols are thought to be *decomposable* into a set of *semantic primitives*, which are the simplest representational elements. The primitives are typically assumed to be grounded and derive their meaning from a direct relationship to a represented world outside the cognitive system rather than indirectly through decomposition into other symbols.

Perceptual Primitives

One example of decomposition into semantic primitives is the system of articulatory features used to open this chapter. The representation of a phoneme consists of a set of primitive features, each of which corresponds directly to an element of the speech production environment, such as voicing or place of articulation. The assumption that phonemes can be decomposed into primitive features has led to a search for aspects of the speech signal that correspond to primitives (Jakobsen, Fant, & Halle, 1963). These aspects of the speech signal are the connection between symbols and the world, a connection that grounds the primitives. To date, identifying aspects of the auditory speech signal that are markers of phonetic features has proved difficult (Blumstein & Stevens, 1981). If the relation between this possible representing world and the represented world of speech sounds is not discovered, the decomposition of phonemes into primitive features may turn out to be a powerful linguistic tool, but not a reflection of psychological reality.

The use of primitives is common in models of visual perception. The discovery of neurons that fire selectively to lines of particular orientations,

(A)

(B)

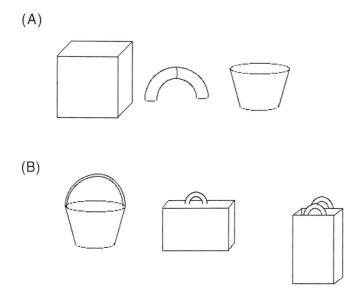

FIG. 3.3. A: A simple set of geon primitives like those proposed by Biederman (1987) in his model of visual object recognition. B: A set of objects that can be created from a set of geons (b).

to lines that move in particular directions, or to even more complex features like edges (as previously described) suggests that, at some level, visual input may be analyzed into features. Biederman (1987) suggested that the representation of visual objects consists of generalized cones, which he called *geons*, connected by relations between them (relations between representational elements are discussed in chap. 5). Some sample geons are shown in Figure 3.3A. According to this theory, the object recognition system has a limited number of geons that serve as the basic representational vocabulary; Biederman posited 36 geons as the basis of his theory. Figure 3.3B shows how various objects can be constructed from a set of geons.

Geons embody two important parts of representational systems that posit a set of primitive elements. First, the limited vocabulary of 36 geons can be combined by using spatial relations to form about 154 million objects made of 3 or fewer geons.[9] This range of objects is certainly sufficient to account for the number that humans can discriminate. Second, geons are posited to be true primitive elements in that they are assumed to represent perceptual properties outside the cognitive system. Geons themselves are recognized via *nonaccidental properties* of objects, visual as-

---

[9]I discuss the importance of relations in perceptual representations at length in chapter 6.

pects of objects that do not change their form substantially through rotations of objects. Examples of nonaccidental properties are parallel lines and collinearity (broken line segments that would form a single line if connected). In the case of parallel lines, for example, many rotations of an object in space still yield an image in which the lines are (nearly) parallel. Geons are only one theory of the primitives underlying object recognition. Other proposals have focused on different aspects of visual objects like defining major axes and radii of objects (Marr, 1982). This issue is taken up again in chapter 6.

There is something quite appealing about perceptual primitives. In particular, because the represented world is outside the organism, it is easy to see that primitives may ground a representation. One need only find a connection (i.e., a set of representing rules) that correlates the primitives to the environment. Perhaps all concepts, even quite abstract ones, can ultimately be decomposed into a set of perceptual primitives. As I discuss in chapter 9, many cognitive linguists have suggested that abstract concepts are understood in terms of perceptual (or emotional) domains (e.g., Gibbs, 1994; Lakoff & Johnson, 1980). Although it is not entirely clear how all abstract concepts can be decomposed into physical or bodily terms (e.g., Murphy, 1996, 1997), it remains an intriguing possibility.

Conceptual Primitives

Proposals of representational primitives are not limited to perceptual systems. Many researchers have focused on developing a set of conceptual primitives (E. V. Clark, 1979; Fillmore, 1978; Miller & Johnson-Laird, 1976; Norman & Rumelhart, 1975; Schank, 1972, 1975). Most systems of conceptual primitives assume structured representations like those I discuss later in the book. To illustrate the notion of primitives, I discuss E. V. Clark's (1979) semantic feature hypothesis of word meaning. (I return to structural theories of primitives in chap. 7.)

According to the semantic feature hypothesis, word meaning is determined by a set of primitive features associated with a word. These features can be acquired independently. For example, when a child first learns the word *dog*, he or she may learn the features [+ animate] and [+ four legged]. This set of features underspecifies the concept *dog*; thus, the child overextends the word *dog* to cows, horses, cats, and other four-legged animals. In this notation, features are enclosed by brackets and are listed along with a plus sign that denotes that they are known to be true of a concept (i.e., [+ feature]) or a minus sign that denotes that they are known to be false of a concept (i.e., [– feature]).

New features are added to words to account for differences in meaning between words. A key pragmatic component of Clark's theory of lexical development is the *principle of contrast*. The assumption behind this principle is that children learning a lexicon assume that no two words have exactly the same meaning (i.e., that no two words are associated with exactly the same features). For example, if a child has associated the features [+ animate] and [+ four legged] with the word *dog* and the child then hears the word *cow*, this word can also apply to animate things with four legs. By the principle of contrast, however, either the word *cow* or the word *dog* (or both) is given features that allow the meanings to be differentiated. The child may associate the features [+ animate, + four legged, + moo] with cow and the features [+ animate, + four legged, + bark] with dog. Once this specification occurs, a child does not overgeneralize words as often as he or she did before.

E. V. Clark (1979) applied this featural analysis to concepts that can be specified by *count nouns* (i.e., nouns that refer to countable objects like *dog* and *cow*), but she also applied it to other concepts like those that can be specified by prepositions. For example, she suggested that children first learn that the preposition *before* applies to time, so that it is given the feature [+ time]. Later, the child realizes that this preposition relates events that do not occur at the same time and so extends the representation of *before* to [+ time, − simultaneous]. Finally, as the child contrasts *before* with other temporal prepositions like *after*, he or she reaches a representation consisting of [+ time, − simultaneous, + prior].

Another interesting aspect of the semantic feature hypothesis is that the features can be about aspects of the represented world (e.g., [+ animate] or [+ time]) but also about more abstract aspects of language usage. For example, the English words *brag* and *boast* may seem to be a counterexample to the principle of contrast. For most people, these words mean basically the same thing. Clark, however, suggested that these words differ in *register*; that is, in the audience for which they are appropriate. It seems more suitable to say:

I stood on the corner and *bragged* about my bowling score.   (3.2)

than to say:

I stood on the corner and *boasted* about my bowling score.   (3.3)

because *boasted* is a more formal term than *bragged*. Clark suggested that semantic features can contain information about aspects of language like register, aspects that allow the meaning of one word to be distinguished from the meaning of another. Similarly, features may represent differences in dialect, so that the word *soda* can be recognized as appropriate for use on the East Coast of the United States to refer to carbonated soft drinks, whereas the word *pop* can be recognized as appropriate for use in the Midwest of the United States for the same concept.

Semantic features are assumed to be primitives because they are used across a variety of concepts. All word meaning is thought to be composed of the meanings of a set of primitive features. Furthermore, no two words are permitted to have the same featural representation. If two words are given the same feature set, the language system searches for a way to extend at least one of the representations to make the sets nonidentical. Clark acknowledged that a limitation of her theory is that a complete set of semantic features for any language cannot currently be specified. Thus, although the semantic feature hypothesis posits that concepts are composed of primitives, it does not give a full account of what the primitives are.

Earlier, I noted that an important function of primitives is to provide grounding for more complex concepts, but it is not entirely clear how semantic features serve that function. One possibility is that there are correspondences between these primitives and perceptual information (perhaps even other perceptual representations). Another (rather implausible) possibility is that these conceptual primitives actually represent specific perceptual instances. With features like [+ time], which refers to the abstract property of time, this solution seems unlikely to work. Ultimately, the success of any system of primitives rests on an ability to ground symbols, and thus, the difficulty grounding a set of primitives can be seen as an important limitation of a theory of conceptual primitives.

General Issues About Primitives

Even if it was possible to specify a set of primitives for a language, there still must be a set of reasoning processes that carry out the implications of sentences. For example, in the sentence:

John gave Mary a necklace.   (3.4)

the representation must make clear that the act of giving involves a change of possession of an object (in this case, a necklace). The representation must also make clear that in this case, the physical location of the necklace is also likely to change location. It is tempting to add a feature like [+ change-location] to the representation of the word *give*, but other instances of giving do not involve the same change in location, as in:

John gave Mary a house.   (3.5)

in which there is a change of possession without a change in location. If a system of representation is truly to capture the subtleties of the implications that people draw during text comprehension, these issues must be dealt with. This problem is not trivial: The general issue of determining what changes given an action has been called the *frame problem* in AI, and is often thought to be one of the most difficult problems that cognitive science has to solve. (I return to the frame problem in chap. 9; see also Ford & Hayes, 1991; Ford & Pylyshyn, 1996.)

A second important issue involves the level of abstraction most suitable for representing things during normal processing. Discussions of conceptual primitives have never been entirely clear as to whether it is best to decompose information automatically into primitives or to represent things at a higher level of abstraction and decompose only when necessary. By representing things at a higher level of abstraction, I mean having representational elements that correspond to semantically complex concepts like *give* or *trade*. The advantage to representing these complex concepts directly is that their primitive representation requires a lot of representational information. Storing only primitives may place too large a memory load on the cognitive system. Thus, it may be advantageous to represent things at a higher level of abstraction some of the time. Always representing things in terms of a small set of primitives implies that it is easy to see similarities between distant domains, but although people sometimes see analogies between domains, they often do not notice similarities between distant domains.

J. D. Fodor, J. A. Fodor, and Garrett (1975) formulated a related argument: They suggested that if concepts were always decomposed into their primitives, it should be more difficult to process concepts requiring more primitives than to process those requiring fewer. For example, it should be harder to process the sentence:

John chased the frog. (3.6)

than to process the sentence:

John caught the frog. (3.7)

because many linguistic analyses have suggested that chasing something involves the intention to catch it, and thus the concept of catching is subsumed in the concept of chasing. Intuitively, however, these sentences seem about equally easy to process. On the basis of evidence like this, J. D. Fodor et al. concluded that there is unlikely to be a fixed set of properties into which all concepts are decomposed.

The alternative to decomposing concepts automatically into primitives is to represent some information without decomposing it. This solution also has its price. Imagine representing the concept *dog* with a symbol DOG and the concept *cow* with a symbol COW. These symbols are distinct (they have different names) and not at all similar. Only when these elements are broken down into their more primitive elements does the similarity between them become evident (i.e., when they are both seen as involving features like [+ animate] and [+ four legged]). Thus, operating over abstract representations risks missing similarities between concepts. Any decision about how to represent a concept has implications for what is easy and hard to do with it. The right way to approach this problem depends in large part on the domain in which a model is being developed.

GENETIC ALGORITHMS

So far, I have discussed only very simple processes associated with featural representations. For example, I have described how sets of features representing two objects can be compared by using elementary set operations. As a demonstration of a more complex process, I examine a set of computational procedures called genetic algorithms (Holland, 1992; Mitchell, 1996; Whitley, 1993), which require an assumption of feature independence to work. Genetic algorithms are inspired by transformations observed in genetic processes just as the earlier described connectionist models were inspired by patterns of connection and activity in networks of neurons. Genetic algorithms are useful for finding combinations of features that are beneficial to have in a complex environment. For example, someone looking to invest money can use a genetic algorithm to search for a combination of features that are predictive of growth in a company.

Genetic algorithms are loosely based on real genetic processes. In particular, genetics assumes that the units of heredity (the genes) are located in arbitrary positions along chromosomes. Any gene can take on multiple values, called *alleles*. Organisms reproduce by passing their genes to a new generation. In the case of asexual reproduction, the offspring gets all the genes of the previous generation, but some genes may change because of a mutation. Organisms best fitted to their environment are most likely to reproduce, and new generations of organisms should have an over-representation of the fittest organisms relative to less fit organisms. Finally, when an organism reproduces sexually, there may be mixing of the genetic material of two organisms. A number of possible mixing strategies can be used to combine genes. Animals like humans have two complete sets of genetic material in the form of pairs of chromosomes, and sections of chromosomes can be swapped in a process called *crossover*.

Genetic algorithms are designed by analogy to the simplified genetic model just described (see Holland, 1992, for an extensive description of this analogy). In a genetic algorithm, an object in a domain is represented by a set of features, which consist of a set of characters in a string. Figure 3.4A shows an example of a string, which is analogous to a chromosome

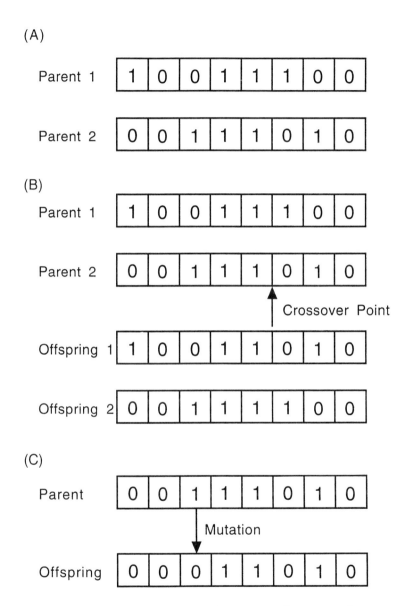

FIG. 3.4. A: Two parent strings in a genetic algorithm. B: Two parent strings producing two child strings with a crossover after the fifth element. C: A parent string producing a child string with a mutation.

of an organism. Each position along a string (analogous to a gene) can have a value (analogous to an allele). In the terminology used earlier in this chapter, the string represents a set of dimensions of variation and feature values for these dimensions.[10] In many systems, each element in a string is a different feature dimension, although in some complex systems, combinations of a few values are jointly interpreted as features.

As an example of how a genetic algorithm can be used, suppose there is a large database of information about corporations whose stock is publicly traded. The information may include profits, outstanding loans, and the length of time the corporation has been publicly held. To predict how the value of the stock for such a company will change in the next year, one can find combinations of attributes that are predictive of increasing stock prices, select arbitrary combinations of features, and then evaluate these combinations by checking the database for stocks with these combinations to determine whether the average stock price of such companies rose or fell. If there are many potentially relevant attributes of companies, searching the entire set of combinations would take too long, and so it would be nice to have an intelligent process for deciding which combination of features is best. This search can be done with a genetic algorithm.

The search starts with some number of strings (the *population*) whose values are chosen randomly. Thus, each string has an arbitrary combination of features. The goodness of each string (its *fitness*) is determined by calculating the mean price change of stocks with this collection of features. Then, a new generation of strings is created by first ordering the initial set of strings by their fitness score. Pairs of strings are randomly selected to be parents of new offspring (with replacement) with a probability that reflects the fitness ratings (the more fit the string, the more likely it is chosen). These two strings are added to the next generation of strings. With some probability, the two parent strings are crossed as shown in Figure 3.4B. When a pair of strings is crossed, all the values after some point (also randomly determined) are switched between strings. This operation is analogous to the process of crossover described earlier. Finally, as shown in Figure 3.4C, each individual string entry can be mutated (e.g., changed to its opposite value) with some second probability. This operation is analogous to genetic mutations that have also been observed in nature.

In this way, a new population of strings is created, and the process repeats. The strings are again evaluated, and again a new generation of

---

[10]In some genetic algorithms, the impact of values occurs only indirectly, a finding analogous to the phenotype in genetics. In genetics, two organisms may have the same genotype (as in identical twins), but manifest different surface characteristics on the basis of other factors like environmental richness.

strings is created. Because the fittest strings are over-represented in each new population, the average fitness of the strings increases. Different strings with good fitness probably derive their fitness from having good values on different features. Thus, the crossover operation, which recombines strings, sometimes stumbles on a good combination and thereby generates a string with a higher fitness level than its parent strings. This new string is likely to become over-represented in subsequent generations because of its high fitness. Finally, the random "mutation" of features may also introduce beneficial values that increase the fitness of a string. In this way, genetic algorithms provide an effective way to search a large space of possibilities efficiently. As discussed by Mitchell (1996), genetic algorithms have been used for both engineering applications (such as predicting the stock market) and scientific applications (like simulations of real populations).

Here, I have just described a simple genetic algorithm. There are many ways that this type of system can be extended. The representation need not involve binary units; the units can each take on many values. The mapping of the representing world of units in the string to the represented world can be complex. The algorithm used to select new members of the next generation can also be made complex and can be designed to selectively favor the best strings from an old generation. Finally, there are a host of additional "genetic" operations that can be applied to strings in addition to the crossover and mutation operations described here. Many of these additional operations are also inspired by transformations that actual genes may undergo, but this is not a requirement of genetic algorithms. These changes can allow a genetic algorithm to search in complex domains, and they add new transformations that help a genetic algorithm find better combinations of feature values.

Genetic Algorithms and Cognitive Models

Genetic algorithms have been applied to cognitive tasks. One classic example is the prisoner's dilemma game, which involves choices by pairs of people. Participants are asked to assume that they and a partner have just committed a crime and that both have been caught. Each one is held in a separate cell and is asked to testify against the partner in exchange for a reduced sentence. Each is told that the partner is being offered the same deal. The structure of the game is shown in Figure 3.5. If one agrees to testify and the partner refuses, he or she is given probation, and the partner receives a stiff sentence (say 5 years). If one agrees to testify and the partner does as well, both get moderately high sentences (say 4 years). If one refuses to testify and the partner testifies against him or her (in the reverse of the first scenario), he or she gets a stiff sentence (5 years), and the partner goes free. Finally, if both refuse to testify, they can be convicted

Player 1

	Defect	Cooperate
Defect	P1: 4 years P2: 4 years	P1: 0 years P2: 5 years
Cooperate	P1: 5 years P2: 0 years	P1: 2 years P2: 2 years

(left label: **Player 2**)

FIG. 3.5. Structure of the prisoner's dilemma game. Each player has been accused of a crime, and each has the option to testify against his or her partner (defect) or refuse to testify (cooperate). The payoffs for the game are shown in the matrix.

only of a lesser charge, and both receive a light sentence (say 2 years). Researchers have used this game extensively in studies of game theory to examine aspects of cooperation. Clearly, it is in the best interests of the pair to cooperate with each other and refuse to testify; this tactic minimizes the number of years that the pair must serve. For any individual, however, if he or she is guaranteed that the partner does not testify, the optimal strategy is to defect against the partner, testify, and thereby receive probation, while the partner goes to prison for a stiff sentence.

In the most interesting version of the prisoner's dilemma game, multiple "rounds" are played sequentially to allow players to use information about the partner's previous behavior to decide what to do in the next round. A simple strategy of tit for tat is more effective than almost any other when playing a sequence of games. When using this strategy, players cooperate with their partner in the first round, and on each subsequent round they just do what their partner did on the previous round. This strategy punishes defections by partners immediately and also rewards cooperation.

Axelrod (1987) studied whether a genetic algorithm would develop some version of the tit-for-tat strategy. The strings in this system consisted of information about the previous three games played in a sequence. Each of the 64 positions in the string represented a different set of outcomes of the previous three games.[11] For example, the first position represented a situation in which both players cooperated with each other in all three games. If the value in a given position was a C, then the system was recommending that the player cooperate again in the next round, and if the

---

[11]Actually, the strings had 70 places, but the other 6 were used to determine what to do in the first two games.

value was a *D*, then the system was recommending that the player testify (or in the language of the prisoner's dilemma, *defect*). The initial strings were randomly generated. Strings were evaluated by having these "strategies" played against eight strategies that people often use when playing the prisoner's dilemma. In 40 different runs of the program, Axelrod found that the program often developed a strategy in which it would reciprocate, as the tit-for-tat strategy would recommend. Because the algorithm found some ways to exploit the particular set of rules it was tested against, its strategy was not completely tit-for-tat.

This genetic algorithm is clearly capable of searching efficiently through a large set of possible strategies to find one that is effective. The assumption of feature independence used by genetic algorithms, however, does seem to limit their psychological plausibility. In this example, the strings consist of the 64 possible outcomes of three consecutive prisoner's dilemma games. The choice of whether to cooperate or testify in the following round is made independently for each of the 64 outcomes. The strategies that people develop do not have this independence. The tit-for-tat strategy reduces the amount of information that needs to be remembered to determining what the partner did on the previous game and doing that. These strategies tend to group similar cases together rather than treating them all independently.

The assumption of feature independence is crucial to the effective performance of genetic algorithms. These algorithms acquire their power through genetically inspired operations like crossover and mutation. Such operations require that it be possible to arbitrarily switch parts of two strings or to arbitrarily change the value of one element in a string via mutation. If the value on one element in a string was actually determined by an element in another string or if there were structural relations among elements (as in the representations I discuss in later chapters), these operations cannot be carried out. Thus, genetic algorithms work because of the assumption of feature independence (see Lenat & Brown, 1984, for a similar discussion).

This use of independent features is also the source of weaknesses in genetic algorithms. With problems in which the solution requires finding and maintaining building blocks of solutions, genetic algorithms can have great difficulty (see Forrest & Mitchell, 1993; Mitchell, 1996, for a discussion of these "royal road" problems). The algorithms have no way of isolating particular parts of the string as being important for the perceived fitness of the string. As a result, they cannot ensure that these aspects of the string are not disrupted by subsequent operations. Nor can the algorithms focus attention on other areas that may be profitably changed to increase the fitness of the string. For search problems involving specific building blocks, representations with more explicit structure may be useful.

SUMMARY

Features are a simple form of representation using discrete symbols. Discrete symbols typically have sharp boundaries, but in some cases the boundaries are fuzzy. When features have fuzzy boundaries, there are often several whose boundaries overlap as in the feature detectors in the visual system described earlier. Because the features are symbols, they can be accessed and used by the processes that operate on them. One example of feature use was in comparison, in which the comparison process can determine both *that* a pair was similar (because it shared a certain number of features) and also *how* it was similar (by virtue of the particular features it shared).

There is only a limited structure to featural representations. In particular, features can be organized into dimensions. When a dimension is substitutive, the presence of one feature along a dimension blocks the presence of any other feature along that dimension. This structure was also evident in genetic algorithms, in which each "gene" can have many different "alleles."

The virtue of this limited structure is that processes acting over features can treat each feature in a representation as independent of all the other features in the representation. That is, the process does not have to worry about what other features are present or how features are related to each other during processing. For example, A. Tversky's (1977) contrast model used elementary set operations to determine the commonalities and differences of a pair. Even genetic algorithms, which use processes more complex than those of elementary set operations, still treat each feature independently. This independence allows genetic algorithms to search through a potentially large set of feature combinations efficiently. The cost of this feature independence is that genetic algorithms often fail on problems that require clusters of important features to be kept together.

The discussion of symbols led naturally to an examination of how symbols can be grounded to give them meaning. In this vein, I discussed decompositional models in which complex features can be decomposed into more primitive features until eventually the most primitive features are reached. It is assumed that primitive features can be grounded in some way, perhaps by referring to perceptual information. Thus, the meaning of any feature can be determined either because it is grounded or because it can be decomposed into more primitive features that are grounded. The notion of primitives is important to consider for all symbolic models of representation, even those that make more complex representational assumptions than the ones made by featural representations.

Network Models

WHAT'S IN A NETWORK?

In this chapter, I am concerned with representations that have more structure than those discussed in chapters 2 and 3. These representations all have some kind of *network* structure. A network consists of *nodes* and *links*; for example, an airline may create a network to illustrate the routes it flies and the distances between cities it flies to. A network representation of this type is shown in Figure 4.1. The nodes in this diagram represent cities the airline flies to; each node is labeled with the name of the city it represents. The links represent flights that the airline makes; each link is labeled with the distance of the flight. This kind of network can be used to determine routes between cities and the total flying distance required to travel from one city to another: A trip from Los Angeles to New York requires only a single flight of 2,451 miles. On this airline, a trip from San Francisco to Washington, D.C. requires at least three flights. Flying from San Francisco to Chicago to New York to Washington, D.C., requires 2,776 miles of air travel.

In the network in Figure 4.1, the links are *undirected*. Undirected links are used when the relation represented by the link is *symmetric*. In this example, if there is a direct flight from one city to another, the airline also has a direct flight from the second city back to the first. It would seem odd for an airline to fly directly from one city to a second (e.g., from Chicago to New York), but not to fly the return trip directly. Network

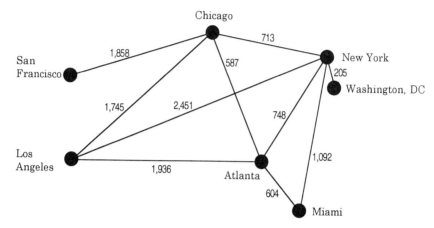

FIG. 4.1. Network diagram showing airline routes for a fictitious company. The nodes represent cities and are labeled with the city name. The links represent flights the company makes and are labeled with the flying distances between cities.

models, however, can also be used when the relation between two nodes is *asymmetric*. When the relation between nodes is asymmetric, then the links are *directed*. Directed links are usually drawn on network diagrams with arrows, which indicate that the relation holds in the direction an arrow points, but not in the reverse direction.[1]

The node and link structure of the networks and the labels on the nodes and links are critical aspects of the representing worlds of these networks. Other aspects of the diagram in Figure 4.1 are not essential. This diagram was drawn to vaguely resemble a map (much like the map constructed from flying distances in Figure 2.2), but the spatial layout of the nodes and the physical distances between nodes and links are not part of the representing world of network models. Only the set of connections and the labels are used by the processes that operate on semantic networks.

In this chapter, I focus on three aspects of networks with nodes and links. First is a semantic network. Early semantic network models consisted of networks with nodes, links, and labels. Processing in these networks often involved passing markers across the links between nodes to model text comprehension and access to words in the lexicon. After describing these initial models, I discuss extensions to this initial proposal focusing on the automatic spread of activation through a network. Finally, I examine

---

[1]The terms *directed* and *undirected* are borrowed from graph theory in mathematics. The networks that have been used in psychology and artificial intelligence are all types of graphs, and the mathematics of graph theory has been used to develop procedures for processing information using networks.

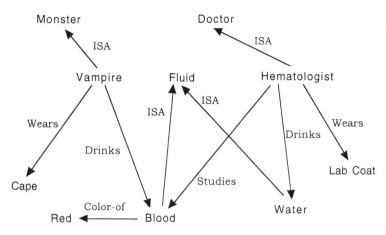

FIG. 4.2. Sample semantic network with nodes related to *Vampire* and *Hematologist*.

parallel constraint satisfaction networks, which also use nodes, links, and spreading activation. Parallel constraint satisfaction models are related to the connectionist models described in chapter 2.

SEMANTIC NETWORKS

An important class of representations in cognitive science is semantic networks, which have nodes that are *labeled* and links that are both *labeled* and *directed* (Quillian, 1968). Nodes in the network correspond to concepts, in which the labels specify the concept denoted by the node just as the labels specified the city represented by the node in Figure 4.1. Figure 4.2 shows a sample semantic network surrounding the concept *vampire*. Each node has a unique label that distinguishes one from another, and the links also have labels. The label on the link specifies a relation between the nodes connected by the link. For example, the *vampire* and *monster* nodes are linked by a class inclusion relation with a link labeled *ISA* (e.g., "A vampire ISA monster"). Class inclusion is a relation stating that one category is a subset of another. Any relation that can hold between a pair of nodes can be used as a label for a link. The label *drinks* specifies that an object specified by one node drinks a substance specified by a second node (as in the *drinks* link between *vampire* and *blood* in Figure 4.2). Finally, these links are directed. As discussed previously, the direction of the link is specified by the arrow on the link and represents the fact that this relation is asymmetric. The *ISA* link from *vampire* to *monster* points from *vampire* to *monster* in accordance with the fact that all vampires are monsters, but all monsters are not vampires.

An early motivation for using semantic network models was storage efficiency. To illustrate, consider assessing the truth of the following two sentences:

Dogs have fur.   (4.1)

and

Dogs breathe air.   (4.2)

Sentence 4.1 seems to be a fact about dogs. It may seem reasonable to have a link in a semantic network between the dog node and the fur node to specify that dogs are covered with fur. In contrast, there need not be a direct link between dogs and air to specify that dogs breathe air. This fact is true, but the connection is indirect.

These indirect connections can be established in semantic networks through *inheritance.* In particular, some categories (like *dog*) are members of more general categories (like *mammal*). One can connect the knowledge of some facts to general categories rather than to specific ones. Thus, if mammals breathe air and dogs are a subcategory of mammals, dogs can inherit the property of breathing air from animals. Class inclusion relations (i.e., *ISA* relations) support the inheritance of properties. Properties can be inherited from any more general category of which a given category is a member. Poodles breathe air, because all mammals breathe air and poodles are mammals. The same object may inherit properties from categories at many different levels of abstraction. For example, one can determine that dogs breathe air because they are mammals and that they are composed of molecules because they are physical objects.

The ability to inherit properties means that the storage of properties in a semantic network can be efficient. One need only link a given property to the node for the most general category about which it is true. Any more specific category for which the property is true inherits the property by virtue of being connected to the more general category by *ISA* links. In this way, one can avoid constructing links between a property and every category it is related to.

The notion of storage efficiency deserves more attention. The idea that objects inherit properties because of their membership in more general categories allows one to learn facts about one object and then infer these facts for other objects about which they were not explicitly stated. One need not learn directly that all dogs breathe air and all cats breathe air and all moles breathe air and all sloths breathe air. Simply finding out that all mammals breathe air and that a particular animal is a mammal is enough to determine that it breathes air. Nevertheless, there is no reason to believe that the human cognitive system is maximally efficient (Collins & Loftus, 1975). Early semantic network models (e.g., Quillian, 1968) suggested that the fact that people know many things forces them to be reasonably efficient in the use of memory, and so people often store properties at the most general level at which they are true and then allow all subcategories to inherit the property from a supercategory.[2] For properties that are usually true, one may store the property at a general level and store the exceptions specially. For example, one can store the fact that all birds have feathers by allowing the property "has feathers" to be inherited by all subcategories of bird. One can store strongly characteristic properties like "flies" with birds, whereas properties like "does not fly" are stored with exceptions like penguins.

The assumption of maximal efficiency is too strong to be correct. The focus on efficiency was due in part to the tools available at the time these models were developed. When semantic networks were developed as computer models in the late 1960s, computers were large and slow and had very little storage capacity. Under these circumstances, efficiency was paramount, because storing redundant information was wasteful of precious space. In contrast, computers are now small and fast and have vast online and long-term storage facilities. As anyone who has loaded a new version of a computer program can attest, there is no longer a premium on efficient storage of information in computer programs. Because computer technology has often been used as a metaphor for the processing capacities of the mind, it seems no more imperative to assume that humans are efficient in their storage of knowledge than computers are.

Even though redundancy in cognitive systems no longer seems like a technological problem, there are still barriers to creating links between every property and every category about which it is true. The problem is that making inferences takes some amount of time and effort. If a semantic network has many objects organized into class-inclusion hierarchies, the addition of new facts to the network creates a vast array of other new facts that are suddenly known to be true. For example, suppose one knows about 100 different birds and learns that birds have hollow bones. Moving down the *ISA* hierarchy, one can attach the fact "has hollow bones" to all 100 subcategories of birds (and to all subtypes of these subcategories, and so on). This possibility is called *forward chaining inference*, because one makes inferences at the time that the information is added. The advantage of forward chaining inference is that retrieving a new fact is fast in the future: If I exhaustively make the inference that all subclasses of birds (and

---

[2]Quillian's theory, particularly as elaborated by Collins and Quillian (1972) and later by Collins and Loftus (1975), made it clear that the networks were not supposed to be maximally efficient, but that they allowed some redundant information to be stored.

all subclasses of these subclasses) have hollow bones, I can quickly retrieve this fact about any bird. The cost, of course, is that it may take a long time to attach this fact to every subclass of birds, and each time I learn that a new object is a bird, I must add many new facts to its representation.[3]

If the cost of forward chaining inference is too great, the cognitive system could delay inferring a particular fact until it is needed. In this situation, if someone asks whether robins have hollow bones, the system must first check to see whether the fact is known directly. If not, *ISA* links can be followed, checking at each supercategory to see whether this fact can be inherited. The process stops when the fact of interest is found, or when the top of the hierarchy is eventually reached. This type of inference is called *backward chaining inference*. The advantage of backward chaining inference is that there is very little cost to learning a new fact, but later processing may take a long time, because much information about objects must be derived rather than being stored directly with the objects for which it is true. Many artificial intelligence (AI) proposals for large knowledge bases use some combination of forward chaining and backward chaining inference (Lenat & Guha, 1990).

Processing in Semantic Networks

To this point, I have talked primarily about the structure of semantic networks without regard to how information is processed in them. In early proposals about semantic networks, the central form of processing involved finding intersections between concepts in the network. Intersections can be found by using a marker-passing algorithm. A marker-passing algorithm is like sending scouts through new terrain, where each scout places a distinctive tag (called a *marker* or an *activation tag*) at each place he or she visits. These scouts begin at the nodes for the concepts in the sentence being processed. At each processing cycle, the scout at a given node visits every node connected to the node where he or she is, places a marker at each node, and checks to see whether a scout for another concept has placed a marker there already. On subsequent cycles, markers are passed recursively to more distant nodes through the links from the nodes reached on the first pass. The search is halted when a node receives markers from both initial concepts (i.e., when the scout reaches a node that already has a marker from the other concept) or after some specified time elapses

---

[3]Another problem with rampant forward chaining inference is that it increases the amount of processing that must be done when a false belief is discovered. For example, if a forward chaining inference system is told that all birds need trace amounts of uranium to survive, the system adds this fact to all known subclasses of birds. If this fact is later retracted (or shown to be false), some process must remove the appropriate link connecting bird to uranium and also the links between all subclasses of birds and uranium.

(i.e., the scouts get tired and want to return home). The path between the nodes is used to describe the relationship between the concepts.

For example, imagine that someone with the semantic network in Figure 4.2 was processing the sentence "A vampire is like a hematologist." Processing this sentence requires figuring out how a vampire is like a hematologist. Initially, the *vampire* and *hematologist* nodes are activated, and each sends activation to nodes to which it is connected. *Vampire* sends activation to *Cape, Blood,* and *Monster.* The fact that each of these nodes is connected to *Vampire* with a different link does not matter. Likewise, *Hematologist* sends an activation tag to *Doctor, Lab Coat, Water,* and *Blood.* The intersection of activation tags for *Vampire* and *Hematologist* at *Blood* leads the program to analyze the links to the intersected concept. A system using this network would conclude that a vampire is like a hematologist in that the former drinks blood and the latter studies blood. Semantic network models assume that the process of finding intersections through passing markers is a central mechanism in sentence comprehension.

Sending an activation tag across a link is thought to take some amount of time (Collins & Quillian, 1972). It generally takes longer to search along a long path than to search along a short path. The amount of time needed to traverse a link is not assumed to be constant for all links, however, and in some cases it may be possible to traverse a long path with links that transmit information more quickly than to traverse a short path with links that transmit information slowly. In particular, links that are important or criterial for a concept are assumed to allow shorter traversal times than do links that are less important or less criterial. Sending an activation marker across a link is assumed to facilitate subsequent processing along that link and other links with the same label. That is, activating an *ISA* link is assumed to facilitate processing of class-inclusion relations, even those between different concepts from the ones processed initially.

Semantic networks have been used as the basis of models for explaining *priming* effects in semantic memory. Priming occurs when processing of one concept affects the processing of a subsequently presented concept. Priming generally involves a facilitation of processing, although under some circumstances, it can actually involve an inhibition (e.g., Neely, 1976). A common finding in psychological experiments is that a brief presentation of a word facilitates the recognition of a word with a related meaning. One commonly used technique for demonstrating priming of concepts is lexical decision, in which a subject is shown a prime and then a string of letters and is asked to say whether the string of letters is a word. In this task, people shown the word "nurse" are faster to verify that the string DOCTOR is a word than are people given a neutral prime like a string of asterisks (Meyer & Schvaneveldt, 1971; Meyer, Schvaneveldt, & Ruddy, 1975). Another common finding is that processing a particular aspect of one stimulus can facilitate processing that same aspect for another stimulus. For example, processing the sentence "Fire engines are red" can facilitate later processing of the sentence "Grass is green." This facilitation may reflect activation of the "color of" link in a semantic network (Collins & Loftus, 1975).

In a semantic network, priming has a straightforward explanation. On an experimental trial, a subject may briefly see the word "nurse". At the presentation of the word "nurse," the concept node for *nurse* is activated in the semantic network. Activation tags are then sent to the nodes connected to *nurse*, and tags are sent from those nodes to the nodes to which they are connected. As discussed previously, the speed of transmission of the tags depends on the strength of the connection. This spread of activation continues until the second target string of letters (e.g., DOCTOR) is presented. It is assumed that if the concept node for *doctor* has been activated through its connection to the concept *nurse* (either directly through an associative link or indirectly through a connection to common nodes), then the string DOCTOR is recognized more quickly than if the node was not activated. Presumably, a neutral prime (like a string of asterisks) does not pass an activation tag to *doctor*. Thus, the semantic network model predicts that recognition of the word *doctor* is faster following a semantically related prime than following a neutral prime.

Testing the Basic Proposal

Early proposals about semantic networks spawned a flurry of research in cognitive psychology to test their psychological plausibility. This empirical work focused on several central aspects of these models. As discussed earlier, semantic networks were originally posited as knowledge representation systems suitable for explaining phenomena in text comprehension. Because text comprehension is a difficult business, many experimental studies focused on narrower assumptions of the model. Studies focused on the basic claim that activation spreads through a network and thereby facilitates the processing of related concepts. In addition, many studies have examined the claim that activation takes more time to spread over longer paths than over shorter paths. Research has also focused on the assumption of efficiency and has examined the extent to which information is stored redundantly in a semantic network. I review some of this evidence in this section.

I have already mentioned that primes can facilitate the recognition of semantically related words. The relations between the words that prime each other can be rather broad: Pairs like *doctor* and *nurse* are associates. Priming is also obtained for concepts on a taxonomic hierarchy: Robin primes *bird*. The link between a category and its parent taxonomic category is typically stronger than is the link between the parent and its child. Thus, *robin* primes *bird* more than the reverse (Collins & Quillian, 1972). The relation between prime and target need not be semantic to get facilitation: Words that sound alike can also prime each other (*phonological* priming) as can words with letters in common (*orthographic* priming). To capture these latter results, a semantic network model must be extended to incorporate aspects of the words themselves in addition to relations between concepts.

Studies of sentence verification have made clear the need for links that vary in their strength. Imagine a network that is strictly hierarchically organized. A simple network of terms connected by *ISA* links is shown in Figure 4.3. Here, *robin, sparrow, chicken,* and *penguin* are all instances of birds, and all are connected to the *bird* node through *ISA* links. If all links have the same strength, it should take the same amount of time to pass an activation tag from the *ISA* links connecting each instance of bird to the *bird* node, without any difference in speed to verify that various instances of birds are in fact birds. In contrast to this prediction, category verification studies have often found a relationship between the typicality of an instance and the speed with which it is verified as being a member of a category (Rips et al., 1973). For example, *robin* (a typical bird) is verified as an instance of the *bird* category faster than is *chicken* (an atypical bird). For these data to be explained by a network model, it is important to assume that links have different strengths.

Studies of sentence verification also make clear that networks are not designed for optimal conservation of storage space. Again, consider the sample network in Figure 4.3. All instances of birds are connected directly to the *bird* node and indirectly to the *animal* node through its connection to *bird.* All instances of mammals are connected to the *mammal* node directly and to the *animal* node indirectly through its connection to *mammal.* With this strict hierarchy, it should take less time to verify that an instance of the category *mammal* is a mammal than to verify that it is an animal and less time to verify that an instance of the category *bird* is a bird than to verify that it is an animal. In contrast to this prediction, Rips and colleagues (1973) found that it actually takes *more* time to verify that most instances are members of the category *mammal* than to verify that they are instances of the category *animal* (see also E. E. Smith et al. [1974]; Collins & Quillian [1972]).[4]

To account for these findings with a model that uses a semantic network, assumptions about minimal storage must be relaxed. One possible account is to connect concepts to more than one more general (i.e., superordinate)

---

[4]A developmental perspective on semantic networks suggests that this finding is not so surprising. Most children are exposed to the category *animal* before they are exposed to the category *mammal.* There is no reason to think that learning a category intermediate in abstraction between two other categories causes the direct links between the first two categories to be removed. Thus, learning about mammals need not remove the direct *ISA* link between instances of animals (i.e., dogs and cats) and the node for *animal.*

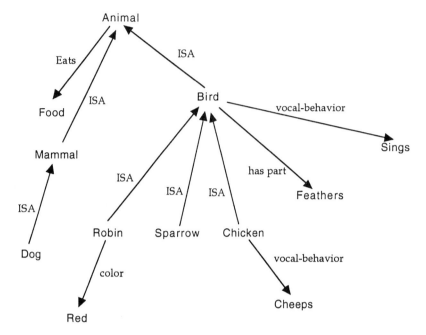

FIG. 4.3. Sample semantic network with knowledge about birds and animals.

category by using *ISA* links, rather than connecting them only to the category immediately more general. For example, the *bear* node could be connected by an *ISA* link to the *mammal* node and by a second *ISA* link to the *animal* node. A second possibility is to adopt a solution similar to the one posited by the featural model of E. E. Smith et al. (1974) described in chapter 3. In that model, objects were described as sets of features, and the category verification process consisted of a comparison of the features of object pairs, in which the initial comparison involved all features and later comparisons involved only core features. In a semantic network, concepts have links to many nodes corresponding to features true of those concepts. Initially, when activation spreads through this network of features, related concepts become highly activated and potentially yield fast responses. If the activation falls in an intermediate range, the search can be restricted to *ISA* links, similar to focusing on core features. In this respect, the feature model and a semantic network model are nearly indistinguishable (see Collins & Loftus [1975] for a similar discussion).

Finally, some findings seem less compatible with the assumptions of semantic networks discussed so far. These findings involve the damping of activation to a concept, also called *inhibition*. In one classic study, Neely (1976) found that if the prime was semantically *unrelated* to the target and the interval between the presentation of the stimulus and the presentation of the target letter string was long, the time to respond that the string was a word in a lexical decision task was actually longer than is observed for a neutral prime. Presenting the prime *hockey* could inhibit responses to the string DOCTOR in a lexical decision task. This finding suggests that semantically unrelated concepts are actually driven below their resting level of activation. Explaining findings of inhibition requires additional mechanisms beyond those discussed so far. In particular, there must be some way to decrease the activation of a node.

As for the initial goal of language comprehension, it is unclear how a spreading activation model can account for concept access in online language comprehension. A classic study by Swinney and Hakes (1976) provided a useful illustration. In this study, researchers read aloud to participants a passage in which there was an ambiguous word but the passage strongly biased one reading of the word. For example, the passage might read: "Rumor had it that for years, the government building had been plagued with problems. The man was not surprised when he found several spiders, roaches and other *bugs* in the corner of the room." When the ambiguous word (*bugs*) was heard, a string of letters was presented for a lexical decision task. The letter string was either related to the contextually biased meaning (e.g., ant), related to another meaning of the ambiguous word (e.g., spy), or unrelated to the ambiguous word (e.g., sew). When the lexical decision task occurred immediately after the ambiguous word, both words related to the contextually biased meaning and to the other meaning of the ambiguous word were facilitated relative to the unrelated word. In contrast, when the lexical decision task was presented three syllables after the ambiguous word, only the contextually related meaning of the ambiguous word was primed. Thus, selection of the correct word sense also seems to inhibit the spread of activation through the semantic network for unrelated concepts. Accounting for online language comprehension data like these is also likely to involve mechanisms that inhibit all meanings of a word except the one selected.

To summarize, the initial formulation of semantic networks was used as the basis of models of text comprehension. In these models, it was assumed that finding intersections among concepts in the network could be used to determine the meaning of a sentence. Of course, sentence meaning involves more than just finding intersections between known concepts. In many cases, language is used to provide new information about a situation, and the sentence constructs new knowledge, rather than just stating relations among known concepts. Additional processing mechanisms are required to allow semantic networks to model this situation.

One place in which semantic networks have been used successfully is in models of the activation of concepts by language. Many studies have demonstrated that one concept can facilitate the access to a related concept. Semantic network models use the process of spreading activation to model the way that one concept can activate another. Although the simple use of markers to pass activation from one node to another has had some success modeling lexical priming, additional mechanisms are needed to model the fine details of processing. I turn to some extensions of the basic processing assumptions in semantic networks in the next section.

Extending Network Assumptions: Activation and Activation Tags

Collins and Loftus (1975) made many changes in the basic assumptions of the network model that laid the groundwork for significant work to follow. In particular, they assumed that activation was spread through the network in a manner similar to the connectionist models described in chapter 2. On this view, activation is a continuous value possessed by a node rather than a marker indicating that the node has been activated. Activation from one node is passed to neighboring nodes via links. The links retain a criterial weight as Collins and Quillian (1972) assumed, but now an activated node raises the activation level of nodes to which it is connected as a function of both the activation of the initial node as well as of the strength of the links between nodes. It is further assumed that the activation of a node decreases over time, so that if the source of activation of a node is removed, the node's activation gradually decreases to a baseline level.

An example of the spread of activation in a network with continuous levels of activation is shown in Figure 4.4. Here, the ovals are nodes, and the arrows are links. The thicker the arrows, the stronger the connection between nodes. Activation at a given node is shown by the darkness of the oval. Figure 4.4A depicts the state of a network presented with the sentence "A vampire is like a hematologist." The nodes for *vampire* and *hematologist* have activation, but the other nodes in the network do not. At the next time step, shown in Figure 4.4B, activation has spread from the active nodes to those it is connected to. Because the *ISA* links in this figure are assumed to be stronger connections than are the other links, the *monster* and *doctor* nodes are more strongly activated than are the *lab coat, water*, and *cape* nodes. The node representing *blood* is strongly activated because it is connected to both the *vampire* and *hematologist* nodes and thus receives activation from both sources. If this example were carried further, the *fluid* node would also begin to get activation from both the *water* and *blood* nodes. In addition, the activation levels of each node would begin to decay. In this way, only nodes that receive activation from many sources tend to remain active. The other nodes get a brief boost of activation and then decay to their resting state (shown in white in Figure 4.4).

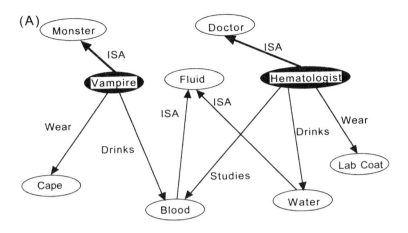

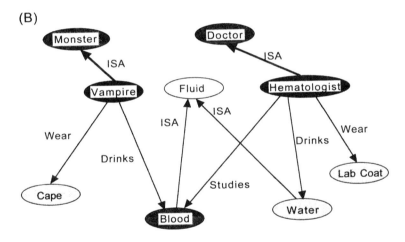

FIG. 4.4. Example of the spread of activation through a semantic network with continuous levels of activation. The strength of connection is shown by the thickness of the arrows. The degree of activation of a node is shown by the darkness of the node. A: The state of the network just after exposure to the sentence "A vampire is like a hematologist." B: The state of the network as activation begins to spread through it.

This network model emphasizes the activation of nodes and the strength of connections between nodes. Although there are still labels on the links between nodes, they are less important to the model than they were under the earlier assumptions. This change reflects a shift in the emphasis of these models from models of text comprehension to models of priming in semantic memory. For this model, it is assumed that the greater the degree of activation of a node, the easier to access the concept conveyed by that node in the future. Facilitatory priming reflects that the activation of a node is greater following some priming stimulus than following some neutral prime.

J. R. Anderson (1983b) also adopted a network model in which nodes have a level of activation measured on a continuous scale. Like the proposal by Collins and Loftus, Anderson's model assumed that activation spreads across links to other nodes and that the links have different connection strengths. Anderson explicitly thought of this network as the long-term memory structure of an individual, so that short-term or *working* memory consisted of those units with positive activation. Short-term memory is the set of concepts that are active at any moment and are available to be used by cognitive processes that are currently operating.

Because the activation level of each element decays over time in the absence of continued activation from other units, there is a limited amount of activation in the network at any given time. Thus, working memory has a limited capacity. More recent work has assumed a limit to the amount of activation that can be provided by active sources in memory, and thus a limit to the capacity of working memory (J. R. Anderson, 1993; J. R. Anderson, Reder, & Lebiere, 1996). J. R. Anderson (1983a) clearly maintained that working memory should not be confused with the amount of information reported in short-term memory tests. In his classic paper, Miller (1956) found that people can report only about seven independent bits of information in short-term memory tasks. Anderson suggested that the amount of information reported is a function of both the active information in working memory as well as the interaction of the information with processes that report it.

The continuous activation version of semantic networks makes a number of predictions that can be tested. One particularly interesting prediction is the *fan effect*. Fan is defined as the number of nodes connected to a given node in memory. The more that activation from a single node must be spread out (i.e., fanned out) among other nodes, the less of an impact this node has in activating other nodes. In empirical studies, fan is typically varied by varying the number of facts that people learn about different items. For example, if I learn one fact about John Doe (say, that John Doe eats ice cream) and two facts about Richard Roe (say, that Richard Roe likes the New York Giants and that Richard Roe owns a dog), the fan for John Doe is lower than the fan for Richard Roe. Anderson suggested that the fan of an element affects the element by dividing the activation flowing from the unit among the various links that emanate from it. Thus, if a node with fan one sends an amount of activation A down its link, a node with fan two sends activation $A/2$ down each link. More generally, the amount of activation going down the links coming from a node is A/f, where f is the fan of that node. Thus, the higher the fan of a node, the less activation it passes to nodes to which it is connected and the longer it takes to retrieve and use these nodes in subsequent processing.

Consistent with these predictions, a variety of findings have suggested that high fan items take longer to respond to than do low fan items. J. R. Anderson (1983a) described an experiment in which participants studied a set of subject–verb–object sentences (e.g., "The cat ate the pizza"). The objects in the sentences always had a fan of one (i.e., they were unique), whereas the subjects and verbs differed in their fan (i.e., they could appear in many sentences). The only constraints on the stimulus materials were that a particular subject and verb appeared together only once and the subject and verb in a sentence had the same fan. Participants were then given two tests. In the recognition test, they saw a sentence and were asked whether it appeared in the memory set. In the recall test, participants were given the subject and verb and were asked to produce the object. The data are shown in Table 4.1. In both tasks, the latency to respond increased with the fan of the subject and verb. This effect was much stronger in the recall task, for which participants could rely only on the subject and verb, than it was for the recognition task, for which participants could focus on the unique object. These data provide clear support for the predicted fan effect.

As many examples in this chapter demonstrate, the assumptions of semantic network models have often been tested with response time tasks that probe the amount of time needed to respond to questions. Theories of working memory must also account for the way people perform in complex situations. Such studies have often been carried out using a dual-task paradigm in which people are asked to carry out two tasks at the same time and the difficulty of one or both tasks is varied. Subjects' performance on both tasks is examined as a function of the difficulty of the tasks.

J. R. Anderson and colleagues (1996) used a dual-task paradigm to test the proposal that working memory is limited by a cap on the amount of activation that can spread through a network at any time. In their study, one task involved solving simple algebra problems, and the other task involved remembering a set of digits. The idea was that making the algebra problems more difficult to solve and increasing the working memory load

TABLE 4.1
Demonstration of the Fan Effect

Fan	Recognition Task	Recall Task
1	1.35 sec	1.54 sec
2	1.58 sec	2.07 sec
3	1.70 sec	2.96 sec

Note. Fan refers to the fan of subjects and verbs in the sentences. From J. R. Anderson (1983a). Copyright © 1983 by Harvard University Press. Reprinted with permission.

(by asking participants to remember more digits) would adversely affect people's performance on the algebra problems. Subjects' data would then be compared to the performance of a computational model (described later).

In the study, the easy problems required only one transformation, as in solving the equation:

$$4x = 8 \qquad (4.3)$$

for x. The difficult problems required two transformations, as in solving the equation:

$$3x - 2 = 4 \qquad (4.4)$$

for x. Subjects were asked to solve these problems while remembering a set of digits. On each trial, the subject was asked to remember either two, four, or six different digits. People were able to remember the shorter (two- and four-digit) strings of numbers correctly with high accuracy, although their accuracy on these strings was higher when they were solving easy problems than when they were solving hard ones. There was a sharp drop in recall performance for the long (six-digit strings). In the equation-solving task, subjects accurately solved the easy problems regardless of the length of the string they were supposed to remember. For the hard problems, solution accuracy was uniformly worse than for the easy problems, and subjects had particular difficulty solving the hard problems when they had to remember long strings of numbers.

J. R. Anderson et al. were able to fit these data by using a version of the ACT-R model. The ACT-R model has two components. One is a semantic network that spreads activation between nodes connected by links, with a strict limit on the amount of activation that can arise from elements that are attended to. That is, working memory is limited by placing a cap on the amount of activation that can flow through the network. The second part is a *production system*, which allows the model to carry out steps in solving a problem by following rules. (I discuss production systems in more detail in chap. 5.) The purpose of the production system is to carry out the steps needed to solve algebra word problems and to access and output the set of numbers for the recall task. Anderson et al. were able to model subjects' data in this task by using ACT-R, a result suggesting that working memory can be conceptualized as the activation in a semantic network and that the limit on working memory is a limit on the amount of activation that can flow through the network.

There are two reasons that both a spreading activation mechanism and a rule-following mechanism are required in ACT-R. The spreading activation mechanism provides an efficient mechanism for searching through an established conceptual structure, but a complete reasoning system needs to be able to construct new knowledge. In addition, it needs to be able to carry out complex processes like solving algebra problems. Both processes require that behavior be guided by the information that is active. (In chap. 5, there is an extended discussion of production systems making clear that the rule carried out at any given moment is a function of what is currently active in memory.)

Some Critiques of Semantic Networks

I have discussed semantic networks that can be characterized as networks consisting of nodes and links. The nodes are labeled with the concepts they represent, and the links have labels representing relations that hold among concepts.[5] I have focused attention on simple modes of processing in these networks in which activation is spread through the network. This spread of activation can be used to search for paths connecting concepts, or it can be used to model the activation of concepts during language comprehension. I have also assumed that complex processes (like production rules) can be added to a semantic network, but these processes go beyond the scope of my focus in this chapter.

One criticism of semantic networks formulated in this way is that the links are used inconsistently in the network (Woods, 1975). For example, in Figure 4.2, some links represent class inclusion relations. Others represent actions that an agent participates in (e.g., a vampire drinks blood). Yet other links represent adjectival relations (e.g., the color of blood is red). It is true that each of these is a relation and that the links play the role of relating pairs of nodes, but the links are not uniform in the types of relations that they represent. Thus, a semantic network representation seems to gloss over distinctions among types of relations that a representational system may want to make.

Another criticism of semantic networks is that they are primarily concerned with relations among elements in the representing world rather than the connection between the representing world and the represented world (Johnson-Laird, Hermann, & Chaffin, 1984). A key characteristic of semantic networks is that processing uses existing elements in a network that is often assumed to contain what is stored in long-term memory. This assumption is problematic, because many aspects of meaning depend on understanding the outside world. For example, Medin and Shoben (1988) showed that people often use their knowledge of the world when interpreting combinations of concepts. Many people thought a wooden spoon was large,

---

[5]In fact, it is possible to construct semantic networks in which only the links are labeled. See Johnson-Laird, Hermann, and Chaffin (1984) for a discussion of this issue.

even though spoons are not typically thought of as large, and wooden things are not typically thought of as large. Instead, people seemed to think of specific instances of spoons made of wood and to determine that they are large (relative to other spoons). A semantic network would have difficulty with conceptual combinations like this, because it has extensive information about the relations among concepts in the network but it has no mechanisms for processing information about the represented world. Thus, in cases where there are *emergent properties* of combinations (like *large* for wooden spoons), a semantic network is likely to run into problems.

Finally, as discussed earlier, semantic networks tend to be static; they are taken to be the set of concepts already possessed. Most of the effort in developing processes that act on semantic networks has focused on ways of using the networks to access information or to process paths between concepts. Much less work has focused on ways of constructing new semantic knowledge during language comprehension. This gap is unfortunate, because much of what people do when they comprehend language is to construct new connections between concepts. They read things to learn new information and not simply to verify facts that they already know. It is important to note that processes that construct semantic networks are not incompatible with the idea of semantic networks as a type of representing world, but these constructive processes have typically not been studied in the context of semantic networks.

It must also be emphasized that many limitations of semantic networks are real if one assumes that the primary processing mechanisms operating on them involve a spread of activation and an analysis of paths between nodes. In fact, the basic assumptions described in this chapter can be augmented in many ways (see Johnson-Laird et al., 1984, for a discussion of some modifications). These extensions turn semantic networks into the kinds of structured representations I discuss in chapters 5 to 7.

INTERACTIVE ACTIVATION AND PARALLEL CONSTRAINT SATISFACTION MODELS

Researchers have also applied the spreading activation mechanism used in semantic network models in models of other processes ranging from letter recognition to analogy to person perception to theory change in the history of science. These models can be grouped under the heading of interactive activation models, using the moniker established by McClelland and Rumelhart (1981) in their influential model of letter recognition. These models derive their power from using spreading activation to satisfy several simultaneous constraints on a problem at once. Hence, they have also been called *parallel constraint satisfaction* models.

Such models are one type of *localist connectionist model.* In chapter 2, I discussed distributed connectionist models in which the representations consist of patterns of activation across a set of units and no individual unit can be identified as a representation of a specific element in the representing world. In a localist connectionist model, the individual nodes in the network do represent specific things in the represented world. The links between nodes are set up to enforce constraints believed to hold in the domain of the model.

The semantic networks described in the previous section were developed as computer models of language comprehension (Collins & Quillian, 1972; Quillian, 1968). As a result, the terminology for describing these networks was borrowed from computer science and mathematics (e.g., nodes in a network connected by links). Localist connectionist models owe some of their heritage to semantic networks, but they also are tied to neuroscience. Thus, these models borrow terminology from both camps. Links between nodes with a positive weight are often called *excitatory* connections. Parallel constraint satisfaction networks take an additional type of link from neuroscience—the *inhibitory* connection. An inhibitory connection between nodes has a negative weight so that high levels of activation of one node strongly inhibit (or decrease) the activation of a second node. In the rest of this chapter, I discuss the basic properties of interactive activation models and describe a few representative models as examples of the strengths and weaknesses of this approach.

The Interactive Activation Model of Letter Perception

The ability to recognize letters is a key perceptual ability underlying the capacity to read. Intuitively, letter recognition may seem simply a function of combining low-level features of letters into larger groups that allow one letter to be distinguished from another. For example, as shown in Figure 4.5, one can think of the letter *P* as one set of features, the letter *B* as another set of features, and the letter *R* as yet another set of features. These features may overlap to some degree, but the task of identifying a letter is simply to find the right mapping between the features in the stimulus and the letters.

Unfortunately, data from psychological studies have shown that letter recognition is not that simple: Many phenomena do not fit neatly into such a simple featural view. One critical finding is the *word superiority effect,* which demonstrates that letters are identified more quickly in the context of words than out of context. Thus, although words may seem to increase the processing load and make letter recognition more difficult, it is actually easier to recognize a letter when it is embedded in a word than to recognize

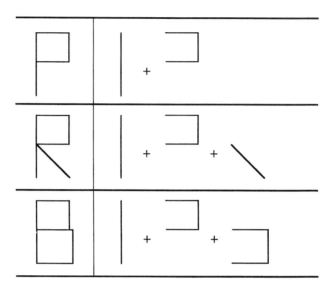

FIG. 4.5. Stick figure letters similar to those used in McClelland and Rumelhart's (1981) interactive activation model.

it in isolation. This advantage extends to pronounceable nonwords, strings of letters that *could* be words but are not, like *blick* or *frin*.

To account for data like these, McClelland and Rumelhart (1981) proposed an interactive activation model that uses many of the mechanisms of spreading activation discussed in this chapter. The model, which is illustrated in Figure 4.6, consists of a network of nodes organized into three layers: *features, letters,* and *words.* Thus, each layer has nodes that represent properties of the same type. The feature layer consists of nodes representing features of letters. There are separate sets of features for each letter in a given position in a word. The original model recognized four-letter words and so had four sets of feature nodes. The letter layer consists of the 26 letters of the English alphabet. Again, there are four sets of letters, one for each position in the word. Finally, the word layer consists of a lexicon of four-letter words. The original model had 1,179 four-letter English words in its lexicon.

Just as in the semantic network models described earlier, the nodes in the interactive activation network are connected via links that allow activation to be passed from one node to another. The feature nodes are given connections with positive weights (*excitatory* connections) to letters that contain the feature, and connections with negative weights (*inhibitory* connections) to letters that do not contain the feature. Thus, the presence of a feature promotes the recognition of letters that contain the feature, and inhibits the recognition of letters that do not contain it. For example,

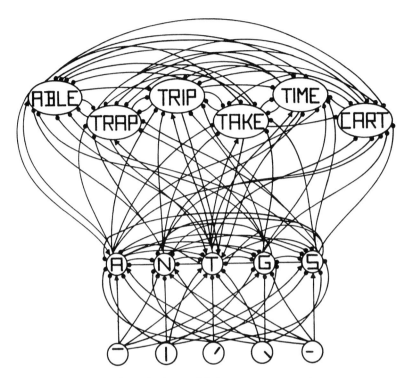

FIG. 4.6.   Interactive activation model. Arrows represent excitatory connections between nodes, and circles represent inhibitory connections between
nodes. From J. L. McClelland and D. E. Rumelhart (1981). Copyright ©
1981 by American Psychological Association. Reprinted with permission.

in Figure 4.6, there are excitatory connections between the feature horizontal line on the top and the letters A, T, G, and S, and an inhibitory
connection between that feature and the letter N.

In the letter layer, there are inhibitory connections between the letters at
the same position of the word. These inhibitory connections reflect that
letters are mutually exclusive at each position in a word. If the first letter is
determined to be an A, it has also been determined *not* to be a G. The letter
nodes are also connected to the word nodes. There are excitatory connections between each letter node and nodes for words in the lexicon with the
letter at that position. There are inhibitory connections between each letter
node and nodes for words in the lexicon without the letter in that position.
For example, the node for an initial letter A has an excitatory connection to
the node for the word ABLE, but an inhibitory connection to the word TRAP.
In the word layer, nodes for each word have inhibitory connections to other
words. For the letter layer, this pattern reflects that a string of letters
corresponds to only a single word. Finally, of critical importance to this

model is the fact that the connections between nodes can pass activation in both directions (i.e., they are two-way connections). Thus, letters pass activation to words to assist in the recognition of words, but words also pass activation back to letters and thereby assist in the recognition of letters.

Processing in the model begins by activating the features of a presented word and then continues in time slices that update the activation of nodes in the network. At each step, the activation of a node consists of any external activation that the node receives (which only happens for feature nodes) as well as the inputs to the node from other nodes in the network. These inputs are determined by summing the activation of nodes connected to each node, modified by the weight of the connection between nodes. In this way, processing begins by passing activation from the features presented to the letter layer. At subsequent time slices, activation is passed from the letter layer to the word layer (as well as back to the feature layer). Once word nodes are activated, they begin to spread activation back to the letter layer, and thereby each layer of the network can affect processing in other layers. At some point, a letter reaches a level of activation high enough to cause it to be recognized. The amount of time that the network processes a particular situation is assumed to be related to the number of cycles in which the weights on nodes are updated.

The interaction between nodes allows the model to explain data from studies of letter recognition. Because the letter layer receives input from both the feature layer and the word layer, letter recognition is a function of both the features presented as well as the words that the model knows. Even strings of letters that are not actual words but are close to actual words receive some extra activation from the word layer, as a function of the activation of words that are close to the string of letters provided. The model is also able to deal with degraded initial input. If ink spilled on a page and caused some features to be obscured, the missing features can be "filled in" by allowing the model to guess the word spelled by the string of letters and then to feed activation back to the letter layer and from there to the feature layer.

The performance of this model allows several constraints on letter recognition to be used simultaneously. The data from studies have suggested that letter recognition is influenced by both the perceptual features of the word presented and the known words in the lexicon. Letter recognition is facilitated by having features consistent with the letter in the visual input (hence the excitatory connection between the feature nodes and letter nodes for letters containing the feature) and by the presence of words that contain the letter (hence the excitatory connection between word nodes and the nodes for letters contained in the word). Finally, it is assumed that both letter recognition and word recognition are competitive, and so there are inhibitory connections between elements in a level.

The network itself is an instantiation of a theory of letter and word recognition, not a theory by itself. That is, the constraints on letter and word recognition were determined in advance by theorists, and then the network was constructed in accordance with the proposed constraints. As an instantiation of this theory, the connection weights in the network are positive when the influence is assumed to be positive and negative when the influence is assumed to be negative. There are no mechanisms for fine control over the constraints as they operate. A constraint that is assumed to be strong can be given a large connection weight, and a constraint that is assumed to be weak can be given a small connection weight, but there is very little temporal control over when particular constraints become active. The only sequencing of constraints in the interactive activation model is that activation starts in the feature nodes, and it takes a few time slices before activation in the word layer can feed back to the letter layer. In general, however, constraints do not become active only in specific circumstances. Rather, all constraints are mixed together, and activation is allowed to pass through the network.

Other Parallel Constraint Satisfaction Models

This general parallel constraint satisfaction approach has been applied to a number of different problems in psychology. In this section, I illustrate the use of these models with two additional examples. One is a model of explanatory coherence (Thagard, 1989), and the second is a model of person perception based on the principles of the explanatory coherence model (Read & Marcus-Newhall, 1993). These two examples are designed to highlight both the strengths and the weaknesses of the parallel constraint satisfaction approach. (See Holyoak & Thagard [1995] for a description of several other parallel constraint satisfaction models.)

Explanatory Coherence. Philosophers and psychologists have speculated about the factors that make a particular explanation a good one. In the context of the history of science, Thagard (1989) proposed seven principles of coherence which he incorporated into a parallel constraint satisfaction model of causal explanation. The principles he proposed are symmetry, explanation, analogy, data priority, contradiction, acceptability, and system coherence. *Symmetry* means that if one statement is consistent with another, the second is consistent with the first. Likewise, if one statement is inconsistent with a second, the second is inconsistent with the first. *Explanation* implies that the set of propositions in an explanation must all be mutually coherent and that fewer explanatory postulates are better than many. *Analogy* asserts that analogies are useful for generating explanations. *Data priority* requires that descriptions of data be treated more strongly than are explanatory postulates. *Contradiction* means that explanatory postulates should not contradict the things being explained. *Acceptability* asserts that explanations explaining a broad range of facts are better than explanations explaining a narrow range of facts. Finally, *system coherence* suggests that the coherence of an explanation arises from the coherence of its parts rather than as an emergent property of the explanation as a whole. Clearly, these constraints need not all point in the same direction. One explanation may be broader than another, but the second may involve fewer postulates than the first.

To model the simultaneous influence of multiple constraints, Thagard implemented this view of explanatory coherence in a computer model, ECHO, which sets up a constraint satisfaction network. The network used by the model consists of facts to be explained and explanatory hypotheses that do the explaining. For example, Thagard (1989) described a network that was given some facts known when the oxygen and phlogiston theories were being debated as well as propositions that described the two theories. The network was created with nodes corresponding to each piece of evidence; these nodes were sources of activation in the network (as the feature nodes in the interactive activation model described earlier were sources of activation). Facts were sources of activation, because the explanatory coherence model assumes that facts are of paramount importance in explanation. The postulates of the oxygen theory were given excitatory connections to the facts they explained, because a theory should explain facts. In addition, excitatory connections were placed between all the postulates of the oxygen theory, because postulates of a single explanation should be mutually supportive. For the same reasons, the postulates of the phlogiston theory were given excitatory connections to the facts they explained and to each other. In addition, inhibitory connections were placed between postulates of the phlogiston theory which contradicted known facts, because a good explanation should not contradict known facts. Finally, inhibitory connections were placed between postulates of the oxygen theory and postulates of the phlogiston theory, because explanation is essentially a competition among competing hypotheses.

The network was constructed so that the oxygen theory explained more facts than did the phlogiston theory and only the phlogiston theory contradicted known facts, but the phlogiston theory involved fewer postulates. Thus, the constraints on explanatory coherence were not all satisfied best by the same explanation. In the ECHO model, the amount of activation emanating from a node representing part of an explanation is divided by the number of hypotheses involved in the explanation to implement a preference for explanations with fewer postulates. In the simulation, activation is divided in fewer ways across the postulates of the simpler phlogiston theory than across the postulates of the more complex oxygen theory. When activation is allowed to spread through the network until it settles, the postulates of oxygen theory have high activation levels, and the postulates of phlogiston theory have low activation levels. This result is consistent with the historical fact that the oxygen theory was accepted as a better explanation of the available data than was the phlogiston theory. This run of the simulation demonstrated that a large broad theory consistent with the available data and not contradicting any of them was preferred to a smaller, narrower theory that did contradict some available data.

This example demonstrates that a constraint satisfaction network can be used to implement multiple constraints being satisfied in parallel, but it is not clear that ECHO can be taken as a psychological model of explanation. The particular set of facts described here is unlikely to be a representation that any individual scientist was likely to have had. Rather, these facts are ones that the scientific community at the time had available. Furthermore, explanation (particularly in science) is an active process in which new facts are searched for precisely because of the explanation being constructed. In contrast, a parallel constraint satisfaction model is given full information and has no capacity to search for new information. Thagard's model of explanatory coherence is probably best viewed as a description of the forces that lead a particular explanation to be taken as coherent, rather than as a model of the psychological processes that an individual goes through when deciding on an explanation to accept.

Person Perception. Although the ECHO model falls somewhere between psychology and philosophy of science, the style of model embodied in ECHO, as well as some of its specific proposals, have been used in psychological models. In particular, they have formed the basis of a research program on how people evaluate new individuals that they meet. Much research in social psychology has focused on how people determine the personality characteristics or traits of new people. Such dispositional inferences are considered helpful for deciding how to interact with an individual, for explaining past behavior, and for predicting behavior in new situations. One model of the process of making dispositional inferences draws heavily on Thagard's work on explanatory coherence (Read & Marcus-Newhall, 1993; Read & Miller, 1993).

According to this view, dispositional inferences are made in order to provide a coherent explanation of a person's behavior. Read and Marcus-Newhall (1993) condensed Thagard's seven constraints into four central constraints on coherence in social inference: breadth, simplicity, recursive explanation, and competition. *Breadth* suggests that explanations accounting for many facts are better than explanations accounting for few facts. *Simplicity* implies that the fewer assumptions required to construct an explanation, the more it should be preferred. *Recursive explanation* states that an explanation is better if its assumptions also have explanations than if its assumptions are unsupported. Finally, *competition* suggests that explanations compete and that the presence of a good explanation weakens the support for other explanations of the same set of facts.

One reason that parallel constraint satisfaction models are popular in social psychology is that they provide a mechanism for implementing classic theories. For example, Heider (1958) suggested that forces in social relations are resolved to achieve a balanced state in which there is no pressure for change. Heider described a scenario that gives an example of an imbalance:

> Bob thinks Jim [is] very stupid and a first class bore. One day, Bob reads some poetry he likes so well that he takes the trouble to track down the author in order to shake his hand. He finds that Jim wrote the poems. (p. 176) (4.3)

In this situation, opposing forces are at work. On the one hand, Bob thinks Jim is a bore, but on the other hand, he has just discovered that Jim is the author of poetry that he likes. Somehow, he must resolve this discrepancy to bring his opinions into "balance." Subjects given a passage like this typically either change the value of the poetry (e.g., it wasn't so good after all), or they change Bob's opinion of Jim (e.g., he wasn't so boring after all). The intuition underlying balance theory is strong. There does seem to be an opposition of forces in this example. Nevertheless, balance theory (and other consistency theories; see Read & Miller, 1993) fell out of favor with psychologists, because they lacked good mechanisms for describing how forces were balanced. One appeal of parallel constraint satisfaction models is that they provide a mechanism for implementing models with a strong kinship to these classic theories.

The model developed by Read and his colleagues is meant to be taken as a model of the psychology of social explanation. The facts in this domain consist of behaviors exhibited by individuals. The explanatory postulates are possible personality traits that may define the people being observed as well as their motivations and goals. In the network model, observed behaviors as well as goals, motivations, and personality traits are represented as nodes in a constraint satisfaction network. Traits, goals, and motivations are given excitatory connections to observed behaviors that they explain and inhibitory connections to observed behaviors that they contradict. Possible behaviors can also be added to the network by using background knowledge about the relationship between traits and observed behaviors. Elements of competing explanations are linked via inhibitory connections. Finally, a preference for simpler explanations is implemented in the network by dividing the activation of a node that forms part of an explanation by the number of elements (e.g., traits, goals, and motivations) involved in the explanation.

As an example, I can create a network to resolve the imbalance in Example 4.5. This network is shown in Figure 4.7. The basic facts that were in conflict were that Bob thought Jim was boring yet Jim wrote good poetry. These facts are connected by an inhibitory link, because they are inconsistent. There are (at least) two possible inferences that can help resolve this dispute. One is that Jim's poetry is not so good, and the other is that Jim is not boring. Each of these inferences is consistent with one fact and inconsistent with another. The two inferences are mutually inconsistent, and so they get an inhibitory connection. Finally, people may have causal beliefs about social interactions. One such belief shown in the figure is that poetry is a good indicator of the sensitivity of an individual. This belief may be consistent with the inference that Jim is not boring and inconsistent with the inference that Jim's poetry is not good. If the two known facts (at the bottom of Figure 4.7) are given activation and this activation spreads through the network, the inference that Jim is not boring after all becomes active and inhibits the inference that Jim's poetry is not

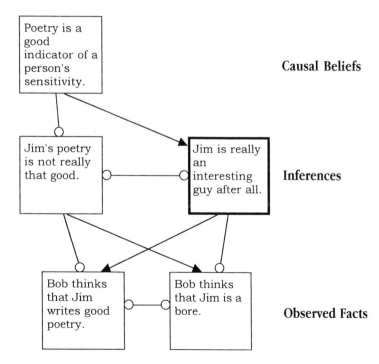

FIG. 4.7. Parallel constraint satisfaction network for making dispositional inferences about a story. Arrows represent excitatory connections, and circles represent inhibitory connections.

good. In this way, an imbalance of social forces is resolved. The parallel constraint satisfaction network provides a way to implement this balancing of forces.

This model is assumed to be a description of the process people go through to make dispositional inferences and to make predictions about behaviors that may be observed in the future. There are, however, two parts to the process of making these inferences. First, there is some process that sets up a network like the one in Figure 4.7. This process must have some knowledge about the behaviors that are consistent with different explanations. It must also be able to determine which explanations are mutually consistent and which are mutually inconsistent. Once this process constructs a constraint satisfaction network, activation runs through it until it settles. There is no mechanism for directing the flow of activation through the network; thus, this model assumes that dispositional inferences are made automatically. To the extent that dispositional inference involves some controlled or rule-governed processes (beyond those needed to build the network), additional mechanisms must be added to the model in much the same way as the assumptions about spreading activation were coupled to a production system in Anderson's model of working memory and problem solving described earlier in this chapter.

In addition to spelling out the processes that construct the constraint satisfaction network, other information needs to be considered in models of dispositional inference as well. Chronically accessible personality traits and personality traits activated by recent processing seem to be important determinants of dispositional inferences in similar tasks (Bargh, Lombardi, & Higgins, 1988). In addition, dispositional inferences are often based on characteristics of significant others who are similar to the new person in some way (Andersen & Cole, 1990). These factors have a clear impact on person perception, and the mechanisms that underlie these influences must be reconciled with the constraint satisfaction approach. Constraint satisfaction models may often have to be combined with other mechanisms to achieve an explanation of psychological phenomena.

SUMMARY

Many models in psychology involve the assumption that information is organized into a network consisting of nodes representing concepts and links representing relations between concepts. Semantic network models use these networks as a proposal for the structure of long-term memory. Memory is searched automatically by passing activation across the links. This structure allows the activation of one concept to activate many other concepts as well. A more general formulation of network models assumes that nodes represent concepts of interest to some psychological model and that connections reflect the constraints operating among these concepts. If a constraint operates to promote a pair of concepts, the connection is excitatory; if a constraint operates to promote one concept at the expense of another, the connection is inhibitory. Once the network is set up in accord with the constraints assumed to control a domain, activation is allowed to pass through it in much the same way as activation passes through semantic networks.

Both of these models focus on automatic processing. The spread of activation is assumed to take place without conscious awareness and without conscious control. Models of phenomena that are assumed to involve both automatic and controlled processes generally require a combination of mechanisms. Models like J. R. Anderson's (1983a, 1993; Anderson et al., 1996) ACT combine a semantic network with a rule-based production system to carry out complex problem-solving tasks. Models like Thagard's (1989) ECHO use rule-based processes to set up a constraint satisfaction network that models the simultaneous satisfaction of multiple constraints by passing activation through the network.

Finally, I have focused on the spread of activation through networks and the analysis of intersections between nodes. The combination of a semantic network with a rule-based system like ACT-R makes this representational system equivalent to the structured representations I discuss in the next three chapters.[6] These structured representations require complex processes that are sensitive to the way elements are related. For this reason, I have treated spreading activation separately from other processes. Because network models lend themselves to the spread of activation, it is natural to include such mechanisms in network models.

---

[6]Semantic networks can even be constructed to permit the representation of quantified statements like "Some dogs live in houses." (I discuss methods for representing quantified statements in chapter 5.)

Structured Representations

STRUCTURE IN MENTAL REPRESENTATIONS

What is the scope of a representational element, for example, a representation for the concept *robin*? If the representation contains the feature *red*, does this feature describe the whole bird or just part of it? The extent or domain of a representational element is its scope. Every representation I have discussed so far contains some assumptions about the scope of its representational elements.

For the spatial and featural representations discussed in chapters 2 and 3, the scope of the representational elements was implicit. In mental space models, concepts were represented as points in a multidimensional space. In models derived from multidimensional scaling techniques, the dimensions of the space were assumed to have some meaning. Each point had a value along each dimension of the space, and each dimension value was restricted in scope to the point in space corresponding to a particular concept. If a psychological dimension represents the color of an object, the point for *robin* occupies a region corresponding to *red* on the color dimension. This representation of *red* has some ambiguity, because the dimension value is associated with the point representing the concept as a whole, and it is difficult to represent that only some part of the robin is red.

In featural models, concepts were represented by sets of features, and each feature described only the concept denoted by the feature set. A given feature might be part of a substitutive dimension, so that having one value of a feature precluded the object's having other values along the same dimension. In the case of a representation for the concept *robin*, each feature in a set applies to the whole concept, and to represent that the whole robin is red, the feature *red* is added to the feature set. It is difficult to represent that a feature is true of only a part of an object. Features themselves have no means for restricting their scope (e.g., restricting the scope of *red* to the breast of the robin). For this reason, representational schemes have made the scope of representational elements explicit.

Semantic networks, like those discussed in chapter 4, are one type of representation in which the scope of representational elements was made explicit. Because each node is connected to other nodes via labeled links, the scope of the relation described by a link is restricted to the nodes that it connects. Figure 5.1 shows a piece of a network representing the fact that a robin has a red breast. Here the connection between robin and breast makes it clear that the breast is a part of the robin. Another connection between breast and red makes it clear that the breast is red, although other parts of the robin may be other colors. Thus, the semantic network contains explicit information about the scope of representational elements.

In chapter 4, I focused on processes in network models that spread activation across links. In these models, labels were important primarily for interpreting paths between nodes found when activation tags intersected. The processes discussed in chapter 4 were not concerned with the scope of the representational elements. In chapters 5 through 7, I discuss structured representations in which the processes acting over these representations are sensitive to the scope of the representational elements. In this chapter, I introduce terminology for describing structured representations and describe some of their basic characteristics. Then, I present processing assumptions that have been used in conjunction with structured representations in psychology and logic. In chapter 6, I extend these basic principles by examining the use of structure in models of perception and imagery. In chapter 7, I describe the use of structured representations in

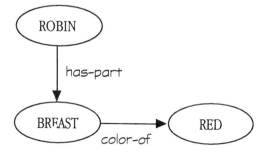

FIG. 5.1. Simple semantic network demonstrating that the scope of the links is determined by the nodes to which they are connected.

conceptual representations, notably scripts and schemas, to complete the introductory tour of structured representations.

THE BASICS OF STRUCTURED REPRESENTATIONS

Determining the scope of representational elements is a critical aspect of the notion of representation. Because the scope of most elements seems intuitively obvious, it is easy to underestimate the importance of this aspect of representation. Figure 5.2 shows a pair of geometric configurations that are clearly different. One pair is a striped square above a shaded circle, and the other is a striped circle above a shaded square. Nonetheless, if I listed a set of features that describe these configurations without worrying about the scope of the representational elements, then I may find that the same set of features can describe both configurations. Figure 5.3A shows sets of features that describe both configurations in Figure 5.2. I have conveniently divided this feature list into sections to make it clear which features belong to which objects in Figure 5.2. An actual feature list would not have this structure, and one would know only that the same set of features describes both configurations.

In a structured representation, one creates the scope of representational elements by allowing elements in a representation to take *arguments* that restrict their scope. For example, I can describe the square in the left configuration in Figure 5.2 with the statement:

striped (square). (5.1)

In Example 5.1, *striped* is a representational element, and *square* is its argument; the scope of the property *striped* is restricted to describing a

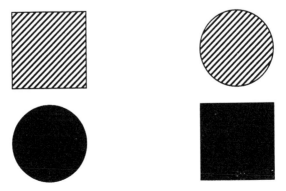

FIG. 5.2. Geometric configurations.

square. This representation is a *predicate* because it represents something true (or false) in the represented world. Predicates with one argument (like the one in Example 5.1) are *attributes*, which typically represent descriptive properties of their argument.

Another important type of predicate is the relation, which is a predicate with two or more arguments. Relations are used to represent relationships that hold between elements in a represented world. For example, the predicate:

$$\text{above (square, circle)} \tag{5.2}$$

represents the spatial relationship between the square and the circle in the left configuration in Figure 5.2. The same representation in graph form appears in Figure 5.3C, which shows a graph of structured representations for the two configurations in Figure 5.2. In this figure, predicates are connected to their arguments by links. Although arrows can be used to show the directions of the links, they are usually omitted for the sake of clarity.[1]

Finally, not all statements in a structured representation are predicates: Not all statements are things whose truth in the represented world can be determined. Statements evaluated for something other than their truth are called *functions*. For example, the size of an object in the represented world can be described by the function:

$$\text{size (circle).} \tag{5.3}$$

In this example, *size (circle)* is a function because it cannot be determined to correspond to a true or false state of the represented world. Instead, *size (circle)* has some value in the represented world.

One can treat this function as a representation and consider it a placeholder for the size of the circle if, for example, one is making an analogy between one object that is larger than another and a sound that is louder than a second (Gentner, Rattermann, Markman, & Kotovsky, 1995). In this case, one can represent the difference in size as:

$$\text{greater [size (object\_1), size (object\_2)]} \tag{5.4}$$

and the difference in loudness as:

$$\text{greater [loudness (sound\_1), loudness (sound\_2)].} \tag{5.5}$$

---

[1]Exactly which direction the links should point is a matter of some debate. In this book, I assume that the links point from the predicate to its arguments.

(a)

Angled   Round
Striped   Striped
Medium Sized   Medium Sized

Round   Angled
Shaded   Shaded
Medium Sized   Medium Sized

Above   Above

(b)

Square-Above-Circle   Circle-Above-Square
Striped-Above-Shaded   Striped-Above-Shaded

Square-on-top   Round-on-top
Round-on-bottom   Square-on-bottom

(c)

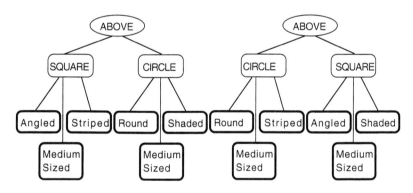

FIG. 5.3. A: Features representing the geometric configurations in Figure
5.2. B: Configural features that can be added to the feature representation.
C: Graph of structured representations of the geometric configurations.

This representation highlights the fact that the size in Example 5.4 is
similar to the loudness in Example 5.5. The specific value of the size of
the object or the loudness of the sound does not matter, only the fact that
the object has a size and the sound has a loudness.

   In other cases, one might want to evaluate the function. Presumably,
the function *size (circle)* is associated with a process for determining the
size of the circle, so one can find its value (e.g., medium-sized). The evaluation of functions is an important part of computer programming; in languages like LISP, functions can be used both as representational ele-

ments (as in Examples 5.4 and 5.5) and as processes. In this way, the
distinction between representation and process gets blurred.

Constants and Variables

The predicates described so far have arguments that represent specific
elements in the represented world. These elements are often called *constants*, a term borrowed from logic. Constants are used when the elements
described by a predicate are known, but it is also possible to represent
situations in which the particular elements that are arguments to a predicate are unknown. In this case, one uses *variables* in the representation; a
variable is a placeholder whose value is unknown, like a box that is eventually filled with a value. For example, I can represent the general fact
that something is above something else by using this statement:

$$\text{above } (?x, ?y). \tag{5.6}$$

In this statement, $?x$ and $?y$ are variables whose values are unknown. A
statement consisting of predicates whose arguments are constants (or variables that are bound to some value) is called a *proposition* because it denotes
a possible state of affairs in the represented world. In structured representations, the meaning of a proposition is compositional and is determined by the meanings of the proposition's constituent elements.

Variables in a structured representation can be free to take on any value
or can be restricted to certain types of values. In computer programming,
many languages use *type restrictions* on variables. In PASCAL, for example,
a variable may be restricted to take on integer values, real number values,
or even strings of characters. Type restrictions on variables have also been
incorporated into structured representations, often as a low-cost way to
make sure that something being represented is likely to be interpretable.
For example, if a system tries to create a representation in which the
predicate *marry* $(?x, ?y)$ is applied to inanimate objects, one may need to
investigate another type of meaning (perhaps a metaphorical meaning).
Type restrictions, sometimes called *case roles*, are also common in linguistic
models (e.g., Fillmore, 1968).

Type restrictions on variables ease the specification of processes in a
domain. If predicates are guaranteed to have arguments of a particular type,
rules formulated to reason about these predicates can make assumptions
about the predicates' arguments. In chapter 9, I discuss qualitative process
(QP) theory (Forbus, 1984), which was designed to reason about physical
systems. In this system, the predicates that describe quantities require their
arguments to be quantities. Because of this type restriction, all rules about
quantities can assume that the predicates supposed to describe quantities

actually do describe quantities. Thus, one need not have each rule check the arguments of the predicates to find out what they are. There are, however, potential costs to this use of type restrictions. First, the set of types must be known in advance so that the case roles can be created. If new case roles are added after some knowledge has already been entered into the system, old knowledge may not obey new case-role restrictions. Second, it is necessary to specify the processes checking the arguments to ensure that they obey the case roles when representations are constructed. Thus, as discussed previously, adding a new complexity to a representation (like type restrictions) requires new machinery to process it.

Number and Type of Arguments

Structured representations are not limited in the number of their arguments. Any element can be identified by the number of arguments that it takes. Elements with no arguments are called *constants* if the value is known and *variables* if it is unknown. Elements that take a single argument are called *unary* elements; those that take two arguments are called *binary* elements. In general, the *arity* of an element refers to the number of arguments that it takes.

In the examples discussed so far, the arguments to predicates and functions have all been constants or variables. A predicate whose arguments are all constants or variables is called a *first-order* predicate. Predicates may also have arguments that are other statements with arguments. The sentence "Mary kissed John causing John to hug Mary" can be represented as:

$$\text{cause } [\text{ kissed (Mary, John), hug (John, Mary) }]. \tag{5.7}$$

In this case, both arguments to the relation *cause* $(?x, ?y)$ are themselves relations. The *cause* $(?x, ?y)$ relation in Example 5.7 is a *second-order* predicate because it contains at least one argument that is a first-order predicate. More generally, the order of a predicate is one greater than the order of the highest order element that is an argument to that predicate. As discussed next, higher order relations are often used to represent important conceptual relations like causal relations.

Why Use Structured Representations?

Structured representations make explicit the relations between elements in a situation, and they allow complex representations to be constructed through the combination of simpler elements. The simple configurations of shapes in Figure 5.2 illustrate this issue; the sets of features in Figure 5.3A represent these configurations with lists of features. As discussed earlier, the feature lists describing the left and right configurations actually contain the same set of features. If the representations of these configurations were truly the same, the configurations would be perceived as identical. Because they are not so perceived, something must be done to the representation to allow the configurations to be differentiated.

One extension to the feature lists in Figure 5.3A includes an additional set of *configural features*, like those in Figure 5.3B. These features encode large-scale configural aspects of the scenes like the fact that there is a square on top of a circle in the left configurations, and a circle on top of a square in the right configuration. This clearly solves part of the problem. Now the representation has explicit information about the relationships between the shapes, and the configurations are no longer seen as identical. Configural features are themselves features, which either match a feature in a second representation or do not. There are no partially matching features. The absence of partial matches is a problem because one can adopt a very large set of possible configural features. Any pair of attributes can potentially enter into a configural feature for every binary relation that holds for the configuration: square-above-circle, round-above-angled, striped-above-shaded, or even square-above-shaded or shaded-and-medium-sized-above-round. In addition, configural features can specify only part of an existing relation like square-on-top or round-on-bottom. These configural features are useful for finding similarities between configurations with only a partial match. The problem with configural features is that the number of possible configural features grows exponentially as the number of elements and relations to be represented grows (e.g., Foss & Harwood, 1975).

Structured representations provide an alternative to feature lists for representing situations like the one in Figure 5.2. Because representational elements contain connections to their arguments, the same element can be reused with different arguments to represent different situations. Because graphs contain the same information as the formulaic notation used in Examples 5.1 through 5.7, the representation in Figure 5.3C can be written as:

above (square, circle)
angled (square)
striped (square)
medium-sized (square)
round (circle)
shaded (circle)
medium-sized (circle). (5.8)

With the structured representation for representing this situation, similar configurations can use similar representational elements with different sets of arguments. The circle above the square in the right configuration can be represented by using the same relation as the square above the circle with the arguments reversed. In this way, there is a partial match between these representations, and the attributes of the shapes are explicitly attached to the elements they describe. Thus, in the left configuration, it is not just that something is shaded, but rather that a circle is shaded. The common relation leads to the perception of differences in the arguments to the relation. I expand this point next.

Evidence for the Importance of Structure

In the previous section, I suggest that structured representations are more efficient than are feature lists, but as discussed in chapter 4, people are not always maximally efficient. Thus, it remains to be demonstrated that structured representations make predictions that are consistent with people's behavior. Indeed, research in perception suggests that people sometimes err when perceiving objects in a manner suggesting they may not bind attributes to the right objects. In a classic set of studies, Treisman and Schmidt (1982) found *illusory conjunctions* of features. An illusory conjunction occurs when people report seeing an object with a particular conjunction of features when, in fact, the pair of features was not initially part of the same object. For example, they may report seeing a blue *N* when they had actually been shown a blue *S* and a red *N*. In one study, researchers quickly flashed to the subjects a display with two numbers and some colored letters and asked them to report the digits and whatever else they saw in the scene. Under these conditions, people reported a number of illusory conjunctions. Indeed, on some trials subjects actually reported seeing colored numbers, even though they were always shown the numbers in black. These data suggest that colors and shapes are initially processed separately and bound together only later in processing. During initial processing, a perceptual feature need not have a scope that corresponds to the scope of the property in the represented world. It may require visual attention to ensure that the perceptual properties of objects are bound together properly.

In normal circumstances, of course, people do not observe these illusory conjunctions, and research on similarity has supported the assumption that cognitive representations are structured. In a simple study by Markman, Gentner, and Wisniewski (1998), we gave people a forced-choice task. We showed them a standard and two comparison figures and asked them to select the comparison figure that was most similar to the standard. The stimuli and results appear in Figure 5.4. We presented subjects with eight forced-choice triads in a random order. In Figure 5.4, the comparison figures in the middle column were preferred to those in the right column by a majority of subjects (at least 8 out of 10 in this study, $p < .05$ by sign test).

The first triad (top row) demonstrates that people find configurations with similar objects in them to be more similar than are configurations

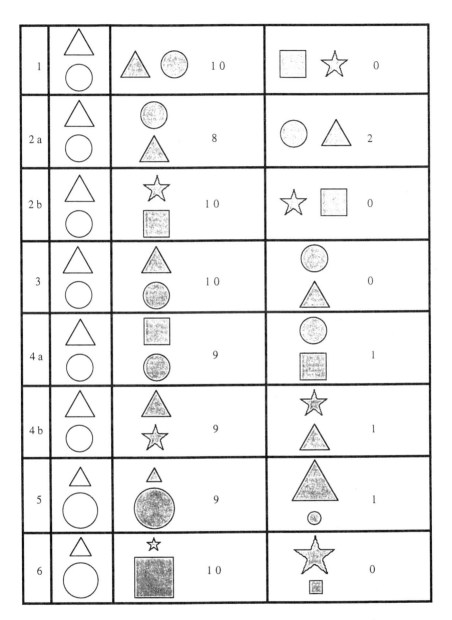

FIG. 5.4. Stimuli from a study of similarity of geometric configurations. Ten subjects reported which comparison figure in the right-most two columns was most similar to the standard in the left-most column. The numbers are the number of subjects selecting each alternative. The favored alternative always appears in the middle column.

with dissimilar objects. In the next two triads (2a, 2b), people prefer configurations with the same relation to those without the same relation, even when the objects that play similar relational roles are different. In Triad 2a, there is a triangle on top and a circle on the bottom in the standard and a circle on top and a triangle on the bottom in the preferred comparison figure. In Triad 2b, the shapes in the comparison figures are different from those in the standard altogether. So far, these results are equally compatible with either featural or structured representations. Both featural representations and structured representations simply have to assume that having features describing similar objects make a pair of configurations similar, and features describing relations (without considering relational roles) also make a pair of configurations similar.

With Triad 3, the situation grows more complex: Similar objects in the same relational roles make a pair more similar than similar objects in different relational roles. To account for this pattern, a featural view needs to have global configural features like above-triangle-circle, but such global configural features are insufficient, as demonstrated by Triads 4a and 4b. Here, having only one similar object playing the same relational role in the target and the comparison figure makes the configurations more similar than having no similar objects playing the same relational roles. In addition to global configural features, a featural view must assume that there are other configural features like circle-on-the-bottom and triangle-on-the-top to account for people's choices in these triads.

Triad 5 demonstrates that people also prefer consistency across a number of different relations in a scene. In the standard, the triangle is above the circle and is also smaller than the circle. Subjects preferred a comparison figure that preserves both these relational commonalities over one that preserves only one. If a featural view were to represent this new relation, a new (and large) set of configural features must be added to handle the new relation. Finally, Triad 6 demonstrates that this preference for relational consistency holds even when none of the actual objects in the standard and the comparison figure is similar. Thus, people can process multiple relational similarities in the absence of any similarity between the objects.

**How Do Structural Representations Account
for These Findings?**

To this point, the study illustrated in Figure 5.4 suggests only that featural representations provide an unwieldy and unsatisfying explanation for the pattern of data observed. How does a structured representation account for these data? In order to understand similarity in the case of structured representations, it is necessary to pay more careful attention to how structured representations are processed. In chapter 3, I described A. Tversky's

(1977) contrast model, which modeled similarity comparisons as the comparison of feature lists. In this model, feature representations were just sets; the elementary set operation of intersection could be used to find the common features of a pair, and the operation of set difference could be used to find the distinctive features of a pair.

With structured representations, the situation grows more complex: Now, the comparison process must be sensitive to the argument structure of the representations. Models of similarity assuming structured representations have adopted a *structural alignment* framework (Gentner & Markman, 1997). Structural alignment is a process derived from studies of how people understand analogies (Gentner, 1983, 1989; Gentner & Markman, 1997; Hesse, 1966; Holyoak & Thagard, 1989, 1995; Keane, Ledgeway, & Duff, 1994; Markman & Gentner, 1993a, 1993b; Medin, Goldstone, & Gentner, 1993). This research is strongly related to Gentner's (1983, 1989) structure-mapping theory. The structural alignment process is substantially more complex than is the simple set operations that were sufficient to compare features lists, because this process must be sensitive to the connections among relations and attributes and their bindings.

In the structural alignment process, people seek a match between structured representations that is rooted in *semantic similarity* and maintains *structural consistency*. The use of semantic similarity implies that at least some matching elements must have identical names, an assumption ensuring that any perceived similarity is rooted in at least one semantic commonality between representations. For example, if the two representations in Figure 5.3C are compared, the *above* (?x, ?y) relations can be matched because they have the same name. Any match must also be structurally consistent, where structural consistency involves two constraints: *parallel connectivity* and *one-to-one mapping*. Parallel connectivity states that if two elements in a representation are placed in correspondence, their arguments must also be placed in correspondence. In Figure 5.3C, placing the *above* (?x, ?y) relations in correspondence causes the square in the left representation to be placed in correspondence with the circle in the right representation because both are the first arguments to the *above* (?x, ?y) relation (i.e., both are on top). Likewise, the circle in the left representation can be placed in correspondence with the square in the right representation because both are the second arguments to the above relation (i.e., both are on the bottom). One-to-one mapping requires that each element in one representation be placed in correspondence with at most one element in the other representation. Thus, placing the square in the left representation with the circle in the right representation because both are on the top precludes also placing the square in the left representation in correspondence with the square in the right representation because both are angled. To see *both* the similarity of the square to the circle because each plays a common relational role *and* the similarity of the square to the square because both are angled, the structural alignment process must calculate two distinct mappings, each of which has a unique set of object correspondences. This process has been embodied in different computational models that take as input structured representations and yield a set of correspondences between the domains (Falkenhainer, Forbus, & Gentner, 1989; Holyoak & Thagard, 1989; Hummel & Holyoak, 1997; Keane et al., 1994).

The structural alignment process allows a straightforward explanation of the results of the study in Figure 5.4. For example, the configurations in Triad 4a can be represented[2] as:

Standard:	above (triangle, circle)
Comparison Figure 1:	above (square, circle)
Comparison Figure 2:	above (circle, square).

(5.9)

With these representations, both comparison figures have a common relation with the standard, but parallel connectivity requires that the arguments of the relations also be placed in correspondence. The second argument of Comparison Figure 1 in Figure 5.4 matches that of the standard; the second argument of Comparison Figure 2 does not. Hence, Comparison Figure 1 has an extra commonality that Comparison Figure 2 lacks.

One can give similar explanations for all the triads in Figure 5.4. Readers may draw a set of representations to verify that the structural alignment view of similarity predicts judging Comparison Figure 1 more similar to the standard than is Comparison Figure 2 for all the triads. One additional example, however, is helpful. Triad 5 can be represented as:

Standard:	above (triangle, circle)
	smaller (triangle, circle)
Comparison Figure 1:	above (triangle, circle)
	smaller (triangle, circle)
Comparison Figure 2:	above (triangle, circle)
	smaller (circle, triangle).

(5.10)

In this case, when Comparison Figure 1 is compared to the standard, both the *above* (?x, ?y) relation and the *smaller* (?x, ?y) relation can be matched, because each of these relations maps the triangle to the triangle and the circle to the circle. In contrast, when Comparison Figure 2 is compared

---

[2]The attributes of objects are omitted from these representations for clarity. It is assumed that placing a pair of objects in correspondence also places the attributes in correspondence. Similar objects are seen as similar because they have matching attributes.

to the standard, either the *above* (?*x*, ?*y*) relation or the *smaller* (?*x*, ?*y*) relation *but not both* can be placed in correspondence because matching these two relations involves different object correspondences. Matching the *above* (?*x*, ?*y*) relations places the triangle in the standard in correspondence with the triangle in the comparison figure and the circle in the standard with the circle in the comparison figure. In contrast, matching the *smaller* (?*x*, ?*y*) relation places the triangle in the standard in correspondence with the circle in the comparison figure and the circle in the standard in correspondence with the triangle in the comparison figure. By one-to-one mapping, both sets of correspondences cannot coexist. Thus, the match between the first comparison figure and the standard is preferred.

Structure and Determination of Commonalities and Differences

The structural alignment view of similarity has implications beyond simply accounting for people's ability to make comparisons involving relations. In particular, making use of the connection between elements and their arguments allows for the possibility that commonalities and differences are related. In chapter 3, I described the contrast model and stated that the sets of common and distinctive features are assumed to be independent. In contrast to this assumption, the structural alignment view assumes that commonalities and differences are deeply connected.

Figure 5.5 shows another set of geometric configurations along with graphs of structured representations that can describe these configurations. If these configurations are compared, they may look similar because there is something above something else in each of them. On this view, the commonalities of the configurations include something above something else in each; striped, medium-sized things on top; and checked, medium-sized things on the bottom. Because the scenes look similar on the basis of the common *above* (?*x*, ?*y*) relation, the circle in the left configuration is placed in correspondence with the square in the right configuration. Likewise, the square in the left configuration is placed in correspondence with the circle in the right configuration. The elements placed in correspondence (e.g., the circle and square on top) are perceived as different because they were placed in correspondence by virtue of a commonality. Thus, they are *alignable differences*. In contrast, the triangle in the left configuration has no correspondence at all with anything in the right configuration. Elements in one representation with no correspondence at all with elements in the other (like the triangle) are called *nonalignable differences*.

The distinction between alignable and nonalignable differences may be easier to see by considering an alternative form of structured representation

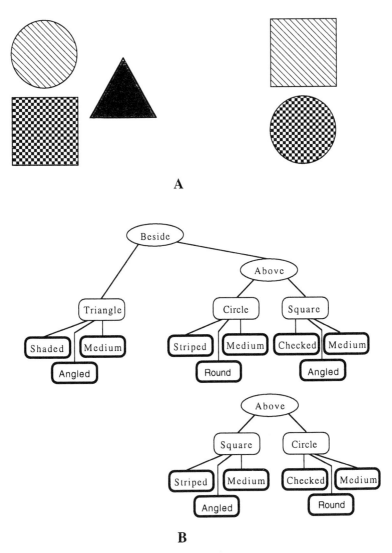

A

B

FIG. 5.5. A: Simple configurations of objects; B: simple relational structure describing the configurations. From "Comparisons," by A. B. Markman and D. Gentner, 1996, *Memory and Cognition, 24*(2), p. 236. Copyright © 1996 by The Psychonomic Society. Reprinted with permission.

called *conceptual frames* (Barsalou, 1992; Lenat & Guha, 1990; Minsky, 1981). As shown in Figure 5.6, a conceptual frame highlights the dimensional structure of the item represented. In its simplest form, a frame consists of a number of binary relations between a concept, a dimension along which the concept varies (a *slot* or an *attribute*), and a value that fills the dimension for that concept (a *filler* or *value*). Although the frame is just a collection of these binary relations, this aspect of frames is obscured by the fact that frames are typically written like the one in Figure 5.6, in which the concept heads the list and the slots and their fillers are listed below it (Hayes, 1979).

In a comparison of conceptual frames, an alignable difference can be thought of as a matching slot between two concepts with a mismatching value. In contrast, a nonalignable difference can be thought of as a slot of one concept with no corresponding slot in the other. In Figure 5.6, the concept *robin* has a slot *eats* that is filled with what it eats. If a robin is compared to a chair, the concept *chair* probably would not have an *eats* slot, because the action of eating does not make sense for chairs. Because there is no equivalent slot for *eats* in the concept *chair*, the fact that robins eat worms would probably be seen as a nonalignable difference in a comparison of robin and chair.

The distinction between alignable and nonalignable differences has been explored in numerous studies (Gentner & Markman, 1994; Markman & Gentner, 1993a, 1996, 1997; Markman & Wisniewski, 1997). In one set of studies, researchers asked subjects to list the commonalities or differences of pairs of similar words (e.g., yacht/sailboat) and pairs of dissimilar words (e.g., shopping mall/traffic light). Not surprisingly, people listed more commonalities for pairs of similar words than for pairs of dissimilar words, but they also listed more alignable differences for pairs of similar

robin	
ISA:	bird
has-part:	wings, head, beak, legs, feathers
locomotes-by:	flying, walking
eats:	worms, bugs
home:	nest
makes-noise:	sings

Elements in **bold** are concept names.
Elements in *italics* are slot names
Elements in regular type are fillers

FIG. 5.6. Sample conceptual frame.

words than for pairs of dissimilar words. A person might say that a yacht and a sailboat differ because sailboats have sails and yachts have motors, that yachts are more expensive than sailboats, and that yachts often travel longer than do sailboats. There are few obvious alignable differences for shopping mall and traffic light, although one might say that a traffic light has red, amber, and green lights, and a shopping mall has primarily white lights.

In contrast to the pattern of listed alignable differences, people listed more nonalignable differences for pairs of dissimilar words than for pairs of similar words. In general, researchers using this commonality- and difference-listing methodology have found a positive correlation between the number of listed commonalities and the number of listed differences across a wide range of stimuli, including pairs of concrete nouns, pairs of abstract nouns, pairs of verbs, and pairs of pictures. For example, one might say that a yacht has deck chairs on it, but a sailboat does not. In contrast, almost any property of a shopping mall has no correspondence with a traffic light and vice versa. One could say that a shopping mall has stores and a traffic light does not, that a shopping mall has places to eat and a traffic light does not, that a traffic light controls what cars do and a shopping mall does not.

A second important aspect of the distinction between alignable and nonalignable differences is that alignable differences are a more focal output of the comparison process than are nonalignable differences. A. Tversky's work on the contrast model suggested that commonalities are generally more important to the perceived similarity of a pair than are differences. Structural alignment also assumes that differences related to commonalities (the *alignable differences*) are more important to perceived similarity than are differences not related to commonalities (the *nonalignable differences*). In support of this view, Markman and Gentner (1996) found that people's similarity ratings were affected more by variations in alignable differences than by variations in nonalignable differences.

Other cognitive tasks that involve comparisons also seem to favor alignable over nonalignable differences. In one study, researchers asked people to choose between pairs of video games that were described by different properties (Markman & Medin, 1995). After making a selection, the subjects justified their choices. The justifications were more likely to include properties that were alignable differences between the games than to include properties that were nonalignable differences. Investigators obtained this finding whether the properties were perceived to be important or unimportant elements of the options (Lindemann & Markman, 1996). Thus, people may systematically ignore information they believe to be important when the information is nonalignable with what they know about other options.

OTHER USES OF STRUCTURED REPRESENTATIONS

Representations with bindings between elements have been a part of many cognitive models both in psychology and computer science. Because these representations are generally more complex than are feature lists or spatial representations, the processing assumptions of the models are likewise more complex. In this section, I first discuss production system models, which have been used as general architectures for understanding cognitive skills. Then, I turn to the use of structured representations in logic. This work is particularly important, because, although it is probably implausible as the basis of a psychological model, it does introduce the idea that a representation may not refer to a specific individual, but may delimit a class of individuals. Because much research in artificial intelligence has used logic, it is worth being familiar with some basic principles of representation in logic.

Production Systems

Production systems are general computational models of cognitive processing that assume cognition involves the acquisition and execution of rules governing behavior (J. R. Anderson, 1983a, 1993; Newell, 1990). In this section, I discuss only the general principles underlying production systems. Proposals about production systems differ in the specific mechanisms they use to model cognitive processes. Readers interested in the application of production systems to psychology should refer to excellent introductions of the ACT-R system (J. R. Anderson, 1993) and the SOAR system (Newell, 1990), which are two of the best worked-out production system models of psychological processing.

   The basic element of a production system is the *production rule*, which consists of a *condition* and an *action*. The condition is a state of affairs that must exist for the rule to be applicable. The action is the thing to be done if the rule is applied (rule application is often called rule *firing*). The entire condition of a rule must be satisfied for a production to be eligible to fire. If only some parts of the condition are satisfied by the current state of the world, the rule may not be applied. For example, a simple production rule may be:

   IF (you are at the street corner) and (there are no cars coming)
      and (you want to get across the street),
   THEN (begin walking across the street).   (5.11)

This example is oversimplified because elements like "you are at the street corner" must be defined explicitly enough for the presence of this state to be detected. This rule clearly applies only if all of its conditions are met. If you are at a street corner and there are cars coming, it is dangerous to cross the street. If you are at a street corner and there are no cars coming but you do not want to cross the street, then you should not cross.

Often, many possible rules can be applied in a given situation. A production system must decide which rule to apply in situations in which more than one rule is applicable. Different production system models use different strategies for making this choice: perhaps the rule that was fired most recently or the most specific rule applicable (i.e., the one with the most parts to its condition).

Production system models use structured representations. Their representation of the world typically consists of relations and attributes. The condition part of a production rule is made up of relations and attributes that must be active in working memory for the rule to fire. The action part of a production rule specifies changes to be made in working memory (e.g., setting new goals, adding new facts) and actions to be taken in the world (e.g., instructions to effectors that operate on the world). J. R. Anderson's (1993) ACT-R system doing simple addition will be used to illustrate the operation of a production system. J. R. Anderson provided a complete description of this system as well as a computer implementation of it. The basic elements of the production system for doing arithmetic are shown in Figure 5.7.

To define a production system for any domain, there must be a knowledge base and a set of rules for acting in the domain. In the case of addition, there must be facts that define what an addition problem is, facts that define what numbers are, and facts that define the known facts about addition and goals. For example, in Figure 5.7, there is a definition of the structure of a column in a production system, as well as an example of a specific column that may appear in an addition problem. There are also definitions of addition facts (like 6 + 3) and definitions of values of specific numbers. All these facts are written in a frame notation. As discussed earlier, frames can be thought of as binary relations connecting the concept to the value via a relation defined by the slot. Thus, memory in this production system corresponds to several different binary relations.

Acting on these facts are a number of production rules. The system can carry out only actions that have rules defining them. To process a column, the system must have the goal to answer a problem and must focus on a particular object in the problem, in this case a particular column in the problem. The column is defined as an array on the left side of Figure 5.7. The notation *?num* means that the value from the fact is substituted in the *variable* defined by *?variable name*. In production systems, a variable can take on different values each time a rule is applied. As discussed previously, variables are typically contrasted with *constants*, whose values remain fixed

FACTS

fact--
  isa: addition-fact
  addend1: number
  addend2: number
  sum: number

6 + 3 --
  isa: addition-fact
  addend1: six
  addend2: three
  sum: nine

six--
  isa: number
  value: 6

column--
  isa: array
  toprow: number
  bottomrow: number
  answerrow: number

column1--
  isa: column
  toprow: six
  bottomrow: three
  answerrow: blank

current-goal--
  isa: writeanswer
  column: column1

PRODUCTION RULES

PROCESS-COLUMN

Condition

goal
    isa: addition-problem
    object: column

column
    isa: array
    toprow: ?num1
    bottomrow: ?num2
    answerrow: blank

fact
    isa: addition-fact
    addend1: =num1
    addend2: =num2
    sum: ?sum

Action

New-Goal

Write-answer
    answer: =sum

FIG. 5.7. Facts and production rules from J. R. Anderson's example of simple addition.

with each application of a rule. Once the variable has been bound, its value can be referred to as = *variable name.* Thus, the condition of the PROCESS COLUMN production in the right column first must have the goal to solve an addition problem and must focus on a column with numbers in its first two rows and a blank answer row. It must also have an addition fact in memory corresponding to the numbers in the first two rows of the column. The sum of the column (obtained from the known addition fact) is then bound into the new variable sum. If these conditions hold, the action may be carried out. In this case, a new goal is established to write the answer into the bottom row, where the answer to be written is the sum derived from the addition fact. The sum itself cannot just be written into the column because it may involve a carry, and separate procedures for dealing with sums greater and less than nine must be established.

Obviously, the production that processes a single column is only one element in a system doing simple addition. There must be productions that begin by finding the right-most column, productions that shift attention to the next left-most column after the current column has been processed, productions that write the answer, and productions that know how to deal with carries. There also must be facts supporting the productions, like the facts for all 100 of the two-addend one-digit addition facts. Although this amount of information seems great, it is consistent with the observation that students in grade school spend a lot of time learning basic arithmetic facts so that they can solve complex arithmetic problems.

There are three main things to take away from this simple production system. First, the representations have to be structured. Because it is important to be able to represent which numbers are in which column, the scope of each representational element must be known. This problem cannot be solved with only a list of features. Second, much information goes into the ability to solve even a simple problem. Doing arithmetic involves a large number of basic facts and procedures. Production systems leave out other important aspects of addition such as the ability to visually recognize the numbers. People who do arithmetic often make marks on paper, such as small numbers to indicate carries, to facilitate the task. This interaction of perceptual and motor skills in solving cognitive problems is often not addressed in production system models, because most such models are not connected to sensors (i.e., organs that sense the world) and effectors (i.e., mechanisms that influence the world). Instead, they assume that there are sensors providing input in a format amenable to the production system and effectors taking instructions in the form generated by the production system. (I return to this issue in chap. 10.)

Production systems use the concept of variables, which at first have no defined value and only acquired values during processing. Variables allow the same rule to be applied to a variety of situations by simply allowing a value to be bound to each variable. For example, in the PROCESS COLUMN production in Figure 5.7, the variables allow the production to be applied to a column with any numbers in it and to take whatever sum is known to result from the combination of any pair of addends. Variables go beyond the power of the representational systems described in previous chapters. In featural and spatial representations, for example, one can represent the properties of a particular individual or class of individuals but not a hypothetical individual. As discussed in the next section, variables are crucial for allowing a system to represent hypothetical individuals and groups, such as the quantifiers *all, some,* and *none.*

In chapter 4, I noted that production systems can be combined with spreading activation models of memory to explain the effects of working memory on cognitive processing. This combination can occur by assuming that each fact in memory (like those on the left side of Figure 5.7) has some level of activation associated with it. The probability of any given production's firing is proportional to the activation associated with the elements that appear in the condition of the rule. Thus, if all facts in the condition of a rule are strongly activated, the probability of the rule's firing is very high. If there are elements in the condition of the rule that are not at all activated, the rule is unlikely to fire. In this way, a semantic network with spreading activation can explain aspects of processing that involve the automatic spread of activation through memory, whereas a production system can explain rule-governed and goal-directed processes.

Quantification in Logic

Structured representations are an important part of systems of logical reasoning. Logic representations have been studied extensively; if a statement can be represented as a logical sentence, rules of logic can be carried out to predict what happens next or to infer properties of objects. A person may assert:

IF it is raining,
THEN it is cloudy.   (5.12)

If the person later learns that it is raining, he or she can immediately infer that it is cloudy, because of the logical inference schema *modus ponens*:

IF P, THEN Q
$$\frac{P}{Q}$$ (5.13)

In addition, if a person knows that it is not cloudy, he or she can infer that it is not raining by using the logical inference schema *modus tollens*:

IF P, THEN Q
$$\frac{\neg Q}{\neg P}$$ (5.14)

where $\neg Q$ means "not (Q)." The beauty of these deductive inference schemas is that if the premises are true (e.g., if it is really the case that the rule IF P, THEN Q holds and it is really true that P) the conclusion must be true (it must really be the case that Q). The truth of the conclusion is guaranteed by the form (i.e., the syntax) of the rule without reference to its content. With any rule of the form If P, then Q, for *any* facts P and Q, the schemas *modus ponens* and *modus tollens* are valid. The many deductive reasoning schemas and proof procedures that have been developed have been the basis of cognitive models. Logic-based models have been applied most often in artificial intelligence (AI) (McCarthy, 1968), but some logic-based psychological models have been developed as well (Braine, Reiser, & Rumain, 1984; Rips, 1994).

The desire to have techniques yielding knowledge bases that are logically consistent and that contain facts known to be true is certainly a reasonable motivation for pursuing research on representations for doing logic. There is an additional aspect of logic systems, however, that allows them to represent an individual whose identity is not important. The representational systems described in previous chapters have allowed representations of individual items. The represented items may be specific objects in the represented world, such as a neighbor's pet cat. The items may also be categories of objects in the represented world, such as cats in general. In a spatial representation, each item was represented by a point in a multi-dimensional space; in a featural representation, each item was represented by a set of features.

Consider, however, the lyric from the Eagles' song "Heartache Tonight," "Somebody wants to hurt someone." Who wants to hurt someone? Whom do they want to hurt? Listeners cannot know, and in a sense, do not care. The statement "Somebody wants to hurt someone" does not name an unknown generic individual; it merely posits the *existence* of somebody who fits the characteristic of wanting to hurt someone. With a later lyric in the same song, "Nobody wants to go home now," a similar issue arises. Listeners do not want to have to name each individual present at the event in question and somehow represent that the individual does not want to go home. Rather, they want to make a generic statement that applies to everybody.

Logic makes a provision for statements of this kind through the use of *quantifiers*. In particular, two quantifiers are important: the *existential* quantifier $\exists$, which means "There Exists," and the *universal* quantifier $\forall$, which means "For All." When used to define the values of variables, these quantifiers allow them to refer to individuals. The meaning of a statement like "Somebody wants to hurt someone" then reduces to a quantified statement that describes the characteristics of individuals for which the statement is true. For example, I can represent this sentence as

$\exists$ (?x), $\exists$ (?y): person (?x) and person (?y) and not [equal (?x, ?y)] and wants-to-hurt (?x, ?y).   (5.15)

This statement means that there exist two people (bound to the variables $?x$ and $?y$) such that both are people, and x wants to hurt y.[3] Who x and y bind to in this example is unimportant. If this sentence is true, it is enough to know that there are people who exist and who satisfy these constraints. A similar case can be made for "Nobody wants to go home now," which I can represent using the existential quantifier as:

$$\text{not } [\exists \ (?x): \text{person } (?x) \text{ and wants-to-go-home } (?x)]. \qquad (5.16)$$

This sentence can be read as meaning that it is not the case that there is some person who wants to go home now.[4] On the surface, this reading somewhat differs from "Nobody wants to go home now," but it works out to the same thing.

This section does not begin to do justice to the elegance and complexity of first-order logic. There are many excellent introductions to first-order logic and the role of quantification in logic representations for those who want more information (e.g., Barwise & Etchemendy, 1993a). In the context of this chapter, however, the main aspect of logical representations that is of interest is the use of quantified variables. By using variables and constraining them with the existential and universal quantifiers, one can represent individuals so that the identity of the individual is less important than are the constraints that the individual must satisfy. The ability to do such quantification is important in a variety of situations, such as language comprehension. Mechanisms for doing this quantification are important representational tools for many tasks, even those for which formal logical systems may be inappropriate.

---

[3]This representation is meant to illustrate the use of quantifiers. A predicate like wants-to-hurt $(?x, ?y)$ is too fine grained to be useful. In a working system, it is better to decompose this complex predicate into a set of basic predicates, each of which is useable in a range of representations. This decomposition easily shows the similarity between different representations (e.g., one can recognize that wants-to-hurt $[?x, ?y]$ and wants-to-dance-with $[?x, ?y]$ both involve desire). It becomes complicated to say that a state of affairs is desired without embedding one predicate inside another, but such embedding is not allowed in a first-order logic. One way to do this embedding is to define the event *hurts* $(?x, ?y)$, to posit the existence of some element z that is the event *hurts* $(?x, ?y)$, and then to state that x desires z. This would change the sentence in Example 5.15 to $\exists \ (?x), \exists \ (?y), \exists \ (?z)$: person $(?x)$ and person $(?y)$ and event $[?z, \text{hurts} \ (?x, ?y)]$ and desires $(?x, ?z)$ where event $(?x, ?y)$ is a predicate that defines the first argument to be an event.

[4]The same issue discussed in footnote 4 applies to Example 5.16 as well. To represent Example 5.16 using more general predicates, one creates a new event of going home occurring now and then states that person x does not want this event to take place. For example, not $[\exists \ (?x), \exists \ (?y)$: person $(?x)$ and event $(?y, \text{go-home} \ [?x])$ and (desire $[?x, ?y])]$.

HIGHER ORDER RELATIONAL STRUCTURE

Structured representations gain some of their power from the ability to create increasingly complex representations of a situation by embedding relations in other relations and thereby creating higher order relational structures. These higher order structures can encode important psychological elements like causal relations and implications. In Example 5.15, I created a representation of a quantified statement that somebody wants to hurt someone and used the arbitrary predicate wants-to-hurt ($?x$, $?y$) for this representation. One would probably not want to use this predicate in a representation, because it is likely to apply in only a small range of circumstances. Unfortunately, to encode this situation using only first-order relations is quite difficult (see footnote 4 for one possibility).

The problem with representing "Somebody wants to hurt someone" arises from the fact that there is a state of the world that is *desired* by someone. Desire is a *propositional attitude* (Dennett, 1987; J. A. Fodor, 1981), a psychological state that someone can have about some proposition. Other propositional attitudes are *believe* and *know*. These propositional attitudes are difficult to represent using only first-order predicates, because the object of the propositional attitude is itself a relation. They become much easier to represent with higher order relations. Example 5.15 can be recast with higher order relations as:

$$\exists \ (?x), \ \exists \ (?y): \text{person } (?x) \text{ and person } (?y) \text{ and}$$
$$\text{desire } \{?x, \text{ cause } [\text{do } (?x, \text{ action } 1), \text{ hurt } (?y)]\}. \qquad (5.17)$$

This representation contains two higher order relations. The first, which corresponds to the propositional attitude of desire, takes two arguments: the person who desires the state of affairs and the desired state of affairs. The second higher order relation expands the notion of what it means to hurt someone. In particular, it is a causal relation in which the antecedent to the causal relation is that some person carries out some action and the consequent to the relation is that person y is hurt.[5]

In this example, the higher order relations encode important facts about the domain. Relations like propositional attitudes and causal relations are central and often bind into a single structure many facts known about a domain. Higher order relations bring coherence to a domain; without them, there are only lists of facts, and it may be difficult to determine

---

[5]Even this representation is flawed, because it does not do a good job of representing the temporal aspects of the situation. For example, person y was not hurt before the event but is hurt afterward. To remedy this situation, I can add some time point (call it t) such that before time t person y is not hurt, and after time t y is hurt. This solution allows reasoning about temporal relations among events (see Charniak & McDermott, 1986).

TABLE 5.1
Summary of Stories Used to Test the Role of Systematicity in Analogy

	Target: Robots	
Base: Tams	Version 1	Version 2
Consume minerals with underbellies. *Exhaust minerals in one spot and must relocate on the rock.* **So stop using underbellies.**	Gather data with probes. *Exhaust data in one place and must relocate on planet.* **So stop using probes.**	Gather data with probes. *Internal computers overheat when gathering a lot of data.* **So stop using probes.**
Born with inefficient under-bellies. *Underbellies adapt and become specialized for one rock.* **So underbellies cannot function on new rock.**	Designed with delicate probes. *Robots cannot pack probes to survive flight to a new planet.* **So probes cannot function on new planet.**	Designed with delicate probes. *Probes adapt and become specialized for one planet.* **So probes cannot function on new planet.**

Note. Key facts are shown in boldface; matching causal information is shown in italics.

what information is important. Thus, being able to represent things as higher order relations may provide one avenue for helping the cognitive system to focus attention on important information. The idea that higher order relational structures lend coherence to, and are the source of important information in, a domain is called the *systematicity principle* (Gentner, 1983, 1989).[6]

Systematicity has been shown to influence the way people process analogy and similarity comparisons. Earlier I discussed evidence that people's perception of similarity is influenced by structure in concept representations. Related work has focused on the importance of systematicity in comparison. In one study, Clement and Gentner (1991) told people

---

[6]Actually two different things have been called *systematicity* in the cognitive science literature. Gentner's (1983, 1989) sense of systematicity is that the similarity of two domains is thought to be higher when these domains match along higher order relational structure than if they match along only isolated first-order relations. The second use of systematicity is also related to structured representations (J. A. Fodor & Pylyshyn, 1988). This use of systematicity says that the ability to think some thoughts is lawfully connected to the ability to think other thoughts. For example, if I can think the thought "John kissed Mary," I can also think the thought "Mary kissed John." According to Fodor and Pylyshyn, this systematicity arises because mental representations are structured and compositional (i.e., the components can be freely combined). For example, "John kissed Mary" can be represented as kissed (John, Mary). There should be no problem reversing the arguments to this relation to yield kissed (Mary, John) or "Mary kissed John." Although both terms address aspects of structured representations, they are not quite the same aspect.

stories that had causal relations in them, one pair of which is illustrated in Table 5.1. The base story tells of organisms (the Tams) that feed off minerals from rocks by using their underbellies. The story had two central facts, as shown in the table. First, when the Tams deplete the minerals in one spot, they must relocate to a second rock and then stop using their underbellies. Second, their underbellies become specialized to a particular kind of rock and cannot function on another kind. After reading this first story, researchers gave subjects one version of a second, analogous story about robots on a distant planet (e.g., Version 1 in Table 5.1), in which the robots gather data with probes. In the story, neither of the causal consequents (shown in boldface in Table 5.1) was given. One causal antecedent was analogous to an antecedent in the Tam story (e.g., the data in one location were exhausted), and one was not (e.g., the robots cannot pack the probes to survive a flight). After reading the stories, workers asked subjects to make one new prediction about the robots in view of the similarity with the Tams. People were far more likely to infer the consequent with the matching causal antecedent (e.g., that the robots stop using the probes) than to infer the consequent without a matching causal antecedent (e.g., that the probes cannot function on a new planet). The reverse pattern was observed when participants were given Version 2 of the robot story. This finding is an instance of systematicity: People carried over information from the first story to the second only when the new information was governed by a higher order relation that was connected to matching facts between the stories. This finding has been replicated in other studies of analogical inference (Markman, 1997; Spellman & Holyoak, 1996).

Systematicity is not restricted to analogical inference; it also seems to be true of similarity-based inductive inferences. Lassaline (1996) asked participants to rate the strength of several inductive inferences. In these inductive inferences, some facts were known about one object, and some other facts were known about a second object. For example, a subject might know that facts A, B, and C were true of the first object and facts A and D were true of the second object. Then, investigators asked subjects to rate the likelihood that another property of the first object (B) was also true of the second. In some cases, a causal relation connected the property to be inferred to a property shared by the two objects (e.g., participants were told that A causes B). In other cases, there was no such causal relation. People judged that inferences in which the causal relation was present were stronger than were inferences in which the causal relation was not present. That is, when there was a causal relation in the first object linking properties A and B, the inference that the second object had property B was deemed stronger than when there was no causal relation linking A and B in the first object. These results suggest that systematicity helps focus people on information that is important in a situation.

Although there is evidence that systematicity constrains cognitive processing, particularly in analogy and inference, other evidence has also suggested that people do not have unlimited ability to embed one relation in another. In particular, researchers have looked at both children's and adults' ability to represent propositional attitudes (especially belief). Studies with children have focused on their ability to solve false belief tasks (Perner, 1991; Wellman, 1990). Typical false belief studies with children have involved describing situations to children in which a person is in a room and an object (e.g., a candy bar) is placed in some location (e.g., a cupboard). Then, the children are told that the person leaves the room, and while the person is out of the room, the object is moved to a new location (e.g., a bread box). Researchers asked children where the person will look for the candy bar when he or she returns to the room. When children are about 3 years old, they respond that the person will look in the location to which the object was moved (e.g., in the bread box), even though the person had left the room before the candy bar was moved and could not know where it was. Thus, children of this age seem to have trouble separating what they know (e.g., that the candy bar is in the bread box) from what the character knows (e.g., that the candy bar is in the cupboard).

By the time children are about 5 years old (and on into adulthood), they respond that the person will look in the original location (e.g., the cupboard). There has been some controversy over the age at which children respond correctly. The results in these tasks are influenced by the way the question is asked, but it clearly takes some time for children to develop the ability to represent other people's beliefs. This task requires that a child represent a propositional attitude explicitly:

$$\text{believe [John, location (candy bar, cupboard)]}, \qquad (5.18)$$

even though the proposition that the character believes does not correspond to what the child knows to be true about the world.

If studies of this type were the only ones to bear on this issue, children's representational abilities would seem to gradually develop sophistication like their abilities to represent relations among propositions.[7] Research with adults, however, has suggested that people are not always accurate in tasks involving reasoning about other people's beliefs (e.g., Keysar, 1994; Keysar & Bly, 1995). Keysar (1994) presented adults with passages describing a situation in which a woman recommends a restaurant to a man because she has just enjoyed a wonderful meal there. When the man goes

---

[7]Perner (1991) provided an interesting discussion of the minimum representational abilities that a child must have to be able to properly solve particular false belief tasks.

to the restaurant, the food and service are terrible. The next day, he leaves her a note saying, "The restaurant was marvelous, just marvelous." The researchers asked the subjects how the woman will interpret this note. Many people suggested that the woman would interpret it as sarcasm, even though she had no way of knowing the man had a bad meal there. The finding that even adults seem to have some difficulty keeping track of other people's beliefs qualifies the simple developmental story about propositional attitudes. The ability to represent other people's beliefs does not seem to develop to the point that flawless performance on false belief tasks ensues. Rather, the ability to keep track of other people's beliefs requires some effort, particularly in the complex settings studied by Keysar. Without the motivation to expend this effort, people may not choose to represent others' beliefs. At present, there is no good theory about why representing propositional attitudes requires effort.

STRUCTURED REPRESENTATIONS AND CONNECTIONISM

Structured representations seem incompatible with connectionist models like those discussed in chapter 2. As described there, simple distributed connectionist models essentially use spatial representations. New vectors are compared to old vectors by using the dot product, which determines the degree of one vector that projects on another (in a high-dimensional space). In general, spatial representations like those in connectionist models using the dot product as the main measure of similarity are inappropriate as models of the structural comparisons described in this chapter, because they do not consider the relations between predicates and their arguments. Researchers have, however, developed more complex connectionist architectures that implement structured representations.

To create a structured representation in a connectionist system, the model must be extended in time or space to accommodate bindings between elements. Investigators have used both types of extensions. An example of a model's extension in space is Smolensky's tensor product model (Halford, 1992; Smolensky, 1990). In a tensor product model, elements to be bound together are first represented as N-dimensional vectors, in which each element is given a unique pattern of activity. To bind together two vectors, their outer product is taken. (The outer product was discussed in chap. 2, when I described the storage of associations in a simple network.) The outer product of two N-dimensional vectors yields an $N \times N$ matrix. To create the tensor product vector, the columns of the matrix are concatenated sequentially. The first column forms the first N rows of the vector, the next column forms the next N rows, and so on. Thus, a tensor product vector has N^2 units. For example, to represent the proposition red (ball), I take the vector for red:

$$\mathbf{f}_{\mathbf{red}} = \begin{bmatrix} 1 \\ 1 \\ -1 \\ -1 \end{bmatrix} \tag{5.19}$$

and the vector for ball:

$$\mathbf{f}_{\mathbf{ball}} = \begin{bmatrix} 1 \\ -1 \\ 1 \\ -1 \end{bmatrix}, \tag{5.20}$$

then take their outer product to yield:

$$\mathbf{A}_{\mathbf{red\ (ball)}} = \begin{bmatrix} 1 & 1 & -1 & -1 \\ -1 & -1 & 1 & 1 \\ 1 & 1 & -1 & -1 \\ -1 & -1 & 1 & 1 \end{bmatrix}. \tag{5.21}$$

Then, I simply take the columns of this matrix and extend them out to form a vector as follows:

$$\mathbf{f}_{\mathbf{red\ (ball)}} = \begin{bmatrix} 1 \\ -1 \\ 1 \\ -1 \\ 1 \\ -1 \\ 1 \\ -1 \\ etc. \end{bmatrix}. \tag{5.22}$$

The tensor product can be used as a vector in another association. Because the tensor product is essentially an outer product, if the vector for red is presented to the system again, the vector for ball can be extracted by multiplying this outer product matrix with the vector (as discussed in chap. 2). Thus, the tensor product extends the dimensionality of the representation to bind pairs of vectors together.

It is important to consider what makes pairs of tensor product vectors similar to each other. It would be interesting if comparing pairs of tensor product vectors (by taking their dot product) would yield patterns of similarity similar to those obtained in studies of structural similarity, like those described earlier in this chapter. Holyoak and Hummel (in press) provided a formal account of the similarity of pairs of tensor product vectors. They demonstrated that the dot product of a pair of tensor product vectors is simply the product of the dot products of the constituent vectors of the tensor product vector. That is, the dot product (dp) of a tensor product vector that binds a pair of vectors a and b to a second vector that binds together the vectors c and d is:

$$dp\ (ab,\ cd) = dp\ (a,\ c) \times dp\ (b,\ d). \tag{5.23}$$

Thus, if corresponding constituents of a pair of tensor product vectors are extremely dissimilar (e.g., if vectors b and d have a dot product near 0), the dot product of these tensor product vectors is very small, regardless of the similarity of the other constituents. This pattern of similarity diverges from the pattern observed in people who, for example, can see similarities in relations even when the arguments to the relations are not at all similar.

A related approach to tensor products involves circular convolution (Metcalfe, 1991; Metcalfe-Eich, 1982; Plate, 1991). Like tensor products, circular convolution first involves taking the outer product of a pair of vectors. This outer product matrix is then reduced back to an N-dimensional vector by adding together the elements on the reverse diagonals of the matrix. Figure 5.8 shows how an outer product matrix can be turned into a four-dimensional vector. As with tensor products, a circular convolution can be combined with one of the elements in the binding to yield the other element. This example demonstrates how a circular convolution can be carried out.[8] To represent a situation with many different bindings, different circular convolutions can be added together. To retrieve something from a memory consisting of a set of circular convolutions, the *circular correlation* operation can be used. In circular correlation, one takes the outer product of the circular convolution vector and a probe vector and adds the elements using the forward diagonal (i.e., going from the upper left to the lower right in Figure 5.8). This operation yields the vector associated with the probe vector if prior associations were stored. Although

---

[8]Some implementational details must be incorporated into the models to get them to work. For example, the elements of each vector must be created so that the activation of its units is independently distributed with a mean of 0 and a variance of $1/N$ (where N is the number of dimensions). This distribution is necessary because there is no unique mapping between a circular convolution and a single pair of vectors creating it.

Circular Convolution

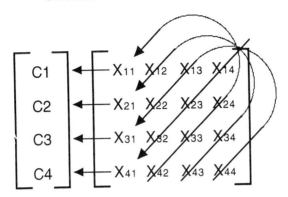

FIG. 5.8. Circular convolution operation used to bind pairs of vectors.

circular convolutions provide another way to bind pairs of vectors, the similarity of a pair of circular convolutions is influenced by the similarity of its components in much the same way as are tensor products (Holyoak & Hummel, in press). Thus, dot product comparisons of circular convolutions do not seem to be a good model of people's use of structural similarity.

Tensor products extend a model in space because representing a binding between two elements, each of which is represented by an N-dimensional vector, requires N^2 units. Circular convolution representations extend the model in space more subtly. Each binding between vectors occupies only N units, but the use of many N-dimensional vectors to bind elements together requires a high-dimensional space so that vectors do not interfere with each other. At most, N orthogonal vectors (which do not interfere with each other) can be placed in an N-dimensional space. If the vector elements are randomly generated, the capacity of such networks is generally much lower (often around 10% of the dimensionality).

A second way of extending connectionist models to incorporate structure is to extend them in time. In these models, the structure unfolds over time in processing. One type of extension uses recurrent networks (Elman, 1990; J. B. Pollack, 1990). Figure 5.9 shows two types of recurrent network architectures. In each case, a new input is associated with some output through a layer of *hidden units* using the back-propagation learning routine (Rumelhart, Hinton, & Williams, 1986). Back propagation extends the simple learning procedure described in chapter 2 to permit more complex sets of associations. The key aspect of recurrent networks is that a set of context units is added to the network. The first time an association is learned, an arbitrary pattern is given to the context units. For each subsequent association, the previous pattern on either the output units or the

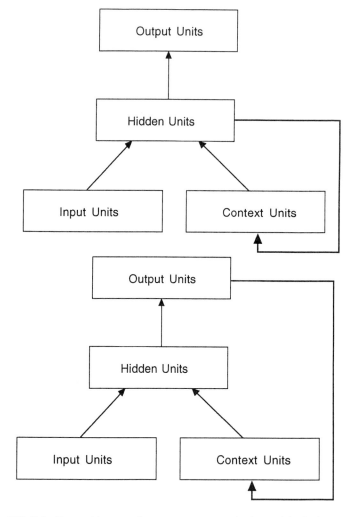

FIG. 5.9. Two architectures for recurrent connectionist models. In the top architecture, the hidden units are used as context; in the bottom architecture, the output units are used as context.

hidden units is used as a context. This use of context allows the network to encode sequences and retrieve them later. The sequences are not available all at once but must be decoded over time by reinstating an old context and finding the output associated with it. The retrieved context units can be fed back as input to retrieve the whole sequence. Thus, the extension of these models in time makes the structure in the representation available to the system only over the course of processing and not at any individual moment.

For example, I can teach a recurrent network to produce the letters of the alphabet in order. To do this task, I give an input pattern for the beginning of the sequence, with no values on the context units. I associate this input with a pattern for the letter *a*. In this way, the model learns that the beginning of the sequence was the letter *a*. Then, I associate my context units (say the pattern of activation in the hidden units from the previous trial), along with the pattern for the letter *a*, with the letter *b*. I continue training in this way, until I reach the end of the alphabet. After these associations are learned, I can retrieve the letters of the alphabet in order by giving the model the input pattern for the beginning of the sequence on the input units, to yield the association *a*. Then I can generate the rest of the sequence by feeding the context units and the output back to the input units and finding the next learned association.

A final way to represent structure in a connectionist model is the use of temporal binding of units (Hummel & Biederman, 1992; Hummel & Holyoak, 1997; Shastri & Ajjanagadde, 1993). This model differs from distributed connectionist models because it uses a *localist* representation scheme. Like the parallel constraint satisfaction models described in chapter 4, localist representations assume that each unit has some meaning. Figure 5.10 shows a sample network. To represent a proposition like *loves* (John, Mary), the system must have units for the relation *loves* and the objects *John* and *Mary*. The system must also have units for the relational roles of *loves* (e.g., the *love-agent* and *love-patient* units in Figure 5.10). The binding between relations and arguments occurs over time. In particular, it is assumed that units active at the same time are bound together. Thus, at one time, the units for *loves, love-agent,* and *John* are active together (Figure 5.10B). At another time, the units for *loves, love-patient,* and *Mary* are active together (Figure 5.10C). Other relations are represented by other patterns of unit activation. As for recurrent networks, temporal synchrony as a method of binding makes the structure in the representation over time.

As demonstrated in this section, extensions to connectionist models allow them to encode structured representations. Extensive research has been devoted to examining the uses of these structured representations. They have been used successfully as models of data from memory experiments (Metcalfe, 1991, 1993; Metcalfe-Eich, 1982). Workers have achieved some success in developing models of reasoning (Shastri & Ajjanagadde, 1993) and analogical mapping (Halford, Wilson, Guo, Wiles, & Stewart, 1994; Hummel & Holyoak, 1997), although these models often do not perform to the level of existing symbolic models (Gentner & Markman, 1993, 1995). The thrust of this section, however, is that just because some cognitive processes involve structured representations, this fact should not be taken as evidence of the inappropriateness of connectionist models as

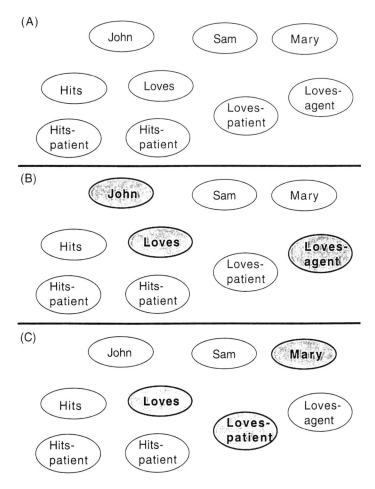

FIG. 5.10. Example of dynamic binding by temporal synchrony. A: Localist connectionist units. B: Units active at the same time representing that John is the agent of a *Loves* relation. C: Units active at the same time representing that Mary is the patient of a *Loves* relation.

models of cognition. Instead, it is possible to implement structured representations using connectionist mechanisms.

SUMMARY

Structured representations contain explicit connections between elements. These bindings provide information about the scope of representational elements. Representational structure allows elements to be combined by entering them as arguments of other elements. Structured representations also permit systematicity in which higher order relational structures are developed to represent important information (like causal relations).

The use of structured representations requires more complex processes than did the simpler representations discussed in chapters 2 to 4. Simply comparing a pair of such representations requires a structural alignment process that attends to the bindings between predicates and their arguments. The advantage of such complexity is that this representation process pair can account for the fact that people distinguish between alignable differences (which are related to commonalities) and nonalignable differences (which are not). This process, however, is computationally expensive; when many comparisons must be carried out, a simpler representation and process may be required.

Finally, structured representations can be implemented in different ways. Most examples in this chapter focused on predicate calculus representations, in which symbols were concatenated to form representational structures. Another prominent representational system is frames, which are based on the attribute–value structure of objects. Finally, it is also possible to extend connectionist models in either time or space to account for structure in representations. In the next two chapters, I examine the applications of structured representations to perceptual representation (chap. 6) and conceptual representation (chap. 7).

Chapter 6

Structure in Perceptual Representations

PERCEPTUAL REPRESENTATION AND PERCEPTUAL EXPERIENCE

For those of us who are normally sighted, the visual world is one of the most compelling facets of psychological experience. Without effort or attention, merely opening our eyes reveals a coherent sense of the outside world. Visual experience provides information about the three-dimensional layout of the world and about the size, shape, color, texture, and motion of objects, and this information is rapidly integrated with information from other perceptual modalities.

Visual perception is the prime example of a central paradox in cognitive science: What is difficult for people to do is easy for computers, but what is easy for people to do is difficult for computers. The apparent ease of visual perception belies the massive amount of processing needed to transform the two-dimensional patterns of light that strike the two retinas into detailed visual experience. The huge processing load of visual perception is obvious from two converging lines of evidence. First, studies of the anatomy and functionality of the brain reveal that a significant amount of the cortex of the human brain is involved in visual processing. Second, computational models of vision have proved difficult to construct. Creating robots that see is not simply a matter of attaching a video camera to a computer and writing a simple program. Substantial research has been devoted to specific problems like extracting edges from scenes and finding corresponding aspects of the visual images received by each eye (e.g., Horn, 1973; Kosslyn, 1994; Marr, 1982).

The complexity of visual processing is important to bear in mind because the representations that people have presented in models of vision and perception may seem inconsistent with visual experience. Conscious visual experience is seamless: Objects have obvious relative sizes and positions in space. It is not obvious, however, how multiple representations are integrated to form such a uniform and compelling view of the world. I do not provide a theory of the unity of perceptual experience or even attempt to summarize the literature on visual perception; that effort would require a book to itself. Instead, I follow up the themes of chapter 5 by discussing structured representations that have been presented in models of visual perception. I begin with a discussion of structured representations in perception and object recognition and extend my discussion to include visual imagery. I end with an examination of the relation between perceptual representation and spatial language.

STRUCTURE IN VISUAL REPRESENTATION

In chapter 5, I introduced structured representations, which involve explicit links that encode relationships among properties of objects. Attributes take the entities they describe as arguments; relations explicitly relate two or more other representational elements (which could be objects, attributes, or even other relations). This structure seems intuitively plausible for many complex concepts. For example, as I discuss in chapter 7, events seem to have a natural structure that involves distinguishing between the various actors in an event and encoding the actions they perform as well as carrying information about causal relations to explain why these actions are carried out.

The intuitive basis for structured representations of visual scenes is less obvious. The unitary perceptual experience of seeing does not seem (at first glance) to be compatible with representations involving relations and connections to the things they relate, but the notion of perception as a veridical "picture" of what is in the world begins to fade as one looks closely at perception. Gestalt psychologists (e.g., Goldmeier, 1972; Wertheimer, 1923/1950) carried out classic work on the ability of the human perceptual system to organize the world. Their work demonstrated that perception is not simply a true readout of the outside world. Instead, the perceptual system imposes a structure on the world.

Figure 6.1A shows two lines, each composed of seven black dots that, in each line, are evenly spaced (Goldmeier, 1972). The two lines differ only in the relative spacing of the dots, which are much closer together in the bottom row than in the top. Perceptual experience of these rows is different, however: The bottom row appears to be organized into a line much more strongly than does the top row, which looks like a group of

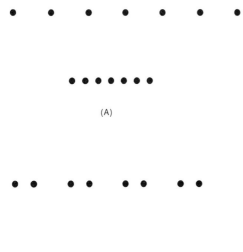

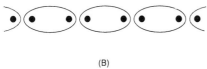

FIG. 6.1. Sample items demonstrating Gestalt principles. A: material and form; B: grouping.

dots all lined up. Goldmeier (1972) suggested that there is a tension
between seeing the *material* and the *form* of a percept. In this example,
the dots are the material, and the line is the form. Increasing the proximity
of the dots increases the likelihood that the perceptual system promotes
seeing the line (i.e., the form) rather than just a collection of collinear
dots (i.e., the material).

Figure 6.1B shows another way that the perceptual system can organize
a stimulus. In the upper row of this figure, the dots seem to be organized
into four groups of two, where the groups are defined by their proximity;
thus, the perceptual system seems to group elements that are near to each
other. In the lower row, however, the same dots have ovals drawn around
them so that the ovals enclose dots that are far apart. In this case, the dots
in each oval seem grouped together, even though the spacing between
the dots is the same as in the upper row of the figure (Palmer, 1992).
Thus, the perceptual system uses elements of the stimuli in the world to
make guesses about what is in the world, and the percept reflects these
guesses. The percept is thus a representation of the stimulus, but not a
veridical copy of it.

The Gestalt psychologists formulated several "laws" of perception char-
acterizing the types of elements that were likely to be grouped together,
but they did not present detailed descriptions of perceptual representations.
Later researchers began to suggest how perceptual representations were

structured. In Figure 6.2 there are many possible ways that the top configuration can be broken into component parts; two possible breakdowns are shown at the bottom of the figure. For the present purposes, what is most important is that the middle decomposition seems more natural than the bottom decomposition. This intuition was confirmed by participants in a set of studies by Reed (1974). Participants were shown a figure like the top one in Figure 6.2, and were asked to verify whether the next part shown was contained in the pattern. Participants responded more quickly and accurately to some parts (like the middle one in Figure 6.2) than to others (like the bottom one in the figure), a result suggesting that the figures were being decomposed into parts. Palmer (1977, 1978b) carried out a similar set of studies.

Another proposal about the way the perceptual system imposes structure on the visual world comes from Leyton (1992), who suggested that the perceptual system is specially attuned to symmetries in the world. The door of a new car often is smoothly curved; a dent in this smooth curve is immediately obvious and calls attention to a force that has acted on the object. In contrast, no point on the smooth curve of the door of an unblemished new car calls for attention, because there is no visual evidence of causal forces acting on the door. The perceptual system may interpret visual input in terms of causal forces acting on an item, and asymmetries may be markers of these causal forces. I will return to this proposal later.

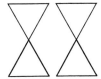

FIG. 6.2. Sample configurations similar to those used by Reed (1972) and subcomponents of the configurations.

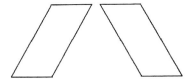

The idea that the visual system constructs representations of the world is also suggested by the nature of vision itself. When talking about vision, it is often handy to ignore the fact that visual scenes are processed through a succession of fixations. Nevertheless, the visual system is not like a video camera that takes in all information in some (reasonably wide) angle in the direction in which it is pointed; the eyes constantly move, scan the scene, and focus on particular aspects of the world. This scanning is necessary because the retina of the eye is not uniform. Instead, it has different sensitivity at different points. There is a high degree of concentration of light-sensitive cells in a small area in the center of the retina called the fovea with fewer light-sensitive cells in the periphery. Further, the relative density of color-sensitive cells is greater in the fovea than in the periphery. The net effect of this structure is that the stable perception of the visual world is a product of the integration of many fixations (as well as the suppression of the smeared images that occur as the eyes move). It is possible that the visual information from a pair of successive fixations is matched through a point-by-point matching of successive images, but this method would be computationally intensive and subject to problems from changes in low-level factors like light intensity. The process of finding correspondences between successive fixations is probably augmented with higher level representations of the objects in the world, in addition to information about lower level aspects of scenes.

These examples do not support any particular model of representation in perception. They simply demonstrate that the perceptual system imposes a structure on the input it receives and that these biases are consistent with the assumption that the perceptual system decomposes visual objects into parts. In the next section, I discuss some specific proposals that have been made for structured representations in perception.

Structured Representations of Objects

Objects are a particularly important aspect of visual experience. It seems a trivial observation that our world is segmented into objects, even for very young children (Spelke, 1990). Yet, much work must be done on the pattern of light that reaches the eye to determine which aspects of a scene are coherent objects. Because of the salience of objects in vision and the importance of vision for recognizing objects in the world, many theories of perceptual representation have focused on object representations. Most of these theories are primarily concerned with object recognition.

Marr (1982) suggested the general form of a theory of object representation suitable for object recognition. His proposal focused on a *3D model representation* with three central assumptions. First, object recognition takes place with representations defined in *object-centered coordinates*. Representing something in object-centered coordinates means that the location of each point in an object is defined relative to other parts of the object itself rather than to the person viewing the object. For example, in object-centered coordinates, the head of the schematic human figure in Figure 6.3 is given relative to other parts of the person like the torso and arms.

Marr's assumption that object representations have object-centered coordinates is interesting because representation in early visual processing is probably *viewer centered*. A viewer-centered representation is one in which the relative locations of elements are defined with respect to the viewer. For example, from where I am sitting right now, there is a green Gumby figurine at eye level, and just below that is the top edge of my computer monitor. If I move, the viewer-centered locations of these objects move as well. If I stand on my head, the edge of the monitor is above the feet of the Gumby figurine. Early in the visual process, the retina receives only a pattern of light, from which the visual system must extract key information, such as sharp discontinuities in the intensity of the light, that might signal edges of objects. Object-centered representations cannot be created until the visual system determines what patches of light are likely to form coherent objects. According to Marr, extracting information like edges or textures occurs in viewer-centered coordinates, but object recognition involves matching current input to stored representations of objects seen previously. As an observer's viewpoint changes, the features in the image change as well. Thus, if the representations used for object recognition are cast in viewer-centered coordinates, there have to be many different views of each object in memory to account for the ability to recognize objects from a variety of perspectives. Marr suggested that it is more efficient to store object-centered object representations.

The second main assumption of Marr's 3D model representation is that it involves generalized cones and the relations among them. A generalized cone need not be cone shaped: The term *generalized cone* denotes that objects need not be cylinders (which have circles of the same radius at each end). Instead, the cross-section of a generalized cone may get wider or narrower along its main axis (i.e., the longest axis of the cone). A generalized cone abstracts across the details of a solid shape. For example, if a cylinder is used as the representation of a metal garbage can, it may abstract over the fluting that is a common design on these cans. These generalized cones are the primitive elements of the 3D model representations, and Marr selected them because he assumed that determining cones from information available in lower level visual processes was a straightforward process.

More than one generalized cone can be combined into the representation of an object to store more complex shapes. Figure 6.3 shows

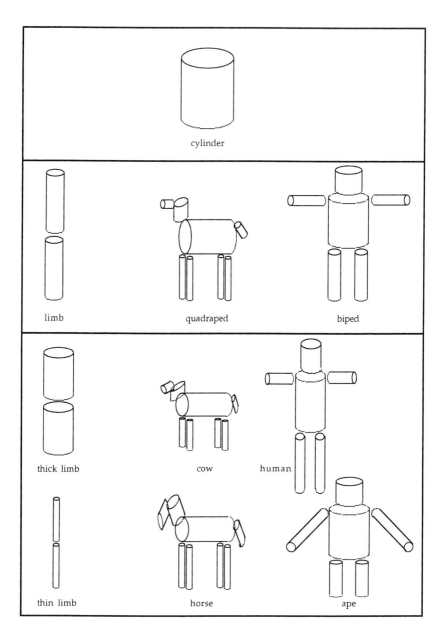

cylinder

limb   quadraped   biped

thick limb   cow   human

thin limb   horse   ape

FIG. 6.3. Objects represented by using a three-dimensional model constructed from generalized cones. Drawn after Marr (1982).

several objects formed from combinations of cones. Representations containing two or more cones must also have relations that determine the relative positions of the cones, although Marr was not specific about the nature of these relations. He assumed that the relations could be stated in terms of vectors. In particular, each generalized cone was assumed to have a major axis, typically the longest axis of the cone. The point of contact of the major axes of two cones and the angle between them define the relation between pairs of cones in the representation.

The representations in Figure 6.3 are highly abstracted from the details of visual objects. The human figure in the middle of the third row has the basic components (head, torso, arms, legs), but lacks many other aspects (including parts like hands, fingers, and feet as well as color and textural features). On the basis of people's ability to identify line drawings and stick figures, Marr assumed that many color and textural details are not required for object recognition. Specific aspects of shape probably do need to be represented, and Marr assumed that the 3D model representations were hierarchically structured, with more specific representations of components being nested in more abstract representations. An example of hierarchical structure is shown in Figure 6.4. In this figure of a human, the arm is decomposed into a pair of cones joined at the elbow. The wrist and hand can likewise be nested in this description. On this view, associations between more specific and more general representations of the same aspect of an object can be used during recognition.

Marr assumed that object recognition involves finding homologies between the representation of a new object in the visual field and the representation of stored objects. The new representation is compared to previously stored representations, and correspondences, of both common parts and common relations, are found between them. Although Marr did not

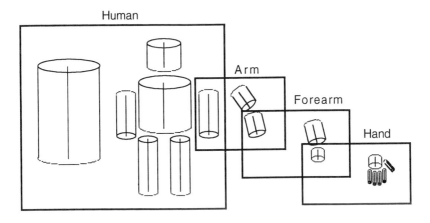

FIG. 6.4.   Hierarchical structure of 3D models. Drawn after Marr (1982).

spell out this process, it seems similar in spirit to the process of structural alignment described in chapter 5, in which elements in pairs of structured representations are placed in correspondence.

Biederman proposed a related view of representation for object recognition (1987; Hummel & Biederman, 1992). His theory, called recognition-by-components, also focused on the role of primitives and the relations among them in object recognition. A brief description of this theory was presented in chapter 3 when I introduced the notion of primitives. In Marr's theory, the primitive volume elements were assumed to be generalized cones, but no constraints were placed on what sorts of generalized cones they were. In most of Marr's work, cylinders stood for the generalized cones. Biederman extended this work by positing a specific set of primitives consisting of 36 generalized cones that he called *geons*. The geons can be developed by changing properties of a prototypical generalized cone as shown in Figure 6.5. A prototypical geon like a cylinder can vary along a number of dimensions: Instead of round edges, it can have straight edges; instead of a straight axis, it can have a curved axis; instead of parallel sides, it can have sides that expand or sides that expand and then contract like a cigar. Finally, the geon can have complete rotational symmetry like a cylinder, it can have reflectional symmetry like an oval, or it can be asymmetric. Combinations of these properties define the basic set of 36 geons.

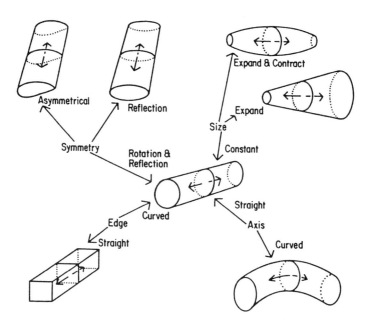

FIG. 6.5. Geons and the properties that derive them. From I. Biederman (1985). Copyright © 1985 by Academic Press. Reprinted with permission.

Geons can be grounded in simple aspects of the visual world; in particular, they can be recognized by attending to *nonaccidental properties* of images, which are evident in views of objects from a variety of vantage points. For example, if two edges in an object are parallel, they appear to be roughly parallel when viewed from a variety of angles; thus, parallel lines are a nonaccidental property. Other nonaccidental properties are symmetry and the straightness and collinearity of lines. Geons differ from each other in terms of their nonaccidental properties; for example, a cylinder differs from a cone and a cigar by having straight parallel lines along its major axis. Because geons are based on nonaccidental properties, they should be easy to identify across a variety of views of an object. In this way, geons ease the identification of objects from multiple viewpoints. The focus on nonaccidental properties also helps explain why objects can be difficult to identify from certain vantage points. Figure 6.6A shows a line drawing of a bucket, which is fairly recognizable. Viewing the bottom of the bucket when it is turned over, however, is a different matter: One sees two concentric circles (Figure 6.6B). These concentric circles are not a nonaccidental property; they are accidental because they are seen only when looking down at the bucket when it is turned over. Objects can be very difficult to identify in configurations with compelling accidental properties.

Objects are not represented with a single generalized cone but are composed of many geons. When an object is represented by many geons, its representation is structured by having relations that describe the spatial configuration of the object. Different objects can have the same set of geons in their representations related in different ways. With a small set of geons and relations, many objects can be represented in much the same way that a finite vocabulary of words and a syntax for combining these words can be used to construct an infinite set of sentences. Biederman suggested that information about the relationships among geons is contained at the vertices of edges in objects, where geons tend to come together. The top image in Figure 6.7 shows an object with line segments

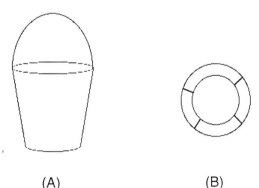

FIG. 6.6. A: Typical view of a bucket with nonaccidental properties. B: Bottom view of a bucket with salient accidental properties.

(A)   (B)

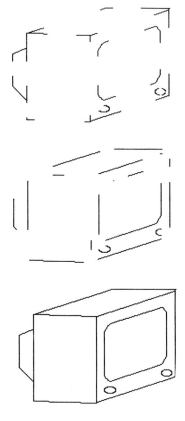

FIG. 6.7. Drawings of a television set; line segments removed from between the vertices (top figure) or at the vertices (middle figure).

removed only between vertices. The middle object has line segments removed at the vertices. The top figure seems easier to identify than the middle one, consistent with the assumption that information about relations between elements is captured at vertices. Biederman (1987) provided a number of examples demonstrating this phenomenon.

The theories of object recognition developed by Marr and Biederman both assume that visual object representations consist of primitive elements and relations between them. These primitive elements are identified by nonaccidental properties of visual images. In this way, the viewer-centered representations of early vision can be translated into object-centered representations that are more suitable for object identification. Comparing the representation of a new object to the representations of objects already in memory involves some process of structural comparison. One possible candidate for this process is the structural alignment process described in chapter 5. Structural representations seem most appropriate for describing objects with easily discernible parts like tables, chairs, or standing animals. Objects that do not have obvious part structures like loaves of bread or bushes may not be well characterized by structural descriptions (Ullman, 1996).

Metric Information in Visual Object Representations

The previous discussion focused on structural descriptions in the recognition of visual objects. These structural descriptions have a nice property of abstracting away from the specific image in the world and allowing the determination of commonalities that can be masked by differences in specific properties of the forms of objects. For example, one can match the legs of two images of birds, even if they differ slightly in length or thickness. Matching these parts requires some abstraction away from the specific forms of the images.

Despite the advantage of abstracting away from image properties, one also needs some information about metric aspects of the visual world. For example, as I write, my coffee cup is next to my computer and in front of my telephone (in viewer-centered coordinates). If I reach to pick up the cup, I do not simply reach next to my computer; unless I reach a certain distance from it, I may knock over the cup or pick up something else. Knowing that there is a handle on the left side of the cup can be useful, but it is also important to know the particular location of the handle. This information is important for grasping the cup and also for helping me to identify the cup as mine rather than as someone else's. This metric information may be quite difficult to talk about but may still be represented (Schooler & Engstler-Schooler, 1990).

Kosslyn (1994) suggested that relational and metric information are treated separately in the visual system. He posited that the right hemisphere of the brain is specialized to handle metric representations of objects, whereas the left hemisphere system is specialized to handle qualitative relational information. I do not attempt to evaluate this claim here except to note the need for a quantitative representation of space in perceptual representations, and the possibility that distinct brain systems process this information.[1]

Ullman (1996) stressed this point and suggested that a variety of representational and processing systems must work together to permit objects to be recognized. Although he conceded that structural descriptions of objects are useful in many situations, he thought that some object recognition requires representations that store metric information. This style of representation may be particularly important when objects are defined by changes in contour rather than by a set of parts. For example, the tool in Figure 6.8 does not have any good parts associated with it, but Ullman

---

[1]The idea that representations contain both metric information and more structured information was also a part of early dual-coding theories of memory (Kieras, 1978; Posner, Boies, Eichelman, & Taylor, 1969).

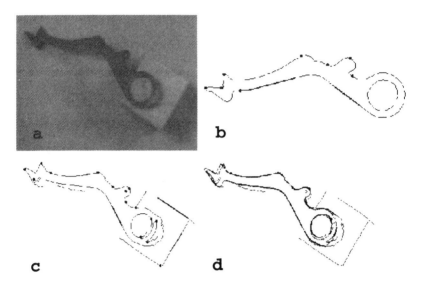

FIG. 6.8. Example of image alignment. From D. P. Huttenlocher and S. Ullman (1990). Copyright © 1990 by Kluwer Academic Publishers. Reprinted with permission.

suggested that stable features of the object can be determined by finding extremes in curvature and centers of enclosed regions (like those shown in Figure 6.8B). These features can be used to compare the object to stored image representations in memory, and the image can be stretched and rotated to make the images match as best as possible. After performing this process, which Ullman calls image alignment, the degree of match between the stored and new images can be determined by summing the distance between each point in the new image and the closest point in the stored image. The object can then be identified as an example of the class depicted by the best-fitting image in memory.

The structural description methods of representation avoided the problem of viewpoint dependence by creating object-centered representations. The image alignment model of object recognition is viewpoint dependent. To allow objects to be recognized from many different viewpoints, Ullman suggested that many different images of the same object are stored and that the current image is compared to many images of the same object as well as to images of different objects (see also Tarr & Pinker, 1989).

By storing images in visual memory, the visual system can have access to metric information about objects not available from the representations posited by most structural description theories. For example, imagine trying to identify specific models of cars. All of these cars are likely to have the same parts (wheels, body, windows, doors). For most cars, the parts are likely to be related in about the same way (the wheels are under the body of the car; the windows are set into the doors). What differs is metric information about the cars. A Volkswagen Beetle can be distinguished from a Honda Civic because of differences in the curvature of the roof, not because of the presence of specific parts or even qualitative differences in size. Further, as discussed earlier, motor movements require more specific information about the distances in the visual world than is available from a structural description.

Ullman proposed that both object-centered representations (like structural descriptions) and viewer-centered representations are used by the visual system to mediate object recognition. On this view, a combination of the image alignment process and a structural description process may provide a robust mechanism for visual object recognition. A combination of approaches to representation may be more powerful than any single representation-process pair. In general, multiple complementary mechanisms may work to solve difficult cognitive problems. This proposal for redundancy is not a cop-out on the part of researchers who cannot find the "right" answer; as I discuss in chapter 10, this redundancy is fundamental to thinking about hard cognitive problems. Different kinds of representations have different strengths and weaknesses, and a combination of representational approaches is the only way to assure that a system provides a robust solution to the problems it is designed to answer.

Causal Information in Visual Object Representations

The previous two sections focused primarily on visual representations used for object recognition. These representations make an assumption that is easy to miss: that the point of visual representation is to store information about what the world outside looks like. There must be explicit representations of properties like edges, boundaries, or relations between parts of objects. This assumption seems plausible enough, although it is not necessary. Gibson (1950, 1986) argued that enduring representations of the properties of images in the visual world are not needed. Instead, he argued that people perceive aspects of the world in terms of their *affordances*. On his view, the goal of perception is to provide functional information about objects in the world such as whether things can be grasped, picked up, or walked around. (I discuss Gibson's views about perception further in chap. 10.)

Visual representations may involve determining properties beyond the sizes and shapes of objects or their parts. One interesting theory of this type was developed by Leyton (1992), who argued that the purpose of vision is to extract causal information from the environment. He argued that symmetry in the world is a sign of the absence of causality and that asymmetries in the world reflect past causal forces. A simple example of this causal view is shown in Figure 6.9. At the right is a square. A square is symmetric in a variety of ways: All the sides are the same length, and all the angles are equal. A rectangle, like the one just to the left of the square, has two sides that are longer than the other two. Leyton suggested that the visual system interprets the longer sides as having been expanded by some force. Similarly, a parallelogram has angles that are not equal. Leyton argued that these can be interpreted as coming from a rectangle that has been sheared. Finally, the tilted parallelogram at the far left in Figure 6.9 has angles that diverge from the vertical and horizontal planes that help define the visual field. Leyton argued that this tilted parallelogram is interpreted as having been rotated by a force. On this view of vision, visual representation is not meant for representing perceptual properties of the visual world but rather for representing causal forces in the world.

Leyton presented a detailed grammar of the forces likely to have acted on objects to create shapes. For example, a protrusion in a circle, like that shown in Figure 6.10A, can be detected as a set of changes in the curvature of the object. This protrusion can be interpreted as an inner force that has pushed outward. In contrast, an indentation in a perimeter can be interpreted as a resistance from the outside. In Figure 6.10B, the indentation in the center is viewed as the product of a resisting force pushing inward. The protrusions on either side of the indentation show evidence of forces pushing outward on either side of the resistance. For example, if one sees a dented car, then, just as in Figure 6.10B, one may view it as the product of a force pushing inward. Attention is drawn to this asymmetry because it is the locus of causal information in the environment.

The detection of axes of symmetry in objects occurs broadly in vision but can also take place in object recognition. Leyton suggested that the determination of axes of symmetry in complex objects in combination with smoothing of small local perturbations on the surface of objects can lead to a representation that contains generalized cones like those suggested by Marr and Biederman. On Leyton's view, these generalized cones are

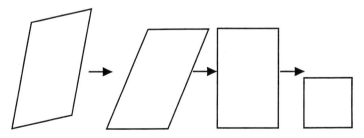

FIG. 6.9. Causal transformations of a rotated parallelogram derived from asymmetries like those discussed by Leyton (1992).

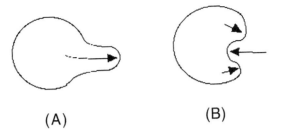

FIG. 6.10. A: Circle with a protrusion; B: Circle with an indentation.

used because they are easily derived from the detection of axes of symmetry and not because of the presence of nonaccidental properties or because cylinders are useful approximations of object shapes that make good primitives. Finally, the detection and explanation of asymmetries can occur for objects without good "parts," objects that Ullman (1996) suggested may not be amenable to representation by structured visual representations.

An interesting aspect of Leyton's theory is the recognition that visual perception itself requires the detection of asymmetries in the environment, although in this case the asymmetries are in the environment of light. If a steady uniform beam of light is shined at the eye, there is nothing to see. Only when light bouncing off surfaces causes asymmetries in the pattern of light that hits the eye is there anything to detect. Color involves the asymmetric absorption of some wavelengths of light rather than others. Rotation of an object in space leads to the compression of an image selectively along the dimension of rotation. Uniform fields that recede into space lead to increases in the density of points. In all these ways, the visual system uses asymmetries in the environment as cues to important aspects of the visual world. According to this view, asymmetries in visual representation are marked as elements to be explained in the process of comprehending a visual scene.

It is probably going to far too assume that the only important thing in visual representation is information about causal forces in the world. One important aspect of vision is that it provides information about the world in the absence of a specific goal for how the information is used. People may want to navigate in the world or to identify objects or to ponder the aesthetic value of a pattern. The visual system provides information suitable for all these tasks. In contrast, any functional approach, whether based on affordances or on the extraction of causal information, assumes a set of goals that the organism may have relative to the information. Any information not relevant to these goals is unavailable. Although it is probably helpful to get causal information about forces in the world, it cannot be the only information yielded by the perceptual system.

STRUCTURE IN MENTAL IMAGERY AND MENTAL MODELS

One of the fiercest battles about representation in cognitive science was fought over mental imagery. Just to ground the phenomenon of interest, answer the following three questions.

Who was president of the United States during the Civil War? (6.1)

How many windows were in the front face of the house you lived in when you were 10 years old? (6.2)

Which is higher, the top of a collie's head or the bottom of a horse's tail? (6.3)

All three questions seem answerable, but Question 1 is qualitatively different from the other two. Answering "Abraham Lincoln" requires accessing a stored fact that one was likely to have been told (perhaps many times). In contrast, answering Questions 2 and 3 probably does not involve accessing stored answers. One may never have pondered these questions before. Many who answer these questions report using mental imagery. For Question 2, they may form a mental image of the house they lived in at the age of 10 and then count the windows in the image, or they may take a mental tour of the house and count the windows in each room. For Question 3, people often imagine a collie and a horse standing side by side and compare the height of the top of the dog's head to the height of the bottom of the horse's tail.

This self-report of the utility of mental imagery has spurred numerous investigations of people's ability to use and manipulate mental images. As discussed in chapter 2, early researchers of imagery examined whether people can carry out the same transformations on mental images as they can on real images, such as rotating or stretching them. Shepard, Metzler, and Cooper (Cooper, 1975; Metzler & Shepard, 1974; Shepard & Cooper, 1982) presented subjects with pairs of two- and three-dimensional objects and asked them to make same–different judgments. On some same trials, identical objects were rotated slightly either in the plane of the image or in depth. The time to respond to these items was linearly related to the difference in orientation. Regression lines fitted to these data yielded a slope of about 2 milliseconds per degree of rotation. The data suggested that people carry out these same–different judgments by mentally rotating the objects to a common orientation before comparing them.

In another classic set of studies, Kosslyn, Ball, and Reiser (1978) had people learn a map of a fictitious island. After learning this map, the investigators asked people to imagine the map and to travel from one landmark to another. Scanning times for this mental map were longer for objects far apart on the map than for objects near together, a result suggesting that mental scanning involves traversing the region between landmarks. Zooming in on the map so that its mental image was large yielded longer scanning times than did zooming out on the map so that its mental image was small. These data suggest that mental images are like real images in many ways.

The debate that raged in cognitive science involved determining in what way a mental image resembled a real image. On one side, there was ample evidence that mental images could be transformed like real images and that they contained some amount of metric information (that is, information about the distances between points in the image). On the other side was the problem that if a mental image was simply a copy of a real image, there would need to be some process that could "see" the mental image and process it. Otherwise, there is a danger of an infinite regress of images: There would have to be a homunculus looking at the internal image, and the homunculus would have an image in his or her head, and there would be a homunculus to read that image, and so on. Furthermore, not all tasks that can be done with real images can also be done with mental images. For example, it is not possible to count the stripes on a mental image of a tiger, even though the stripes on a real image can be counted (Pylyshyn, 1981).

Proposals for the representations used in mental imagery have begun to resemble proposals for the representations of visual objects (Hinton, 1979; Kosslyn, 1994; Tye, 1991). Indeed, Kosslyn (1994) suggested that the visual system used mental images to assist in object recognition. For example, an activated mental image can help fill in obscured details from the visual world. On this view, it should be no surprise that mental images use the same kinds of representations as do visual object representations. Kosslyn further pointed out that one reason why people may not be able to carry out all the same operations on mental images that they can on visual images is that some operations on real images require multiple fixations. Multiple fixations are not possible on mental images, because the mental image is processed in visual buffers that are used to facilitate the integration of visual information from different fixations. Counting the stripes on a tiger requires scanning across the tiger, making a number of successive eye fixations, and counting the stripes along the way. The mental image cannot be similarly scanned, because the image is processed in areas of cortex far down the line from the retina.

In addition to arguments that mental images can play a role in object recognition, there are also demonstrations of imagery phenomena compatible with the presence of structure in mental imagery. Hinton (1979) produced a compelling example: He asked people to hold a finger about 1 foot off the surface of a table and then to imagine a cube with one corner touching the finger and the diagonally opposite corner touching the table at the point of the table directly below the finger in the air. The imagined cube should appear to be standing on its corner. Then Hinton asked people to point to the other corners of the cube. Whoever is unfamiliar with this example should try to accomplish it.

It is quite difficult to do this task correctly. A picture of a wire-frame cube standing on its edge is shown in Figure 6.11A. Many people point to only four corners in the air, even though there are six more corners of the cube (in addition to the ones touching the table and the finger). People often put these four corners on the same plane arranged in a square. As shown in Figure 6.11A, the remaining six corners are not in the same plane, but are arranged in a shape like a crown. Hinton suggested that people have difficulty with this task because of the way their representations of the cube are structured. The default structure is as a pair of squares separated by edges. Hinton repeated the cube task by asking people to imagine a cube on a table in front of them with one face pointing at them. Then they were to imagine tilting the cube away from them so that it rested on its back edge, with the diagonal edge vertically above it (as in Figure 6.11B). When asked to point to the corners of the cube in this task, people had no difficulty. This

(A)

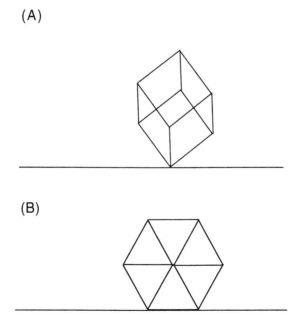

(B)

FIG. 6.11. A: Cube resting on one point with the diagonal point directly above it; B: Cube resting on one edge.

finding is compatible with the default structure. A second possible representation that people can generate is as two tripods extending from opposite corners, where each tripod is rotated by 60 degrees, and the alternating legs of the two tripods are connected to form the remaining edges of the cube. This structure requires keeping track of more edges than does the double square representation and hence is more difficult to process. Of central importance for this discussion is simply that mental images do appear to have structure and that different ways of structuring an image can change the relative ease of processing the image.

As previously discussed, researchers have suggested that visual object representations contain information about relations among parts as well as metric data that encode specific information about distance and geometric properties. Likewise, there is some evidence that mental images have information about both structural and metric properties. If mental images had information only about parts and relations among parts, it would be very difficult to form a mental image and then find emergent properties of the image. In contrast to this prediction, Finke, Pinker, and Farah (1989) gave people simple descriptions such as this:

> Imagine a capital letter H. Rotate the figure 90 degrees to the right. Now place a triangle at the top, with its base equal in width to that of the figure. What is it? (6.4)

With descriptions of this type, on nearly 50% of trials on which they were able to do the correct transformation, people interpreted this item as a tree. These identifications required a different segmentation of the object into parts than was given in the initial description. Thus, people's ability to interpret these mental images as pictures suggests that some amount of metric information was also incorporated into the images.

It is unclear how visual representations and mental images preserve metric information. One possibility is that images involve some kind of array representation, in which the image is stored as a two-dimensional array of pixels with filled points distinguished from empty points (see the discussion of Knapp & Anderson's, 1984, model in chap. 2). Ullman's (1984, 1996) image alignment mechanism involves this kind of array representation. Kosslyn (1994), who also suggested that metric spatial relations are important to visual processing, was vague about the way metric information is represented.

The potential problem with array representations of metric information is that processes operating over them must be defined. An array does preserve geometric relations like angles between lines and contains more precise information about the relative location of elements in an image than is contained in general categorical relations like *beside* or *near*. Some process must actually calculate the angle between the lines or determine the relative distances between elements for an array representation to be useful.

Defining processes that operate successfully on arrays has proved difficult. One reason for this difficulty is that arrays are limited in their spatial resolution, and transformations of objects in arrays tend to lose information. The processes that transform images in an array have to reason about the behavior of each element (pixel) independently, rather than use a higher level description of the object being transformed. Figure 6.12 illustrates the problems with local transformations. In this figure, I rotated a square in a computer drawing package through 180 degrees in 12 unequal steps. The 90- and 180-degree rotations are marked on the figure. Each of these rotations is no longer a clear square; the lines become progressively more diffuse with successive rotations. To get a computer drawing package to make smooth rotations of figures requires a mathematical description of the object as a square rather than a pixel representation of it. Because of this difficulty in transforming images, it has been difficult to provide accounts of phenomena like mental rotation by using array representations.

One issue that I have ignored in this discussion is the status of the mental image itself. When many people have performed tasks that involve mental imagery, they have reported having a conscious experience similar to the experience of looking at objects in the world (although perhaps

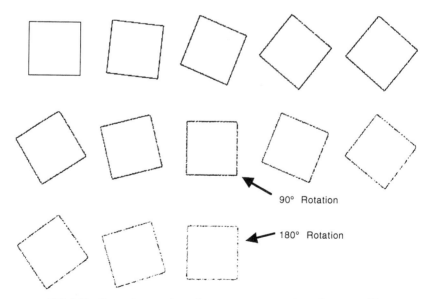

FIG. 6.12. Successive rotations of an array representation of a square. The 90° and 180° rotations of the square marked on the figure are no longer clear squares like the original.

not as rich). Some have argued that the conscious experience of the mental image is crucial to the use of imagery; others have argued that the experience occurs as a byproduct of the processing done while performing imagery tasks. Although this debate is interesting (and is captured in many references cited in this section), it is not relevant to the representational issues at hand. Mental images have representations, and these representations are quite similar to those required by the visual system for other tasks. This observation provides no way of resolving the importance of the conscious experience of mental images.

To summarize, mental images are not simply pictures in the head; they use the same kinds of representations that were proposed in discussions of visual objects. Mental imagery seems to rely on structural representations in which parts are bound together by relations. The particular structure used to represent an item determines what mental transforms are easy and difficult to do on the image. Despite the centrality of structured representations in imagery, some information about geometric properties, which allow the creative use of imagery to find emergent perceptual properties, must also be preserved.

VISUAL REPRESENTATION AND LANGUAGE

There is often a tension between perception and language. The common adage "A picture is worth a thousand words" attests to the difficulty of giving precise descriptions that capture the essential aspects of visual information in language. Nonetheless, there is an important relationship between visual representation and language. People can talk about space, and indeed notions of space seem to pervade language use. Language may direct attention to aspects of visual scenes that are likely to be important. In this section, I examine two places in which visual information and spatial language interact. First, I discuss the use of spatial language in general and then explore the use of spatial models to interpret discourse about scenes with a spatial extent.

Spatial Language

Although there are many ways to talk about space, an intriguing aspect of language is the system of spatial prepositions. Prepositions are a class of words that specify relations among elements in sentences. Most languages have only a small number of prepositions (particularly relative to the number of nouns and verbs), and so they are easy to study exhaustively. For this reason, authorities have intensively studied preposition systems of a variety of languages, and other work has contrasted the prepositions used across languages. In this section, I begin with a cursory overview of linguistic work on prepositions to motivate the discussion of spatial representation and then examine the relation between this work and proposals for visual representation.

An Overview of Prepositions. Many prepositions in language have a primary meaning that is spatial. The English prepositions *on, in, over, above, behind,* and *near* are primarily spatial terms, although they can be used in a variety of other circumstances as well (Lakoff, 1987; Lakoff & Johnson, 1980). Prepositions exist in all known human languages, and all languages have many prepositions that deal with space. Despite this similarity, prepositions in different languages treat space and objects in space differently. In this section, I examine a few general characteristics of spatial prepositions and their relation to perceptual representations.

Many researchers have pointed out that prepositions take an abstract functional view of space (Bowerman, 1989; Cienki, 1989; Herskovits, 1986; Landau & Jackendoff, 1993; Regier, 1996; Talmy, 1983; Vandeloise, 1991). First, spatial language involves spatial relations between elements. These elements are often objects (The airplane is *above* the house), well-defined parts of objects (He has a good head *on* his shoulders), or locations (Chicago is *near* Lake Michigan). Second, prepositions typically distinguish between their arguments. One, which I call the *landmark*, is typically more fixed in location or prominent than the other (which I call the *trajector*).[2] Third, only some aspects of objects and of space seem to matter for prepositions. Talmy (1983) pointed out that prepositions may provide information about the relative width of the dimensions of objects but not the specific shapes. For example, one can say:

John paddled *across* the lake. (6.5)

or

John walked *across* the tennis court. (6.6)

despite the fact that tennis courts are typically rectangular but lakes are not as regularly shaped. These sentences are better used, however, as descriptions of statements for situations like those in Figure 6.13A, in which the trajectory of motion traverses the shorter dimension of the landmark than for situations like the one in Figure 6.13B, in which the trajectory of motion traverses the longer dimension of the landmark. These cases are better described using prepositions like *up* or *down* as in:

---

[2]There are many possible ways to refer to these roles.

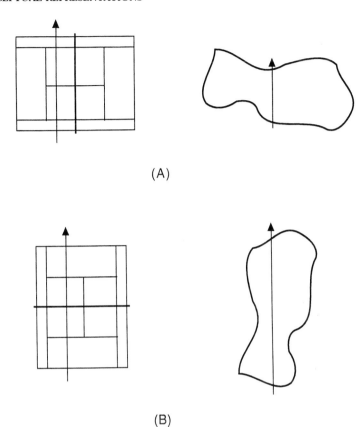

FIG. 6.13. (A) Good and (B) bad examples of movement *across* a surface.

John walked *up* and *down* the tennis court.   (6.7)

The shape of objects can be eliminated altogether for prepositions that treat one of the elements as a point. Herskovits (1986) suggested that the preposition *at* treats the landmark as a point. Large locations must be far away for this preposition to be used properly. While standing on a lake shore looking at a boat, one cannot say:

The boat is *at* the lake.   (6.8)

but one can use this sentence if he or she is in Manhattan and the boat is on a lake in upstate New York. In the latter case, the lake is far enough away to be treated as a point.

The preposition *at* has a number of other related uses as well (Herskovits, 1986). Not only does it suggest nearness to some point; it also often carries the assumption that the landmark is used for its intended function. Thus, the sentence:

> Betsy is *at* her desk.   (6.9)

implies that Betsy is working at her desk. The sentence:

> Ed is *at* the store.   (6.10)

carries with it more of a sense that Ed is shopping than does the related:

> Ed is *in* the store.   (6.11)

These examples demonstrate that prepositions carry with them information about both spatial relations associated with objects and the way that actors interact with objects.

Two other aspects of prepositions are important for this discussion. First, as the discussions of *across* and *at* should make clear, prepositions can refer either to trajectories or to static relations between elements. Second, there are many ways of conceptualizing spatial relations, and existing languages use different ways. A number of linguists have pointed out that a speaker of English located at the point of the observer in Figure 6.14 would say:

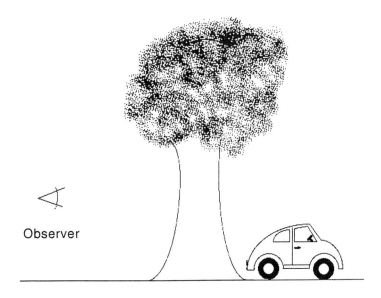

FIG. 6.14. Demonstration of the deictic use of the English preposition *behind*.

The car is *behind* the tree.   (6.12)

whereas a speaker of the African language Hausa would use the equivalent preposition for "in front of" (Vandeloise, 1991). English and Hausa differ in what is considered to be the front of an object in relation to a *deictic center* (where a deictic center is a location, like the current position of the speaker, which must be fixed before the rest of the relation can be interpreted).[3] In English, the front of an object is the one facing the deictic center, whereas in Hausa, the front of an object is the face oriented in the same direction as the object at the deictic center. Some of these aspects of preposition use are likely to reflect the representations underlying prepositions; others may reflect convention in a particular language (Herskovits, 1986; Regier, 1996).

Representation of Spatial Information in Spatial Language. There are two varieties of proposals for the representations of prepositions: logic based and perception based. Logic-based repare exemplified by the work of Miller and Johnson-Laird (1976). In their analysis of the relation between language and perception, they provided predicate calculus representations like those discussed in chapter 5. These authors stated that the preposition *at* can be represented by the general schema:

at $(?x, ?y)$ holds if INCLUDES $[?x, \text{REGION} (?y)]$.   (6.13)

That is, the preposition *at* should be used if the object bound to the variable x is included in some region defined by the variable y. This representation does seem to capture the general structure of statements about space for which *at* is used. The use of logic as a representation for prepositions has the property of providing a rigorous definition for each preposition.

The particular definition of *at* presented by Miller and Johnson-Laird has some flaws. For example, it does not help to distinguish why the sentence:

Lucas is *at* the garden.   (6.14)

does not sound grammatical, but if it is stipulated that Lucas is watching a basketball game at Madison Square Garden, then the sentence:

---

[3]The linguistic notion of *deixis* involves pointing with words (E. V. Clark, 1979). For example, the deictic term *there* specifies a point in space relative to the speaker. The deictic center is the location from which the pointing takes place. This point is typically the location of the speaker.

Lucas is *at* the Garden.   (6.15)

is perfectly appropriate. As discussed previously, Herskovits (1986) suggested that *at* treats the landmark as a point, although the landmark is typically a region. A simple predicate calculus description does not capture this geometry fully and does not account for the observation that *at* implies that an object is being used for its intended purpose as in Example 6.9.

Some of these problems can be circumvented by additional work on the representations. For example, additional senses of *at* can make it clear that, as discussed earlier, *at* often refers to objects used for their intended purpose. Further, Miller and Johnson-Laird's representations for prepositions were developed primarily through an analysis of English prepositions. Extensive analysis of prepositions cross-linguistically has suggested some commonalities in the distinctions made by prepositions across languages, and the primitive relations used to describe prepositions should probably be designed to account for both commonalities and differences in prepositions across languages (Cienki, 1989; Regier, 1996; Vandeloise, 1991).

An alternative to predicate calculus representations like those developed by Miller and Johnson-Laird has focused on the relationship between spatial language and perceptual representations. Landau and Jackendoff (1993; Jackendoff, 1987) stated that there are similarities in the abstractions made by prepositions and the visual representations proposed by Marr (1982). As already discussed, the 3D model representation proposed by Marr assumes that object representations are hierarchically organized structures in which the fine details of object shapes are abstracted to generalized cylinders with relations between cylinders. Jackendoff (1987) observed that, just like Marr's 3D models, prepositions highlight important intrinsic axes of objects. Linguists have pointed out that crabs are said to walk "sideways," because their main axis of symmetry defines their front and back and their direction of motion is perpendicular to this axis of symmetry. Thus, a crab would not walk into an object placed *in front of* it.

Further, Landau and Jackendoff (1993) noted that prepositions abstract across objects in a manner similar to that proposed in models of visual representation. Just as proposals like those of Marr and Biederman assumed that generalized cones can describe real objects despite fine variations in their surface detail, so too do prepositions abstract away from the fine detail of objects. For example, one can say:

The Palisades Interstate Parkway runs *along* the Palisades.   (6.16)

even though the road near the cliffs along the Hudson River is straight and the cliffs are not. The preposition can be used because the border between the Palisades and the Hudson River can be conceptualized as a straight axis that abstracts across the local surface variations. Indeed, as discussed in the previous section, beyond some information about the relative width of objects (which helps determine its axes), very little shape information is incorporated into prepositions at all. Landau and Jackendoff suggested that this similarity between observations about spatial prepositions and proposals for visual representations is not accidental. Visual representations constrain the information supplied to prepositions. This use of visual representation helps ground the meanings of the prepositions.

The notion that visual representation can constrain the acquisition of prepositions was examined in a computational model that Regier (1996) developed. This model uses a technique called *constrained connectionism*, in which the input is developed by making assumptions consistent with what is known about visual representations. This input is then fed to a standard connectionist network (like those described in chap. 2), and a set of prepositions is learned. The model was explicitly designed to learn prepositions from a number of different languages, to see whether the assumptions about visual representation could provide constraints on the kinds of prepositions that do and do not appear in different languages.

The architecture of the model is shown in Figure 6.15. As shown in the diagram, the input to the model consists of simplified movies of motions between objects. The movies each have two objects in them, which are labeled *trajector* (TR) and *landmark* (LM). The model then performs a perceptual analysis of the movie to provide an assessment of the properties of the current movie (labeled *Current* in the figure). This current state is further analyzed to find both the *Source* and the *Path* of the motion. This information is used as input to a set of trainable connection weights that learn how the perceptual analysis is related to the prepositions in the language being learned.

The model assumes that all information needed to learn the spatial prepositions of a language can be determined from a perceptual analysis of the scenes of the movie. This analysis finds the outer boundaries of the trajector and landmark and then determines the angle between them. In addition, for each frame of the movie, the model determines whether any part of the object is inside the landmark (and if so, how much). The output of this visual processor consists of information about the relative center of mass of the trajector and landmarks, the relative position of trajector and landmark in the final scene, the extent of the trajector's and landmark's overlap (if any), and information about whether the trajector passes through the area of the landmark at any point during the movie.[4]

---

[4]The connections in the modules that perform this perceptual analysis are all trainable, so that the model can optimize its focus on perceptual properties for the language it is learning.

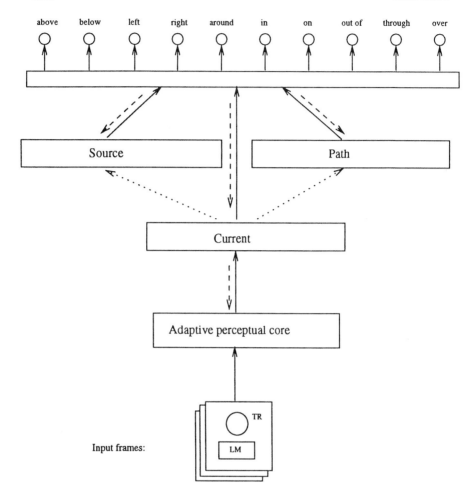

FIG. 6.15. Architecture of Regier's constrained connectionist model of preposition learning. From T. Regier (1997). Copyright © 1997 by Academic Press. Reprinted with permission.

The data, which constitute the basis of the spatial representation of prepositions, are then fed to a set of trainable connection weights that learn to map these features of the movie onto the prepositions of the language that the model is being taught. Different runs of the model have been taught prepositions from English, Russian, German, Japanese, and Mixtec, each of whose prepositions break the world up in different ways. The model is capable of learning the distinctions made by these languages.

Regier's model assumes that a few key elements of spatial information are critical for understanding most prepositions. The relative center of mass of the objects is particularly important: It provides information about the static location of pairs of objects. The use of center of mass reflects the fact that prepositions are only very generally influenced by object shape. In particular, the center of mass of an object is in the center if the object is symmetric, but asymmetries in the object pull the center of mass toward an edge of the object and provide rudimentary information about its shape. The model also uses a category representation of whether the objects come in contact or overlap. This information too is important, because a preposition like *above* can apply only to objects that are not touching. In addition, categorical information about whether one object is wholly contained by another is important. For example, the preposition *inside* requires that one object be completely in the other. Interestingly, the preposition *in* does not have the same requirement: One can say:

The apple is in the bowl.   (6.17)

even if it is the topmost apple in a large pile that is supported by a bowl. In this case, the enclosing surface of the bowl is treated as if it rises up to include the whole pile. In sum, of the large amount of information that could have been used as the basis of preposition representations, Regier's model assumes that only a small subset of it is actually incorporated into the visual basis of prepositions.

An interesting aspect of Regier's model is the way it deals with the absence of negative evidence in language learning. Many theorists have pointed out that language learning is particularly difficult, because children receive only positive instances of sentences and rarely get negative feedback (see Pinker, 1991, for an extended discussion of this issue). Regier, having taken a cue from researchers who suggested that children treat words as mutually exclusive, assumed that a positive instance of one preposition is implicit negative evidence for all other prepositions (E. V. Clark, 1987; E. M. Markman & Wachtel, 1988). Words are not truly mutually exclusive, however. For instance, the prepositions *above* and *over* can be used interchangeably in some circumstances. Thus, the negative evidence provided by the use of another preposition to describe a scene is weaker than is the positive evidence provided by the use of the preposition to describe it. This assumption allows the network to learn a variety of prepositions without receiving any negative instances (i.e., without seeing an instance labeled as "not *over*"). In this way, the model provides an implementation of E. V. Clark's (1979) principle of contrast described in chapter 3.

This model provides an interesting first step toward understanding how people learn spatial prepositions, although several issues still remain to be explored. For example, the model currently is told which object is the landmark and which is the trajector, but the use of spatial language may highlight the spatial relations between objects, and people may come to view objects as trajectors and landmarks because of the way they use them in language. This model cannot capture other aspects of prepositions like the use of *at* to refer to objects being used for their intended function. These problems should be viewed as an incompleteness in this approach rather than as a flaw, because this model is still in the process of being developed. For example, the meaning of *at* that implies intended function may be achieved by giving this model inputs from other sources.

Summary. Prepositions describe spatial relations between objects in the world and in this way bear a resemblance to structured representations of visual objects, which also contain information about spatial relations. Furthermore, like visual representations, prepositions seem to be sensitive to major axes of the objects involved in the preposition, but insensitive to local variations in the contour and texture of objects. These parallels have led some investigators to speculate that the structure of prepositions in language is guided by the structure of visual representations. The link between spatial prepositions and visual representations seems reasonable, although it is clear that other information about objects is also included in prepositions, like their functions and relative salience in the world.

If visual representations form the basis of spatial language and prepositions, this possibility may have an important impact on people's ability to use language to talk about abstract properties as well. Researchers like Lakoff and Gibbs and their colleagues have proposed that the representation of many abstract concepts, such as emotion and valence, is structured by perceptual experiences (Gibbs, 1994; Lakoff, 1987; Lakoff & Johnson, 1980). Lakoff and Johnson (1980) provided many examples of how the goodness of things in the world is mapped to their spatial position with the general metaphor GOOD is UP such as:

Paul was in high spirits this morning. (6.18)

or

Jack was really down about his test scores. (6.19)

To the extent that spatial language is rooted in perceptual representations, this phenomenon may suggest how representations of abstract concepts are grounded in perceptual experience. (I discuss the use of concrete domains as metaphors for abstract concepts again in chap. 8.)

Representations of Spatial Configurations

Prepositions are not the only way that language describes space: People also give and receive descriptions of spatial configurations. Although some workers have explored how people coordinate their descriptions of space (e.g., Schober, 1993, 1995), in this section I focus on proposals for the representation of spatial configurations that have been described.

One proposal for the way that people understand descriptions of spatial situations is through the construction of spatial mental models (Mani & Johnson-Laird, 1982).[5] For example, if I describe a configuration of tableware on a table, I may say:

The fork is to the left of the plate.
The dessert spoon is behind the plate.
The glass is behind the dessert spoon. (6.20)

A person reading this description might create a mental model of the configuration with this structure:

$$G$$
$$D$$
$$F \quad P,$$ (6.21)

where F is the fork, P is the plate, D is the dessert spoon, and G is the glass. Having such a mental model allows the inference of properties that were not stated directly in the description, such as: The glass is behind the plate.

A spatial mental model is an abstract spatial description of a set of objects. The objects themselves are only given placeholders. The plate is not assumed to be round or breakable; it is simply an object that occupies a point in space. Space is assumed to be represented in an array that preserves simple spatial relations between objects. Each model that is constructed places the objects at some position in space, but more than one model may be consistent with a given description. For example, with the description:

The fork is to the left of the plate.
The dessert spoon is behind the plate.
The glass is behind the plate. (6.22)

the model in Example 6.21 can be constructed, but so can the following model:

---

[5]I thank Philip Johnson-Laird for providing me a copy of his computer program space-4, which constructs spatial mental models from text descriptions.

> *D*
> *G*
> *F   P.*   (6.23)

Without further disambiguating information, one cannot know which model is most appropriate.

These spatial models may be important for remembering simple configurations for short periods. For example, a person remembering where the car is parked when going to a shopping mall may create a simple mental model with a few landmarks and the spatial relations between them. These spatial models can also be helpful for understanding complex discourse involving spatial relations (Glenberg & Kruley, 1992; Glenberg, Kruley, & Langston, 1994). For example, in a story, if an actor puts down an object and moves to a new location, one can infer that the actor is no longer near the object. In practice, these mental models require effort to construct. There is some evidence that people reading text build models only when they are necessary for understanding a passage (McKoon & Ratcliff, 1992), but they can use information about spatial relationships to understand discourse.

Research on the relationship between spatial models and language has also focused on complex scenes and maps (Franklin, Tversky, & Coon, 1992; Taylor & Tversky, 1992, 1996). In one study, Taylor and Tversky (1992, 1996) asked people to describe areas depicted in maps. They found that people used both *survey* and *route* descriptions of the scenes. Objects were discussed in survey descriptions with spatial relations between objects and between an extrinsic source of reference (e.g., using direction terms like north, south, east, west). In contrast, route descriptions referred to spatial locations of objects relative to a moving frame of reference, which was generally assumed to be the speaker. Route descriptions were most common when maps had a single route and landmarks in the map were approximately the same size. Survey descriptions were most common when maps had multiple paths and there were landmarks of varying sizes. Survey descriptions were more common when describing maps than when describing areas that people had learned about by navigating through them.

The studies of spatial descriptions highlighted two interesting facets of spatial representation. First, the locations of objects are almost always referred to relationally. In a survey description, the relations are relative to some external frame of reference (like the cardinal directions) or to particular other objects in the scene. For example, one says:

> The car is *at the front of* the church.   (6.24)

Here the church serves as the frame of reference. In route descriptions, relations also dominate, but they are given in terms of the individual following the route, as in:

When you get to the church, the car will be *in front of* you. (6.25)

In 6.24, the basis of the relation is the speaker, who is serving as a deictic center. Thus, like prepositions, descriptions of spatial scenes seem to abstract away from particular metric aspects of spatial scenes.

Perceptual relations are important for two reasons. First, relations are likely to hold between a pair of objects for a wide range of views, whereas metric information changes as soon as any object being described moves. Second, the determination of precise metric information is difficult: Calculating the distance between two objects being observed requires knowing the precise distance from the observer to them as well as the precise distance between them in the image. Thus, spatial relations provide important information about a pair of objects without requiring extensive calculations of metric information.

As a second facet of spatial representation, people give descriptions of visual scenes relative to their own visual experience in acquiring the scenes. Thus, as Taylor and Tversky (1996) found, survey descriptions were more common with maps, and route descriptions were more common with areas that the describer had learned by navigation. People's visual experience has an important impact on the way they structure their descriptions of spatial scenes. Being presented with an overview of a spatial layout promotes a conceptualization in terms of an external frame of reference, whereas experiencing the spatial layout by traversing through it promotes a conceptualization in terms of routes. This pattern is consistent with observations that people often learn routes between landmarks in new areas they must navigate before learning a global spatial layout.

SUMMARY

This survey suggests that relations are important in perceptual representations and spatial language. There is evidence that people use object-centered representations containing spatial relations among parts. The same structured representations that are important for vision also seem to be important for visual imagery, a finding that may explain some limitations of imagery ability. Finally, relations are also important for spatial language. Spatial prepositions, perhaps the most basic form of spatial language, involve relations between generalized objects and focus on relations between objects or between objects and paths. Complex spatial language also makes use of structured representations. People can represent the relative spatial locations of objects described in discourse. This ability may involve the construction of spatial mental models of scenes. The construction of these mental models may also be informed by people's specific visual experiences.

Chapter 7

Structured Concept Representations

OBJECTS AND EVENTS

The division in human concepts between objects and events is very obvious. Events and objects are different ontological kinds. Objects have a prominent spatial extent: They generally do not change rapidly over time but instead are enduring aspects of the physical landscape. They may undergo developmental changes (as when children grow up), but these changes operate slowly. Even concepts with aspects that change rapidly, like a flame, tend to refer to stable aspects of an object like its general color, shape, and size rather than to individual tongues of flame that change rapidly. In contrast, events have a prominent temporal extent: They track the movements and interactions of different objects over some specified time. For example, the event of going on a date involves relationships between two people and a location, as well as between other objects like a means of transportation.

One manifestation of the distinction between objects and events is the division between nouns and verbs in language. Nouns usually refer to objects (both concrete and abstract), and verbs usually refer to events (and states and actions). This linguistic division is not absolute: There are nouns for events like *football game* or *TV show*, and there are verbs that refer to states like *exists*. Nevertheless, the distinction between nouns and verbs does mirror the distinction between objects and events.

The prototypical object is perceptual (as discussed in chap. 6), and the perceptual system is designed to find objects in the world and to create representations of them (Spelke, 1990). The object representations discussed in chapter 6 had a number of characteristics in common. They typically consisted of a collection of parts (e.g., generalized cylinders or generalized cones) and spatial relations among them. The object representations were largely self-contained and did not refer to representations of other objects. Instead, there were many internal relational connections among parts and perhaps a hierarchically organized set of more specific representations nested in more abstract ones. Gentner (1981a) referred to the relative degree of internal relational connection among components of a representation versus the degree of external relational connection to components outside the representation as *relational density*. She suggested that object concepts have a high relational density because most of their relations involve connections among parts in the representation.

In contrast to objects, events seem to involve connections external to the event itself. In fact, an event implies a set of relations that hold among various objects. Consider the event of going to the movies on a date. When I was in high school, the typical movie date involved me, my big green car, a date (otherwise, the event was going to the movies with a pack of rowdy friends), and a movie. I would *drive* my big green car to my date's house to pick her up. The two of us would *drive* to the movie theater. Together, we would *watch* a movie. An event representation seems to differ critically from an object representation in that it relates a set of objects together. In contrast, my representation of my big green car does not consist of many relations between the car and other objects or people but instead involves internal relations between parts and descriptive attributes that help to identify and use it. For example, my car was green, and it had wheels, an engine, and seats as parts. In Gentner's (1981a) terminology, events have a low relational density because there are more relational connections from the event to elements external to it than there are connections between elements within the event itself. This idea of relational density becomes important later in this chapter when I talk about verbs and their connection to event representations.

I begin with a brief discussion of object concepts building on the discussion of perceptual representations in chapter 6. The bulk of this chapter focuses on event representations. First, I introduce the important representational constructs of *scripts* and *schemas*. Then, I present some advances on the basic structure of scripts. Finally, I focus on the parallel between object concepts and nouns and between event concepts and verbs and discuss some differences between nouns and verbs.

OBJECT CONCEPTS

I take a broad notion of object. An object is an enduring entity in the represented world. Objects can be perceptual entities or abstract concepts. The basis for many object concepts is a perceptual representation. Concrete object concepts often have a perceptual representation (of the type discussed in chap. 6) that describes the relative spatial relations among the parts of objects and may also contain information about other perceptual features like color and texture.

Paradoxically, even abstract concepts may have some perceptual representation. Cognitive linguists (e.g., Gibbs, 1994; Lakoff, 1987; Lakoff & Johnson, 1980) have suggested that abstract concepts like anger can be conceptualized through concrete situations such as heated liquid in a container. On this view, phrases like:

He was boiling mad.   (7.1)

or:

He blew his stack.   (7.2)

communicate the emotion of anger in terms of a physical process. According to cognitive linguists, people understand abstract domains (like emotions) only by casting them in terms of concrete situations. This position is rather extreme; there may be other avenues for understanding abstract concepts. Indeed, Murphy (1996) argued that there must be other ways to understand abstract concepts because the understanding of physical systems like heated fluid in a container develops late whereas children have some comprehension of anger relatively early in life. Nonetheless, even if there are multiple routes to understanding abstract concepts, metaphoric extensions of concrete situations to abstract concepts may still be an important way of representing the latter. (I return to this issue in chap. 8.)

Although perceptual information is an important part of object concepts, there must also be conceptual knowledge. For example, in addition to objects' appearance, people know about their functions. They can identify something as a car or even as my big green car but also know that cars can be driven by people, that they have internal combustion engines, and that they require gasoline to operate.

The basis of conceptual information is clearly different from that of perceptual information. Perceptual information comes from sensory experience whereas conceptual knowledge comes from interacting with objects and from cultural transmission. People may discover facts about objects while interacting with them, or others may tell them particular features about the objects. Despite this difference in source, both perceptual and conceptual information can be structured in the same way. In particular, both can consist of attributes and relations among elements in a representation.

The coexistence of perceptual and conceptual information in object concepts is apparent in the structure of people's categories. In chapter 4, I discussed semantic networks and pointed out that the class-inclusion relation ISA is an important organizing force in concept representations. For example, the lime green 1972 Oldsmobile Cutlass Supreme that I had in high school was a coupe; a coupe is a car, and a car is a vehicle. The car itself can be classified properly in any of these categories (e.g., coupe, car, or vehicle). One reason for these nested categories at different levels of abstraction is that each highlights different features. The expression *lime green 1972 Oldsmobile Cutlass Supreme* highlights perceptual features including the car's color and shape, although conceptual features like *gas guzzling* are also important. A more abstract classification, like *car*, highlights general perceptual features such as a shape common to most cars as well as properties such as doors, wheels, and windows (B. Tversky & Hemenway, 1984). This level of abstraction also highlights conceptual information such as the use of a car to drive or the fact that cars need gasoline to operate. Finally, an even more abstract classification such as *vehicle* involves general features like function (Murphy & Wisniewski, 1989; Rosch, Mervis, Gray, Johnson, & Boyes-Braem, 1976). Because each of these categories highlights different features, using different levels of abstraction when talking about categories can allow people to communicate different things about the same objects (Brown, 1958). All levels of abstraction, however, incorporate a mix of perceptual and conceptual information.

Although different ways of classifying the same object can highlight different types of information about it, the same kind of structured representations can encode both perceptual and conceptual information. According to the alignment process for comparing structured representations discussed in chapter 5, comparisons yield commonalities and two kinds of differences: *alignable differences*, which are mismatching representational elements placed in correspondence on the basis of commonalities, and *nonalignable differences*, which are elements in one representation that have no correspondence at all to the other.

One set of studies examined comparisons of objects at different levels of abstraction (Markman & Wisniewski, 1997). People listed the commonalities and differences of pairs of very specific categories like *sports car* or *family car* (called *subordinate categories*), pairs of somewhat more abstract categories like *car* or *bus* (called *basic-level categories*; Rosch et al., 1976), and pairs of quite abstract categories like *vehicle* or *furniture* (called *superordinate categories*). Subjects found pairs of categories in a superordinate (such as *car* and *bus*, which are both *vehicles*) easy to compare, and they listed many commonalities and many alignable differences for these comparisons. In contrast, subjects found pairs of categories in different superordinates (such as *car* and *sofa*, members of the superordinates *vehicle* and *furniture*, respectively) difficult to compare, and they listed few commonalities or alignable differences for these comparisons. More important for the present discussion, the commonalities and differences that people listed were both perceptual and conceptual properties. People making comparisons of categories in a superordinate often talked about perceptual properties like parts (e.g., cars and buses both have wheels). They also described functional properties (e.g., cars and buses are both driven) as well as class-inclusion relations (e.g., cars and buses are both vehicles). This pattern of results suggests that concrete objects' representations are structured and also that the information in these structured representations is both conceptual and perceptual.[1]

To summarize, conceptual information appears to be structured similarly to perceptual information in object categories. The proposal that object representations are structured suggests that there are many internal relational connections in an object. These internal relational connections consist of perceptual as well as conceptual and functional relations. This dense internal relational structure gives coherence to object concepts by ensuring that the perceptual and conceptual aspects making up object concepts are strongly interrelated. Finally, because the same kind of representational structure describes both conceptual and perceptual aspects of objects, the same comparison process can determine perceptual and conceptual similarities among items.

EVENTS

As just discussed, object and event representations differ in their ontological status, but they also differ in their uses. People use object representations for identifying and using objects. I must recognize a car as a car and also recall why I want to use one and how I go about using it. In contrast, people use event representations for planning, prediction, and narrative comprehension.[2] In high school, my date representation allowed me to plan ahead to have enough money to pay for a movie or to go to

---

[1] There is also evidence that representations of abstract concepts are structured (Markman & Gentner, 1993a). In particular, commonality and difference listings done with pairs of similar abstract nouns yield many commonalities and alignable differences.

[2] Structured representations have been part of several different models of text comprehension (e.g., Kintsch & Van Dijk, 1978), but here I focus on the role of event representations in text comprehension.

a diner afterward. I could use this representation to predict whether the date was likely to end with a kiss or a friendly hug. Finally, if I read a story about two high school kids on a date and learn that they are at the movies, I can assume that one of them picked the other up and drove to the movies. I can assume this without being told, because this information is part of my event representation for a date. Because of the different uses of object and event representations, it is not surprising that they are also structured differently.

How exactly can event representations be structured? This question has been addressed by Schank and Abelson's (1977) classic work on scripts and by subsequent elaborations on this view. In the following sections, I describe scripts and some elaborations as well as the ways that these representations can be created and used. Finally, I discuss some limitations of scripts.

Scripts

A primary motivation for developing an elaborate system of event representations arises from the sparseness of narratives. For example, in many movies, a character enters a bar and orders a drink. In the next scene, the character is stumbling through the streets singing. The audience is expected to infer that the character entered the bar, had a number of drinks, and then left the bar and that the narrative has continued with the events occurring after the character left the bar. For that matter, the audience is expected to infer mundane things as well, such as that the character did not have to serve the drinks and that money was used to pay for the drinks. The audience need not see each drink the character takes; it is enough to see him (or her) staggering in the street to infer that the character had the drinks. The filmmaker relies on a shared script about sitting in a bar and drinking and expects the audience to recognize the appropriate script and to fill in the missing details. If there is an important deviation from the script, the filmmaker includes a scene depicting the deviation; otherwise, the audience may fill in the missing information incorrectly. For example, if the film is a comedy and the character stumbles drunkenly through town after one sip of a drink, the audience must understand that the character had only one drink or the humor is lost.

Schank and Abelson (1977) approached this problem by positing that people represent events with *scripts*. A mental script, like the script of a play, is composed of chains of scenes that determine what a set of actors does in a given situation. The events are temporally ordered and causally connected. That is, the script contains information about both the time sequence of events and also about the reasons that particular events are carried out. Thus, the script for "Getting drunk at a bar" may involve entering a bar, ordering a drink, consuming the drink, paying for the drink, repeating the ordering, consuming, and paying sequence until the primary actor is intoxicated, and then leaving the bar. The script also has a role for someone to serve the drinks as well as roles for other patrons at the bar. In addition to this temporal information, there is causal information, such as knowledge that alcoholic beverages cause intoxication but that a moderate to large number of drinks is required before the main actor shows signs of intoxication.

The sequence information is useful for filling in missing information during narrative comprehension. Seeing a character enter a bar and order a drink in a movie invokes the script for being in a bar. When the scene changes to the character stumbling in the street, the audience can infer that the character is drunk, and that the character had many drinks at the bar. Likewise, after reading:

> John walked into the bar and sat on a stool. He turned to the
> bartender and asked for a beer; then he turned to the man
> sitting next to him and began his tale.   (7.3)

we are not surprised by the presence of either the bartender or the other person sitting at the bar. Both are part of the script for going to a bar. Because many scripts are culturally shared, they can be invoked during narratives to limit what has to be said. A story about John getting drunk does not have to include each drink, because people know that the sequence of ordering, drinking, and paying is repeated. Nor need they figure out why John does not pour the drink for himself, because there is information in the script that someone does it for him.

Causal information is useful for helping to understand violations of a script. One knows that many drinks and some time are required for a person to get intoxicated, because a person must consume a certain amount of alcohol to get drunk, and it takes time for the alcohol to enter the bloodstream and affect behavior. If a character in a movie sips a drink and suddenly shows signs of drunken behavior, the audience detects a causal violation that (at least the first time) is likely to be seen as humorous. This causal information may also allow people to see permissible variations in a script. If one knows that a person must consume an alcoholic drink to get drunk, then free substitutions of any alcoholic beverage are allowed, but substitutions of nonalcoholic beverages are not permissible. The causal information is helpful because one need not store every possible drink in the script. Thus, a man who walks into a bar and drinks eight snifters of brandy in rapid succession may be doing something unfamiliar, but he is not violating the causal structure of the script as would a woman who enters a bar and rapidly drinks eight glasses of seltzer.

Schank and Abelson pointed out that there is not just one generic script for a situation, but rather many related scripts that describe similar events. For example, the script for getting drunk at a bar is related to the script for getting drunk at a fancy restaurant in that both require repeated actions of ordering and consuming an alcoholic beverage. The sequence of events differs subtly, however; the bar script requires paying for each drink as it is ordered, whereas the restaurant script allows all of the drinks to be paid for at the end. There is also a causal difference: Drinking to intoxication is accepted (and perhaps expected behavior) at many bars, but it is not accepted behavior at many restaurants. Thus, the reactions of other patrons to a drunk individual are expected to differ in the bar and restaurant versions of this "getting drunk" script. Because of such subtle differences, Schank and Abelson referred to separate *tracks* that handle frequently encountered variations of a script.

A key element of scripts is that they are related to an actor's goals. The causal information that links the actions in a script must refer to the goals of the actors. The bar requires patrons to pay for each drink as it arrives, because the bar is in the business of serving alcohol to make a profit and the owner must get paid to make a profit. The character who enters the bar to get drunk has the goal of being intoxicated and takes a series of actions to reach this goal. If someone tries to stop the person from drinking, the ensuing discussion is related to the attempted blockage of one actor's goal. Thus, unlike object representations, event representations are critically bound to the goals and motivations of the actors.

The importance of goals in scripts makes them particularly useful in planning. Someone with a familiar script as the basis for a plan can use the goal information to create new sequences of events when a sequence of events specified by a script cannot be carried out. Suppose John has just broken up with his sweetheart and wants to get drunk. He plans to take a bus to a nearby bar and drink beer until he is drunk. When he arrives at the bar, he finds that it has closed, but across the street he spots a restaurant that serves alcohol. When he goes there, he finds that it serves wine, but not beer. Because his aim is to drink an alcoholic beverage and wine contains alcohol, John can substitute wine for the beer in his initial plan. Thus, the causal information in John's script for getting drunk is critical for the successful completion of his plan. Even when many low-level actions cannot be carried out as planned, the overall goals can be satisfied by substituting other actions that achieve the same end.

Scripts are thus sequences of actions that contain information about the actors involved in an event, the typical sequence of actions in the event, and the goals of the various actors. Scripts can fill in missing information in narratives by assuming that the typical sequence of events was carried out without incident when a narrative moves from one scene to another. Scripts can also explain unanticipated events, either by determining that they satisfy an actor's goal in a different way or by highlighting that a particular actor's goal has not been satisfied. Finally, scripts can be used for planning by providing an accessible sequence of actions to be carried out; a script can also be adapted to changing circumstances by focusing on the goals to be satisfied by each action rather than on specific actions.

The initial formulation of scripts has been extremely influential in cognitive science. Scripts have been used to explain how people make action slips by suggesting that if a familiar script is activated, it may be carried out automatically, even if the actor wanted to perform a variation of the script (Heckhausen & Beckmann, 1990). For example, if Sally wanted to pick up milk on her way home, she might decide to stop at a convenience store that is along the route she takes to drive home. As she drives from her office to her house, she may become preoccupied with other thoughts and find herself pulling into her driveway without the milk, because her typical script (of driving straight home from work) was carried out to completion. This analysis assumes that deviating from a standard script requires cognitive effort, the source of which is that, whereas familiar scripts satisfy frequently activated goals, deviating from a script requires interpolating a new goal into the automatized sequence. Cognitive effort is needed to maintain this unfamiliar goal in working memory.

Scripts also seem to have a profound impact on people's memory for situations. The literature on this topic is too vast to summarize here, but a few examples give a flavor of the general findings. In one study, Bransford and Johnson (1972) asked people to read the following vague passage:

> The procedure is actually quite simple. First you arrange things into different groups. Of course, one pile may be sufficient depending on how much there is to do. If you have to go somewhere else due to lack of facilities, that is the next step, otherwise you are pretty well set. It is important not to overdo things. That is, it is better to do too few things at once than too many. In the short run this may not seem important, but complications can easily arise. A mistake can be expensive as well. At first the whole procedure will seem complicated. Soon, however, it will become just another facet of life. It is difficult to foresee any end to the necessity of this task in the immediate future, but one can never tell. After the procedure is completed, one arranges the materials into different groups again. Then they can be put into their appropriate places. Eventually they will be used once more and the whole cycle will have to be repeated. However, that is a part of life. (p. 722)

With some people, the investigators did not describe the topic of the passage before subjects read it; with others, the researchers told subjects the topic after they read it. A final group was told before reading it that the passage was about doing laundry. Only this last group was able to recall a significant amount of the passage later, a finding suggesting that activating the proper schema is important for making sense of a discourse. Having a script helps organize points in memory and facilitates later recall. Similar studies have demonstrated the same point (R. C. Anderson & Pichert, 1978; Bower, Black, & Turner, 1979; Bransford & Johnson, 1973).

A study by Sulin and Dooling (1974) produced a second representative finding. This study focused on whether people with familiar schemas might actually misremember a passage they had read earlier. In this case, subjects read the following passage:

> *<Person X>'s need for professional help.* <Person X> was a problem child from birth. *She was wild, stubborn, and violent./She was deaf, dumb, and blind.* By the time <X> turned eight, she was still unmanageable. Her parents were very concerned about her mental health. There was no good institution for her problem in her state. Her parents finally decided to take some action. They hired a private tutor for <X>. (p. 256)

For half the people, Person X was named Helen Keller, and for the other half, Carol Harris (an unfamiliar name). For half the people, the first sentence in italics (She was wild . . .) was used, and for the other half, the second sentence (She was deaf . . .) was used. After reading this passage, subjects took a recognition test in which they saw each sentence of the passage one at a time. The key sentence was replaced with the one they had not seen, and subjects rated how confident they were that they had seen the sentence in the original passage. Subjects who read the passage with the name *Helen Keller* were more confident that they had seen the sentence "She was deaf, dumb, and blind" when they had not than were subjects who were tested on the sentence "She was wild, stubborn, and violent." The opposite pattern was observed for subjects who read the passage with the unfamiliar name *Carol Harris*. These results suggest that people's previously existing schema influenced their memory of the passage and made a sentence that had not been seen before seem familiar.

Despite the influence of scripts, this formulation raises questions that have no obvious answers. For example, how are people reminded of the appropriate script? When John walks into a seedy bar, how is it that one activates the "getting drunk" script and not the "doing laundry" script? How does one keep track of the various related scripts? The notion of parallel tracks seems insufficient to cope with the wide variety of scripts that exist. For example, some bars allow a person to pay at the end; others require that one pay for each drink as it comes. At some bars patrons are expected to get drunk; at others, drunkenness is inappropriate. Some bars serve food; others do not. Bars in general are related to restaurants; there are many different restaurants from fast food to haute cuisine, each with subtle variations in the expected set of events. In view of this variety of event knowledge, how is the information organized?

Finally, there seem to be levels of abstractions of events in the same way that there are levels of abstraction of object categories. The event of going to a bar can be viewed as a specific instance of an event at a specific bar at a specific time (analogous to a lime green 1972 Oldsmobile Cutlass Supreme) or as a general trip to a bar to get drunk or even as a general event of getting intoxicated in some way. Scripts seem to occupy a medium level of abstraction eliminating specific details of particular circumstances, but still maintaining many details about a situation. If having both specific and general knowledge structures about events is useful, some change to the notion of scripts presented here needs to be made. In the following sections, I discuss elaborations to scripts that have been made to address these issues.

Scenes, Scripts, MOPs, and TOPs

Schank (1982) recognized the shortcomings in the original formulation of scripts. To organize the range of information that must be involved in event representations, he extended the concept of scripts by assuming that any event is encoded at different levels of abstraction and that these levels are interrelated. The use of levels of abstraction was helpful for organizing parallel "tracks" in scripts and for allowing specific episodes to act as reminders of general events. In this section, I describe Schank's work in more detail.

The general framework of this multilevel representation for events is shown in Figure 7.1. At the base of this framework is the script, which now is no longer a general event representation but a representation of a very specific event that contains details about particular locations in which actions take place. Scripts, in Schank's view, were much narrower than previously. Before, a script referred to an entire event (e.g., going to a bar to get drunk, going to a restaurant, or taking a trip by train). In the revised view, scripts referred to specific subevents within a larger event such as ordering a drink at a particular bar, getting seated at a particular restaurant, or purchasing tickets for the train at Penn Station in New York. Scripts contained details specific to particular contexts. For example, the script for buying tickets at Penn Station involves information about where ticket counters are located. This script differs in subtle ways from other strongly related scripts such as the script for buying tickets at a suburban train station. Scripts incorporate specific information in recognition of the fact that this information is important for carrying out actions, particularly in frequently encountered situations.

As shown in Figure 7.1, *scenes* are generalizations of scripts and are similar to scripts in that they also encode small episodes from larger events. Scenes, however, strip away particular details of specific contexts. Purchas-

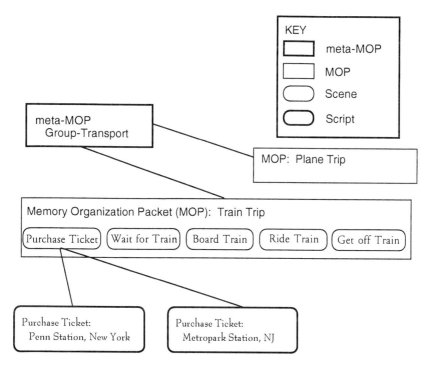

FIG. 7.1. Memory organization in Schank's (1982) dynamic memory. Event representations consist of scripts, scenes, MOPs, and meta-MOPs.

ing a train ticket at a large city station or at a small suburban station is generalized to the same scene. The organizing force is the satisfaction of a subgoal of a larger event. A ticket is needed to board a train, and the scene for purchasing a ticket includes information about its purpose. Thus, if this scene is skipped, the failure of the goal can be noted.

The central construct in this view of event representation is the *memory organization packet* or MOP. A MOP plays the same role that scripts played earlier: They organize a set of scenes into an event. Traveling by train is a MOP that consists of scenes like purchasing a ticket, waiting for the train, boarding the train, giving the ticket to the conductor, riding the train, and getting off the train when reaching the destination. This sequence is shown in Figure 7.1. Because the scenes contain information about the goals they serve, a system can reason about what to do if a scene in a MOP is skipped. For example, failing to purchase a ticket before boarding a train requires buying a ticket from the conductor to satisfy the condition of having a ticket to board a train. Someone without a scene for purchasing a ticket from the conductor after boarding a train may perform the original actions for buying a ticket and thus miss the train.

The last major component of this system is the meta-MOP, which organizes sets of MOPs for related events with similar structures. For example, taking a train trip is a lot like taking a trip on a Greyhound bus or taking a plane trip. In each of these events, there are subevents of purchasing a ticket, waiting for the transportation, boarding, traveling, and leaving. These general commonalities may be overlooked without a global structure pointing out their similarities. It is difficult, however, to have a structure that describes only the most general level, because there are significant differences between these forms of travel. Plane trips require going through a security check that is not required for bus or train travel. If events must be organized at only a high level of abstraction, a mechanism is needed for describing when a security check is needed. Instead, by having events described at many different levels of abstraction, subevents that are required only in specific contexts can be stored where they are needed.

Solving the Problems With Scripts. Differentiating between scripts, scenes, MOPs, and meta-MOPS allows this view of event representations to avoid many of the problems with scripts raised earlier. Obviously, this representation was constructed with the issue of levels of abstraction in mind. In particular, there are four explicit levels of abstraction allowing specific information about events to be stored while still making clear the similarities between distinct events. One similarity between events involves their being specifications of the same abstract memory structure. Two scripts can be seen as similar because they are specifications of a common scene. Likewise, two MOPs can be seen as similar because they involve the same types of scenes and hence can be described by a common meta-MOP.

This organizational structure also facilitates the organization of parallel tracks in scripts. For example, there are many different ways to purchase tickets at a train station. Most train stations have people who sell tickets. Some train stations have vending machines. Still others allow purchasing tickets by mail, phone, or the Internet. Each option for buying tickets can be stored as a separate script that specifies how the scene of purchasing tickets is carried out. Because MOPs are organized by scenes and scenes are created around subgoals that must be satisfied, it is easy to combine different specific scripts to represent a particular event. According to the old view of scripts, a whole new track for a script had to be created whenever new events were idiosyncratic to a particular context. In the newer formulation, a new script is created with the specific information and is attached to the appropriate scene.

Finally, by keeping track of specific information about particular contexts (in scripts), subgoal information (in scenes), and global sequence information (in MOPs and meta-MOPs), this view gives some insight into how people are able to find the appropriate event information in memory when a new situation is encountered. One way to be reminded is in a bottom-up manner by encountering specific information that cues a particular script. For example, a person entering a train station in Paris may see a vending machine for purchasing tickets and may be reminded of Penn Station in New York; thus the person can adapt an old specific script to a new situation (see also Alterman, 1988). Because scripts are connected to abstract representations of events, general potential goals are activated on the basis of specific situations.

Another way to be reminded is by a top-down route through the presence of a general goal that serves as a reminder of a particular situation. When faced with the problem of traveling inexpensively from New York to Boston, the general event of train travel can be found, because traveling (inexpensively) is associated with the MOP of train travel. Once the MOP has been found, the connections to more specific information about travel can be followed to form a plan for traveling by train. Thus, this view of event representation permits both bottom-up and top-down remindings.

Failure-Driven Learning. An important motivation for this view of event representation is to explain learning. Schank (1982) suggested that *expectation failure* is an important impetus for learning and that event representations are used to make predictions about which events occur next. When the predictions turn out to be correct, nothing new needs to be learned, but when expectations are violated, a learning situation arises. For example, although riding the Underground in London is much like riding a train (or even a subway) in New York, the first time that a person rides the Underground, he or she may be surprised at having to insert the ticket into the gate to exit. (Riders of subway systems other than that of New York are familiar with this policy.) Thus, a New Yorker riding the Underground for the first time meets with an expectation failure, which can be resolved by adding a script for exiting the Underground (Alterman, 1988). This change may also require an additional scene for exiting a subway system, which may not have been considered an important event in New York.

The general importance of expectation failure in cognition has been widely noted (e.g., Bruner, 1990). Indeed, it is the basis of narrative. A novel would be uninteresting if it described only typical events. Novels are interesting because their stories deviate from expected patterns of events. Storytellers can leave out typical events and provide only enough information to help readers gain access to the proper script; then they can introduce information about deviations from the script. After an expectation failure has been encountered and something has been learned, a repetition of the failure is no longer surprising; it is simply an instance of the previously encountered situation. As Schank (1982) suggested, memory is *dynamic*; situations are never viewed the same way twice because they are filtered through previous experience.[3]

Thematic Organization Points. The memory organization described here has one additional level of abstraction not yet discussed. Schank (1982) proposed a global abstract form of representation called a *thematic organization point* or TOP. TOPs encode general goal and outcome relations without any supporting event structure. For example, there may be a TOP for a general situation like an event that fails because an important precondition has not been satisfied. Disparate events including being denied admission to a footrall game for not having a ticket, being unable to start a car because it is out of gas, and being denied registration for a course because one has not taken a prerequisite are all instances of this general situation. The idea behind encoding these very general goal relationships is that people are sometimes reminded of situations on the basis of very abstract relationships between them.

Dyer (1983) proposed a similar abstract representation in a model of text comprehension. This model recorded general expectation failures by using *thematic abstraction units* or TAUs. Like TOPs, TAUs involve only very general goals and the way in which a goal failed to be satisfied. Specific information about events themselves are omitted from the TAUs. As shown in Figure 7.2, TAUs can be summarized by adages like "the pot calling the kettle black" or "don't count your chickens before they hatch." According to Dyer, TAUs are used during narrative comprehension to recognize the general pattern of a story. Once a story is recognized as an instance of a particular TAU, it is easier to keep track of events and characters because a higher order relational structure binds the narrative together (see also Gentner & Toupin, 1986). Finally, TOPs and TAUs record expectation *failures*. They need not record situations in which events unfold as they are supposed to; normal event representations (like MOPs) serve that purpose.

Summary

Event representations must contain information about the sequence of subevents that constitute the event, about the goals satisfied by the events and subevents, and about the relations that hold between goals. An influential theory of event representations is scripts, whose initial formulation assumed a basic knowledge structure that contained the information about event sequences as well as the goals connecting events. This theory was

---

[3]Indeed, Schank (1982) criticized his early text comprehension programs for never getting bored, even though they were presented with the same passages repeatedly.

TAU-Pot calling kettle black

TAU-Counting chickens before they hatch

X is guilty of some transgression T

X expects some event E

Y is guilty of some transgression T

X plans event Y assuming E

X publicly accuses Y of T

X commences carrying out Y before E

E does not occur spoiling Y

FIG. 7.2. Two examples of TAUs that record expectation failures.

expanded to account for people's ability to store both specific information about particular episodes and general information about similarities between events that appear dissimilar on the surface. Specific information is included in scripts and is generalized into scenes. Scenes are organized into MOPs, which contain information about general event sequences and goals. Meta-MOPs organize MOPs into clusters that relate similar events together. Finally, very abstract knowledge structures like TOPs and TAUs can be used to recognize situations in which there are general goal failures. MOPs and TOPs/TAUs serve complementary functions. MOPs provide higher order relations to bind together events that occur as they normally do. TOPs and TAUs provide higher order relations that bind together events that violate expectations.

EVENTS AND VERBS

To this point, this chapter has focused on representations of events themselves. As discussed earlier, events can be contrasted with objects, which have representations with many connections between their parts. Events also have many connections between their parts, but the parts are subevents, and the connections are related to goals of actors. Events can also be described in another way. In many sentences, objects and actors are described by nouns, but events and actions that they take part in are described by verbs. Nouns and verbs are universal aspects of language; not only do nouns and verbs play different roles in sentences, but they appear to be represented differently (Gentner, 1981a). In this section, I first discuss ways that primitive elements of events and verbs can be represented. Then, I discuss some conjectures about verb representation. This section is brief primarily because there is much less research on verbs than on nouns. Although workers have offered interesting speculations about the nature of verb representations, there is little consensus about the appropriate way to represent verbs.

Primitive Events

One area of psychology in which researchers have significantly explored events and verbs has been that of conceptual primitives (Miller & Johnson-Laird, 1976; Norman & Rumelhart, 1975; Schank, 1975). Theorists of text comprehension have recognized that verbs provide the glue holding together actions and actors involved in sentences. Because of the important organizational function of verbs, a theory of primitives that form the basis of verbs would provide an important backbone for a full theory of text comprehension. The proposals for conceptual primitives are all structured representations, because an important function of verbs is to specify the relationships among elements in a sentence. In this section, I discuss Schank's (1975) primitive actions. I use this work as an example, because I have discussed Schank's work on scripts and memory organization earlier in this chapter. The interested reader is encouraged to look at the other sources referred to in this section as well.

Schank (1975) posited 11 primitive actions, although he was more committed to there being a small number of primitive actions rather than to the 11 particular actions that he suggested. Indeed, in later work (e.g., Schank & Abelson, 1977) the number actually increases somewhat. The 11 primitive acts and their definitions are shown in Table 7.1. The primitive acts are grouped into clusters. The largest cluster consists of actions that agents can perform: PROPEL, MOVE, INGEST, EXPEL, and GRASP. In addition, there are three actions of transfer, PTRANS, ATRANS, and MTRANS. These transfer actions differ only in what is transferred. PTRANS changes the physical location of an object, ATRANS changes some abstract relation associated with an object (such as who owns it), and MTRANS moves an idea from one head to another. There are two instrumental actions, SPEAK and ATTEND, which govern production of sound and

TABLE 7.1
Primitive Acts in Conceptual Dependency Theory

Act	Definition
PROPEL	To apply force to a physical object.
MOVE	To move a body part.
INGEST	To take an object inside an animate body.
EXPEL	To force something out of an animate body.
GRASP	To grasp a physical object.
PTRANS	To physically transfer an object from one location to another.
ATRANS	To transfer an abstract property from one agent to another.
MTRANS	To transfer a mental entity from one mind to another.
SPEAK	To produce a sound from a source in some direction.
ATTEND	To direct a sense organ to a stimulus in the environment.
MBUILD	To construct or combine a mental entity (thought).

attending to external stimuli, respectively, and one mental action, MBUILD, which involves creating or combining thoughts. Each of these primitive acts is actually shorthand for a relation. For example, PTRANS takes arguments that determine the object whose location is being changed as well as the initial and final locations.

As an example of how these primitive actions work, consider the verbs *give*, *trade*, and *buy*. The simplest of these verbs is *give*, which involves the transfer of possession of an object from one person to another (ATRANS) as in the sentence:

John gave Mary a compact disc. (7.4)

ATRANS is used in this sentence because possession is an abstract relationship. From this sentence, *give* may seem to require a change of location as well (PTRANS), but the transfer of physical location is not necessary as in the sentence:

Columbia University was given the General Electric Building recently. (7.5)

in which only ownership changes hands (the building stays where it is).

The verb *trade* is more complex than *give*, as it involves a reciprocal transfer of ownership (ATRANS) with ownership of one item passing from Actor A to Actor B and ownership of a second item passing from Actor B to Actor A. Thus, the representation of *trade* involves two instances of ATRANS. This use can be illustrated with the sentence:

John traded the compact disc for the pencil box. (7.6)

Finally, the verb *buy* is more complex than *trade*; although both verbs involve two changes of ownership (ATRANS), for *buy*, one is required to be money or some mechanism of transferring currency. Thus, if one says:

John bought the compact disc with the credit card. (7.7)

it means that he paid for it with a credit card. If one says:

John bought the compact disc with the pencil box. (7.8)

the pencil box was not traded for the compact disc, but rather something else occurred (such as "John bought the compact disc that came bundled with the pencil box and paid for it by transferring money to the previous owner").

The use of a system of primitives also allows one to see that verbs have some similarity across domains. I have already noted that the verb *give* involves a simple change of possession (ATRANS). Analogously, the verb *move* involves a simple change of location (PTRANS), and the verb *tell* involves a simple change in the location of an idea (MTRANS) as in:

John tells Mary a secret.   (7.9)

In this case, the mental location of the secret moves from John to Mary. There is one disanalogy between MTRANS and PTRANS, however. If an object moves from point A to point B, it is no longer at point A, but if an idea moves from head A to head B, it now exists in both heads at once.

Schank's system of primitives, like E. V. Clark's (1979) semantic features discussed in chapter 3, have no specific perceptual grounding. Thus, there must be additional work with this system to understand how these primitives ground the representations. The theory does, however, suggest how a complex set of verbs can be developed from a simple set of actions.

Internal Structure of Verb Representations

Gentner (1982) suggested that concrete nouns differ from verbs in that concrete nouns refer to bounded spatial entities that are easily partitioned from the environment whereas verbs refer to events that are difficult to separate from the environment. Although the perceptual system seems designed to segment objects out of the visual array (as discussed in chap. 6), it seems not to give privileged access to events that have both a spatial and a temporal extent. In this section, I discuss three important aspects of verbs: first, the information about events incorporated into verb representations; second, the importance of causal relations in verbs; third, the difference between relational connections within a concept, characteristic of nouns, and relational connections between concepts, characteristic of verbs.

There are many aspects to events, and not all of them can be captured using a particular verb (Talmy, 1975). For example, in the sentence:

The bottle floated in the river.   (7.10)

the manner in which the bottle moved is specified by the verb (i.e., it bobbed up and down on the surface of the water), but the direction and speed of motion, which are likely to be part of a floating event, are not specified. These would require additional phrases added to the sentence as in:

The bottle floated slowly in the river toward the cave mouth.   (7.11)

Finally to make matters even more complex, different languages incorporate different information about events into verbs. As pointed out by Talmy (1975), verbs in Spanish tend to incorporate the direction of motion into the verb and to leave the manner of motion to be specified by other phrases. In contrast, English (as in sentence 7.11) puts the manner of motion into the verb but leaves the direction to be specified by other phrases. In Spanish, the sentence "The bottle floated out of the cave" is:

La botella salio de la cueva, flotando.   (7.12)

which can be translated literally as "The bottle exited the cave floating." This analysis suggests that verbs themselves cannot be used as the underlying representations for events, because significant information that people can have about an event is not captured by a given verb. Nonetheless, people are able to describe the missing information by using other linguistic devices (like prepositional phrases).

Although verbs do not capture all there is to know about event representations, they describe complex relational structures rather than single components of the underlying event representation. In particular, verbs often describe complex causal relations that hold among a causal agent, a patient, and perhaps some objects that are acted on. For example, Gentner (1981b) presented the relational structures shown in Figures 7.3A and 7.3B as plausible structured representations for the sentences:

Ida gave her tenants the clock.   (7.13)

and

Ida sold her tenants the clock.   (7.14)

respectively.

These representations come from work on a memory model developed by the LNR research group (Norman & Rumelhart, 1975). The representation in Figure 7.3B is obviously more complex than is the one in 7.3A; selling involves a reciprocal transfer in which the clock goes from Ida to her tenants:

(change[poss(Ida, clock), poss(tenants, clock)]).   (7.15)

Money goes from the tenants to Ida:

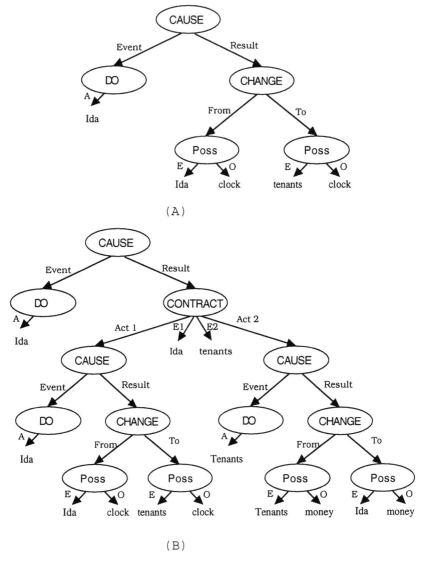

FIG. 7.3. Representations of A: "Ida gave her tenants a clock" and B: "Ida sold her tenants a clock."

$$(\text{change}[\text{poss}(\text{tenants}, \text{money}), \text{poss}(\text{Ida}, \text{money})]),\tag{7.16}$$

whereas giving requires only the transfer in 7.15. Both representations involve causal relations. In the representation of *give* in Figure 7.3A, the causal relation relates the event of Ida performing some action to the change in possession of the clock from Ida to the tenants. Ida herself does not cause the giving; an action that she takes causes the transfer. That is why the event part of the causal relation contains the predicate DO, rather than simply having Ida as the first argument to the causal relation (see Munro, 1975, for additional discussion of this point).

As a test of the psychological reality of these structures, Gentner (1981b) presented subjects with sentences containing simple verbs (like *give*) and complex verbs (like *sell*) and later asked them to recall the sentences. The sentences with more complex verbs (e.g., *sell*) were better recalled than were sentences with less complex verbs (e.g., *give*), a result suggesting that complex verbs are represented by more relational structure than are simple verbs.

As previously discussed, in the representations in Figure 7.3, the highest order relation is causal. Many verbs have causality as an important part of their representation. For example, the verb *give* involves causing a change in an object's location from one place to another, and the verb *kill* involves causing something to die. In addition to causal information that is a central part of the meaning of a verb, causal information is also implied by many verbs. Au (1986) found that people tend to attribute causality to individuals playing specific roles in a sentence (although the particular individual seen as the causal force depends on the verb). For example, for verbs denoting an event of experiencing, the stimulus is perceived to be the causal agent. For the sentence:

John bored Mary.   (7.17)

John is the stimulus seen as causing Mary's boredom (although possibly everything bores Mary and hence she is the causal force). The attribution of causality to John in Example 7.17 does not reflect a tendency to make the subject of the sentence the causal agent. In the sentence:

John esteemed Mary.   (7.18)

Mary is seen as causing John's esteem, even though she is the object of the verb. For verbs denoting actions, there is a similar pattern, but it is clearest for verbs whose action is directed at the object of the sentence when stated in the active voice. For example, for the sentence:

John reproached Mary.   (7.19)

Mary is seen as doing something that led to John's reproach. In Au's data, sentences in which the action is directed by the subject of the sentence (when stated in the active voice) as in:

John hit Mary.   (7.20)

do not give a clear sense of who is the causal force. In Example 7.20, John
may be the causal force (e.g., he likes to hit people), or Mary may be the
causal force (e.g., she stole John's toy in the sandbox). Indeed, in Au's
studies, people asked to write completions for sentences like those in 7.20
were about evenly split as to whether the subject or object was the causal
force. These results suggest that the interpretation of verbs in sentences
includes information about causal forces.

The structured representations pictured in Figure 7.3 highlight the point
that verbs (and event representations in general) consist of relational connections among elements outside the representation of the verb (Gentner,
1981a; Gentner & France, 1988). In Example 7.14, the verb *sell* binds
together Ida, her tenants, and a clock in a series of relations. In contrast,
noun representations seem to involve relations among elements that are
part of the object itself. This point can be demonstrated by considering
the *mutability* of properties of nouns and verbs (Gentner & France, 1988;
Love & Sloman, 1995). Gentner and France (1988) found that the meanings of verbs are more mutable than are the meanings of nouns. That is,
when people read a sentence that cannot be interpreted literally, they are
more likely to change the meaning of the verb than of the noun. For
example, people considered the sentence:

The lizard worshiped.   (7.21)

as more likely to suggest a meaning of a reptile basking in the sun (thereby
changing the meaning of *worshiped*) than to suggest a meaning of a des-
picable person going to church (thereby changing the meaning of *lizard*).
Gentner and France suggested that this greater mutability of verbs than
of nouns arises because verb representations have a lower relational density
than do nouns.

This interpretation is reinforced by studies of the mutability of individual
properties of nouns (Love, 1996; Love & Sloman, 1995). In these studies,
researchers asked people which properties of nouns are easiest to change,
for example, whether it is easier to imagine a robin that is not red or a
robin that does not eat. People typically responded that it is easier to
imagine a robin that is not red than one that does not eat, a result suggesting that the property *red* is more mutable than the property *eats* for
robins. In other tests, people were probed to find out which properties of
nouns were related to other properties of the same nouns. In general,
properties that are more mutable are related to fewer other properties of
the noun than are properties that are less mutable. Thus, a feature is
mutable when it is connected to few other features, so that changes in

that feature do not require changes in other features. This finding suggests that the greater mutability of verb meanings than of noun meanings arises because there are fewer relations among properties in verbs than there are in nouns. In this way, changing a feature of a verb does not require significant changes in many other properties.

Like scripts (and their more complex descendants), verb representations seem well characterized as having structured relational representations. Like scripts, verbs involve causal relations among elements. Nonetheless, verbs do not contain the same range of information as do scripts; verbs often need additional phrases to describe information about events not captured by the verb itself. Finally, when compared to nouns, verbs seem to have a less dense internal relational structure. Rather than there being extensive relations among elements in a verb representation, a verb seems to involve connections to elements outside the verb itself, such as the actors and objects involved in it. One result of this low internal relational density is that the meanings of verbs are mutable. Thus, verb meanings are more likely to change than are noun meanings in the face of pressure to make sense of a seemingly anomalous sentence.

Structure of the Verb Lexicon

How is the verb lexicon organized? Earlier in this chapter, I discussed the hierarchical organization of object categories. Because many object categories are named by nouns, it has been assumed that the noun lexicon is organized hierarchically as well. In contrast, verbs appear to be organized differently (Gentner, 1981a; Huttenlocher & Lui, 1979). There is no clear consensus at this point about how the verb lexicon is organized, but there have been some proposals.

Miller and Fellbaum (1991) proposed that verbs are hierarchically organized but that the hierarchies of verbs are not as deep as those of nouns. They also suggested that the organizing relations are different for noun and verb hierarchies. Noun hierarchies are organized by class-inclusion (i.e., ISA) relations. Thus, one can say:

A robin is a bird. (7.22)

Class inclusion-relations make no sense when applied directly to verbs, however. One cannot say:

To jog is to run. (7.23)

Miller and Fellbaum proposed that verb hierarchies are based on *troponymic* relations, in which specific verbs are related to general verbs through noting a key dimension of difference such as:

To jog is to run *slowly*.   (7.24)

In this case, the verbs differ in the manner in which the action is carried out, but verbs can differ in other ways, such as the direction of motion or implied causality.

A hierarchical organization of verbs has been implemented in Miller's WordNet program. WordNet is a massive lexical database organized around the semantics of the words in it. A key aspect of WordNet is its use of a *relational semantics* (Fellbaum, 1993) or a *conceptual-role semantics* (as discussed earlier in this chapter and in chap. 1). That is, words are not decomposed into primitives to determine their meaning (as discussed in chap. 3) but the meaning of words is determined by the relations between a word and other words in the system. These relations can be class-inclusion relations (or troponymic relations in the case of verbs) as well as causal relations, synonymy and antonymy relations, and also meronymy (i.e., Item X has Item Y as a part). WordNet assumes a hierarchical organization for verbs by explicitly connecting different verbs by troponymic relations.

Some interesting observations about the hierarchical organization of the verb lexicon emerge from WordNet (Fellbaum, 1993). First, verbs appear to have a level of abstraction at which there are many contrasting verbs. For example, many verbs describe walking that differs in its manner such as *march, saunter, limp,* and *strut.* In contrast, there are fewer contrasting verbs at higher levels of abstraction. For example, *walk* and *run* are both at the same level of abstraction, but there are not many other types of human movement at this same level of abstraction. Second, there are few verbs more specific than those at the level of abstraction that has many verbs. For example, it is quite difficult to think of troponyms of verbs like *march* (e.g., goose-step).

An alternative proposal for the structure of the verb lexicon is that it does not involve hierarchies at all but is organized like a matrix (Hutten-locher & Lui, 1979). The matrix view capitalizes on the observation that there are many similarities between verbs that come from distant semantic fields. For example, verbs involving actions have an agent that carries out the action, a patient that is the recipient of the action, and an object involved in the action. This similarity in overall structure is also true of transfers of physical objects, transfers of information, and violent acts. A matrix view of verb organization assumes that this high degree of similarity in structure for verbs that differ semantically implies no real hierarchies in the verb lexicon.

How can one decide whether the verb lexicon is organized as a matrix or with hierarchies? One set of studies by Pavlicic and Markman (1997) used a commonality and difference listing task analogous to the one used by Markman and Wisniewski (1997) to study the structure of noun hierarchies. As discussed earlier, nouns from the same hierarchy are easy to compare, and people can list many commonalities and many alignable differences for them. In contrast, nouns from different hierarchies are difficult to compare, and people can list few commonalities or alignable differences for them. If verbs are also hierarchically organized, a similar pattern should be observed for comparisons of verbs as was true for comparisons of nouns, but if verbs are organized into a matrix structure, all verbs should be about equally comparable. In a study in which people listed the commonalities and differences of pairs of verbs, people listed more commonalities and alignable differences for verbs from the same hierarchy than for verbs from different hierarchies (although people listed many fewer properties overall for verbs than they did for nouns). This result suggests that verbs are not organized as a true matrix. Rather, at first glance, it appears that there are hierarchies in the verb lexicon.

These data are not completely compatible with a hierarchical view of verb organization, however. In the study with nouns, people found it very difficult to list the differences between a noun and its immediate superordinate (e.g., it was hard to list differences between a robin and a bird). This difficulty seems to be a result of the class-inclusion relation. People do not want to list the differences between a robin and a bird, because they want to say that a robin *is* a bird. Because properties can all be inherited through class-inclusion relations (as discussed in chap. 4), there cannot be properties of birds that are not properties of robins, unless particular exceptions have been stored explicitly (such as that penguins do not fly). In contrast, people had no difficulty listing differences between a verb and troponyms of the verb (e.g., it was not difficult to list differences between *to walk* and *to march*). Thus, although verbs do not appear to be organized in a matrix structure, they also do not appear to be organized in true hierarchies. Much additional work remains to be done, but the evidence suggests that verbs are organized into semantic clusters rather than into strict hierarchies. These clusters are defined by a variety of relations including troponymy, synonymy (and antonymy), and meronymy.

Events and Activities

As already discussed, the distinction between nouns and verbs is correlated with the distinction between objects and events, but it is not identical to it. One particularly interesting class of nouns consists of terms for activities. Activities are events that are described by nouns, events for which a verb can be used to denote action that makes up the activity. For example, *walking* (a gerund) is an activity, and the verb *to walk* denotes the action involved in the activity.

Activities differ from regular nouns in that they do not appear to be organized into class-inclusion hierarchies but instead into hierarchies with the relation *kind of* (Rips & Conrad, 1989). For example, it does not seem right to say:

Walking is moving. (7.24)

but it does seem right to say:

Walking is a *kind of* moving. (7.25)

To move down a hierarchy, the appropriate relation seems to be *part of.* For example, one can say:

Moving is a *part of* walking. (7.26)

Rips and Conrad (1989) examined the *kind of–part of* structure of activities by using words for mental activities like thinking, reasoning, and deciding. According to these researchers, people believe that specific activities (e.g., crying) are kinds of more general activities (e.g., having emotions), whereas general activities are parts of specific activities. This work further reinforces the idea that events (and activities) are represented differently from objects.

Despite this difference, there is some evidence that events have a basic level just as objects do (Morris & Murphy, 1990). As labels for basic-level categories are generally used to describe an event, basic-level event labels are also frequently used to describe events. For example, an event is more likely to be described as *shopping* than as *food shopping* or *clothes shopping.* As members of basic-level categories share parts, members of basic levels of events share common subevents. For example, food shopping, clothes shopping, and shopping for electronics all involve selecting and paying for items. Thus, people solve the problem of selecting a level of abstraction for events similarly to the way they do for objects. As a default, they select a middle level that preserves the basic set of subevents.

STRUCTURED AND NONSTRUCTURED REPRESENTATIONS

In this section, I contrast the strengths and weaknesses of structured representations with those of unstructured representations discussed in chapters 2 and 3. Some cognitive processes are probably best characterized as operating over unstructured representations, whereas others are best characterized as involving structured representations. Thus, one need not assume that choosing structured representations for a model of a particular task involves a commitment to structured representations for models of every task. It may be better to assume that cognitive models are representationally pluralistic.

Structured representations allow the storage of detailed information about spatial and conceptual relationships among elements. When people reflect on visual scenes or concepts, this relational information seems to be important. Furthermore, the prized human abilities of language, reasoning, analogy, and problem solving all apparently involve the ability to see relationships and to reason about similarities and differences in relationships between different situations. Models that do not permit the storage and use of relations seem to miss something fundamental about cognition (J. A. Fodor & Pylyshyn, 1988).

Although relational knowledge is important for understanding cognitive processing, the ability to reason with and about relations comes at a cost: Processes operating over structured representations are computationally intensive and require time to carry out. Relations take arguments, and good reasoning requires assessing both the particular types of representational elements involved in a situation and the specific bindings between predicates and arguments. For example, when a preschool teacher is trying to keep order in her classroom, it matters whether "Lucas hit Solomon" or "Solomon hit Lucas."

There is evidence that the process of binding objects to relations takes time. In one set of studies, Ratcliff and McKoon (1989) asked people to read sentences consisting of two people and a relation (e.g., "John met Mary"). Later, they showed subjects sentences and asked them whether these sentences appeared in the earlier set. If subjects were asked to respond quickly (i.e., faster than 700 ms), they correctly rejected sentences with new actors who had not appeared in the original set (e.g., they could say that "Randy fed Jackson" was not in the earlier set). Subjects did not distinguish between sentences with the objects bound correctly to the verb (e.g., "John met Mary") and sentences with the objects bound incorrectly (e.g., "Mary met John") until after at least 700 milliseconds had elapsed. This finding suggests that constructing and comparing relational structures requires some time. Goldstone and Medin (1994) obtained a similar result when looking at people's similarity judgments.

This processing cost is high. Many processes have to take place quickly, and the cognitive system cannot rely on structured representations to carry out all cognitive tasks. At the same time, the cognitive system cannot do without structured representations; people are sensitive to relations and relational bindings in many situations. One road to take is to explore the role of both structured and unstructured representations in cognitive processing.

Researchers can aim to develop cognitive models in which different stages of processing involve different representations of a situation (see also Sloman, 1996). Every representational scheme discussed in this book has its strengths and weaknesses. Although it seems logically parsimonious to try to find *the* representational system underlying cognitive processing, there is no reason to think that things are represented in only one way. An unconstrained proliferation of representational systems may make the cognitive system unwieldy, but a fruitful approach to the study of cognition is to search for a small number of representational systems that can support cognitive models by explaining both processes that take place quickly and those that require more effort. (I return to this point in chap. 10.)

General and Specific Information in Representations

REPRESENTATION AND ABSTRACTION

In chapters 6 and 7, I turned from defining new representational types to examining how one particular representation, structured representation, can represent perceptual and conceptual information. Nonetheless, chapters 2 through 7 were primarily concerned with questions like "How are representations of different types structured?" and "What processes are often used with particular representations?" Chapters 8 and 9 focus primarily on issues of content of representations. Although I have discussed content to some degree already, some general issues about the content of representations are important to address. In this chapter, I examine the degree of abstractness associated with representations. Chapter 9 focuses on a particular kind of specific instance information: mental models.

The issue of abstraction is important in thinking about representation. In this book, I have characterized representations as involving a representing world that stands in a consistent relation to elements in a represented world. The degree of abstraction of an element in the representing world is simply the range of different items in the represented world represented by that element. For example, a symbol representing the concept *catfish* is less abstract than a symbol representing the concept *fish* because it refers to a narrower range of items in the represented world. Likewise, a symbol representing the concept *fish* is less abstract than a symbol representing the concept *animal*. On this view, all representations are abstractions to some degree; there are always aspects of the represented world not captured in the representing world (and hence distinct items in the represented world treated as the same in the representing world). Thus, the degree of abstraction focuses on how much information is captured by a representation.

For an extreme example, Braitenberg (1984) described some simple vehicles that exhibit primitive behaviors. The vehicle pictured in Figure 8.1 has a single wheel at the back and a sensor at the front. The sensor is sensitive to some aspect of the environment, say light. The more photons that hit the sensor, the more current it generates. When electricity is sent to the motor, it causes it to turn. A vehicle like this moves when there is a light somewhere in front of it and does not move when there is no light in front of it. This vehicle exhibits only a crude behavior and has only a crude representation. The more photons, the more current that flows. This representation is transient; when the light source is taken away, the sensor stops producing current. There is no memory for past lights; the stopped vehicle does not daydream of a time when photons were plentiful.

This representation is not only crude; it is also extremely abstract. The sensor is sensitive to any photon-producing thing in the environment. Thus, neon signs, distant stars, Zippo lighters, and welding torches are all treated equivalently. The information that allows people to distinguish between a Zippo lighter and a welding torch (a helpful distinction at the encore of a rock concert) is not part of the representing world of the Braitenberg vehicle.

At the other end of the spectrum, imagine a thumbprint recognition security system (of the type seen in many science fiction films). Such a machine has a detailed representation of a person's thumbprint. When an object is placed on the machine's sensor, its image is compared with stored representations, and the door opens only when the object on the sensor matches a stored thumbprint. In this case, the representation is highly specific: Only a few objects in the world correspond to this object (namely, one person's thumb and really good replicas of it). This representation is still an abstraction. If it were not an abstraction, only one

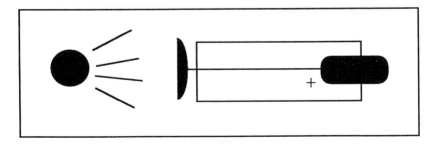

FIG. 8.1. A Braitenberg vehicle that is sensitive only to the presence of light.

thumb would match the stored representation (and the plots of many science fiction films would be foiled).

Although these examples are contrived, they do illustrate the notion of abstraction. What is interesting about research in cognitive science is that much of it has assumed that representations are rather abstract. For example, the scripts described in chapter 7 are generalized events. They do not refer to a specific event but to the sequence of occurrences that make up an event of that type in general. Likewise, the mental space representations of concepts described in chapter 2, like those described by Rips, Shoben, and Smith (1973), have points in a space corresponding to concepts like *cat* and *horse* (see Figure 2.4). These nodes are supposed to represent concepts at a level of abstraction specified by the label rather than by specific instances. For one more example, many researchers have suggested that categories are represented by *prototypes* (Posner & Keele, 1970; Reed, 1972; Rosch & Mervis, 1975). As discussed in chapter 3, a category prototype is supposed to be a "central tendency" of a category. The prototype need not be an actual member of the category; it is a generalization that captures the properties typical of the category. The prototypical bird, for instance, is small, has feathers, flies, and sings. A person need not have seen a single bird with precisely these characteristics, but the prototype is an average of the birds that the person has seen.

A fundamental assumption that appears to underlie this use of abstraction is that a representation is useful for future reasoning only if the important elements of a situation are abstracted away. New situations are never identical to past occasions. If the representation of a category or event contains too many details about previous episodes, it is difficult to find past experiences that apply in a new situation. It is difficult to distinguish which differences between the current situation and past ones are important and which are not. This difficulty interferes with the use of past experiences that are retrieved. For example, a particular past experience of going to a restaurant may have involved getting crayons at the table to draw on the placemat during the wait for the food. If this instance was retrieved during a new trip to a restaurant, some mechanism would be needed to suppress the confusion that would occur when crayons were not brought to the table at the restaurant.

Despite the apparent need for abstract representations, there has been a surge of interest among cognitive scientists in the use of specific instance information in cognition and reasoning. This work has suggested that in many situations people do not rely on abstract representations but use information about specific instances or scenarios. The basic assumption of this research is that specific instances are indeed useful for reasoning as long as processes are designed to find the relevant information in a situation at the time of processing. On this view, when new knowledge is acquired (and when new situations are experienced), it is impossible to foresee all possible uses of this information in advance. If a lot of specific information about an instance is stored at the time of acquisition, more information is available for future reasoning.

In this chapter, I begin with a discussion of some data that suggest cognitive processing operates over representations that contain specific instance information. Then, I discuss three proposals for the use of specific instance information in cognition. First, I review research on case-based reasoning, which assumes that new problems can be solved by referring back to specific previous instances. Second, I return to the role of concrete metaphors as ways to conceptualize abstract concepts (discussed briefly in chap. 6). Finally, I discuss exemplar models, which assume that categories are represented by specific examples encountered in the past.

THE PRIORITY OF THE SPECIFIC

In many areas of cognitive science, researchers have assumed that reasoning processes approach a logical ideal. The appeal of deductive logic, for example, is that a set of rules can allow a system to reason about any domain. The deductive reasoning schemas described in chapter 5 are powerful because they guarantee the truth of the conclusions when the premises are true *for any set of premises with the structure specified by a schema*. Thus, deductive schemas are ways of reasoning about anything. The appeal of logic in artificial intelligence (AI) is that if a logic is sufficiently powerful, people need not understand the domain about which they reason; they simply have to structure the knowledge about the domain in the appropriate way, and the highly abstract rules of logic do the rest. This appeal to abstract reasoning abilities is also implicit in other accounts of cognition. For example, Piaget assumed that the ultimate end state of cognitive development was *formal operations*, in which adults could reason logically about many different situations by applying a single set of abstract rules across domains.

Despite the appeal of logic, humans clearly are not good at even the simplest logical puzzles. The Wason selection task described in chapter 1 is a logical task in which people must successfully use the reasoning schemas *modus ponens* and *modus tollens*. Recall that in this task, investigators showed subjects four cards and told them to decide which cards must be turned over to test the rule "If there is a vowel on one side of the card, there is an odd number on the other side" (see Figure 1.1). Although subjects generally correctly turn over the card with the vowel on one side (recognizing that *modus ponens* applies), they rarely turn over the card with the even number on the other side (which requires reasoning by *modus tollens*). This failure is striking, especially because (as discussed in chap. 1) subjects presented with an isomorphic problem set in a familiar context (e.g., people drinking in a bar) solve the problem with ease. Many studies have demonstrated that people are much better at solving problems with a particular logical structure when the content of the problems is in a familiar domain than when it is in an unfamiliar domain (Johnson-Laird, 1983; Johnson-Laird, Legrenzi, & Legrenzi, 1972).

What benefit can a familiar domain provide for reasoning? One possibility is that people recognize a new event as an instance of a familiar event and then do exactly what they did in that situation. The problem with this possibility is that people would have great difficulty when operating in situations not exactly like those they had encountered before. A second possibility is that people reason by using rules that are intermediate in abstraction between detailed representations of the events in specific situations and highly abstract domain-independent rules. Another proposal is that people form rules about common social interactions, and they bring their knowledge of social situations to bear when solving a new problem (Cheng & Holyoak, 1985, 1989; Cosmides, 1989). To demonstrate this point, Cheng and Holyoak (1985) gave people a version of the Wason selection task in an unfamiliar domain (entrance visas to a new country), but used a familiar social rule (permission). In this case, the rule was that if the visa says "entering" on one side, it includes cholera on the list of diseases on the other (the cover story had made clear that the list of diseases was a list of inoculations that a passenger had received). Thus, people could consider this task as an instance of needing permission to carry out an action. Cheng and Holyoak found that more subjects were able to solve the Wason task correctly in this situation than were subjects given the same rule without the rationale for the rule (i.e., without telling them that the list of diseases was a list of inoculations). This study suggests that people use rules derived from familiar situations to reason about common social situations.[1]

Of course, logic is only one kind of abstract reasoning system. Data like those on the use of social reasoning suggest not that there are no abstract

---

[1]There has been considerable debate about where these rules come from. Cosmides (1989) suggested that humans are born equipped with a capacity to learn rules of social exchange because of evolutionary history. Cheng and Holyoak (1989) proposed that social interaction may be sufficient to create these rules. In general, it is difficult to resolve debates about the evolutionary basis of cognitive processes, because the evidence for the evolutionary explanation is the presence of a particular behavior (e.g., social reasoning ability) and a plausible evolutionary story.

rules, but that the rules are not maximally abstract. Instead, there seem to be a set of rules tied to familiar situations. Workers have showed that many cognitive processes that could function with abstract rules are actually carried out by using representations tied to specific episodes (Medin & Ross, 1989). Medin and Ross (1989) suggested that this use of instance information reflects a *priority of the specific* in cognitive processing; that is, the cognitive system is designed to operate by using representations of specific instances that have been encountered rather than by creating abstract rules from experience.

A striking case of the use of specific information came from a study of college students asked to develop word problems for addition and division problems (Bassok, Chase, & Martin, 1998). This domain is interesting, because intuition suggests that semantic content does not affect college students' performance with basic arithmetic. In one study, researchers asked students to generate either addition or division problems and gave them a pair of objects to use in the problems. The objects either came from the same category (e.g., apples and oranges) or were associatively related (e.g., apples and baskets). When college students were asked to make addition word problems involving objects from the same category like apples and oranges, they wrote simple stories in which the objects were aggregated (say, finding the total number of pieces of fruit when given the number of apples and the number of oranges). In contrast, when asked to make addition word problems involving objects that were only associatively related, like apples and baskets, they were uncomfortable writing problems that required dissimilar items to be aggregated. Instead, they tended to use other strategies, such as introducing new objects from the same category as one of the original objects (e.g., having apples and oranges in a basket and finding the total number of pieces of fruit) or even writing the problem with a different arithmetic operation (e.g., using division instead of addition). The opposite pattern was observed for division problems. College students were happy to write division problems for objects that were associatively related (e.g., distributing apples among baskets), but not for objects from the same category (e.g., finding the number of apples per orange). This finding suggests that content influences the way college students think about even very basic abstract domains like arithmetic.

In another illuminating example of the spontaneous use of specific instance information, Regehr and Brooks (1993) gave people a classification task that involved a complex rule. Sample items from this classification task are shown in Figure 8.2. Subjects were shown the items in either Training Set A or Training Set B and were asked to identify the "builders," which were defined by a complex rule like "six legs and an angular body and spots." For this classification task, the complex rule was given explicitly, so that the task

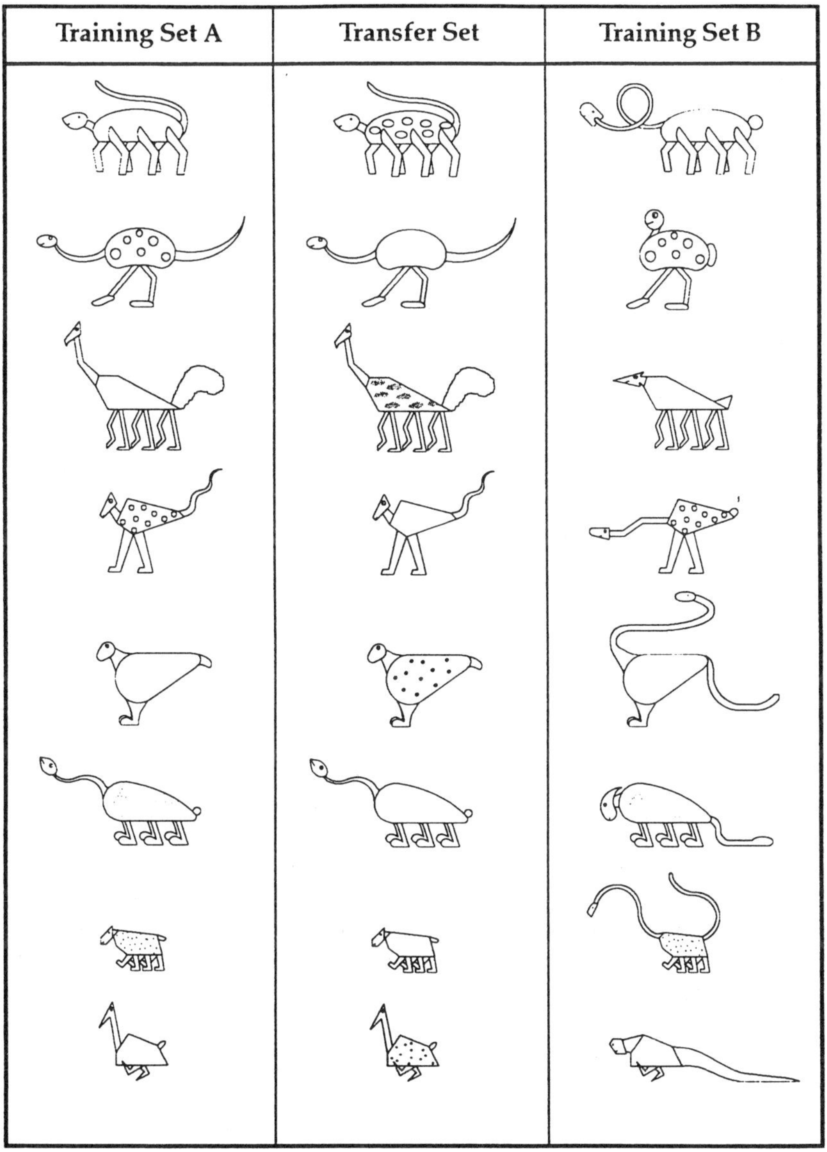

| Training Set A | Transfer Set | Training Set B |

FIG. 8.2. Training and transfer items from a study demonstrating the role of specific instances in a situation that required only application of an abstract rule. From G. Regehr and L. R. Brooks (1993). Copyright © 1993 by American Psychological Association. Reprinted by permission.

required only learning how to apply the rule to specific instances. After a set of training trials in which they practiced applying the rule, people were given a transfer phase in which a new set of items was presented. The transfer items were selected so that some of the items for which the rule did *not* apply were perceptually similar to the items in the training set for those subjects given Training Set A, but not for those given Training Set B.

If people use only the abstract rule, this perceptual similarity should not matter, because only the application of the rule is important. In contrast, if people use specific instance information, people given Training Set A would mistakenly say that the transfer items belonged in the category (because of their perceptual similarity to the training instances), whereas people given Training Set B would not. Indeed, people given Training Set A did make many errors on these transfer items, but people given Training Set B did not. Thus, this finding suggests that subjects did not simply follow a rule but instead answered the new classification questions on the basis of information about specific exemplars seen during training, even though the task required only following an abstract rule. The cognitive system is apparently designed to store specific information about instances that it is exposed to.

I now turn to three proposals for the ways that specific instances are used and address the issue of how to determine the right level of abstraction for representing properties of instances at the end of this chapter.

CASE-BASED REASONING

Perhaps the best worked-out models that use specific instance information for reasoning belong to a branch of AI called case-based reasoning (CBR). The central tenet of CBR models is that the knowledge of an intelligent reasoning system is in the form of cases, which describe specific instances that are typically other experiences in the same problem domain (see Kolodner, 1993; Schank, Kass, & Riesbeck, 1994, for overviews). CBR systems have been applied primarily to problems of planning and explanation, in which the cases in the knowledge base (typically called a *case base*) are previous plans or explanations. In this discussion of case-based reasoning, I first describe the basic components of a CBR system and then one example of a CBR system that illustrates these components in action. Finally, I discuss some limitations of current CBR models and some possible extensions.

Components of a Case-Based Reasoning System

CBR systems are often implemented computer programs that consist of four basic components (see Figure 8.3). First, there is a knowledge base that contains a set of relevant cases. Second, there is a mechanism that retrieves cases from the knowledge base when a new problem is encoun-

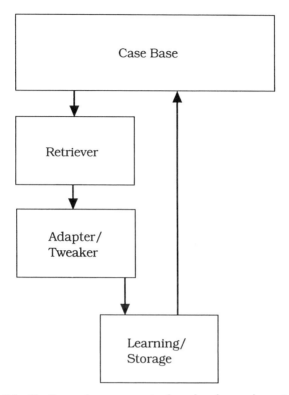

FIG. 8.3. The four major components of case-based reasoning systems.

tered. Third, there is a mechanism that adapts or tweaks the case to make it work in the current situation. Finally, there is a mechanism that takes new situations and adds them to the case base to enhance the functionality of the system.

The heart of a case-based reasoning system is the case base. Each case in the case base consists of a bundle of knowledge about a particular episode. Typically, cases are represented with some form of structured representation. In domains with a consistent set of attributes that one can expect across cases (as in medical diagnosis, where every patient is likely to have had the same set of diagnostic tests), the cases can be represented as frames (see chap. 5). In these systems, cases are described by slots and their fillers. As discussed in chapter 5, however, it is possible to augment these structured representations with relations that provide further information about relationships among elements in the case. For example, causal relations that describe how the value of one slot is related to the value of another can be added.

After a set of cases has been defined, there needs to be a mechanism for retrieving cases from memory. Case-based reasoning systems typically use an *indexing scheme* for this purpose. In an indexing system, particular aspects of memory items are defined in advance to be indices. These indices point directly to the item in memory, and if the index appears in the description of a new problem situation, the case can be retrieved. Many different aspects of a case can be used as indices, for example, the actors or objects in the case. Likewise, key elements of the case, such as goals they satisfy or failures they help avoid, can be used as indices. The use of goals and execution failures helps ensure that the case is retrieved when it is likely to be relevant. Thus, the advantage of an indexing system is that indices allow items to be retrieved when they are relevant to important goals that the system must reach. The potential disadvantage is that the indices must be defined in advance when the case is entered into the case base. Thus, cases can be retrieved only for goals that are known in advance. If a new problem arises, cases relevant to that problem are not retrieved.

After a case has been retrieved from the case base, it must be applied to the current problem. Sometimes, the case can be applied without any further effort. For example, if a person who is cooking macaroni recalls a previous occasion of cooking macaroni, he or she can simply repeat the steps of the previous situation. If the new situation differs in any way from the previous situation, the latter must be altered to be used in the new situation. In many cases, the changes are minor, and the case need only be *tweaked* (Schank et al., 1994). For example, if a person is cooking macaroni and is reminded of a time when he or she cooked spaghetti, the person can substitute macaroni for spaghetti in the retrieved case and then carry out the events. This is not a substantial change, but it does require that the old case be properly aligned with the new case so that the proper substitution can be made.

Large-scale changes to a retrieved plan may also be required. Here, an existing case may be *adapted* to the new situation. For example, imagine cooking macaroni and retrieving a previous situation in which one cooked angel-hair pasta. Because it is so thin, angel hair cooks in only a few minutes; macaroni is thicker and requires more cooking time. If a person follows the angel-hair pasta plan, substitutes macaroni for angel hair, and cooks it for the same amount of time, the macaroni would be too hard. In this situation, other reasoning is necessary. One must know that pasta gets softer as it cooks, and one should change the plan by increasing the cooking time. In this case, one has adapted the old case to the new situation (Alterman, 1988; Hammond, 1990).

The idea that a retrieved example requires cognitive effort to be applied in a new situation has psychological support. Researchers have extensively explored how people solve insight problems (e.g., Sternberg & Davidson, 1995), an example of which is the nine-dot problem shown in Figure 8.4. The problem is to draw four lines through all nine dots in the three-by-three

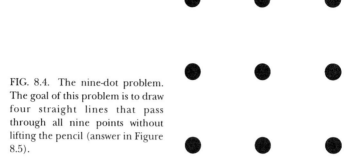

FIG. 8.4. The nine-dot problem. The goal of this problem is to draw four straight lines that pass through all nine points without lifting the pencil (answer in Figure 8.5).

grid of dots without lifting the pencil. The solution to the problem, shown in Figure 8.5, involves drawing lines that go outside the boundaries of the grid. Studies have demonstrated that an important component of the insight experience (i.e., the "aha" experience) that goes along with solving an insight problem is retrieving a relevant case from memory. For example, other problems like the nine-dot problem involve larger grids; the solution to these problems also involves drawing lines that extend beyond the boundaries of the grid, but the specific lines are not the same. Thus, many people report having an "aha" experience with other versions of the nine-dot problem (if they have solved the nine-dot problem itself before), because they are reminded of the nine-dot problem and remember that problems of this type can be solved by drawing lines that go outside the boundaries of the grid. Nevertheless, they still need a lot of time to solve the problem even after having this insight experience; the insight provides an avenue for solving the problem, but does not provide a complete solution (Weisberg, 1995). This result supports the idea that recalling a relevant case from memory is only part of the process of using a previous experience. The retrieved case must also be adapted to the current situation to be used.

When a new situation leads to a tweak or adaptation of an old case, this new situation is a candidate to be stored in the case base as well. In CBR systems, storing the case requires placing its representation into the case memory and indexing it. Typically, CBR systems have an automatic indexing system that specifies particular slots whose fillers become the indices to the new case. As discussed earlier, object, goal, and goal failure information are frequently used as retrieval indices.

Not all these mechanisms are fully implemented in the CBR models that have been developed. Many systems work with a fixed case base that is not updated with new cases. In these systems, the case base was selected to be representative of the problems in the domain, and updating this case base is deemed unnecessary. In many systems, the process of adapting and tweaking is carried out primarily by users of the systems. In these

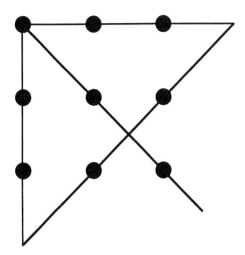

FIG. 8.5. The solution to the nine-dot problem.

programs, the case-based system selects a relevant case and may even suggest possible changes to the case selected. These systems act only as advisers to a human user, who has ultimate authority over how the case is used. Case-based reasoning systems have been applied to real-world problems, including architectural design, autoclave loading, and case law retrieval (Kolodner, 1993).

SWALE: A Case-Based Explainer

As an example of a system that does case-based explanation, I consider SWALE (Schank & Leake, 1989), a program designed to generate explanations of anomalous occurrences based on past events. SWALE contains the four components in Figure 8.3.[2] The program was originally designed to explain the mysterious death of the racehorse Swale, who died after winning the Belmont Stakes. In casting about for an explanation for the death of an athlete, one can look for similar events. SWALE has in its case memory a number of possible similar events such as the death of Jim Fixx, a jogger and author who wrote about the joys of jogging. He had a heart defect and collapsed one day after running. Likewise, one can speculate that Swale had a similar hidden defect that caused him to die after exertion.

In SWALE, memory consists of objects and memory organization packets (MOPs). The objects describe the attributes of objects and relate them on abstraction hierarchies via class-inclusion relations (e.g., Swale was a race-

---

[2]The LISP code for a small version of SWALE, called microSWALE, is presented by Schank, Kass, and Riesbeck (1994).

horse, which is a kind of horse, which is a kind of animal). The MOPs (see chap. 7) describe events (e.g., the events involved in a horse race as well as extra information such as the fact that a horse race requires exertion on the part of the horse). One other memory structure in SWALE is the explanation pattern, a previous explanation that the system has stored. For example, SWALE might know about Jim Fixx. The explanation pattern for Jim Fixx would say that Fixx had a heart defect and that the heart defect caused Fixx's untimely death.

The explanation patterns are the cases in memory that must be retrieved to generate an explanation. SWALE has an indexed case base. The primary indices in the case base are unexpected events. In the case of Swale, the unexpected event is that, whereas a young racehorse is expected to be alive, Swale died. This story is classified as involving an unexpected death which is used as a cue in a search of memory. Explanation patterns in memory are retrieved if they were indexed as unexpected deaths as well. The case of Jim Fixx would be indexed this way (as might a situation like that of the singer Janis Joplin, who died of a drug overdose).

After a case is retrieved, it must be fitted to the current situation. SWALE adapts cases by using a set of tweakers. These tweakers allow objects and events in the explanation pattern to be changed if the current situation has different values for the objects and events, but they do not affect the causal connections between elements in the story. For example, SWALE compares the case of Swale to that of Jim Fixx and notices that Swale was a horse and Fixx was a person. The tweaker looks at its information about horses and people and decides that the difference is not important because horses and people are both animals and can die. After making this change, the program determines that Jim Fixx died after jogging, but that Swale did not jog. Because the MOPs have information that jogging is a kind of physical exertion and that horse races are a kind of race, which is also a physical exertion, this substitution is also allowed. Thus, the differences between the Swale and Fixx cases are not deemed fatal to the explanation, and the Jim Fixx explanation pattern is accepted as a possible explanation for Swale's death. The explanatory aspect of this case would be the suggestion that Swale had a heart defect just as Jim Fixx did. This aspect is the explanation, because it is the relational information that binds together the parts of the Swale story connected to the expectation failure.

More elaborate tweaking may also be necessary. For example, if there was a case in memory for the death of Janis Joplin (who died of a drug overdose), a simple substitution is not possible. Nothing in the immediate story about Swale points to drug use. Instead, other knowledge would have to be brought to bear, such as that athletes sometimes use drugs to enhance their performance. Further, the system would have to know that horses cannot administer drugs to themselves, and another agent would have to be posited for giving the drugs to Swale. In fact, elaborate explanations like this can be generated by Swale if enough object and event knowledge is given to the system. SWALE does not really evaluate the explanations. If it finds a few different explanation patterns that it can tweak, it returns more than one possible explanation for the observed anomaly. Presumably, however, some heuristics can be used to evaluate competing explanations. For example, explanations requiring extensive tweaking should probably be deemed less plausible than are explanations requiring little tweaking.

Finally, after an explanation is generated, it can be incorporated into memory. One strategy that SWALE uses for incorporating new cases into memory is to generalize the initial explanation. After discovering that both horse racing and jogging are forms of physical exertion, SWALE can generate an explanation pattern that assumes that physical exertion is important and that the particular form of physical exertion is not. Likewise, if SWALE notes that Swale and Fixx were both animals but were not both human, the new explanation pattern can be stored as true of animals in general, not just of people. After generalizing the explanation pattern, SWALE can index it. SWALE uses two types of indices for new explanation patterns. First, the explanation patterns are indexed by the anomaly that they explain (in this case an unexpected death). Second, they are indexed by the causal preconditions in the situation. Thus, causally relevant features are assumed to be important for retrieval. In the case of Swale, physical exertion would become an index, as would death (Schank & Leake, 1989).

Discussion and Limitations

Case-based reasoning systems attack complex reasoning problems by looking for previous solutions that are similar rather than by reasoning from abstract principles. The advantage of using similar cases is that these cases are known to work. Jim Fixx really did die from the combination of a heart defect and exertion. Janis Joplin really did die from an overdose. Thus, the explanation in a case is already known to work in at least one domain. If explanations had to be constructed before they were applied, the explanations would first have to be tested to make sure they were plausible.

Case-based reasoning systems also solve a difficult combinatorial problem. Any anomalous situation or planning problem may have an infinite number of possible explanations or solutions. By limiting the search for answers to the set of items in memory, a case-based reasoning system is able to find solutions efficiently. This advantage also limits the system to explanations that bear some resemblance to episodes from past experience. In many real-world domains, however, the combinatorial problem is probably more severe than the possibility that there will be too little good information in memory, and so it is reasonable to use a case-based reasoning approach. Case-based reasoning systems can be augmented with other methods of generating explanations to provide even more powerful engines for solving problems.

The notion that previous cases can help to solve important combinatorial problems seems to be exploited by people in situations in which they are asked to be creative (Ward, 1994, 1995). In particular, people tend to extend existing categories when making novel inventions rather than seeking highly novel solutions to new problems. Ward (1995) pointed out that during the development of the railroad, conductors and brakemen initially rode on the outside of the train, because drivers sat outside on stagecoaches and stagecoaches were a dominant means of transportation when railroads were being developed. Thus, designers extended the design for a stagecoach to this new mode of transportation because the stagecoach had solved important problems for transporting people (e.g., where they should sit, how luggage should be stored). Unfortunately, this design also presented problems; railroad cars had a tendency to derail and tip over. Thus, the design of railroad cars was eventually modified to put the crew on the inside to avoid injuries. Such incremental creativity in invention is common.

Case-based reasoning systems are typically designed as programs that are applied in practical settings. They are not really cognitive models, and the mechanisms they use are not necessarily those that people use to solve the same problems. Although people also seem to use previous examples to solve difficult problems (Gick & Holyoak, 1983; Reed & Bolstad, 1991; Reed, Ernst, & Banerji, 1974; Ross, 1984, 1989), they do not appear to access these problems by using an indexing system like those implemented in CBR models (Gentner, Rattermann, & Forbus, 1993).

There has been significant research on the way that analogs in memory are accessed in the area of analogical retrieval and problem solving (see Reeves & Weisberg, 1994, for a review of this area). The generic research paradigm here is that people are given a previous case or example and some time later are asked to solve a new problem. The new problem is similar to the previous case in some way, and researchers look for evidence that the previous case was used to solve the new problem. In one classic set of studies, Gick and Holyoak (1980, 1983) examined people's ability to use a previous example to solve a new problem. First, they told people a story that would later be useful in solving a problem. The story told of a general who wanted to attack a fortress surrounded by mines, and so he divided his army into small groups and had them converge on the fortress. Later, these people were given a problem to solve. This problem, Duncker's (1945) ray problem, describes a patient with an inoperable tumor that can be destroyed by radiation, but radiation strong enough to destroy the tumor will also destroy the healthy tissue around the tumor. The subjects must find a way to destroy the tumor without destroying the healthy tissue.

The solution to this problem is similar to that in the story about the general. Weak rays should be directed at the tumor from different directions so that they converge on the tumor, destroy it, but spare the surrounding healthy tissue. The striking finding in these studies is that, despite the fact that people had just read a story with a solution that is helpful for the problem, they did not find the earlier story very helpful. In a typical study, 10% of the subjects solved the ray problem spontaneously without being given the story about the general. Gick and Holyoak found that only about 20% of the subjects solved the ray problem correctly when given the story about the general. There are two possible explanations for this finding. First, people may have failed to notice that the story about the general was relevant to the problem. Second, people may have recognized that the story was relevant, but were unable to apply the solution to the ray problem. To distinguish between these possibilities, Gick and Holyoak gave people time to solve the ray problem after reading the story about the general. If they failed to solve it, they were given a hint to use a story they had just read. Given this hint, 92% of the subjects solved the ray problem. This finding suggests that people did not notice that the story was relevant to solving the problem, because they could use it when told it was relevant.

The story about the general is similar to the ray problem only in that both require a common solution to a problem. The troops in the military story are not similar to healthy tissue. The fortress is not similar to a tumor. Thus, this result suggests that people do not retrieve things from memory whose only similarities are in the relations between objects. This pattern of results has been confirmed in studies using similar procedures (Gentner et al., 1993; Holyoak & Koh, 1987; Novick, 1988; Ross, 1984, 1987, 1989).

If people do not retrieve things from memory on the basis of similarities in relations between objects, what do they use to guide retrieval? Much evidence seems to suggest that commonalities in the objects in pairs of situations drive retrieval. In one study demonstrating this point, Gentner et al. (1993) had people read stories. A week later, the same people read other stories and were asked whether they were reminded of any of the earlier stories. Stories with similar characters served as good retrieval cues whether or not they had a similar plot. Stories with dissimilar characters and similar plots served as poor retrieval cues. Related work by Wharton and colleagues (1994) found a small effect of matching relations between cue and memory items. In their study, people read two stories, only one of which had a plot similar to a cue story presented later. The story with the similar plot was more likely to be retrieved than was the story with the dissimilar plot, but only if the stories also had similar characters. Taken together, these studies suggest that the presence of common objects is very important for retrieval.[3] Thus, people do not appear to index previous cases by goals and prominent relations in the way that many CBR models do.

This pattern of data is rather perplexing. It seems advantageous for a person in a new situation to be reminded of episodes with a similar relational structure, because such episodes are likely to be useful in constructing new plans and problem solutions. Although a complete review of this issue is beyond the scope of this chapter (see Forbus, Gentner, & Law, 1995; Hammond, Seifert, & Gray, 1991; Reeves & Weisberg, 1994), at least two important factors make purely relational remindings less attractive than remindings that involve some common objects. First, as discussed in chapter 5, processes (like analogical comparison) that operate over structured representations are computationally expensive. It takes substantial processing resources to place the arguments of matching relations in correspondence. This degree of processing is not feasible for a memory retrieval process that must take into account all items in memory. For this reason, many computational models of analogical retrieval have adopted a two-stage process in which the first stage is computationally inexpensive and operates over nonstructured representations; only later processing is affected by structural elements of the representations like relations (see chap. 10; Forbus et al., 1995).[4]

Second, as interesting as it is to find relational remindings that come from very different domains (like being reminded of the general's story when given the ray problem), these remindings are often not useful relative to mundane remindings of highly similar situations. When a person goes to a supermarket to buy tomato sauce, it is probably best to be reminded of other experiences of buying tomato sauce rather than of situations in which the person was selecting a vacation spot, even though both involve a choice. The specific factors important to choosing a tomato sauce (e.g., spices, thickness) are more likely to be part of a stored tomato sauce purchase than of a stored vacation decision. A similar situation occurs in scientific reasoning, in which the best "analogy" to a current problem often comes from a similar domain rather than a dissimilar one. Dunbar (1997) demonstrated that microbiologists often make analogies from one bacterium to another. These analogies are very rich and useful, but they also involve pairs of domains with many similar surface elements. Thus, case-based reasoning systems that attempt to find far-flung analogies (like SWALE) may be aimed at a problem that is much harder than those that people are generally required to solve to use past experience in their daily life.

---

[3]These are not the only possible cues that can be used for retrieval. Many problem situations are connected to a goal that they address; for these problems, the goal may also serve as a retrieval cue (Seifert, 1994).

[4]A multistage model has also been developed by Thagard, Holyoak, Nelson, and Gochfeld (1990).

METAPHORIC SYSTEM MAPPINGS AND ABSTRACT CONCEPTS

Concrete domains are also useful in the representation of abstract domains. In chapter 6, I briefly mentioned that cognitive linguists have speculated that abstract domains can be conceptualized in spatial terms (Gibbs, 1994; Lakoff & Johnson, 1980). For example, English has a system of meaning that follows the mapping *MORAL is UP*. One can say:

Mary decided to take the high road.   (8.1)

to mean a moral decision, and:

John stooped to new lows with his recent tactics.   (8.2)

to refer to an immoral act. The speculation on the part of cognitive linguists is that space is easy to understand and so it helps people comprehend complex concepts.

Space is not the only concrete domain that has been suggested as a source domain for metaphors for talking about abstract concepts. Gibbs (1994) gives an extended discussion of the metaphor *ANGER is HEATED FLUID IN A CONTAINER*. In this metaphor, the abstract domain of anger is conceptualized in terms of a closed container that contains fluid. As the level of anger increases, the container heats up; the increased pressure on the container may cause it to burst. This metaphor can be seen in the following passage:

Mary's blood was beginning to boil. The longer she watched
John, the more the pressure began to build inside her. She
was unable to vent her anger, and finally blew up at John,
spewing her rage.   (8.3)

In this passage, Mary's anger acts like heated fluid. This account assumes that the action of heated fluid is easier to understand than is that of anger, and it is easier to communicate about anger by using this metaphor than to use language that refers only to abstract emotional concepts. Cognitive linguists did not have to search very far to find metaphors like this one. As shown in Table 8.1, English is filled with metaphors in which physical systems refer to abstract concepts.

Such metaphors are assumed to set up mappings between representational systems (Fauconnier, 1994; Gentner, 1988; Gibbs, 1994; Lakoff & Johnson, 1980). Lakoff and Johnson (1980) and Gibbs (1994) were not very specific about how these metaphors are represented, but Gentner (1988) and Fauconnier (1994) both suggested that metaphors involve finding correspondences between structured relational representations. For

TABLE 8.1
Some Metaphoric Systems for Abstract Concepts in English

Target Domain	Base Domain	Example
Debate	War	John attacked his opponent's weak arguments.
Life	Container	Mary's life was filled with adventure.
Life	Journey	Susan was proud that she passed this milestone in her life.
Love	Physical Force	They were awed at how their feelings drew them together.
Love	Nutrient	In their hour of need, their love sustained them.
Ideas	Commodities	Rod passed his suggestions along to the management.
Ideas	Physical Objects	After many hours, Karen grasped the concept.
State	Person	The United States finally retaliated after being provoked by Iraq.

Gentner, the comparison process is the structure-mapping process described in chapter 5. On this view, the relations among concrete objects can be transferred to the abstract domain.

Fauconnier does not provide a specific comparison process but focuses on metaphor as one of several linguistic devices that involve setting up local domains in discourse. In each of these local domains, the representations are structured. Understanding a metaphor involves setting up one domain for the base of the metaphor and one domain for the target and tracking the correspondences between them.[5] For Fauconnier, language comprehension involves creating subdomains and finding correspondences between them. These correspondences can be simple identifications, as in the case of metonymy, where one object stands for another. For example, understanding the sentence:

The ham sandwich left a big tip. (8.4)

involves identifying the person who ate the ham sandwich with the thing he or she ate and setting up a domain in which the ham sandwich refers to the person. This domain is separate from the "real" world, in which the phrase "ham sandwich" refers to a ham sandwich. The distinction between the real world and the metonymic world can be seen in the sentence:

The waitress spoke to the complaining ham sandwich and
then she took it away. (8.5)

This sentence does not make sense; it uses the phrase "ham sandwich" to refer both to the person (in the metonymic world) and a ham sandwich (in the real world).

---

[5]Fauconnier (1994) referred to these domains as "mental spaces." I avoid this term here to avoid confusion with the mental space representations discussed in chapter 2.

Although there is no doubt that English uses the language of concrete domains to refer to abstract situations, what this fact reflects about ongoing cognitive processes is unclear (Murphy, 1996). Possibly, metaphoric language is a sign of active conceptual mappings between domains. On this view, when people use the metaphor *ANGER is HEATED FLUID IN A CONTAINER*, they activate their knowledge about anger and also about heated fluid and construct a mapping between these domains. A second possibility is that the observed metaphoric language is largely a collection of cognitive fossils enabling people to see metaphors that were active in the past. On this view, people interpret passages like Example 8.3 by using literal meanings of phrases that refer directly to anger, even though someone may have used these same phrases metaphorically before they were incorporated into the language.

Murphy (1996) pointed out several potential problems with the view that abstract concepts are understood only metaphorically. One problem is that many base domains used in metaphors are themselves rather complex and may not be well understood by people using the metaphor. These observed metaphorical systems may involve primarily literal meanings of terms that were once used metaphorically. On this view, many word senses that were once metaphorical are now literal. A second problem is that the metaphor view does not explain which aspects of the base domain are carried over to the abstract target domain. For example, the metaphor *ANGER is HEATED FLUID IN A CONTAINER* does not include the fact that hot fluid thrown from a container can burn those around it. Otherwise, it would make sense to say:

Mary's vented anger scalded John. (8.6)

Thus, although examples of language from concrete domains do seem to be used to express abstract concepts, there is no account of why some concepts are carried from the base to the target and others are not.

This argument should not be taken to mean that active use of metaphor is unimportant in understanding abstract concepts. Rather, the dispute is about the degree to which metaphors in which words for concrete domains refer to abstract concepts involve active processing of the metaphor rather than access of stored meanings relating to abstract concepts.

EXEMPLAR MODELS

Specific instance information has also been important in recent models in psychology. Researchers have examined whether human performance can be modeled by assuming that people store only previous instances (typically called *exemplars*), in which subsequent processing is a simple function of the stored past information. In this section, I review exemplar models of classification, automaticity, and memory and then discuss the representational assumptions that these models have in common.

Exemplar Models of Classification

An important task in the study of category acquisition is classification. In the typical classification task, people are shown a new item and asked to classify it into one of a small number of categories. After making a response, subjects receive feedback and are then given another trial. This process continues until subjects reach some accuracy criterion or perform a particular number of trials. Subjects' performance in these studies is often described by mathematical models. A prominent class of mathematical models for this task is the exemplar model (Estes, 1986, 1994; Kruschke, 1992; Medin & Schaffer, 1978; Nosofsky, 1986, 1987). Exemplar models assume that people store each instance that they are shown as well as the correct category label for the instance. On each new trial, the new instance is compared to all exemplars stored in memory, and a response based on the similarity of the new exemplar to previously seen exemplars is given.

One early exemplar model, which can serve as an example here, is Medin and Schaffer's (1978) context model. The context model assumed that exemplars are stored in memory as collections of features. When a new instance is presented, each of its features is compared with those of all exemplars stored in memory. For each new instance–old exemplar pair, each feature of the items is compared, and a similarity value that ranges between 0 and 1 is given for each feature comparison. Identical features get a value of 1, and less similar features get lower similarity values. The feature similarity values for each dimension are multiplied together to form the overall similarity between exemplars. The probability that a new instance is classified in a particular category is a function of the sum of the similarity values of the new instance to all old exemplars in that category divided by the sum of the similarity values of the new instance to all old exemplars in memory. Most exemplar models of classification have this general structure, although they have been extended with other mechanisms, such as those that allow different dimensions to be given different attention weights (Kruschke, 1992; Nosofsky, 1986, 1987). In Nosofsky's (1986) generalized context model, objects are represented as points in a multidimensional space (e.g., chap. 2), and the similarity of items is a function of the distance between points in that space. The spatial representation allows the dimensions of the space to be stretched or shrunk to reflect changes in the importance of the dimensions as a function of context.

Category A   Category B

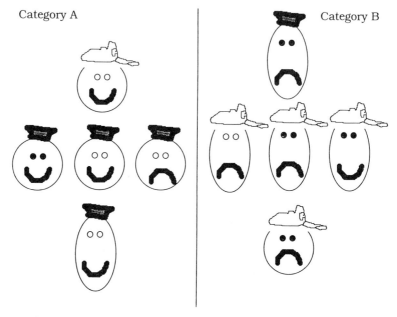

FIG. 8.6. Two categories of faces with prototypes in the middle of each group.

Exemplar models can account for many findings in studies of classification. For example, it is well known that category prototypes are easy to classify. The prototype is typically the "average" exemplar. In Figure 8.6, the prototype is the middle face in categories A and B. Every other exemplar shares three features with this prototype and one feature with the prototype of the other category. As discussed in chapter 2, an interesting finding is that the category prototype may be well categorized, even if it has never been seen during learning (e.g., Posner & Keele, 1970). This finding had been taken as evidence that category acquisition involves the automatic generation of a prototype (that is, of an average exemplar), but exemplar models can also account for this phenomenon. In general, the prototype is similar to many of the instances that are members of the category. Thus, even if the prototype has never been seen before, it is more similar to the exemplars of one category than to those of the other, and hence it is classified correctly.

Exemplar Models of Automaticity

Exemplar models have also been applied to the study of automaticity. Automaticity is achieved in a cognitive skill when the skill can be performed without effort or conscious control. For example, most people can produce basic arithmetic facts automatically. When they must add 6 and 3, they can produce 9 without having to generate the answer through an algorithm (such as starting at 6 and counting up 3). Of course, this automaticity is not achieved easily; it is the result of extensive practice in the domain. For arithmetic facts, teachers often give children hundreds of practice trials for each fact with an emphasis on speed. An early school memory for me is a grade school test in which all 100 two-addend addition facts involving the numbers 0 through 9 had to be completed in 5 minutes. As I recall, the class could not continue to the next lesson until everyone successfully completed this assignment.

Logan (1988) suggested that such automatic processes are carried out by storing individual training instances paired with the response that goes with them. Performance on a task is a race between an algorithm (such as starting at the first addend and counting up to the number of the second addend) and retrieval of a fact from memory. Logan assumed that the more times a particular instance is stored in memory, the faster it can be retrieved. At some point, there are so many instances of a particular fact in memory that the fact can be retrieved faster than the algorithm can be performed. When memory retrieval becomes faster than the algorithm, the skill becomes automatic.

According to this initial instance theory of automaticity, a new instance retrieves only memory instances identical to it. Extensions to this type of model have proposed that merely similar instances can be used as well. In the exemplar-based random walk model (EBRW: Nosofsky & Palmeri, 1997; Palmeri, 1997), instances are represented as points in a multidimensional space (as in the generalized context model just described), in which the similarity of two items decreases with the distance between them in the space. In EBRW, a newly presented instance retrieves items from memory, where the probability of retrieving a given item in memory is larger the greater the similarity between the item and the new instance. This model differs from Logan's instance-based theory in that the response made is not the one associated with the first new instance retrieved. Instead, the model uses a random walk of a particular distance to determine the response.

A diagram of a random walk is illustrated in Figure 8.7. Initially, the response criteria (labeled Response A and Response B) are some distance from the starting point. When an instance is retrieved, the model takes one step toward the response associated with that instance. Then, another instance is retrieved, and another step is taken. This process continues until one of the response criteria is reached. Thus, a response involves many memory retrievals rather than just one. The time needed to respond is based on the number of memory retrievals required before one of the response criteria is reached (or until a competing algorithm finishes processing). The model has been applied successfully to data from tasks de-

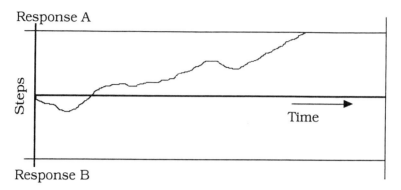

FIG. 8.7. Illustration of a random walk.

signed to examine the development of automaticity (Palmeri, 1997) and classification ability (Nosofsky & Palmeri, 1997).

Exemplar Models of Memory

Both the classification and automaticity tasks described in the previous sections are essentially memory tasks. In both cases, appropriate previous elements must be retrieved from memory to make a response. As discussed in chapter 4, many models of memory tasks have adopted semantic network representations (J. R. Anderson, 1983a; Raaijmakers & Shiffrin, 1981), but some models make assumptions closer to those of the classification and automaticity models described in the previous two sections. A common memory task in cognitive psychology involves showing subjects a list of items (e.g., words or pictures) and then probing their memory for the items in some way. The probes can be direct, as in free recall, cued recall, and recognition tasks, or indirect, as in stem completion tasks (e.g., Squire, 1987).[6] Some memory models are similar to the exemplar models described in the previous sections, in that each memory item is stored as an instance (which may include some information about the context of presentation). The representations used in these exemplar memory models may involve features or points in a multidimensional space. As in the previously described models, the probability that an item will be retrieved is a function

---

[6]In a stem completion task, subjects first read a list of words. Some time later, they are given the first three letters of a word (e.g., STR_____) and are asked to complete the stem with the first word that comes to mind. A word beginning with a given stem is more likely to be given as a completion to a stem if it appeared on a previous study list than if it did not. This task is thought to tap implicit memory, because even people with amnesia, who have no recollection of the previous list, show evidence of having seen the list in a stem completion task (Cohen & Eichenbaum, 1993; Squire, 1987).

of the similarity of the item and a cue for the item, although memory models incorporate many other factors as well.

Random walk models can be applied to data from recognition experiments. Ratcliff (1988) presented a model in which the recognition probe is compared to memory feature by feature. Each feature match pushes the model one step toward the boundary to respond "old," and each feature mismatch pushes the model one step toward the boundary to respond "new." In this case, the random walk model assumes a featural representation of information in memory. Ratcliff further demonstrated that the random walk model can be given a continuous formulation (the diffusion model). In this case, the representation of items is more like a multidimensional space than a set of discrete features.

Another model that focuses on storage of individual items is MINERVA 2 (Hintzman, 1986). In this model, items in a studied list are represented as vectors of features, in which the value of any feature can range from 1 to −1. A sample memory of this type is shown in Figure 8.8. In models like this, it is possible to think of values of 1 as features that are present, values of −1 as features that are explicitly noted as absent, and values of 0 as features that are absent but are not explicitly noted as absent (Markman, 1989). When a memory probe is presented to the model, it is compared with every vector in memory. For each comparison, the dot product (see Equation 2.17) is taken between the probe and the item in memory, and this value is divided by the number of nonzero elements in the vector for at least one of the vectors. This quantity, which ranges between −1 and 1, is a measure of the distance between the vectors in space. The probe is assumed to activate each item in memory proportional to its similarity to the probe. In particular, the activation of each item is the cube of the similarity score, which has the effect of driving moderately small values of similarity toward 0 while preserving the sign of the dot product. Activations of each item in memory when there is a probe are also shown in Figure 8.8.

Two things can be done with these activations. First, the familiarity of the probe can be determined by summing the degree of activation generated by the probe. The greater this activation score, the more familiar the probe. The familiarity can be used as the basis of a judgment that the probe had been seen before. For example, in the memory shown in Figure 8.8, three memory items are activated by the probe. When the activation of these memory items is added together, the probe is judged as familiar, because there are some moderately high levels of activation. Second, one can generate a memory response by taking each feature of the items in memory, multiplying them by their activation, and then adding the values together. The activated features with a memory probe are also shown in

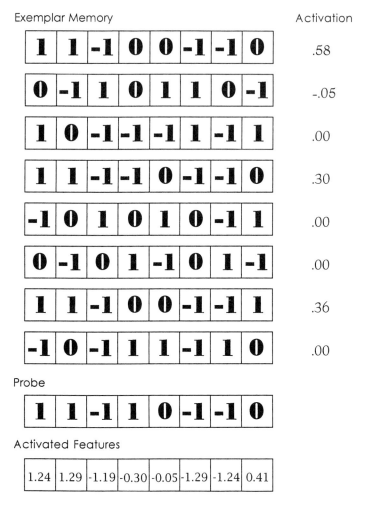

Exemplar Memory   Activation

| 1 | 1 | -1 | 0 | 0 | -1 | -1 | 0 | .58
| 0 | -1 | 1 | 0 | 1 | 1 | 0 | -1 | -.05
| 1 | 0 | -1 | -1 | -1 | 1 | -1 | 1 | .00
| 1 | 1 | -1 | -1 | 0 | -1 | -1 | 0 | .30
| -1 | 0 | 1 | 0 | 1 | 0 | -1 | 1 | .00
| 0 | -1 | 0 | 1 | -1 | 0 | 1 | -1 | .00
| 1 | 1 | -1 | 0 | 0 | -1 | -1 | 1 | .36
| -1 | 0 | -1 | 1 | 1 | -1 | 1 | 0 | .00

Probe

| 1 | 1 | -1 | 1 | 0 | -1 | -1 | 0 |

Activated Features

| 1.24 | 1.29 | -1.19 | -0.30 | -0.05 | -1.29 | -1.24 | 0.41 |

FIG. 8.8. An exemplar memory like that proposed in the MINERVA 2 model. If the probe is compared to the memory, the items in memory are activated to the degree shown in the column labeled "Activation." The features activated in memory are shown at the bottom of the figure.

Figure 8.8. This vector of activated features reflects an average across a variety of items in memory (in this case, the feature values are most strongly influenced by the three highly activated vectors). Because this vector is an average across items in memory, it acts like a prototype. For example, the fourth feature in the probe vector is a one, but when the activated features from memory are found, there is very little activation for this feature. This result suggests that a value of 1 was not the dominant value for this feature in memory. In this way, storage of individual instances can give rise to an abstraction. The model calculates this abstraction during retrieval from memory by using stored information about specific instances.

Exemplar Representation and Retrieval

Exemplar models of classification, automaticity, and memory differ in many of their specific implementational details, but they all seem to share a common set of representational assumptions. In particular, all the models assume either a multidimensional space representation or a feature representation in which the features are independent. In these feature representations, the common and distinctive features are typically not treated differently. Instead, simple feature comparisons are made, and the results of a set of feature comparisons for a given pair are combined in a straightforward way (typically by multiplying the results of different comparisons together).

This commonality among models is not surprising: All the models solve a fundamentally similar problem. All assume that memory consists of a large number of stored instances. In exemplar models of classification and memory, memory apparently consists of all the training stimuli. In exemplar models of automaticity, memory is even larger and consists of all training trials (which can exceed 10,000). For a newly presented instance to be compared against *every* item in memory, the comparison process must be computationally simple. The simple feature comparisons and spatial distance comparisons in the models described in this section all have that property.

These models highlight an interesting contrast in the use of representation. Exemplar models that require comparisons of new instances with a large number of previous cases involve simple representations (i.e., features, spaces, or semantic networks). Likewise, as discussed previously, the early stages of models of analogical retrieval also involve simple representations that can be easily compared with many other representations. In contrast, more complex processes of reasoning, explanation, and metaphor involve structured representations. The representations in case-based reasoning systems and those assumed by models of metaphor are structured and contain explicit relations among elements. At first glance, it might seem difficult to reconcile these two approaches, but the two kinds of representations are designed to carry out different functions and may indeed coexist in the cognitive system (see Sloman, 1996, for a discussion of two types of reasoning processes compatible with this suggestion; this issue is discussed in more detail in chap. 10).

FINDING THE RIGHT LEVEL OF ABSTRACTION

As discussed at the very beginning of this chapter, all representations are abstractions to some degree. A perceptual representation of a face incorporates some but not all of the information available in the light that hits the eye. If a symbolic representation is used, each symbol has a particular scope. A question of great importance to cognitive science, one that has received very little attention, is how the scope of a representation is determined.

This issue can be illustrated with the schematic bugs shown in Figure 8.9 (Yamauchi & Markman, 1998). How should the bug in Figure 8.9A be represented? Is the overall outline important? Should it be broken down into features? Even if it is agreed that the bug can be described by features for the head, tail, body, and legs, what features are appropriate? The overall shape of the legs may be important or perhaps the number of legs. Seeing another example, like the one in Figure 8.9B, does not necessarily help. How the features in these two bugs should be represented depends in large part on what is to be done with the bugs and the relation between them. If the bugs are to be classified, the way that the features are described depends on whether these bugs are in the same or different classes. If they are in the same class, perhaps the number of legs is important; the shape of the legs clearly is not. If they are in different classes, perhaps the shape of the legs should be represented. Deciding when two aspects of the world should be treated as manifestations of a single feature and when they should be treated as two distinct features is a complex process (Medin, Dewey, & Murphy, 1983).

Little research has addressed this issue. Studies of word learning in children have revealed some early biases in the information represented about objects. Some data have demonstrated that when children are given a novel noun in the presence of an unfamiliar object, they extend the label to refer to other objects with a similar shape; this finding suggests

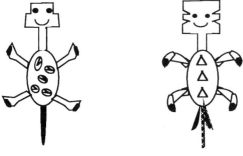

(A)   (B)

FIG. 8.9. Two bugs that illustrate the difficulty of determining how features should be described.

that the overall shape of objects is represented (Imai, Gentner, & Uchida, 1994; Landau, Smith, & Jones, 1988). Workers have focused broadly on the shapes of objects and have not explored the components that may make up shape representation. Perhaps the kinds of representations discussed in chapter 6 might be useful.

Other investigations support the suggestion that the way one feature contrasts with another influences how the information is represented (Schyns & Rodet, 1997; Spalding & Ross, 1994). In one study, Schyns and Rodet (1997) showed people complex perceptual stimuli, which they called Martian cells. Stimuli like those used in their studies are shown in Figure 8.10. There were two classes of cells. One was defined by the presence of a perceptual feature X, and a second was defined by the presence of a perceptual feature that was a combination of perceptual features X and Y (which I call XY). An example of an XY stimulus is shown in the third row of Figure 8.10. Half the subjects in this study saw examples of the X category followed by examples of the XY category. The other half saw the examples in the reverse order (i.e., XY followed by X). After this training, subjects were shown a new stimulus that had both the features X and Y, but they were separate elements, not joined (I call this category X-Y).

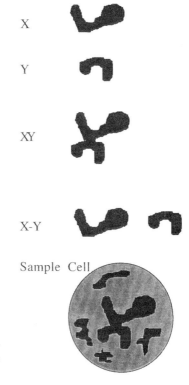

FIG. 8.10. Perceptual stimuli like those used by Schyns and Rodet (1997).

When people saw the *XY* category first, they tended to categorize the new *X-Y* stimuli in the *X* category. This result was probably obtained because these subjects saw the *XY* feature first and treated it as a single indivisible feature. When they then saw the *X* feature alone, they treated it as an indivisible feature. For these subjects, the *XY* and *X* features were diagnostic of the categories. Because they had no representation of the *Y* feature alone, they did not think it relevant when the *X-Y* stimulus was shown, and so the *X-Y* item was categorized in the *X* category.

In contrast, when subjects saw the *X* category followed by the *XY* category during training, they tended to categorize the *X-Y* stimulus in the *XY* category. In this case, seeing the *X* category first gave them a representation of the *X* feature. Then, when the *XY* stimulus was shown, the complex *XY* feature could be broken down into its *X* and *Y* components. These subjects would have category representations in which features *X* and *Y* were both diagnostic of the categories. Thus, when the *X-Y* category was presented, they were able to recognize that it contained both *X* and *Y* elements and hence categorized it in the *XY* category. This study suggests that people's previous history with perceptual items influences the way that they represent the items.

Finally, language may play a role in determining an appropriate level of abstraction for features. In many situations, properties of objects are described in different ways on the basis of how they should be represented. For example, I often take my son to the Museum of Natural History in New York and show him the dinosaur fossils. Pointing to an apatosaurus skeleton, I may say, "That dinosaur ate plants." Later in the visit, we often pass displays of animals local to the northeastern United States, and I may point to a cow and say, "Cows eat grass." When I say that the dinosaur ate plants, I am providing information about its diet but also information about the right level of abstraction for representing this property. I could have said that the dinosaur ate grass (as I did for the cow) or even that the dinosaur ate a particular species of plant. By using the general term *plants*, I signaled that the feature should be represented at a high level of abstraction for dinosaurs (but not for cows). In this way, language may be a powerful force for helping people to determine how features should be represented.

SUMMARY

As this chapter demonstrates, there are many cases in which people could use abstract concepts but instead seem to reason with specific information. In case-based reasoning, rather than storing abstractions that capture only the important relations that hold for a domain, people seem to store specific cases. New reasoning situations involve retrieving past cases and adapting them to the new situation. Analysis of language for abstract concepts suggests that people talk about abstract domains by using the language of concrete situations. This metaphoric language suggests that (at least at one time) these abstract domains were actually conceptualized in concrete terms. Finally, many models of memory-based processes (including classification, automaticity, and retrieval) involve the storage of individual cases that are retrieved directly and used to process new items.

It is clear that specific instance information is important in cognitive processing. Nonetheless, abstractions are also crucial. Generalized structures like MOPs help people see similarities across domains without getting caught up in the fine details of specific situations. Having abstract schemas can be helpful. Earlier in this chapter, I described one of Gick and Holyoak's studies, in which people were unable to retrieve the story about the general's armies converging on the fortress when given Duncker's ray problem. In an extension of this study (Gick & Holyoak, 1983), people were given two analogous stories and were allowed to compare them. Later, they were given Duncker's ray problem. Unlike the first study described, the subjects in this study often solved the ray problem. This finding suggests that the comparison of the two analogous stories allowed people to form a schema for a "convergence" solution to the problem (i.e., that a force should converge on something to allow it to be destroyed). This schema was easier to recall than was the specific case.

The main point is that cognitive representations probably involve a mix of specific and abstract situations. I have focused here primarily on the use of specific cases, because research on knowledge representation has historically focused on abstraction. This chapter is meant to demonstrate that, when thinking about representation, specific cases should be on a par with abstract information, but not that cognitive representations should contain only information about specific instances.

Chapter 9

Mental Models

WHAT IS A MENTAL MODEL?

In chapter 7, I examined the problem of scripts and related representational structures for events. Such representations focused on temporal and causal relationships among objects during events. Most events that I discussed (and indeed most events that have been the basis of work on scripts) are socially or culturally defined events, such as going to the doctor or taking a trip on a train. These representational structures allow people to reason about ongoing events by using knowledge about related events that have already happened.

How do people reason about novel events? Imagine a situation in which a young boy stands at the top of a hill, makes a snowball, and rolls it down the snow-covered side of the hill. A person may never have witnessed an event like this, but one can construct the event and talk about it. One can imagine that the snowball rolls down the hill and gets larger and larger as it rolls, because snow sticks to it. A mental image of this event occurring might be formed. I discussed mental imagery extensively in chapter 6, but this situation goes beyond a mere mental image; it requires reasoning about the physics of the situation to determine how the image changes over time.

Constructing this answer requires a *mental model* of the situation. That is, one must envision a boy on a hill and then use one's knowledge of snow, hills, and gravity to make educated guesses about the snowball's behavior after the boy rolls it down the hill. Mental models of this type are useful for making predictions about the behavior of objects in novel situations that are often like situations encountered before, but not so familiar that a person has an established script for dealing with them.

In addition to reasoning about novel physical systems like snowballs and hills, other instances call for similar kinds of reasoning. For example, text comprehension often involves reasoning about novel situations. As discussed in chapter 6, if one reads a story about a man jogging around a lake, and at some point the man takes off his sweatshirt, places it on the ground, and continues to run, one can recognize that the man and his shirt are at different locations. One need not have an established script for this scenario; a person can construct this situation based on knowledge of the spatial locations of the individuals involved as well as an understanding of space (e.g., that moving away from a stationary object puts distance between the person moving and the object).

Now, consider a third situation that seems unrelated to the other two at first glance. In a complicated abstract reasoning problem, one may encounter the syllogism:

All the Actors are Beekeepers
None of the Chemists are Beekeepers

?   (9.1)

If a person is asked what can be concluded from it, and if the person has taken an elementary course in logic, he or she might conclude that None of the Chemists are Actors. Even if one did not know what follows from these premises directly, one can still generate an answer by reasoning about it. On the surface, the notion of a mental model does not seem helpful in a situation that requires abstract reasoning, but one can try to instantiate this syllogism as a spatial layout of objects and then reason about the objects. For example, one may first imagine a group of actors and imagine that all of them are beekeepers. Next, one may imagine an additional group of beekeepers who are not actors (as the premise that all actors are beekeepers does not require that all beekeepers are actors). After that, one can imagine a group of chemists, none of whom are beekeepers. Having done this, one can examine the mental model, and see that none of the chemists are actors either.

Theories of mental models have been developed for all three kinds of examples described here. At the heart of all of these types of mental models are specific instantiations of situations consisting of objects and relations among them. The relations can be simple (like the simple spatial relations used in mental models of reasoning) or complex (like the mental models of physical systems). I discussed the construction of spatial models of the sort used in the text comprehension example in chapter 6 and do not discuss them further in this chapter. Instead, I examine the use of mental models in logical reasoning tasks and then turn to naive physics and mental models of physical systems.

MENTAL MODELS OF LOGICAL REASONING TASKS

The theory of mental models for reasoning has been developed by Johnson-Laird and his colleagues (Johnson-Laird, 1983; Johnson-Laird & Byrne, 1991; Johnson-Laird, Byrne, & Tabossi, 1989), in response to people's difficulties in reasoning abstractly (as discussed in chaps. 1 and 8). For example, in chapters 1 and 8, I noted that the Wason selection task (see Figure 1.1) is difficult to solve when presented abstractly, but can be solved when put in a concrete context, particularly one with the structure of a common social rule like permission. People find some abstract logical problems easier to solve than others. For example, Johnson-Laird and Byrne (1991) summarized the results of studies that examined people's ability to solve classical syllogisms.[1] For example, people provided a correct conclusion to the syllogism:

All the Archers are Bodybuilders
All the Bodybuilders are Car Owners
?   (9.2)

---

[1]As a brief review, a classical syllogism has two premises. The first premise relates two terms, A and B, and the second premise relates B to a C term. The conclusion must find a valid relation between A and C. The four relations in syllogisms are All X are Y, No X are Y, Some X are Y, and Some X are not Y. There are 64 ways that these four relations and the arguments (in either order) can be assigned to the two premises. Typically, a conclusion is also given, and the task is to determine whether the conclusion follows from the premises. The conclusions can be constructed from the four relations with either assignment of the arguments A and C, and there are 512 possible syllogisms containing two premises and a conclusion. If the task is set up so that there are just the 64 combinations of two premises, 27 have valid conclusions. For the others, there are multiple possible conclusions. For example, for the syllogism:

All Artists are Barbers
Some Barbers are Cooks
?

there is no valid conclusion. One can apparently conclude that Some Artists are Cooks, but it is also possible that some Barbers are not Artists and that only Barbers that are not Artists are Cooks. Thus, it is not possible to draw a conclusion from this form.

(All the Archers are Car Owners) about 90% of the time. In contrast, the syllogism:

Some Bankers are Anglers
<u>None of the Crooks are Bankers</u>
?   (9.3)

received the correct conclusion (Some of the Anglers are not Crooks) only about 20% of the time. If people can reason by using logical rules, it is unclear why there are such vast differences in the ability to solve these problems.

In response to such issues, Johnson-Laird and his colleagues developed a mental models approach to logical reasoning. The intuition underlying this approach is that a deductive reasoning task can be solved by creating a model of the premises and then finding a statement that describes the model. The model consists of spatial relations among objects denoting elements in the premises of an argument. If a statement describing the model that is constructed can be formulated, this statement is the conclusion of the deductive argument. A key aspect of this approach is that a set of premises may have more than one model that is consistent with it, and it is necessary to construct all possible models consistent with the set of premises. A valid conclusion to a deductive argument is one that is consistent with all the models that can be constructed on the basis of the premises.

As an illustration of how this approach works, consider the syllogism in 9.2. The model for the first premise (All the Archers are Bodybuilders) is:

A   B
A   B
A   B
   [B]   (9.4)
   [B]
   [B]

The way to interpret this model is to treat each line as an individual in the model. The letters correspond to descriptions that apply to the individual. A letter in brackets means that the existence of the individual is optional. In this case, the [B] individuals leave open the possibility that there are Bodybuilders who are not Archers. The model can then be extended to the second premise (All the Bodybuilders are Car Owners) by adding:

```
A   B   C
A   B   C
A   B   C
   [B] [C]
   [B] [C],                                                        (9.5)
   [B] [C]
       [C]
       [C]
       [C]
```

where all the Archers who are Bodybuilders are also Car Owners. Also, all the optional Bodybuilders are also Car Owners. Finally, there are some possible Car Owners who are neither Archers nor Bodybuilders. This model leads to the obvious conclusion that All the Archers are Car Owners. For one to make this conclusion, these last Car Owners must be recognized as optional so that a conclusion like "Some Car Owners are not Archers" is not suggested.

An interesting facet of the mental models theory is that it predicts which syllogisms are likely to be easy and which are likely to be difficult. For example, because the model in 9.5 is the only one that can be constructed for the syllogism in 9.2, the syllogism should be easy. As discussed earlier, this prediction is borne out. In contrast, the syllogism in 9.3 is difficult. How can a mental model of this syllogism be constructed? The first premise of 9.3 (Some Bankers are Anglers) can be given a mental model like:

```
A   B
A   B
   [B] '                                                           (9.6)
   [B]
```

and the second premise (None of the Crooks are Bankers) can be added to form the model

```
A   B
A   B
   [B]
   [B]    ·                                                        (9.7)
       C
       C
```

This model is consistent with the conclusions that Some Anglers are not Crooks, Some Crooks are not Anglers, and None of the Crooks are Anglers. A second model can also be constructed, however. In this case, the model for the first premise acknowledges that if Some Bankers are Anglers, there may be some Anglers who are not Bankers:

```
A
A
A   B
A   B   .                                                    (9.8)
    [B]
    [B]
```

When the second premise is added, it is possible that some Anglers are Crooks:

```
A       C
A
A   B
A   B     .                                                  (9.9)
    [B]
    [B]  C
         C
```

This model rules out the conclusion that None of the Crooks are Anglers, but leaves open the conclusions that Some Anglers are not Crooks and Some Crooks are not Anglers. Finally, a third model can be constructed in which the first premise is again modeled as in 9.8, but the second premise now yields a model in which all the Crooks are Anglers:

```
A       C
A       C
A   B
A   B     .                                                  (9.10)
    [B]
    [B]
```

This model rules out the possibility that Some Crooks are not Anglers and leaves only the valid conclusion that Some Anglers are not Crooks (namely those that are Bankers). This syllogism requires examination of three models to find a valid conclusion. Because three models are required, mental models theory predicts that this syllogism is more difficult than the one in 9.2, and indeed it is. In extensive tests of this theory, fewer people solve syllogisms that require three models than solve those that require two models, and fewer solve these syllogisms than solve those that require one model.

This mental models account is not limited to syllogisms. Johnson-Laird and Byrne (1991) extended their theory to deductive problems with many quantifiers in them. For example, the statement:

All the Airplanes are in the same place as some of the Bicycles   (9.11)

can be represented as

A   A   A   B   B
        B   B   B   (9.12)

in which each line represents a location. As for syllogisms, it is possible to combine sets of sentences with multiple quantifiers like Example 9.11 into a deductive argument. Some sets of premises require examining more than one model to reach a valid conclusion, and people find it more difficult to reach valid conclusions for sets of premises that require multiple models than to find valid conclusions for sets of premises that require only one model.

To summarize, the mental models approach to reasoning posits that people approach logical reasoning problems by creating models of the premises. Descriptions of the model derived from a set of premises are the conclusions that can be drawn from the premises. In some cases, many different models are consistent with a set of premises, and one model may rule out a conclusion suggested by another. These problems are difficult because people must keep all the models in mind at once to find a description that applies to all of them. Mental models also seem compatible with content effects in deductive reasoning like those discussed in chapters 1 and 8. Because each element in mental models is assumed to be a specific object, it should be easier to create and maintain a model of a familiar situation than to create a model of an unfamiliar situation. The mental models approach has been applied to a wide variety of reasoning tasks and has been viewed as one of the most complete theories of human reasoning (Evans & Over, 1996).

What Is the Mental Models Theory?

The study of reasoning has a long history in psychology. From the time of Aristotle, authorities have been interested in how people reach the conclusions of deductive arguments. Thus, it should be no surprise that there is intense debate over whether the mental models approach to logical reasoning is a good account of the way people reason deductively. At the center of this debate is an argument about exactly what the mental models theory is. The use of diagrams (like those in the previous section) to illustrate mental models suggests that mental models are connected in some way to imagery. It is dangerous to take diagrams too seriously, however, because some process must act on the mental model to carry out the reasoning process. If a mental model was only a diagram that required someone to look at it, it would be a notational device, not the basis of a model of reasoning.

Having been acutely aware of this danger, Johnson-Laird and his colleagues implemented mental models for reasoning and for constructing spatial descriptions (as discussed in chap. 6) as computer programs. In their programs, the elements in a mental model are symbols, and the program has rules that determine how a model is constructed from premises, how a description is generated from a model, and how new models can assess whether there is a counterexample to a possible conclusion.

This description of the mental models view is significant because many attacks on mental models theory have come from people who subscribe to a natural logic theory of reasoning (e.g., Braine, Reiser, & Rumain, 1984; Rips, 1994). Briefly, natural logic theories suggest that people solving deduction problems use logical rules like those of formal logical systems, and people's reasoning flaws arise because of limited processing capacity, flawed strategies for applying the rules, or the absence of rules needed to solve a particular problem. For example, Rips (1994) suggested that almost everyone knows the inference schema *modus ponens* (at least implicitly), but that few people have learned (or at least act in accordance with) the inference schema *modus tollens*.

A key point raised by many of these researchers is that the mental models approach to reasoning is not qualitatively different from a natural logic approach. Instead, both types of models posit some encoding of the premises of the arguments and some set of rules for examining the premises to formulate or verify a deductive argument. The models differ in their proposals about how the premises are encoded and in the types of rules (or processes) that they suggest are important for reasoning (Evans & Over, 1996; Rips, 1986, 1994).

A potential limitation of the mental models approach is that how to extend it to other forms of reasoning beyond deduction is unclear. As already discussed, the power of deductive inference lies in the fact that, because of the structure of the argument, the conclusions of a valid argument are true if the premises are true. Unfortunately, the absolute truth of premises is generally impossible to establish. Thus, pure deductive reasoning is of limited use in most ordinary circumstances. Johnson-Laird (1983) suggested that the general notion of a mental model may be appropriate in domains like language comprehension, in which the meanings of words are established in part by the context in which they appear, but these proposals for extensions of mental models are not made with the same degree of specificity as are the proposals about deductive reasoning. Thus, it may be that the mental models framework is most useful for understanding human performance on deductive reasoning problems (but see Johnson-Laird & Savary, 1996, for an extension of mental models to probabilistic reasoning).

MENTAL MODELS OF PHYSICAL SYSTEMS

Mental models for logical reasoning tasks have focused on collections of objects in particular spatial locations. The description of the model(s) generated serves as the conclusion for the reasoning problem. People also use complex mental models to describe and reason about physical systems (Gentner & Stevens, 1983). Unlike mental models for reasoning, mental models of physical systems are internal representations of external systems. The represented world for a physical mental model is a physical system in the world; the representing world is a scheme for capturing the physics of the represented world. Finally, a number of computational models of physical reasoning also have procedures for extracting the knowledge in the representation and using it to predict the future behavior of elements in the represented world (Forbus, 1984; Kuipers, 1994). For mental models of reasoning, there is generally no external represented world. Instead, the elements in these mental models are empty (i.e., nonrepresenting symbols that are used to reach a conclusion about the relationship between elements in the reasoning problem).

In this section of the chapter, I discuss psychological evidence for the nature of people's physical knowledge. Although these data have typically not been modeled directly, they do place some constraints on what people find easy and what they find difficult. These constraints have been captured in models of physical reasoning. I then describe some general aspects of mental models of physical systems. Finally, I analyze Forbus's (1984) qualitative process theory (QP theory) in detail as an example of how to represent qualitative information about physical systems and how to reason with this knowledge.

Naive Physics

Psychological research carried out under the umbrella of *naive physics* has been directed at people's understanding of the physical world. Much of this research has been descriptive and has dealt with the extent to which people have a veridical understanding of physical processes and with the depth of their understanding. This work, which has centered on finding flaws in people's reasoning about physical systems, has shown people to have fundamental misconceptions about the way the world works and to possess only shallow knowledge about physical systems.

Some demonstrations of shortcomings in people's physical knowledge seem to involve single phenomena for which people's judgments of what happens in a situation do not match what actually happens. Perhaps the best-known case of an error in naive physics is the belief in curvilinear momentum (Kaiser, Proffitt, & McCloskey, 1986; McCloskey, 1983). The speed and direction of a moving object change only when a force is applied to the object, but in the real world, gravitational forces constantly pull objects toward the earth and frictional forces constantly slow them down. These unseen forces make it appear as if objects must exert a constant force to continue moving and that objects themselves have a memory of the direction in which they are traveling. In a fascinating series of tests, Kaiser, McCloskey, and Proffitt (1986) asked people what would happen in a situation like that shown in Figure 9.1, where a ball rolls into a curved tube and emerges at the end of it. The investigators asked subjects to assume that they were looking down on the tube and then asked them to predict the motion of the ball when it leaves the tube. Despite the fact that the ball has no additional forces acting on it when it leaves the tube and hence shoots out straight (the middle choice in Figure 9.1A), many people predicted that the ball would take a trajectory that (at least partially) continued the path it took inside the tube. Such a path is shown in the left-most trajectory in Figure 9.1A. This finding suggests that people believe objects maintain some memory (momentum) of their previous path. The researchers obtained this finding even when they allowed subjects to roll a ball bearing themselves. Thus, people make errors when they are performing an action, not only when they are solving problems in a pencil-and-paper task.

A similar error in physical reasoning occurs in the water-level problem (Piaget & Inhelder, 1956). In this problem, illustrated in Figure 9.1B, subjects are asked to imagine that the beaker is filled with water and they are asked to draw the surface of the water in the picture. The correct answer is that the water level is perpendicular to the pull of gravity, and the water level should be drawn horizontally (as in the middle item in Figure 9.1B). Nevertheless, 40% or more of adults given this task drew the water level incorrectly, typically as it appears in the left-most beaker in the bottom row of Figure 9.1B (McAfee & Proffitt, 1991). This phenomenon is also apparently not a function of being a pencil-and-paper presentation; it is observed with realistic pictures (McAfee & Proffitt, 1991) and also with animations of jugs pouring water (Howard, 1978).

As a final example, studies have explored people's ability to detect the relative mass of objects that collide (e.g., Gilden & Proffitt, 1989, 1994). In one set of studies, people were shown collisions between two balls that differed in their mass. One ball was initially stationary, and when the other

(A)

(B)

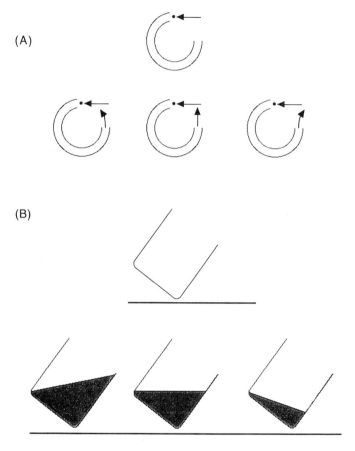

FIG. 9.1. Examples of errors in naive physics. A: Curvilinear momentum;
B: the water-level problem.

ball struck the stationary ball, both balls moved at some speed in some
direction. People's performance in this task was well described by simple
heuristics. If one ball moved faster than the other after the collision, it
was generally judged to be lighter. If one ball ricocheted backward from
the collision, it was generally judged to be lighter. The incoming velocity
of the colliding ball was not used to make mass judgments. These heuristics
often give the correct answer, but people do make errors in their judgments
of relative mass. The important finding from these studies is that people
do not judge the mass of objects on the basis of accepted principles of
Newtonian physics but use rules (heuristics) that may often yield an appropriate answer but may sometimes be wrong.

These phenomena demonstrate that people are not always perfectly
attuned to the physics underlying the action of objects in the world. Yet

people are not thereby ill suited to exist in the world. Because of unseen forces like gravity and friction, the world often seems not to act in accord with Newtonian physics. People are reasonably well equipped to predict the actual motions of objects and to handle objects and liquids. Nonetheless, they do not seem to have quantitative physical models in their heads but rely on fairly simple rules that relate salient properties in the environment.

Mental Models of Physical Systems

Many studies described in the previous section focused on simple events. The tasks have a strong perceptual component, and the problem to be solved often involves information that can be extracted from a visual display of a physical system. Studies of complex physical reasoning, however, have explored how people reason with a mental model of a situation. There is no accepted definition of a mental model in this case, but generally a mental model involves understanding the causal relations among several elements in a physical system. The purpose of representing this information is to facilitate reasoning about change in the system being modeled. The knowledge of these relations allows prediction of how the system operates and allows people to reason about unexpected events (as they must do when diagnosing and repairing broken mechanical and electronic devices). Thus, mental models are larger in scope than the rules and heuristics posited to underlie performance in naive physics tasks.

Mental models have two primary components (de Kleer & Brown, 1983). First, there are objects in the domain. For example, Figure 9.2 depicts a heat exchanger (Williams, Hollan, & Stevens, 1983), used to cool a fluid

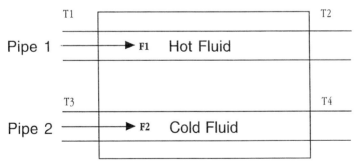

FIG. 9.2. Heat exchanger. The top pipe has hot fluid flowing through it at a rate F1. The bottom pipe has cold fluid flowing through it at a rate F2. The temperature of the fluid entering the heat exchanger through the top pipe is T1, and the temperature of the fluid as it exits the heat exchanger is T2. The temperature of the fluid entering the heat exchanger through the bottom pipe is T3, and the temperature of the fluid as it exits the heat exchanger is T4.

in a machine. Pipe 1 may contain oil used to lubricate the parts of an engine. The oil heats up as it comes into contact with hot engine parts and flows through a pipe into the heat exchanger. There is also a fluid flowing through Pipe 2, and this fluid is colder than the fluid in Pipe 1. The heat exchanger puts the fluids flowing through the pipes in thermal contact so that heat can flow between them. Because heat flows from hotter to cooler areas, heat from the liquid in Pipe 1 flows out of the fluid, into the surrounding heat-conducting material, and into the cold fluid in Pipe 2. Thus, the fluid in Pipe 1 leaves the pipe cooler than it was when it entered (i.e., $T2 < T1$), and the fluid in Pipe 2 leaves the pipe warmer than it was when it entered (i.e., $T4 > T3$). The amount of heat that enters the system is dependent on the flow from the hot pipe ($F1$), and the amount of heat that can be taken out of the system depends on the flow from the cool pipe ($F2$).[2]

In a mental model of this heat exchanger, there are definitions for elements like the pipes (which are paths for fluid to flow). There is also general causal knowledge, like the knowledge that heat flows from hotter to cooler places. These relationships are generally assumed to be qualitative. Thus, although the model predicts that heat flows from one point to another when the first point is hotter than the second point, it does not predict precisely how much heat flows. The mental model combines the parts to form a set of relationships that govern the expected behavior of the system. This process is called *model formulation*. To simulate the behavior of the heat exchanger, the model must specify the relationships among the various quantities that exist in the device. For example, the greater the temperature of the fluid in the hot pipe ($T1$), the greater the temperature of the fluid exiting the hot pipe ($T2$) is likely to be. The greater the temperature of the fluid in the hot pipe ($T1$), the greater the temperature in the exiting cool pipe ($T4$) as well (provided that the entering fluid in the cool pipe was indeed cooler than the entering fluid in the hot pipe [i.e., $T3 < T1$]). The more hot fluid that enters the system (i.e., the higher $F1$), the greater the temperature of the fluid exiting both the hot pipe ($T2$) and the cool pipe ($T4$). The complete model must have relations among all the quantities that affect each other, and it must have boundary conditions on the relations (such as that increases in $T1$ lead to increases in $T4$ only when $T3 < T1$). One possible model for the heat exchanger is shown in Figure 9.3.

Once the model has been formulated, the behavior of the system can be simulated. For example, with the set of relations in Figure 9.3, one can

---

[2]The diagram in Figure 9.2 is schematic. Actual heat exchangers try to maximize the surface area in the region of thermal contact to maximize the amount of heat flowing from one fluid to the other.

```
┌─────────────────────────────────────────────────┐
│  Relations  in  the  Heat  Exchanger             │
│     T2   increases with   T1                      │
│     T4   increases with   T1   if T3 < T1         │
│     T4   increases with   T3                      │
│     T2   decreases with   T3   if T3 < T1         │
│     T2   increases with   F1                      │
│     T4   increases with   F1   if T3 < T1         │
│     T4   decreases with   F2                      │
│     T2   decreases with   F2   if T3 < T1         │
└─────────────────────────────────────────────────┘
```

FIG. 9.3.   A simple qualitative model of the heat exchanger in Figure 9.2.

ask what happens if the flow in Pipe 2 (*F*2) is increased. Under normal circumstances, this change should lead to a decrease in temperature in the exiting fluid in the hot pipe (*T*2) and a decrease in temperature of the exiting fluid in the cold pipe (*T*4). If these changes are not observed, in view of the conditions on the rules, one can speculate that the temperature of the fluid in the cold pipe (*T*3) is not less than the temperature of the fluid in the hot pipe (*T*1). The effects of a variety of changes in temperatures and flow rates can be assessed by using these simple rules.

In support of this way of thinking about mental models, Williams, Hollan, and Stevens (1983) asked people to reason about a heat exchanger like that in Figure 9.2. As people reasoned about various changes in quantities, they were asked to think aloud. Consistent with the mental model depicted in Figure 9.3, people tended to reason by using simple qualitative relationships among components, and their errors in reasoning could be traced to the absence of rules governing the relationships among quantities in the model. White and Frederiksen (1990) suggested that such simple models are useful for automated teaching systems that help people learn to reason about simple physical systems. In their view, many people who reason about physical systems think in terms of zero-order models (i.e., whether a particular quantity is present or absent at a particular location) and first-order models (i.e., the direction of influence of a change in a quantity would be in the system). In this parlance, the simple model in Figure 9.3 is a first-order model because it describes the effects of changes in a quantity. White and Frederiksen further suggested that quantitative models are typically not used. That is, people are unable to reason about the specific values of quantities and the specific degrees of change of quantities in physical systems.

Having a mental model of a physical system allows people to reason effectively about a variety of situations without having to represent all possible interactions among components in advance. The ability to "run" a mental model allows people to specify a set of relationships, and to determine the actual behavior of a system only when it is important to know how the system works (Schwartz & Black, 1996). The model limits reasoning in two important ways. First, the model is only as good as the assumed relationships among components; if there are flaws in these relationships, they show up as errors in reasoning. Second, mental models are assumed to omit many details; if someone has only a first-order model, he or she cannot reason about indirect influences of one quantity on another. Because mental models are qualitative, one can reason only about the direction of change, not about its precise degree. Of course, it is not surprising that reasoning is qualitative: Quantitative reasoning about physical systems requires enormous computational power.

Qualitative reasoning generally permits accurate reasoning with minimal cost, but it can pose a problem when two quantities both directly influence a third quantity in different directions. For example, the pressure of a gas in an enclosed area increases with the temperature of the gas and decreases with its volume (Boyle's law). In a qualitative system, it is impossible to reason about the pressure of a gas in a situation in which the temperature and the volume increase simultaneously.

D. Gentner and D. R. Gentner (1983) provided some evidence of the power of models to mislead. They suggested that people can conceptualize electricity either as analogous to the flow of water through pipes or as analogous to a crowd of people in a constricted hallway. These models can be helpful in many cases. For example, voltage can be conceptualized as the pressure of water flowing through a pipe or as the speed of people walking through a hallway. A resistor in an electrical circuit can be thought of as a constriction in a pipe or a gate in a hallway, either of which limits the flow (of water or people) through the path. Gentner and Gentner pointed out, however, that batteries are easier to conceptualize in the water model than in the crowd model. In the water model, a battery is simply a pump. In contrast, there is no particularly good way of thinking about a battery in the crowd model, except perhaps as a waiting room full of people who want to leave.

The effect of this difference is that people find it easier to reason about configurations of batteries if they use the water model than if they use the crowd model. In the water model, two batteries connected in serial (as in Figure 9.4) can be conceptualized as two pumps, each of which increases the pressure of the water. In this way, there is twice the pressure in the pipe, just as connecting two batteries of the same voltage in serial yields twice the voltage of a single battery. Connecting two batteries in parallel is like having two pumps in parallel. Both push water to the same pressure, and the total pressure in the pipe is the pressure generated by each pipe alone (there is just more available water). Likewise, two batteries of the

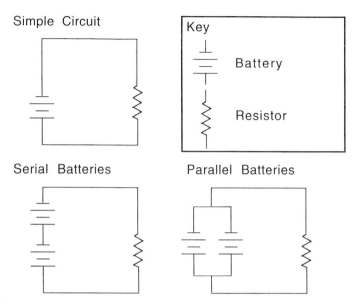

FIG. 9.4. Simple circuits consisting of batteries and resistors.

same voltage connected in parallel yield the same voltage as one battery. In contrast, picturing two waiting rooms connected either in serial or in parallel does not provide much insight into the action of batteries. Consistent with this analysis, people asked to reason about the voltage in circuits with serial and parallel batteries were more accurate when they held the water model than when they held the crowd model.

Errors in people's mental models have been demonstrated to lead directly to errors in real-world decisions. Kempton (1986) interviewed people about how their home heating systems worked. The proper model of a thermostat for a heater (which is held by many people) is that it is set to the desired temperature, and the heat stays on until the room reaches the desired temperature, at which time the heat shuts off. However, a significant number of people have a model of the thermostat that assumes it is like the accelerator of a car. That is, the higher it is set, the more heat that comes out. People with this model believe that setting the thermostat to a high temperature causes the heat in the house to rise faster than setting it to a lower temperature (that is still greater than the temperature in the room). By studying home heating records, Kempton was able to isolate families that appeared to act on the basis of both these models. In some homes, the thermostat was set twice a day (in the morning and at night). In other homes, the thermostat was constantly adjusted up and down during the day. This latter strategy wastes energy and is expensive, but it is consistent with the mistaken accelerator model of the thermostat.

The potentially misleading effects of people's models on their reasoning are as true for scientists as for novices reasoning about electricity. Hutchins (1983, 1995) described the anthropological study of navigation among Micronesian navigators. These navigators are able to sail outrigger canoes hundreds of miles between islands without any instruments used by Western navigators (e.g., logbooks and compasses). They accomplish this feat by a number of means, among them by using stars as guidance for directions and by using landmarks (real and fictitious islands) as a measure of how far they are from their destination. The landmarks are envisioned as moving along the boat, which is conceptualized as being stationary. The landmark islands are seen as being ahead of the boat at the start of the voyage and moving slowly down its length and behind it as the journey is completed.

Early investigators studying Micronesian navigation practices had difficulty understanding how the islands figured into the navigational system, because they assumed that the navigators used the islands to create a bird's-eye view of the journey, in which the boat is conceptualized as moving through space. This assumption is deeply ingrained in Western navigation, in which the course of a vessel is plotted on charts that show an overhead perspective. In this system, landmarks and the boat itself are treated as objects viewed from above, and the function of landmarks is to locate the boat in the plane of the map. The location of the moving boat in relation to a fixed frame of reference is determined by finding the angle between the boat and at least two (usually three) landmarks whose location relative to the frame of reference is known.

It is difficult to see the function of the landmark islands in the Micronesian system from this perspective because the landmark islands seem not to be used to fix the boat's location in space. Instead, the movement of the islands relative to the boat functions as a measure of how much of the journey has been completed. Only when the Micronesian navigational system is conceptualized independently of the Western system do the practices make sense (see Hutchins, 1995, for an elegant description of this navigational system). Hutchins used this example as a warning of the problems that even trained scientists can encounter when they are forced to reason about situations that diverge from their own mental models.

A second issue of importance involves the completeness of a mental model. In the model of the heat exchanger, there was a series of relations among quantities but very little other supporting knowledge. The model had no other information about thermodynamics and so it could not be used to reason about properties of the materials in the heat exchanger. With this model, there is no way of assessing the impact of a change in the type of fluid used in the cooling pipe of the exchanger or of a change in the materials used to build the pipes. Such information could be important to someone looking to improve the performance of the machine, but extensive knowledge including quantitative information is required to answer these questions. Clearly, people in the business of building heat exchangers would know this information and might even incorporate it into their mental models. It is an open question whether people think that their models are incomplete without extensive knowledge or whether they are happy with even a minimal set of relations among the objects in a model.

A quick check of one's own intuitions suggests that an extensive mental model is not always necessary. I have a vague idea of how the engine in my car works: Pistons compress gas and fuel in a chamber; a spark plug creates a controlled explosion that causes gas to expand and drives the piston outward. The pistons are arranged so that the upward motion of some pistons leads to the compression motion of others. There is quite a bit missing in my model. I am not sure I understand the impact of pressing the gas pedal. I am sure I do not understand how the valves in the engine allow fuel to enter the chamber or gas to escape. Yet, despite this marked absence of knowledge, I am happy to drive my car, to fill it with gasoline, and to have the oil and other fluids checked regularly.

Such general intuitions have been examined in an extensive investigation of children's understanding of the solar system undertaken by Vosniadou and Brewer (1992; Samarapungavan, Vosniadou, & Brewer, 1996). In these studies, researchers asked children to discuss the Earth and the solar system. The results showed that children often have some information about the Earth and the solar system (the Earth is round, it spins, and it goes around the sun), but they have not received extensive training in the causal mechanisms involved. As a result, there are significant gaps in children's mental models of the solar system, and they try to fill these when pressed by using knowledge from their own experience. For example, most children say that the Earth is round, but when asked for more information, some children suggest that it is round like a pancake, with the people living on the flat side (see Figure 9.5). This answer conforms to the observation that the ground is flat. Others know that the Earth is round like a ball, but they assume that people live inside the ball and that the stars

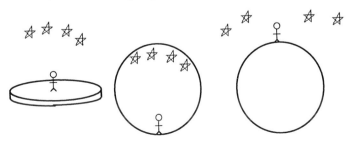

FIG. 9.5. Examples of some children's conceptions of the Earth.

are on the top side of the ball. Still others know that the Earth is a ball and that people live outside it (although it takes time for some to realize that people live all over the surface, not just on the "top"). Eventually, children are exposed to more detailed models of the Earth until they reach the currently accepted scientific model. Children also display misconceptions about what causes the sun to move across the sky and what causes the seasons to change; these also seem to arise from a lack of causal knowledge. The studies demonstrated that children do not have a complete mental model of the solar system. Instead, aspects of the world always lie beyond what they know. Nonetheless, children (like adults) are content to have partial knowledge and may not even notice the limits of what they know until pushed to answer questions that extend beyond these limits. Thus, it appears that mental models are not assessed for their completeness. Instead, people are willing to reason with whatever knowledge they have.

To summarize, mental models of physical systems consist of representations of objects. The objects can be given functional descriptions that outline how they work in a broad mechanism. The model of a whole mechanism is formulated by combining the objects and specifying the relationships that hold among the objects. These relationships are typically qualitative. They specify broad correlations among quantities (e.g., whether the quantities have a positive or negative relationship). Quantitative relationships do not appear to be part of people's everyday mental models. The choice of a mental model influences what kinds of problems are easy or hard to reason about. Finally, mental models are not complete specifications of a system. Rather, they contain enough information to carry out whatever tasks a person typically faces. It is easy to construct situations that go beyond the information people have about a situation and to demonstrate the brittleness of their knowledge about a domain.

Qualitative Process Theory

In the preceding section, I described the general characteristics of a mental model and focused primarily on people's ability to generate and reason about physical situations. In artificial intelligence (AI), there have been many attempts to build systems to represent and reason about physical systems (Bobrow, 1984; Kuipers, 1994). Rather than summarizing the diversity of approaches to qualitative physical reasoning in this section, I go into one such approach in some detail: qualitative process theory (or QP theory: Falkenhainer & Forbus, 1991; Forbus, 1984). This system contains all the basic elements of a system for generating computational mental models and so provides a good example of the issues already raised in this chapter. The system has been incorporated into detailed models of complex physical systems and so is known to work. QP theory was motivated by the desire to understand how people reason about physical systems and hence is meant as a cognitive model as well as a computational tool. In the following subsections, I first discuss the general notion of a process and a process history. Then, I describe the way that the theory represents objects and quantities. Finally, I describe how models are created and how QP theory represents physical processes.

An Overview of QP Theory.   A central goal when reasoning about a physical situation (or for that matter, a social situation) is to understand change. A physical system that does not change is not very interesting. For example, if I put a plate on a table and walk away, I do not need to spend much cognitive effort to reason about what happens to the plate. I assume that if I come back some time later, the plate will still be on the table, and only if the plate is not there (and something has changed) is there any need to reason about the situation. Although the idea that change is important may seem trivial, it is the focus of the *frame problem*, one of the most vexing problems in AI and cognitive science (Ford & Hayes, 1991; Ford & Pylyshyn, 1996; Hayes, 1985). Part of the problem's difficulty lies in its apparent simplicity. The frame problem can be illustrated with a simple scenario.

> Imagine being in a room, sitting on a chair, with a table in
> front of you. On the table are 500 different objects, including
> a revolver, a flashlight, an oil lamp that is lit, a pitcher of water,
> and a ball of string. You move the ball of string to the edge
> of the table, and it drops to the floor.   (9.13)

What has changed in the room? Intuitively, this question seems straightforward. Most people would say that the ball of string has fallen to the floor and is no longer on the table. Nothing else seems to have happened.

Does one manage to restrict attention to the ball of string because it was mentioned in the passage describing the situation? Imagine that situation 9.13 is changed just slightly:

> Imagine being in a room, sitting on a chair, with a table in
> front of you. On the table are 500 different objects, including
> a revolver, a flashlight, an oil lamp that is lit, a pitcher of
> water, and a ball of string. You accidentally tip the oil lamp,
> and it falls over.   (9.14)

In 9.14, the situation seems more dire. There is the possibility of a fire, and some objects on the table may burn. The ball of string is quite likely to burn; the revolver may get hot, but is unlikely to burn. Something else about one's knowledge allows a determination of what changes to consider when reasoning about a physical system. The goal of a system that reasons about physical systems is to determine what changes and what does not.

Despite its apparent simplicity, the frame problem is difficult to solve, because it is analogous to the holism problem already discussed. To determine what changes in a situation, one may need to check each fact to see whether it has an influence on the current situation. Each object in the table in these examples is a potential source of change (not to mention every other object in the fictitious world I have created). For a system to solve the frame problem, there must be a mechanism that limits the elements that are considered when reasoning about change. Of course, checking only a subset of information may lead to errors, but the job of a reasoning system is to find procedures that are reasonably accurate and still to reach conclusions in an acceptable time.

Qualitative reasoning systems like QP theory solve the frame problem by reasoning locally. This local reasoning is done by representing objects (and agents) in the world as *histories* (Hayes, 1985).[3] A history is a spatially bounded object that exists in time (and makes the history four-dimensional: three spatial dimensions and one temporal dimension). In the example of the plate on the table, the history for the plate on the table is bounded spatially by the three-dimensional space filled by the plate and temporally by the time between when it is left on the table and when it is picked up again. This representation can solve the frame problem, because only other objects whose histories intersect with the history of the plate need to be reasoned about. The table that supports the plate intersects the spatial boundary beneath the plate and intersects the time at which the plate rests on the table, and the histories of the table and the plate are intertwined. When the state of the table changes, one must reason about the plate because it has an intersecting history. One need not reason about other objects whose histories do not intersect with those of the table and plate. In Scenario 9.13, when the ball of string falls to the floor, it does not intersect with the histories of any of the objects on the table, and there is no need to consider those objects. In contrast, when the oil lamp falls over, because the oil and flame may spread to other objects on the table and thereby intersect with the histories of all of those objects, they must be reasoned about. Of course, there must be a mechanism that reasons about the behavior of objects that tip over, but that is the goal of physical reasoning systems like QP theory. That is, there must be a detailed specification of how a history is constructed and how the objects that make up a process interact.

---

[3]This is by no means the only proposed solution to the frame problem (see Ford & Hayes, 1991; Ford & Pylyshyn, 1996).

Objects and Quantities. QP theory permits representations of physical systems and reasoning about them by using qualitative representational machinery. There are no statements of exact quantities. Instead, quantitative relations are stated qualitatively. QP theory uses structured representations in which attributes and relations describe objects, quantities, causal relationships among objects, and (qualitative) numerical relationships between quantities.

A key aspect of a physical system to be defined is the set of quantities in it; understanding the behavior of a system often involves reasoning about quantities. One may want to reason about the amount of water in Container 1 in Figure 9.6A. QP theory has methods for representing quantities in qualitative terms. First, something is defined as a quantity type. There are many different types of quantities in physical systems; an amount is a type of quantity. This type of quantity is interesting, because it can take on only values greater than or equal to zero (i.e., never less than

(A)

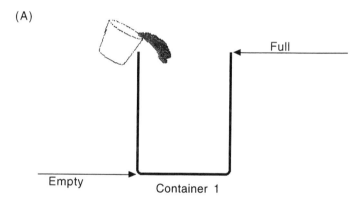

(B)

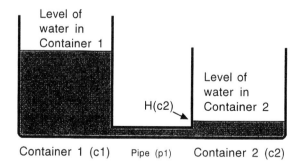

FIG. 9.6. A: Container being filled with water. B: Situation in which water flow is about to occur.

zero). Electrical charge is another type of quantity. Unlike amount, electrical charge can be positive or negative. Elements in a physical system whose quantities are going to be reasoned about must be defined as being describable by the appropriate quantity type. For example, it must be stated explicitly that water has an amount. Because it seems obvious that water has an amount, it may seem like overkill to define this property explicitly. Without defining quantities and objects at this level of detail, however, a reasoner lacks sufficient information to analyze this system later.

Quantities have four parts. The first two are sign and magnitude. Different quantity types permit different ranges of signs. The sign of a quantity of liquid is always positive, because there is never less than nothing of a physical substance, but the sign of the electrical charge of a substance can be positive or negative. Magnitudes of quantities specify the degree of the quantity. The magnitude of the quantity of liquid is the amount of liquid in the container. The magnitude of an electrical charge is the degree of charge. The second two components of a quantity are the sign and magnitude of the derivative of the quantity. This part of the representation specifies the direction and size of the change in the quantity over time. For example, a positive derivative of an amount of water means that the amount is increasing over time, and a negative derivative means that the amount is decreasing over time. The magnitude of the derivative specifies the rate at which the level of the water is changing.

Quantities are typically not described by using exact values. Rather, there is a quantity space, which defines landmark values of a quantity for a given situation. The landmark values are important for reasoning about a particular physical system. In Figure 9.6A, Empty and Full form landmark values of the level of water in the container. The quantity space for a level of a liquid is bounded by zero at one end and positive infinity (∞) at the other. The zero point is important in quantity spaces, because it is the point at which the sign of a quantity changes from negative to positive. The landmark values are important, because they are typically the points at which processes acting on the system become active or are disabled. A model for the container in Figure 9.6A being filled with water may describe the level of water rising as water is added. This process remains active until the water level reaches the Full level, at which time a new process becomes active. In this process, the water level remains the same, but the added amount of water spills over the side of the container.

In a quantity space, it is possible to know of the existence of a system's particular landmark quantities without knowing their relative ordering. For example, a system can know that a liquid freezes at some point and that a liquid boils at some point without knowing which temperature is higher. Although it seems implausible that someone would not know the relative temperatures associated with freezing or boiling, it is possible in complex situations to be unsure of the relative ordering of landmark values.

Time is a key quantity that is treated qualitatively. Although assumed to be continuous, time is represented in discrete steps. It is typically stated in terms of intervals and instants, in which the intervals of interest are the ones bounded by important changes in quantities in the world. Figure 9.6A depicts a container being filled with water at a constant rate. An important time interval for this system is the time interval before the filling of the container. A second important interval begins at the instant when the filling starts and ends at the instant when the water reaches the maximum (full) level of the container. A third important interval begins at the instant when water has reached the maximum level of the container. The intervals are defined on the basis of the value of some other quantity. The exact values of the quantity (the amount of water in the container) are not important, but landmark values like empty and full are (see also Kuipers, 1994).

Relationships Among Quantities.   In QP theory, the relationship between a pair of quantities can be established in a qualitative way. The sign of the relationship between variables is more important than the magnitude of the relation. In addition, the type of influence of one quantity on another is represented explicitly. QP theory distinguishes between direct and indirect influences. *Direct influences* represent situations in which one element in the world is directly applied to another to cause a change in the element. Figure 9.6B shows two containers connected by a pipe. The flow rate from the water source (Container 1) causes the amount of water in the container to decrease. Likewise, this flow rate causes the amount of water in the destination container (Container 2) to increase. These relationships can be written as:

$I-$ [amount-of (water_source), A (flow_rate)]
$I+$ [amount-of (water_destination), A (flow_rate)].   (9.15)

Direct influences can be thought of as specifying specific additive effects in an equation that defines the change in a quantity. For example, the influences in 9.15 specify:

Δ amount-of (water_source) $= \ldots - A$ (flow_rate) $+ \ldots$
Δ amount-of (water_destination) $= \ldots + A$ (flow_rate) $+ \ldots$ (9.16)

where Δ amount-of ($?x$) specifies the change in the amount of a quantity and A ($?x$) specifies the magnitude of the amount of a quantity. These equations have left room for other factors that may also directly influence the amount of water in a container.

In addition to direct influences, there are also *indirect influences*. An indirect influence occurs in a situation in which a change in one quantity is associated with a change in a second, but the first element cannot be applied directly to the second. Indirect influences are represented by using *qualitative proportionalities* (denoted α_Q, in which positive relationships are denoted α_{Q+}, and negative relationships are denoted α_{Q-}). This relation suggests that as one quantity changes, a second quantity changes as well; it does not imply that the first quantity was applied directly to the second. For example, one may be interested in the relationship between the flow rate into the destination container in Figure 9.6B and the level of the water in the container. This relationship is stated:

$$A \text{ (flow\_rate) } \alpha_{Q+} \text{ level (water\_source)}; \tag{9.17}$$

that is, a positive flow rate is associated with an increase in the water level and a negative flow rate with a decrease in the water level. This relationship is indirect; the flow rate changes the amount of water in the container, and the amount of water changes the level. The specific value of the level of the container is determined by factors like the circumference of the container (if it is round). Thus, one can only say that some function relates flow rate to water level such that:

$$\Delta \text{ level (water\_in\_container) } = f[\ldots, A \text{ (flow\_rate)}, \ldots], \tag{9.18}$$

where Δ level $(?x)$ is the change in the level of the fluid in some container and $f(?x)$ is some monotonically increasing function that includes the flow rate in it. The qualitative proportionality is qualified by the idea that everything else in the system has been held constant. If many quantities in a system are changing at once, the relationship specified by a qualitative proportionality may not hold; other arguments to the function in Equation 9.18 may have a different influence on the output of the function.

Model Fragments. Systems are represented by using *model fragments* (Falkenhainer & Forbus, 1991).[4] A model fragment consists of four components: *individuals, operating conditions, assumptions*, and *relations*.

The *individuals* component of a model fragment represents the objects and the relations between them describing the physical system of interest. The process of water flow depicted in Figure 9.6B shows a pair of containers connected by a pipe. There is water in each of the containers. The objects involved in the water flow are the containers (source and destination), the

---

[4]The notion of a model fragment generalizes the concepts of individual view and process, which were originally part of QP theory (Forbus, 1984).

pipe between them (p1), the water in Container 1 (water source), and the water in Container 2 (water destination). When defining the objects, the relevant quantities must be defined as well. The relevant quantities are the amount of water and the level of the water in Containers 1 and 2. In addition, the pipe must be defined as a path that permits the flow of a fluid.

The *operating conditions* are a set of conditions that must hold for this model fragment to be useful for reasoning about the current situation. For example, in a model fragment describing water flow, it is important that the pipe (p1) be open so that water can flow through it. If the model fragment describes a situation of water flow, the level of water in the source container must be higher than the level of water in the destination container. If these conditions are not met, the water flow model does not hold. As another example, to construct a model of the heat exchanger pictured in Figure 9.2, one must assume as one of the operating conditions that the fluid in the cold pipe is in fact colder than the fluid in the hot pipe.

The *assumptions* part of a model fragment describes the assumptions made by the model. A few different kinds of assumptions are important for model fragments. The first provides an ontology for thinking about the process of interest. When reasoning about fluid flow, it is important to know whether the system is trying to reason about fluids or about the behavior of individual molecules, because the explanatory constructs needed to reason about fluid flow are different from those needed to reason about molecular interactions. A second important assumption involves the grain size of reasoning. In Figure 9.6B, one is explicitly interested in fluid flow between two containers. To reason about a large hydraulic system, however, one may use a system of containers connected by a pipe as a subcomponent of the system and assume that its behavior is known. In general, when reasoning about a system, it is important to know the grain size of the elements that are basic components of a system. A final assumption worth making explicit is the approximation for reasoning in a particular case. For example, a physics student may reason about fluid flow by assuming a frictionless environment. This assumption must be made explicitly because it may lead to reasoning errors.[5]

Finally, the *relations* in the model fragment specify the mathematical relations among quantities on the basis of the set of individuals and the assumptions, if the operating conditions in the model are true. In a qualitative simulation, the relations consist of the direct and indirect influences. In a numerical simulation, these relations are precise equations specifying the correlations between variables.

---

[5]See Falkenhainer and Forbus (1991) for an extended discussion of assumptions.

Dynamic Aspects of a Model. After a model is described, its behavior can be simulated in a series of episodes and events. Episodes are situations with a temporal extent; events are instantaneous situations. Typically, episodes describe time intervals in which a process takes place; events describe instants in time that switch from one process to another. For example, earlier I described important time intervals associated with filling the container in Figure 9.6A with water. These episodes (and bounding events) are the history describing the behavior of this system. This history begins with the episode in which the container is empty; the episode continues until the event of beginning to fill the container with water. At this time, the episode of filling the container begins. There is no time between the end of each episode and the beginning of the next event or between the end of an event and the beginning of a subsequent episode. Once the container has begun to be filled, the episode of filling the container begins immediately. The episode of filling the container continues until the event of reaching the full container. At that point, a new episode, consisting of stopping the flow of water or of continuing the flow of water and having water spill over the edge of the container and onto the floor, begins.

Model fragments are used as the basis of simulations of the behavior of a physical system. In an AI model, it is possible to create a complete simulation of the behavior of the system; this simulation determines all possible states of the system and all possible events that lead from one episode to another. Creating a complete description of the behavior of a system is called *envisioning*. This process can be useful for reasoning, but because it requires too much computation, it is not a good candidate for a cognitive process. Instead, cognitive models of qualitative reasoning focus on *simulating* the behavior of a system (de Kleer & Brown, 1983). As discussed previously, simulation involves determining the behavior of a system on the basis of its description. In QP theory, the behavior of a system can be described as a history guided by the operating conditions and quantity conditions in the model fragment. In general, the critical events in a process history occur when changes in the world influence the elements in an operating condition and allow a process to become active or when quantities that appear in the operating conditions of a process go from being equal to unequal (or from unequal to equal). The search for changes in equality relations among quantities in a model is called *limit analysis*.

An example of a history of a process is the situation in Figure 9.6B, in which the source and destination containers have different water levels and a pipe connecting the containers has a valve on it. Initially, the valve is closed, and so there is an episode in which the valve is closed and no water flows. When the valve is opened (an event) and there is more water in the source container than in the destination container, a new episode begins in which water flows from the source to the destination. Because of this event, the operating conditions for the model fragment associated with water flow are now relevant; there is an open path through which the fluid can flow. This flow causes the amount of water in the source to decrease and the amount of water in the destination to increase. The change in the amount of water produces a change in the level of water in each container as well. At some point, the water level in each container is equal (an event), and the flow stops. The situation now reaches an equilibrium in which there is no additional water flow. This equilibrium reflects a case in which an operating condition that was true (i.e., that the water levels were unequal) became untrue. In general, processes become active or cease to be active when operating conditions that were untrue become true or when operating conditions that were true cease to be true. The important transitions in this process occurred when the pipe became an open path and when the water levels in the source and destination containers became equal.[6]

In the interest of clarity, this discussion has glossed over some details. For example, the model of a process must have relations describing that the water is actually contained in the containers. Creating and reasoning with these relations requires domain-specific knowledge about the action of water in containers. The importance of domain-specific knowledge should not be surprising: People have little understanding of the physics of the world in novel domains. Only after experience in a new domain does one have a sense of how objects act. Qualitative physical models similarly require domain-specific information to operate.

QP theory represents physical situations using model fragments. The model fragments describe the objects in the system and relevant relations among them. The model fragments also specify the assumptions made by the model. These assumptions are important to track, because errors in reasoning may occur when a faulty set of assumptions is adopted. Another key component of the model fragment is the set of operating conditions, which specify the circumstances under which the model can be used. Among these operating conditions are preconditions specifying when a particular process is active. Finally, a model fragment contains a record of the direct and indirect influences on quantities that allow the behavior of a system to be simulated. These simulations track changes in quantities, changes that may eventually lead other processes to become active (by

---

[6]The process of generating the behavioral states of a system on the basis of the process description (i.e., envisioning) in QP theory has been implemented in the program GIZMO and its successor QPE (Forbus, 1990). A discussion of the mechanisms involved in this work is beyond the scope of an introductory chapter like this, but the topic is well worth exploring for those who want more details on the processes involved in using QP theory to reason about a physical system.

satisfying their operating conditions) or inactive (by disabling their operating conditions). QP theory permits reasoning about complex physical systems by using only qualitative information about time and quantities. In this way, the theory can be used both as an effective computer model of the behavior of physical systems as well as a model of the way people reason about physical systems.

CONTRASTING TYPES OF MENTAL MODELS

In this chapter, I have reviewed two different types of systems known as mental models. Although these systems differ in significant ways, both are aimed at the problem of reasoning about complex problems by using specific elements. Both mental models have mechanisms for representing and reasoning about novel situations (in contrast to the scripts discussed in chap. 7, which focused on representations of familiar situations). In the case of mental models of reasoning, the specific elements are tokens created for the purpose of solving a problem. In the case of mental models of physical systems, the elements are representations of objects, quantities, and processes.

Keane, Byrne, and Gentner (1997) characterized the difference between these types of models as reflecting a different emphasis on working memory and long-term memory. They suggested that mental models of reasoning are designed to explain how people solve difficult, novel problems. Thus, the primary limitation on processing is the working memory available as the problem is solved, because multiple models may need to be held in mind at the same time. In contrast, mental models of physical systems focus on explaining the behavior of physical systems. These mental models are knowledge intensive: Reasoners must have extensive knowledge about the domain to form a model of a novel system in the domain. This need for background knowledge is a reflection of people's inability to reason about the dynamics of systems in unfamiliar domains. Thus, these models emphasize the way that people store and use models of physical systems that they already know something about. Keane et al. suggested that, although research on these two models has been independent, a rapprochement of the lines of research may lead to insights about how working memory and long-term memory come together in the solution of complex problems.

Using Representation

As I complete this survey of ways to represent knowledge, I want to suggest some general lessons for the study of the mind. In this book, I did not advocate a particular type of representation as *the* way that information is stored. Indeed, it should be obvious by now that there is much debate over how to think about knowledge representation in explanations of the range of behaviors that people exhibit. Instead, my point was to introduce a variety of formats for thinking about representation. Every format has produced insights about how human cognition works, and all of them are likely to be the source of future insights. Thus, rather than advocating a particular type of representation, I have tried to describe what the different approaches are good for. In this chapter, I give seven proposals for the use of representation in cognitive models, proposals that I think are important for research in cognitive science.

These issues are listed in Table 10.1 (see also Markman & Dietrich, 1998). The first three proposals are about representations themselves. Proposal 1 implies that representations must actually satisfy the definition presented earlier: They must represent. Proposals 2 and 3 explicitly admit that there are many types of representations and that many different types may need to be integrated in cognitive models. Proposal 4 focuses on the processes that act on representations. Proposals 5 through 7 stress the relationship between models of representation and the psychological phenomena to be explained: Cognitive models must deal with details, context, and relations between people and the world.

TABLE 10.1
Seven Proposals for the Use of Representation in Cognitive Models

1. Cognitive models must be based on representations that actually represent.
2. Cognitive models must adopt multiple approaches to representation.
3. Cognitive models must use representations at multiple grain sizes.
4. Cognitive models must be clear about the specification of processes.
5. Cognitive models must attend to the details of processing as well as to its gross form.
6. Cognitive models must attend to social context.
7. Cognitive models must attend to the relationship between the individual and the world.

PROPOSAL 1: THE NEED FOR REPRESENTATIONS THAT ACTUALLY REPRESENT

The first proposal in Table 10.1 is that cognitive models must be based on representations that actually represent. Although this statement may seem trivial, most psychological models are simplified to effectively illustrate a particular theoretical position, and it is unclear whether they can scale up to real domains. In these systems, the representational scheme lacks all the components in the definition of a representation given in chapter 1. As defined in this book, representation has four requirements: (1) a represented world, (2) a representing world, (3) a consistent set of relationships between the represented and representing worlds, and (4) processes that make use of the information in the representing world. Most forms of representation described in this book have focused on the structure of the representing world and on the processes using the information in the representing world. The representing world may be a space, with procedures for measuring distance in the space, or a structured relational representation with procedures for comparing pairs of such representations to find their commonalities and differences.

The represented world has often been omitted from these discussions. Investigators have simply assumed that the components of the representing world refer to some represented world. Often, the represented world is denoted by labels given to aspects of the representation. For example, the points in a multidimensional space may be labeled, or the nodes in a semantic network may have words associated with them. In many cases, the representing worlds are actually connected to the represented world indirectly through a user who can interpret the labels on a representation (that is, they have a *user semantics*).

In many practical cases, having representations that actually represent (i.e., having both a represented and a representing world) is not so important. If a researcher wants to predict people's behavior in a particular psychological task, he or she may construct an overly simple model of the task to demonstrate the consequences of a theory. For example, Markman and Gentner (1993b) tried to predict people's behavior in a mapping task. Figure 10.1 shows a sample pair of pictures from these studies. Each picture pair contained a cross-mapping, which occurs when objects in each of a pair of scenes look similar but play different relational roles. When a pair containing a cross-mapping is compared, there is a tension between seeing the pictures as similar because of the objects that look alike and seeing the pictures as similar because of the similarities in relations. In the mapping task, people first rated the similarity of the pair of pictures on a 9-point scale. Then, the experimenter pointed to one of the cross-mapped objects (e.g., the woman in the top picture in Figure 10.1) and asked the subject to point to the object in the bottom scene which "goes with" that object. Typically, people selected either the object that looks similar (e.g., the woman in the bottom picture) or the object that plays the same relational role (e.g., the squirrel receiving food in the bottom picture). In general, subjects were more likely to select the object playing the same relational role when they had just made a similarity judgment than when they had not. Workers have taken this finding as evidence that judging the similarity of a pair of scenes involves a process of structural alignment (like that described in chap. 5), which promotes attention to relational commonalities between the pair.

To provide an explanation for people's performance in this task, structured relational representations for the scenes in Figure 10.1 were created. These representations, shown in Figure 10.2, embody several assumptions about people's representations critical to structure-mapping theory. First and foremost, the representations are structured. Next, the main story in the pictures is represented by the deepest and most connected relational structure (i.e., it is most systematic). Objects that look similar (like the women in the top and bottom pictures) are represented by sets of overlapping attributes. These representational assumptions are the ones taken to be important psychologically.

To construct a model of a cognitive process, other assumptions must be made as well. For example, the relation describing the event of the woman giving food to the squirrel is represented as the three-place predicate:

$$gives \ (woman, \ squirrel, \ food). \tag{10.1}$$

The commitment in this model is to a structured representation of this event. It is possible that people have a single predicate with three arguments that represent the event of giving, but it is also possible that this event is represented by using a fully decomposed representation of the transfer as discussed in chapter 7. Likewise, one assumes that the objects in the pictures are represented with sets of attributes, but no one knows which attributes

(A)

(B)

FIG. 10.1. Pair of pictures containing a cross-mapping. From A. B. Markman and D. Gentner (1993). Copyright © 1993 by Academic Press. Reprinted with permission.

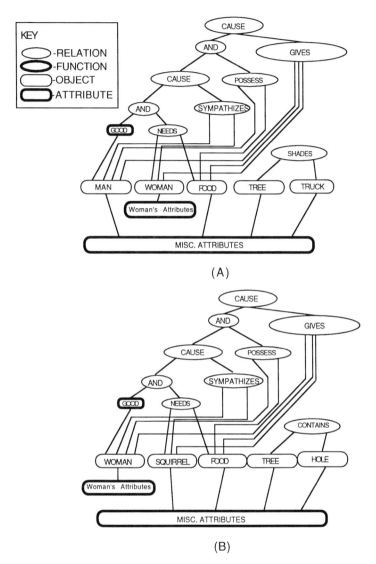

FIG. 10.2. Structured representations of the scenes in Figure 10.1 given to the structure-mapping engine in a simulation of how people compare scenes with cross-mappings.

people use. This is not to say that how people represent events of giving or how they represent particular objects is unimportant. Rather, too little is known about the fine details of people's representations to describe their specific content with any certainty. There is no deep commitment to the assumptions made simply to fill out the details of the representation.

These representations were given to the structure-mapping engine (SME; Falkenhainer, Forbus, & Gentner, 1989), which implements the structural alignment process described in chapter 5. This model takes pairs of structured representations as input and yields sets of structurally consistent correspondences between representations. The program suggested two possible sets of correspondences, shown in Figure 10.3. The preferred interpretation, shown in Figure 10.3A, placed the objects in the pictures

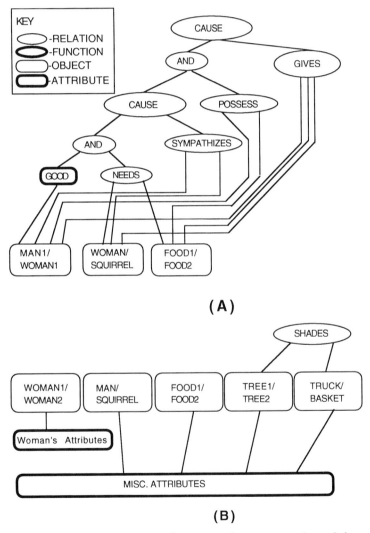

FIG. 10.3. Two interpretations that emerge from a comparison of the representations in Figure 10.2. A: An interpretation that preserves relational similarities. B: An interpretation that preserves object similarities.

in correspondence on the basis of relational similarities. In this interpretation, the woman receiving food in the top scene is placed in correspondence with the squirrel receiving food in the bottom scene. A less preferred interpretation, shown in Figure 10.3B, placed the objects in correspondence on the basis of shared attributes of perceptually similar items. In this interpretation, the woman in the top scene is placed in correspondence with the woman in the bottom scene. Thus, as observed in the data, the relational correspondence was preferred to the object correspondence.

This example makes two important points. First, it can be quite useful to use representations that do not actually represent. The predicate structures fed to SME were assumed to have properties similar to those of people's representations of the same situation. People were assumed to represent conceptual relationships by using a representation with explicit connections between relations and the things they relate. The representations of perceptually similar objects were assumed to be described by similar sets of representational elements. There was, however, no commitment to the actual predicates used in the representation in Figure 10.2. Instead, these representations embodied a set of assumptions about cognitive representations as well as other less crucial assumptions needed to get the model to work. Presumably, as investigators learn more about the way people represent objects and events, firm commitments can be made about these aspects of representations as well.

Although much research can use this strategy, it is important to make progress on the issue of how people actually represent information. There are at least three reasons why it is important to use representations that actually have both a represented world and a representing world. First, much research in psychology focuses on narrow problems. Research on logical reasoning has little contact with research on social reasoning, and research on classification has little contact with research on other aspects of memory. Part of the reason for this narrowness is that cognitive models are often built on minimal representations that are sufficient for understanding the particular task being modeled, but not for other related tasks. By thinking about how a representation may actually connect to something in the outside world, one can arrive at representations that are easily used for more than one task. Creating representations that serve more than one task may place constraints on the structure and content of representations; there is no room for idiosyncratic representational assumptions that satisfy the constraints of only a single task.

A second reason that it is important to think about representations that actually represent is that perceptual and motor tasks demand it. People cannot only reason about complex problems; they can also make their way through the world. Researchers have made significant progress in thinking about conceptual processing by using representations that are mere toys (as in the previous similarity example), but it is increasingly difficult to make process in research on perception and action without thinking about how the information in the world is actually represented. Researchers have complained that symbols and structured representations are an inappropriate basis for models of human cognition (Gibson, 1986; Port & Van Gelder, 1995; Thelen & Smith, 1994; Van Gelder & Port, 1995). Many such attacks have come from people who study perception and motor control. These researchers have abandoned symbols because of difficulties in attaching them in a representing world to actual aspects of the represented world. If psychologists are to develop a more complete understanding of human cognition, they must bridge the gap between higher cognitive processes (like categorization and reasoning) and lower level abilities (like perception and motor control). Accomplishing this task requires finding representing worlds that actually connect to their represented worlds.

A third reason to consider representations with an actual represented world arises from the symbol-grounding problem (discussed in chap. 1). This problem characterizes systems that use a conceptual role semantics (in which many representational elements are given meaning by their relation to other representational elements). Lacking a represented world, a representational system with a conceptual role semantics has no grounded symbols and thus no meaningful symbols.

Of course, not all cognitive models are based on representations without a representing world. Forbus's (1984) qualitative process (QP) theory—a representational system for reasoning about physical systems (described in chap. 9)—has been used to represent and reason about a variety of different domains. Researchers have developed programs that create representations of physical systems from other information about them. In this way, the notations of QP theory have been embedded in models of other tasks. By using QP theory in models that must actually do reasoning about physical systems, a representational scheme can be evaluated with respect to an actual represented world. This kind of explicit attempt to connect representational schemes to specific represented worlds is important for validating particular approaches to knowledge representation.

PROPOSAL 2: MULTIPLE APPROACHES TO REPRESENTATION

If the cognitive system represented information in only one way, this book would read like a pamphlet by Marx and Engels: There would be an orderly progression of proposals for the nature of mental representation culminating in the ultimate form of representation that is right for all models. On this view, previous theories of mental representation would be mere scientific stepping-stones along the way to the one form of representation that serves as the basis of cognitive processing.

There are two reasons why this book does not follow such a progression. First, current cognitive science does not yet point to a single representation scheme as a good candidate for the one true form of representation. From a pragmatic standpoint, cognitive models need to consider a variety of representational types to judge their goodness as the basis of cognitive models. As discussed throughout this book, different approaches to representation have different strengths and weaknesses. When faced with a problem that requires a particular set of characteristics, one should be able to reach into the representational toolbag to pull out a representation that is appropriate for the particular task. Second and more deeply, however, there is little reason to believe that one true form of representation is the only basis of cognitive processing. People display varied abilities, from perception and motor control to language and problem solving. People's behaviors in these abilities do not all seem to be reasonably described by processes acting over a single form of representation.

In chapter 2, I discussed representations that use mental spaces in which items are represented as points or vectors in space. Processing involves geometric operations like measuring distance or projecting one vector onto another. These models have the advantage of procedures (like connectionist learning algorithms) that can create such spaces, as well as efficient processes (like projecting one vector on another) for determining the similarity of pairs of representations. In many spatial models, it is easy to create representations that exist for only short durations. For example, the activation values in a connectionist state vector can change from moment to moment. Thus, spatial representations may be particularly good for models in which the representational states are not expected to be enduring (Port & Van Gelder, 1995). In chapter 1, I discussed Watt's steam engine governor, which represents the pressure in a steam engine by the speed with which the governor spins. The spinning of the governor is a transient representation of pressure. The behavior of mechanical systems like the governor can be described by using systems of differential equations known as dynamic systems (Port & Van Gelder, 1995). When the equations are solved, a graph that relates the behavior of quantities in these equations can be constructed. Such a graph, called a state space, can define the behavior of a complex system by the way it traverses through this state space. Thus, dynamic systems can be construed as yet another type of spatial system (like those described in chap. 2).

One weakness of spatial models is that they cannot explicitly represent information that requires bindings between two or more elements. A second weakness is that they have no good procedures for accessing the commonalities and differences of representations that are compared. Thus, spatial representations can be very useful when efficient processing is needed and when the representational states are expected to be transient, but not when access to specific properties of representations is called for.

Featural representations (described in chap. 3) address some shortcomings of mental space representations. They allow access to specific properties of the representations, because the features are discrete symbols. Processing with these representations can be efficient; the features are independent. For example, genetic algorithms allow search through a massive space of possibilities by allowing recombinations of elements. Because all the representational elements are independent, these recombinations are possible. Thus, for situations in which access to specific elements is needed but relational binding is not, featural representations are useful.

Semantic networks (discussed in chap. 4) are excellent representations for models that require a spread of activation through a system of information. These models are well suited to explanations of situations in which the presence of one concept primes the presence of another. Network representations are also useful for implementing parallel constraint satisfaction models, which allow many different (and possibly conflicting) constraints to be applied to a problem simultaneously. In both cases, the structure of the network guides the automatic spread of activation. Semantic networks need additional processing mechanisms to be used as models of controlled cognition and reasoning. For example, Anderson's ACT system (discussed in chap. 5) uses production rules along with semantic networks to model behaviors like the solution of addition problems.

Structured representations (see chaps. 5–7) provide a way to capture the binding between representational elements. For situations in which it is important to know which features are connected to other features, structured representations are crucial. Applications like understanding sentences, representing the premises of reasoning problems, and solving analogies all seem to involve these kinds of structured representations. This structure comes at a price, however: The processes that act over structured representations are expensive to operate. Even a comparison process like structure mapping requires mechanisms that ensure one-to-one mapping and parallel connectivity (see chap. 5). Thus, structured representations are not appropriate for situations in which fast processing is required or for which a computationally intensive process is not feasible.

It is one thing to argue for diversity and another to actually construct models that use more than one type of representation. Generating models that reconcile different representational formats can be quite difficult; therefore, this approach has not had widespread appeal. An example of both structured and unstructured representations incorporated into a single model is Forbus, Gentner, and Law's (1995) MAC/FAC (Many are called/Few are chosen) model of analogical retrieval. The model is designed to understand how one situation reminds people of another. For example, imagine seeing a man running around his house, trying various methods to rid the house of a bug. On seeing this event, a person may be reminded of the cartoons in which Wile E Coyote futilely chases the Roadrunner, trying various elaborate schemes that fail. Noticing this similarity involves *analogical reminding*, because the first situation prompted the recall of a second situation that was similar to the first primarily in the relations between the objects (i.e., *X* chases *Y* unsuccessfully).

To model analogical retrieval, the MAC/FAC model represents every situation in memory in two ways. First, each situation has a structured predicate calculus representation that links the actors and objects in the event. Second, each situation also has a feature vector representation that encodes only which predicates are incorporated into the representation without taking into account any relational bindings. MAC/FAC posits that retrieval involves two stages. In the first stage (MAC), a new item serving as a retrieval cue is represented as a flat feature representation; the MAC stage is like the exemplar models of memory described in chapter 8. At this stage, the featural representation is quickly compared to featural representations of everything stored in memory, and items with a large number of overlapping features (not counting differences) are passed along to the second stage. At the second stage of processing (FAC), structured representations of the memory items taken from Stage 1 are compared to the structured representation of the memory probe by using the structural alignment procedure in the structure-mapping engine (described in chap. 5; Falkenhainer et al., 1989). This process is more computationally intensive than is the feature comparison, but it allows the model to be sensitive to relational similarities between the cue and items in memory. Any memory items with a sufficient degree of structural similarity to the cue are then retrieved from memory and can be used for subsequent processing.

A primary virtue of this system is that it uses both a featural and a structured representation. The featural representation is used as a first pass to search through a large number of memory items in a small amount of time. The speedy feature comparison process can result in passing along some elements that are not at all structurally similar to the cue. These items are weeded out by the structural comparison process, which performs the computationally intensive structural alignment between two representations on only a small number of representations.

In short, having many different kinds of representations is a boon for cognitive science. Much work has demonstrated the strengths and weaknesses of different representational systems. Indeed, this book is a summary of this effort. Comparatively little research has, however, been devoted to understanding how representational systems can be combined to form powerful models of cognitive processing. This area is important for future research.

PROPOSAL 3: REPRESENTATIONS AT MULTIPLE GRAIN SIZES

How much information is incorporated into each representational element? As discussed in chapter 8, if a representational system has a symbol for *bird*, this element has a wide scope that refers to any item that is a bird. Even more specific features like *red* and *beak* are still fairly abstract. People believe that the red associated with fire engines is different from the red associated with hair or with the breast of a robin. Each of these reds can be represented with the symbol *red*, but something else is clearly needed to account for the fact that people acknowledge the differences between these reds as well as their commonality. Likewise, birds have beaks, but the beak of a chicken looks different from the beak of a toucan. One possibility is that this context sensitivity of features requires using only fine-grained features in representations. Fine-grained features allow different manifestations of a general concept to emerge in different contexts. For example, when representing a beak in the context of a chicken, the fine-grained features describing its shape can differ from those representing a beak in the context of a toucan. This proposal permits a concept (like *beak*) to vary as a function of context but does not explain how people also notice fundamental commonalities between different things called beaks.

One solution to this problem is to assume that cognitive representations for the same item exist at many different grain sizes. Some representational elements may be coarse grained, roughly equivalent to the symbol *beak*, and may represent beaks in general. Other elements may be fine grained and may represent subtle properties that are true for some beaks but not for others. Thus there is more than one way to represent the same item. This redundancy allows models to deal with cases in which context sensitivity is important and also to deal with cases in which invariance across context is important.

One example of how multiple grain sizes can be incorporated into a single model is Hummel and Holyoak's (1997) LISA, a connectionist model of analogical reasoning. LISA uses both distributed vector representations (see chap. 2) and local representations of concepts and structure (see chaps. 4–5). For distributed representations, there is a pool of features for a concept, and a concept is active when some set of its features has a high level of activation. For local representations, labeled nodes correspond to different objects and relations. For example, the concept *John* can be accessed in its general form by activating its node. Activating this node, in turn, activates features associated with this concept. The set of features that is activated is different in different contexts. Thus, LISA is able both to respond to the context of a situation and to abstract from the fine details of a particular situation when necessary. This representational strategy seems appropriate for modeling the way that people process analogies.

The idea that cognitive models need representations at a variety of grain sizes is also consistent with neurobiological evidence of song production in the zebra finch. Behavioral evidence has suggested that these birds' songs have both syllables (typical patterns of notes) and specific notes. Yu and Margoliash (1996) have found that activity in one brain region in zebra finches—the HVc nucleus of the forebrain—is correlated with production of song syllables, whereas activity in a second brain region—the robustus archistriatalis—is correlated with production of individual notes of the zebra finch song. These results suggest a hierarchical control for song in the zebra finch. The fluent operation of the song system requires representations of different grain sizes in a single system. This general principle is likely to operate over a wide range of psychological processes.

PROPOSAL 4: CLEAR SPECIFICATION OF PROCESSES THAT OPERATE OVER REPRESENTATIONS

A central part of the definition of a representation is that some process must extract and use information from it. One reason that specifying the processing assumptions for a given representation is important is that the implications of a representational formalism for psychological models are not clear until the processing assumptions have been laid out. For example, clearly enumerated processing assumptions demonstrate how cognitive systems deal with the holism problem raised in chapter 1. Holism is the idea that the meaning of one concept is defined in part by its relations to other concepts, and all the information in someone's knowledge base is necessary to fix the meaning of any given concept. Most cognitive models deal with this problem by having only a subset of the information in memory active at any given time. This point was made explicitly in chapter 4, in which semantic networks were assumed to have a limited amount of activation flowing through them. In this case, only the active information fixes the meaning of a given symbol at any moment.

This way of dealing with holism is not a philosophical solution but a psychological one. Cognitive systems use methods to constrain the information taking part in a given process under the assumption that only the information available at a particular moment is relevant for processing the current situation. For example, two people may know different things about the 1986 New York Giants, but this difference in knowledge is usually not relevant to the way they process the concept *cat*. Thus, knowledge about the 1986 New York Giants is not normally activated during processing of the concept *cat*.

This issue was also discussed relative to the frame problem in chapter 9. The frame problem involves the difficulty of reasoning about what changes in a new situation. When people want to reason about changes in a physical situation, they should check to see whether every element in the represented world has changed. Because it is not computationally feasible to do this check, systems that reason about the physical world adopt a strategy for limiting the objects examined for change. Solutions to the holism and frame problems both introduce potential errors in reasoning. Communication may become derailed if a speaker activates different knowledge about a concept than does a listener. Likewise, failing to reason about a particular object in the represented world may lead to a mistaken understanding of change in that represented world. A successful cognitive model makes few errors in reasoning, and its pattern of errors mirrors that made by people.

The specification of processes is also necessary because in an important sense, without specifying processing assumptions, there is no representation at all (there is at best only representation potential), so all further discussion begs many important questions. The processing assumptions associated with a model of representation are the properties that decide whether the representation can be applied rigidly to only one situation or can be used flexibly across a variety of situations.

For example, Smolensky (1991) discussed a possible context-dependent representation for a cup. He suggested that representations consist of fine-grained features that he called *micro-features*; the manifestations of a concept in different circumstances differ subtly because of the micro-features that are active. For example, the micro-features of a cup active in the context of a cup with coffee (which may include insulating properties of a cup) may be very different from the micro-features of a cup active in other situations. On the surface, this proposal seems to make clear that a distributed representation can be used as a model of the context dependence of concepts and can provide flexible context sensitivity in representation. Yet Smolensky's proposal does not carry with it any assumptions about how the features are activated or about how a micro-feature representation is used by other cognitive processes (or for that matter how micro-features manage to represent a cup in the first place). On its own, it is not clear what such a representation is capable of doing, and hence it is not clear that it can live up to Smolensky's claims for it. Indeed, Markman, Gentner, and Wisniewski (1998) suggested that vector representations like those used in many distributed connectionist models, when combined with the dot product as a mechanism for comparing vector pairs (Equation 2.7), are not sufficient to model the complexity of human similarity processing. Simple vector representations and dot-product comparisons cannot account for the pattern of similarity judgments displayed in Figure 5.4. As discussed in chapter 5, these data strongly suggest that the comparison process operates over structured relational representations.

Representations like activation vectors are appealing because they seem to embody the flexibility often observed in cognitive processing, but a representation is fluid only if a process allows it to be used flexibly. No representation is fluid by itself. As discussed in chapter 2, vectors are spatial representations; a dot-product comparison process allows only a computation of proximity between two vectors and thereby limits a model's flexibility rather than increases it. Conversely, applying suitable processes to a highly structured representation can make it very flexible. Indeed, the appeal of a universal grammar in linguistics is that it allows infinite productivity from a finite number of elements and rules that contain discrete elements.

One demonstration of the flexibility of using structured representations comes from structured imagination tasks (Karmiloff-Smith, 1990; Ward, 1994, 1995). Researchers in an important area in cognitive science have examined the creative extension of existing concepts (Finke, Ward, & Smith, 1992). How can flexibility in concepts be achieved? People seem to constrain their creativity by extending existing ideas to novel situations. For example, Ward (1994) asked college students to draw novel animals that might live on an alien planet. The animals that people drew tended to maintain the basic structure of animals on Earth. Most constructions were bilaterally symmetric, and many even had the familiar sense organs of known animals. The animals might differ in the number or shape of their parts, but they tended not to diverge strongly from known animals. Even an analysis of alien animals in science fiction revealed that most creatures were structured similarly to animals on Earth.

Structured representations can also exhibit flexibility when they are involved in analogical reasoning. Indeed, Barnden (1994) suggested that analogical reasoning may allow symbol systems to exhibit some of the flexibility often associated with connectionist models that use spatial representations. For example, as discussed in chapter 5, structure-mapping models of analogy and similarity have assumed that the arguments of relations placed in correspondence are themselves also placed in correspondence (Gentner, 1983, 1989; Gentner & Markman, 1997; Holyoak & Thagard, 1995). This principle of parallel connectivity allows nonidentical items to be matched by allowing the arguments of corresponding predicates to be placed in correspondence. Thus, symbol systems are not rigidly required to permit correspondences only between elements with identical symbol names. Just as connectionist models allow responses to vectors that are not identical to those presented during training (see chap. 2), models of analogy allow the recognition of similarities between nonidentical pairs of situations. Missing information in one domain of an analogical correspondence can be filled in on the basis of the structure of the second domain by carrying over relations connected to already matching structure (Clement & Gentner, 1991; Markman, 1997; Spellman & Holyoak, 1996).

The specification of processing assumptions can bring about unforeseen flexibility in other ways. Models of analogical reasoning are able to form multiple interpretations of a single match. For example, people given a "double" metaphor (Gentner, 1988) like "A cloud is a sponge" can generate more than one interpretation (e.g., "Both are fluffy" or "Both can hold water"). Likewise, when given structured representations of this metaphor, models of analogy like SME (Falkenhainer et al., 1989), and LISA (Hummel & Holyoak, 1997) can form both interpretations. These models do so because they can enforce a set of constraints (e.g., structural consistency in the case of analogy) and then start over and form a different interpretation. Interestingly, models that do not strictly enforce constraints, like the ACME model, which uses a process of parallel constraint satisfaction (as discussed in chap. 4), are unable to form multiple interpretations of a comparison (Holyoak & Thagard, 1989). Parallel constraint satisfaction models attempt to form a single interpretation that best satisfies all constraints; hence they cannot form more than one interpretation.

As I have emphasized throughout the book, representations can be discussed only in the context of the processes operating over them. It is not enough to look at a representation and decide that it does (or does not) permit some type of processing. There must be an explicitly designed process that actually makes use of the information in the representation. A benefit of attention to processing is that representations that seem highly inflexible (like structured relational representations) can exhibit quite a bit of flexibility when accompanied by the right kind of process (e.g., an analogical comparison process).

PROPOSAL 5: DETAILS AND GROSS FORM OF BEHAVIOR

Cognitive processing is often much messier and therefore more complicated than theories reflect. Most psychological theories identify a few factors that contribute to the observed behavior under study. In many theories, these factors are represented and combined in relatively simple ways. Such theories agree with good scientific practice; scientists must first see whether simple models suffice before offering complicated explanations. Although this methodology is good, its result is that most psychological models are often not robust enough to explain variability in human performance. For example, if I am asked to list all the words associated with the word *fish*, my list will probably be different from a list that I would give next week (Barsalou, 1989). The specific words reflect my underlying knowledge structures as well as the way that concepts are activated (perhaps through a semantic network, like those discussed in chap. 4). The eventual success of cognitive models rests on the degree to which they can account both for the gross pattern of data observed in studies (e.g., to predict the words most people associate with *fish*) and the fine details of particular patterns of data (e.g., to determine how an individual lists a specific set of words).

As Bruner (1990; L. B. Smith & Sera, 1992) pointed out, cognitive psychologists often study average behavior. They conduct experiments on groups of individuals and average the data that they accumulate. The assumption of such work is that a cognitive central processor governs behavior, and individual variability is less important than is average performance across individuals. Contextual constraints and background differences that give rise to variation in performance between individuals are also important details of cognitive processing, however. As discussed in chapter 1, data that are treated as noise (like variability in performance across individuals) can be meaningful with another set of representational assumptions, as when one is trying to model the fine details of human performance.

Variability in human performance is an object of study in work on expertise. Three facets of expertise bear importantly on discussions of representation. First, expertise is domain specific. This fact is perhaps so obvious that it can be overlooked, but it is crucial from the standpoint of knowledge representation. Experts are experts in a domain, not experts at all things. Thus, experts have learned information and procedures that are selectively helpful in their areas of expertise.

Second, experts are efficient in their ability to represent aspects of their domain relative to novices. Classic studies demonstrating this point have focused on memory in chess experts (Chase & Simon, 1973). Chess experts require less time to reconstruct a configuration of pieces on a chess board than do novices, and experts can remember more pieces from a configuration than can novices. This ability holds for configurations that reflect possible situations from a game, but not for random configurations of pieces. Experts seem to organize chess pieces on the board by information relative to a game (e.g., pieces that are attacking or defending). This organization does not exist for random configurations. Similar findings have been obtained in other domains as well. For example, expert field hockey players are better able to remember the position of field hockey players in a picture than are novices (Allard & Starkes, 1991). These findings suggest that experts can impose a conceptual structure on what they see in their domain of expertise.

Third, experts know different things about their domain of expertise than do novices. Again, this fact may seem too obvious to note, but it is important for understanding representation. Many studies in cognitive psychology have drawn their data from college undergraduates. The results of these studies are taken as evidence of fundamental cognitive processes at work, but these data also reflect college students' level of knowledge about a variety of topics. Systematic differences in performance between college students and experts may reflect differences in knowledge without reflecting differences in processing.

As a demonstration of this point, recent studies have explored how people with different types of expertise classify and reason about trees (Medin, Lynch, Coley, & Atran, 1997). This work contrasted three groups of experts: landscape workers, parks maintenance workers, and taxonomists (i.e., those with scientific training relevant to trees). When asked to sort trees into groups, taxonomists tended to sort into groups based on scientific taxonomies. To a lesser degree, maintenance workers also sorted into groups of taxonomically related trees, but they were less likely to do so than were taxonomists. Finally, landscape workers sorted trees on the basis of their uses in landscaping (i.e., ornamental trees vs. trees to be planted near the street vs. weed trees). Despite these differences in the groupings formed by different types of experts, all were still able to form groups that were consistent with the knowledge relevant to their particular domain of expertise, and all groups of experts could use their categories to reason about trees. For example, they could answer a question like "If a white poplar is susceptible to a new disease, how likely is a weeping willow to be susceptible to this disease?" Thus, these experts seemed to differ primarily in their specific knowledge about trees rather than in their ability to process information in this domain.

In sum, expertise is one area in which variability across people has been treated as an important aspect of research. Studies have demonstrated that knowledge is local to the domain of expertise and that experts can use knowledge to structure their perception of events in the domain. The study of experts enables researchers to tease apart aspects of behavior that reflect workings of the cognitive system from those that reflect differences in knowledge. This analysis simply reinforces the importance of looking both at the average performance of members of groups and at the performance of individuals.

PROPOSAL 6: IMPORTANCE OF THE SOCIAL WORLD

Nearly all the cognitive models described in this book focus on the individual and on the way that individuals represent the world around them, but there is more to human cognition than individual behavior. Humans operate in a dynamic social environment, which influences cognitive processing in a variety of ways, two of which I focus on here: communication and cognitive scaffolding.

One cognitive function that has received substantial attention from cognitive scientists is language. This attention is hardly surprising; the use of language is one of the most striking differences that separate people from other animals. In this book I have discussed how representations of prepositions may be related to the way people represent space (chap. 6) and how verbs may be related to the way people represent events (chap. 7). Each of these discussions focuses largely on the individual and the way that an individual's representations are related to language. I have not been concerned with the primary function of language, to transmit information from one person to another and to establish joint reference to things in the world (H. H. Clark, 1992, 1996; Garrod & Doherty, 1994; Krauss & Fussell, 1996; Nelson, 1988; Tomasello, 1995).

The communicative function of language places strong constraints on how information is represented. For example, establishing joint reference to objects in the world requires attention both to commonalities and to differences related to those commonalities (Markman & Makin, in press; Markman, Yamauchi, & Makin, 1997). People must attend to commonalities because the same word often refers to many similar objects. People must also attend to differences related to the commonalities because establishing reference to unique individuals or specific categories often involves first specifying a category and then modifying the category label to distinguish between members of the category. The same object can refer to many different categories at different levels of abstraction (e.g., poodle vs. dog vs. animal) and with different roles (e.g., animal vs. pet; Brown, 1958). This use of language may also affect how concepts are represented. Thus, things as fundamental as the structure of our categories are likely to be affected by the social context in which the categories are acquired. This is not to endorse a strong Sapir–Whorf view that the structure of the particular language spoken by individuals influences their concepts, but rather to make the more general point that the fact that concepts are developed in a social environment in which they must be communicated has an impact on category structure. The communicative context provides an important force that helps standardize concepts across individuals (Freyd, 1983).

Because people must communicate with other members of their linguistic communities, everyone's concept representations must overlap substantially. Consistent with this suggestion, Garrod and Doherty (1994) gave people a task in which they had to communicate with someone else about locations in a maze. There are many different ways to establish reference to locations in this setting, such as using row and column coordinates or specifying paths. When each person communicated with a number of different people from the same group in this task, the group settled on a single scheme that all members used to talk about locations. Thus, even people who never spoke to each other ultimately used the same communication scheme because they spoke to other people in the same group.

The act of communicating is a joint action pursued by a set of individuals (H. H. Clark, 1996). All participants in communication have an influence on what an utterance means. A speaker may have one intention when speaking, but if the meaning is not adopted by a hearer and ratified in the conversation, the speaker has the option of repairing the flawed communication or letting the meaning taken by the listener stand. Thus, during a conversation, both parties must represent the discourse in a discrete way that allows them to reflect on the match between the intended meaning and the construal of an utterance.

Participants in a discourse may also store a model of what they believe the other participants know. This representation of the other conversational participants allows utterances to be formulated for others appropriately and is also important for other communicative acts like lies. People can lie only if they believe that the other person does not already know the truth and if they think that the other person believes the lie. Through the joint action of conversation, people achieve a shared reality that serves to influence how they represent the interaction between them (Higgins, 1992). Of importance here is that meaning is arrived at dynamically during conversation, but this dynamics is likely to be mediated by discrete representational states that are analyzed by the participants during the discourse.

A second role of the social setting is cognitive scaffolding (Vygotsky, 1986). Typical studies in cognitive psychology have required participants to do a substantial amount of learning on their own. For example, in the standard classification paradigm, participants are presented with objects (or descriptions of objects) and asked to respond with the category to which the object belongs. Participants are given feedback on each trial and eventually learn to distinguish between the categories they are supposed to learn. In contrast, when learning in social settings, people are often given more information (see Markman & Makin, in press, for more discussion of this point). When a parent teaches something to a child, the parent often sets up a situation that is slightly more difficult than the child can master alone, and then the parent guides the child through the learning process (Rogoff, 1990; Vygotsky, 1986). Even when adults learn, there is strong social scaffolding. Hutchins (1995) described how sailors learn the task of navigation. He observed that sailors first take part in simple tasks like reading water depth from a meter. From this vantage point, they can hear the interactions of other crew members and begin to get a feel for the overall navigation task. Over time, they are exposed to other navigation tasks until they are capable of directing the task and carrying out all the separate jobs themselves. As these examples demonstrate, people are rarely called on to develop complex representations in isolation.

Cognitive scaffolding between parents and children is also evident in concept acquisition (Callanan, 1985, 1990). Callanan (1985) examined the way that parents teach children about categories at different levels of abstraction. She found that parents teaching their children about basic-level categories (e.g., dog), or specific subordinate categories (e.g., poodle) tended simply to point to an object and name it. Parents seem to assume that children think a label applied to an object refers to the object and others generally similar to it. In contrast, when teaching children about a general superordinate category (e.g., animal), parents tended to use a strategy in which they first labeled the object with a specific label and then pointed out that it was a member of a general group. For example, parents would say, "See this dog? It is an animal." This strategy suggests that children may have difficulty finding referents for labels that refer to a diverse group of objects and that they must start by giving a specific label to the object. In order for this scaffolding strategy for teaching superordinate categories to work, parent and child must both be able to fix their reference on the basic-level category.

There are two reasons for incorporating the social setting of cognitive processing into models. First, the social setting places constraints on the form of representations. In the case of tasks like communication, representations with discrete symbols that people can reflect on during conversation are necessary to establish meaning with other participants in a dialogue. Second, people often learn concepts in situations in which others work to facilitate this learning. Learning situations are structured so that new representations are constructed collaboratively, often in conjunction with someone else who already has experience in the domain being learned. In this way, people can rely on others to help them determine which aspects of the environment are salient. Because many cognitive models focus only on the individual, the models may assume that the problem of learning new concepts is more difficult than the one that must actually be solved by people in a social environment (Callanan, 1985, 1990; Nelson, 1988, 1996).

PROPOSAL 7: RELATIONSHIP BETWEEN
THE INDIVIDUAL AND THE WORLD

In the previous section, I suggested that by ignoring the social setting in which cognition takes place, some cognitive models focus on tasks that subjects rarely perform in their actual environments. This omission leads to weaker, less explanatory models. In another sense, cognitive models may typically be overly powerful, because they typically ignore the relationship between individuals and their world. As a result, modelers are forced to deploy enduring robust representations for cognitive capacities for which they are not needed.

Considering the relationship between an individual and the world may lead to a different way of formulating the problem that the cognitive system must solve. For example, the models of visual representation discussed in chapter 6 assume that the goal of visual processing is to construct a representation of the image reflected in the pattern of light striking the retina. This representation may then be used for a variety of purposes such as moving through the world, grasping objects, or identifying things in the world. An alternative view was proposed by Gibson (1950, 1986), who had the fundamental insight that the purpose of vision is to provide an organism with information about environmental objects related to the organism's goals. Thus, objects are of interest to an organism primarily because they may be useful for satisfying these goals, or, in Gibson's terminology, objects have *affordances*. According to Gibson's view, the visual system may not need to provide an elaborate representation of the visual world to give information about affordances of objects. Instead, affordances may be perceived directly from visual input.

As an example, imagine a saucepan sitting on a counter in a kitchen. The saucepan has a handle. Given an image of the saucepan, most models of visual processing would try to find the edges in the object and perhaps to describe the saucepan in terms of parts (e.g., a handle, a body) and spatial relations between them (as in chap. 6). In contrast, Gibson suggested that the visual system provides information about the affordances of the object, for instance, that the pot's handle can be grasped.

Gibson's insight is based on the fact that humans (and all other creatures) have bodies and are embedded an environment. Inspired by this approach, several researchers in cognitive science have adopted a "situated action" perspective, which assumes that people need not have a complete representation of the world around them because the world remains in existence and can itself act as an external representation (Agre & Chapman, 1987; Clancey, 1993; Hutchins, 1995; Suchman, 1987). This strategy is likely to be a good one for models of some cognitive processes: All stages of complex cognitive processes need not have explicit and enduring representations when these cognitive processes take place in a complex environment (O'Regan, 1992). Cognitive systems can use information existing in the world to aid in processing.

For example, a cook need not have a complete plan in mind for preparing a dish. Instead, the cook can look at the stove and counters to see where he or she is in the preparation of the current recipe. The presence of dishes, pots, pans, and spices in the kitchen serve as reminders about what steps need to be carried out next. The cook need not remember how long a dish should stay in the oven but can rely on timers or can look at the dish in the oven to see whether it looks like it is done. In all these ways, a cook uses information available in the world to guide the process of preparing a meal without having to represent much information at all.

The importance of embodied cognition is the focus of Glenberg's (1997) work on memory. He suggested that traditional memory tasks studied by cognitive psychologists are flawed because they do not take into account why the human organism needs a memory. On this view, human memory is designed not to recall lists of arbitrary items, but rather to remember information like locations of objects relative to the body. Thus, humans have a capacity to recall information and to structure representations of new experiences to facilitate interactions with the world. Memory is designed to be useful for bodily actions like reaching in space. Thus, understanding the capacities of human memory first requires determining the purposes for which the memory system was developed and the relationship between memory and the body.

Hutchins' (1995) work on navigation discussed earlier, which has focused on the way that cognition develops in a social setting, has also examined how cognition develops in combination with sets of tools designed to aid in the cognitive tasks that are carried out. Hutchins pointed out that a navigator's particular actions when plotting a course for a ship are carried out by using maps, protractors, calculators, and pencils. Given the ship's bearings to fixed landmarks, the navigator plots lines that assess the current position of the ship in water. The time between readings of location and the distance between location points on the chart can be used to calculate the rate of the ship. The tools used for navigation may carry out low-level aspects of the task. For example, the navigator may use a protractor and ruler simply because the task requires drawing a line at a particular angle, but Hutchins argued that, taken as a whole, the set of tools used for navigation actually defines the task that the navigator believes must be solved. For Western navigators, the task is fundamentally assumed to be about determining the location of a moving ship in a two-dimensional plane (viewed from above) with reference to fixed locations in the world. This view of the task is supported by the range of tools that navigators have at their disposal. Hutchins' observation raises two interesting questions for further research. First, what is it about human cognition that makes the particular sets of tools developed effective? Second, in what ways do people represent the tools they use in the course of ordinary processing?

These questions are important for developing accurate models of human cognitive processing. Under normal conditions, people are not cut off from the world around them but use strategies (implicitly or explicitly) for gathering information about the world around them to carry out cognitive tasks. In many laboratory experiments, subjects are studied without the tools they habitually use. This research runs the risk of focusing on cognitive strategies that are not frequently needed—namely, those useful in unfamiliar situations. This limitation may then lead researchers to form models of cognition that are overly dependent on domain-general representations. Cognitive models must preserve the insight that cognition may have few domain-general representations and processes (as discussed in chap. 8). Organisms have bodies and live in environments, and psychologists must take these facts seriously.

A JOURNEY ENDED AND A JOURNEY BEGUN

This concludes the tour of modes of representation. Proposals for the nature of representation are tools needed to construct cognitive models. All theories of cognitive processing make assumptions about how representations are organized. The representations and associated processes determine which things that a cognitive model posits are easy for people to do and which are hard. For this reason, psychologists must choose representational assumptions with care. Cognitive scientists must be careful not to make arbitrary representational choices that may have unintended consequences down the line.

This final chapter provided a set of issues that should be kept in mind when developing a cognitive model. It is not necessary (or even appropriate) to worry about all of them when trying to decide how to model a new task. The social or physical environment may not be relevant when thinking about a particular aspect of a system. Likewise, it may not be necessary to think about how people actually represent a situation. It may be enough to make proposals about the general structure of their representations (Markman, 1997; Ohlsson, 1996). Nevertheless, it is important to step back and think about these issues periodically. Investigators can easily lose sight of their fundamental assumptions when developing a model. By thinking about the broad context in which a model is embedded, we are forced to reconsider these assumptions to ensure that we still believe them to be appropriate. Focusing on these issues is one way to recognize the hidden assumptions that can creep into a research program and that can unwittingly influence the behavior of cognitive models.

References

Agre, P. E., & Chapman, D. (1987). Pengi: An implementation of a theory of activity. In *Proceedings of the National Conference on Artificial Intelligence* (pp. 196–201). Seattle, WA: American Association for Artificial Intelligence.

Allard, F., & Starkes, J. L. (1991). Motor-skill experts in sports, dance, and other domains. In K. A. Ericsson & J. Smith (Eds.), *Toward a general theory of expertise* (pp. 126–152). New York: Cambridge University Press.

Alterman, R. (1988). Adaptive planning. *Cognitive Science, 12*, 393–421.

Andersen, S. M., & Cole, S. W. (1990). "Do I know you?": The role of significant others in general social perception. *Journal of Personality and Social Psychology, 59*(3), 384–399.

Anderson, J. A. (1972). A simple neural network generating an interactive memory. *Mathematical Biosciences, 14*, 197–220.

Anderson, J. A. (1995). *An introduction to neural networks.* Cambridge, MA: MIT Press.

Anderson, J. R. (1978). Arguments concerning representations for mental imagery. *Psychological Review, 85*(4), 249–277.

Anderson, J. R. (1983a). *The architecture of cognition.* Cambridge, MA: Harvard University Press.

Anderson, J. R. (1983b). A spreading activation theory of memory. *Journal of Verbal Learning and Verbal Behavior, 22*, 261–295.

Anderson, J. R. (1993). *Rules of the mind.* Hillsdale, NJ: Lawrence Erlbaum Associates.

Anderson, J. R., Reder, L. M., & Lebiere, C. (1996). Working memory: Activation limitations on retrieval. *Cognitive Psychology, 30*(3), 221–256.

Anderson, R. C., & Pichert, J. W. (1978). Recall of previously unrecallable information following a shift in perspective. *Journal of Verbal Learning and Verbal Behavior, 17*, 1–12.

Arabie, P., Carroll, J. D., & Desarbo, W. S. (1987). *Three-way scaling and clustering.* Newbury Park, CA: Sage.

Au, T. K. (1986). A verb is worth a thousand words: The causes and consequences of interpersonal events implicit in language. *Journal of Memory and Language, 25*, 104–122.

Axelrod, R. (1987). The evolution of strategies in the iterated prisoner's dilemma. In L. D. Davis (Ed.), *Genetic algorithms and simulated annealing* (pp. 32–41). Los Altos, CA: Morgan Kaufmann.

Bargh, J. A., Chaiken, S., Raymond, P., & Humes, C. (1996). The automatic evaluation effect: Unconditional automatic attitude activation with a pronunciation task. *Journal of Experimental Social Psychology, 32*(1), 104–128.

Bargh, J. A., Lombardi, W. J., & Higgins, E. T. (1988). Automaticity of chronically accessible constructs in person × situation effects on person perception: It's just a matter of time. *Journal of Personality and Social Psychology, 55*(4), 599–605.

Barnden, J. A. (1994). On using analogy to reconcile connections and symbols. In D. S. Levine & M. Aparicio (Eds.), *Neural networks for knowledge representation and inference* (pp. 27–64). Hillsdale, NJ: Lawrence Erlbaum Associates.

Barsalou, L. W. (1989). Intra-concept similarity and its implications for inter-concept similarity. In S. Vosniadou & A. Ortony (Eds.), *Similarity and analogical reasoning* (pp. 76–121). New York: Cambridge University Press.

Barsalou, L. W. (1990). On the indistinguishability of exemplar memory and abstraction in category representation. In T. K. Srull & R. S. Wyer (Eds.), *Advances in social cognition* (pp. 61–88). Hillsdale, NJ: Lawrence Erlbaum Associates.

Barsalou, L. W. (1992). Frames, concepts and conceptual fields. In A. Lehrer & E. F. Kittay (Eds.), *Frames, fields and contrasts: New essays in semantic and lexical organization* (pp. 21–74). Hillsdale, NJ: Lawrence Erlbaum Associates.

Barwise, J., & Etchemendy, J. (1993a). *Tarski's world.* Stanford, CA: CSLI.

Barwise, J., & Etchemendy, J. (1993b). *Turing's world.* Stanford, CA: CSLI.

Bassok, M., Chase, V. M., & Martin, S. A. (1998). Adding apples and oranges: Alignment of semantic and formal knowledge. *Cognitive Psychology, 35*(2), 99–134.

Biederman, I. (1985). Human image understanding. Recent research and a theory. *Computer Vision, Graphics, and Image Processing, 32,* 29–73.

Blumstein, S. E., & Stevens, K. N. (1981). Phonetic features and acoustic invariance in speech. *Cognition, 10,* 25–32.

Bobrow, D. G. (1984). *Qualitative reasoning about physical systems.* Cambridge, MA: MIT Press.

Bower, G. H., Black, J. B., & Turner, T. J. (1979). Scripts in memory for text. *Cognitive Psychology, 11,* 177–220.

Bowerman, M. (1989). Learning a semantic system: What role do cognitive predispositions play? In M. L. Rice & R. L. Schiefelbusch (Eds.), *The teachability of language* (pp. 133–169). Baltimore: Paul H. Brookes.

Braine, M. D. S., Reiser, B. J., & Rumain, B. (1984). Some empirical justification for a theory of natural propositional logic. In G. H. Bower (Ed.), *The psychology of learning and motivation.* New York: Academic Press.

Braitenberg, V. (1984). *Vehicles: Experiments in synthetic psychology.* Cambridge, MA: MIT Press.

Bransford, J. D., & Johnson, M. K. (1972). Contextual prerequisites for understanding: Some investigations of comprehension and recall. *Journal of Verbal Learning and Verbal Behavior, 11,* 717–726.

Bransford, J. D., & Johnson, M. K. (1973). Considerations of some problems of comprehension. In W. G. Chase (Ed.), *Visual information processing* (pp. 383–438). New York: Academic Press.

Brown, R. (1958). How shall a thing be called? *Psychological Review, 65*(1), 14–21.

Bruner, J. (1990). *Acts of meaning.* Cambridge, MA: Harvard University Press.

Buchler, J. (Ed.). (1940). *Philosophical writings of Peirce.* London: Routledge & Kegan Paul.

Budescu, D. V., & Wallsten, T. S. (1995). Processing linguistic probabilities: General principles and empirical evidence. In J. Busemeyer, R. Hastie, & D. L. Medin (Eds.), *The psychology of learning and motivation* (pp. 275–318). New York: Academic Press.

Burgess, C., & Lund, K. (1997). Modeling parsing constraints with high-dimensional context space. *Language and Cognitive Processes, 12,* 177–210.

Callanan, M. A. (1985). How parents label objects for young children: The role of input in the acquisition of category hierarchies. *Child Development, 56,* 508–523.

Callanan, M. A. (1990). Parents' descriptions of objects: Potential data for children's inferences about category principles. *Cognitive Development, 5*, 101–122.

Charniak, E., & McDermott, D. (1986). *Introduction to artificial intelligence.* Reading, MA: Addison Wesley.

Chase, W. G., & Simon, H. A. (1973). Perception in chess. *Cognitive Psychology, 4*, 55–81.

Cheng, P. W., & Holyoak, K. J. (1985). Pragmatic reasoning schemas. *Cognitive Psychology, 17*, 391–416.

Cheng, P. W., & Holyoak, K. J. (1989). On the natural selection of reasoning theories. *Cognition, 33*, 285–313.

Cienki, A. J. (1989). *Spatial cognition and the semantics of prepositions in English, Polish and Russian.* Munich: Verlag Otto Sagner.

Clancey, W. J. (1993). Situated action: A neuropsychological interpretation. Response to Vera and Simon. *Cognitive Science, 17*, 87–116.

Clark, E. V. (1979). *The ontogenesis of meaning.* Wiesbaden, Germany: Akademische Verlagsgesellschaft Athenaion.

Clark, E. V. (1987). The principle of contrast: A constraint on language acquisition. In B. MacWhinney (Ed.), *Mechanisms of language acquisition* (pp. 1–33). Hillsdale, NJ: Lawrence Erlbaum Associates.

Clark, H. H. (1992). *Arenas of language use.* Chicago: University of Chicago Press.

Clark, H. H. (1996). *Using language.* New York: Cambridge University Press.

Clement, C. A., & Gentner, D. (1991). Systematicity as a selection constraint in analogical mapping. *Cognitive Science, 15*, 89–132.

Cohen, N. J., & Eichenbaum, H. (1993). *Memory, amnesia, and the hippocampal system.* Cambridge, MA: MIT Press.

Collins, A. M., & Loftus, E. F. (1975). A spreading-activation theory of semantic priming. *Psychological Review, 82*(6), 407–428.

Collins, A. M., & Quillian, M. R. (1972). How to make a language user. In E. Tulving & W. Donaldson (Eds.), *Organization of memory* (pp. 309–351). New York: Academic Press.

Cooper, L. A. (1975). Mental rotation of random two-dimensional shapes. *Cognitive Psychology, 7*, 20–43.

Cosmides, L. (1989). The logic of social exchange: Has natural selection shaped how humans reason? Studies with the Wason selection task. *Cognition, 31*(3), 187–276.

de Kleer, J., & Brown, J. S. (1983). Assumptions and ambiguities in mechanistic mental models. In D. Gentner & A. L. Stevens (Eds.), *Mental models* (pp. 155–190). Hillsdale, NJ: Lawrence Erlbaum Associates.

Dennett, D. C. (1987). *The intentional stance.* Cambridge, MA: MIT Press.

Dietrich, E. (1994). Computationalism. In E. Dietrich (Ed.), *Thinking persons and virtual computers* (pp. 109–136). San Diego: Academic Press.

Dunbar, K. (1997). How scientists think: On-line creativity and conceptual change in science. In T. B. Ward, S. M. Smith, & J. Vaid (Eds.), *Creative thought: An investigation of conceptual structures and processes* (pp. 461–493). Washington, DC: American Psychological Association.

Duncker, K. (1945). On problem solving. *Psychological Monographs, 58*.

Dyer, M. G. (1983). *In-depth understanding: A computer model of integrated processing for narrative comprehension.* Cambridge, MA: MIT Press.

Eimas, P. D. (1971). Speech perception in infants. *Science, 171*, 303–306.

Elman, J. L. (1990). Finding structure in time. *Cognitive Science, 14*(2), 179–212.

Estes, W. K. (1986). Array models for category learning. *Cognitive Psychology, 18*, 500–549.

Estes, W. K. (1994). *Classification and cognition.* New York: Oxford University Press.

Evans, J. S., & Over, D. E. (1996). *Rationality and reasoning.* East Sussex, England: Psychology Press.

Falkenhainer, B., & Forbus, K. D. (1991). Compositional modeling: Finding the right model for the job. *Artificial Intelligence, 51*, 95–143.

Falkenhainer, B., Forbus, K. D., & Gentner, D. (1989). The structure-mapping engine: Algorithm and examples. *Artificial Intelligence, 41*(1), 1–63.

Fauconnier, G. (1994). *Mental spaces.* New York: Cambridge University Press.

Fellbaum, C. (1993). *English verbs as a semantic net.* Unpublished manuscript.

Fillmore, C. J. (1968). The case for case. In E. Bach & R. T. Harms (Eds.), *Universals in linguistic theory* (pp. 1–90). New York: Holt, Rinehart & Winston.

Fillmore, C. J. (1978). On the organization of semantic information in the lexicon. In D. Farkas, W. M. Jakobsen, & K. W. Todrys (Eds.), *Papers from the parasession on the lexicon* (pp. 148–175). Chicago: Chicago Linguistic Society.

Finke, R. A., Pinker, S., & Farah, M. J. (1989). Reinterpreting visual patterns in mental imagery. *Cognitive Science, 13,* 51–78.

Finke, R. A., Ward, T. B., & Smith, S. M. (1992). *Creative cognition: Theory, research, and applications.* Cambridge, MA: MIT Press.

Fodor, J. A. (1981). *Representations: Philosophical essays on the foundations of cognitive science.* Cambridge, MA: MIT Press.

Fodor, J. A. (1986). Why paramecia don't have mental representations. In P. A. French, T. E. Euhling, & H. K. Wettstein (Eds.), *Midwest studies in philosophy: Vol. 10. Studies in the philosophy of mind* (pp. 3–23). Minneapolis: University of Minnesota Press.

Fodor, J. A., & Lepore, E. (1992). *Holism: A shoppers guide.* Cambridge, MA: Blackwell.

Fodor, J. A., & Pylyshyn, Z. W. (1988). Connectionism and cognitive architecture: A critical analysis. *Cognition, 28,* 3–71.

Fodor, J. D., Fodor, J. A., & Garrett, M. F. (1975). The psychological unreality of semantic representations. *Linguistic Inquiry, 6*(4), 515–531.

Forbus, K. D. (1984). Qualitative process theory. *Artificial Intelligence, 24*(1), 85–168.

Forbus, K. D. (1990). The qualitative process engine. In D. S. Weld & J. de Kleer (Eds.), *Readings in qualitative reasoning about physical systems* (pp. 220–235). San Mateo, CA: Morgan Kaufmann.

Forbus, K. D., Gentner, D., & Law, K. (1995). MAC/FAC: A model of similarity-based retrieval. *Cognitive Science, 19*(2), 141–205.

Ford, K. M., & Hayes, P. J. (Eds.). (1991). *Reasoning about agents in a dynamic world: The frame problem.* Greenwich, CT: JAI Press.

Ford, K. M., & Pylyshyn, Z. (Eds.). (1996). *The robot's dilemma revisited: The frame problem in artificial intelligence.* Norwood, NJ: Ablex.

Forrest, S., & Mitchell, M. (1993). Relative building-block fitness and the building-block hypothesis. In L. D. Whitley (Ed.), *Foundations of genetic algorithms* (Vol. 2, pp. 109–126). San Mateo, CA: Morgan Kaufmann.

Foss, D. J., & Harwood, D. A. (1975). Memory for sentences: Implications for human associative memory. *Journal of Verbal Learning and Verbal Behavior, 14,* 1–16.

Franklin, N., Tversky, B., & Coon, V. (1992). Switching points of view in spatial mental models acquired from text. *Memory and Cognition, 20,* 507–518.

Freyd, J. J. (1983). Shareability: The social psychology of epistemology. *Cognitive Science, 7,* 191–210.

Garrod, S., & Doherty, G. (1994). Conversation, co-ordination and convention: An empirical investigation of how groups establish linguistic conventions. *Cognition, 53,* 181–215.

Gati, I., & Tversky, A. (1982). Representations of qualitative and quantitative dimensions. *Journal of Experimental Psychology: Human Perception and Performance, 8*(2), 325–340.

Gentner, D. (1981a). Some interesting differences between nouns and verbs. *Cognition and Brain Theory, 4*(2), 161–178.

Gentner, D. (1981b). Verb semantic structures in memory for sentences: Evidence for componential representation. *Cognitive Psychology, 13,* 56–83.

Gentner, D. (1982). Why nouns are learned before verbs: Linguistic relativity versus natural partitioning. In S. A. Kuczaj (Ed.), *Language development: Vol. 2. Language, thought and culture* (pp. 301–334). Hillsdale, NJ: Lawrence Erlbaum Associates.

Gentner, D. (1983). Structure-mapping: A theoretical framework for analogy. *Cognitive Science, 7*, 155–170.

Gentner, D. (1988). Metaphor as structure mapping: The relational shift. *Child Development, 59*, 47–59.

Gentner, D. (1989). The mechanisms of analogical learning. In S. Vosniadou & A. Ortony (Eds.), *Similarity and analogical reasoning* (pp. 199–241). New York: Cambridge University Press.

Gentner, D., & France, I. M. (1988). The verb mutability effect. In S. L. Small, G. G. Cottrell, & M. K. Tanenhaus (Eds.), *Lexical ambiguity resolution: Perspectives from psycholinguistics, neuropsychology and artificial intelligence* (pp. 343–382). San Mateo, CA: Morgan Kaufmann.

Gentner, D., & Gentner, D. R. (1983). Flowing waters or teeming crowds: Mental models of electricity. In D. Gentner & A. L. Stevens (Eds.), *Mental models* (pp. 99–130). Hillsdale, NJ: Lawrence Erlbaum Associates.

Gentner, D., & Markman, A. B. (1993). Analogy—Watershed or Waterloo? Structural alignment and the development of connectionist models of analogy. In S. J. Hanson, J. D. Cowan, & C. L. Giles (Eds.), *Advances in neural information processing systems* (Vol. 5, pp. 855–862). San Mateo, CA: Morgan Kaufmann.

Gentner, D., & Markman, A. B. (1994). Structural alignment in comparison: No difference without similarity. *Psychological Science, 5*(3), 152–158.

Gentner, D., & Markman, A. B. (1995). Analogy-based reasoning. In M. Arbib (Ed.), *Handbook of brain theory and neural networks* (pp. 91–93). Cambridge, MA: MIT Press.

Gentner, D., & Markman, A. B. (1997). Structural alignment in analogy and similarity. *American Psychologist, 52*(1), 45–56.

Gentner, D., Rattermann, M. J., & Forbus, K. D. (1993). The roles of similarity in transfer: Separating retrievability from inferential soundness. *Cognitive Psychology, 25*(4), 524–575.

Gentner, D., Rattermann, M. J., Markman, A. B., & Kotovsky, L. (1995). Two forces in the development of relational similarity. In T. J. Simon & G. S. Halford (Eds.), *Developing cognitive competence: New approaches to process modeling* (pp. 263–313). Mahwah, NJ: Lawrence Erlbaum Associates.

Gentner, D., & Stevens, A. L. (Eds.). (1983). *Mental models*. Hillsdale, NJ: Lawrence Erlbaum Associates.

Gentner, D., & Toupin, C. (1986). Systematicity and surface similarity in the development of analogy. *Cognitive Science, 10*, 277–300.

Gerrig, R. J., Maloney, L. T., & Tversky, A. (1991). Validating the dimensional structure of psychological spaces: Applications to personality and emotions. In D. R. Brown & J. E. K. Smith (Eds.), *Frontiers of mathematical psychology: Essays in honor of Clyde Coombs* (pp. 138–165). New York: Springer-Verlag.

Gibbs, R. W. (1994). *The poetics of mind*. New York: Cambridge University Press.

Gibson, J. J. (1950). *The perception of the visual world*. Westport, CT: Greenwood Press.

Gibson, J. J. (1986). *The ecological approach to visual perception*. Hillsdale, NJ: Lawrence Erlbaum Associates.

Gick, M. L., & Holyoak, K. J. (1980). Analogical problem solving. *Cognitive Psychology, 12*, 306–355.

Gick, M. L., & Holyoak, K. J. (1983). Schema induction and analogical transfer. *Cognitive Psychology, 15*(1), 1–38.

Gilden, D. L., & Proffitt, D. R. (1989). Understanding collision dynamics. *Journal of Experimental Psychology: Human Perception and Performance, 15*(2), 372–383.

Gilden, D. L., & Proffitt, D. R. (1994). Heuristic judgment of mass ratio in two-body collisions. *Perception and Psychophysics, 56*(6), 708–720.

Glenberg, A. M. (1997). What memory is for. *Behavioral and Brain Sciences, 20*(1), 1–55.

Glenberg, A. M., & Kruley, P. (1992). Pictures and anaphora: Evidence for independent processes. *Memory and Cognition, 20*(5), 461–471.

Glenberg, A. M., Kruley, P., & Langston, W. E. (1994). Analogical processes in comprehension: Simulation of a mental model. In M. A. Gernsbacher (Ed.), *Handbook of psycholinguistics* (pp. 609–640). New York: Academic Press.

Goldmeier, E. (1972). Similarity in visually perceived forms. *Psychological Issues, 8*(1).

Goldstone, R. L., & Medin, D. L. (1994). The time course of comparison. *Journal of Experimental Psychology: Learning, Memory, and Cognition, 20*(1), 29–50.

Halford, G. S. (1992). Analogical reasoning and conceptual complexity in cognitive development. *Human Development, 35*(4), 193–217.

Halford, G. S., Wilson, W. H., Guo, J., Wiles, J., & Stewart, J. E. M. (1994). Connectionist implications for processing capacity limitations in analogies. In K. J. Holyoak & J. Barnden (Eds.), *Advances in connectionist and neural computation theory: Vol. 2, Analogical connections* (pp. 363–415). Norwood, NJ: Ablex.

Hammond, K. J. (1990). Explaining and repairing plans that fail. *Artificial Intelligence, 45,* 173–228.

Hammond, K. J., Seifert, C. M., & Gray, K. C. (1991). Functionality in analogical transfer: A hard match is good to find. *Journal of the Learning Sciences, 1*(2), 111–152.

Hayes, P. J. (1979). The logic of frames. In D. Metzing (Ed.), *Frame conceptions and text understanding* (pp. 46–61). Berlin: de Gruyter.

Hayes, P. J. (1985). The second naive physics manifesto. In R. J. Brachman & H. J. Levesque (Eds.), *Readings in knowledge representation* (pp. 467–485). Los Altos, CA: Morgan Kaufmann.

Heckhausen, H., & Beckmann, J. (1990). Intentional action and action slips. *Psychological Review, 97*(1), 36–48.

Heider, F. (1958). *The psychology of interpersonal relations.* New York: Wiley.

Herskovits, A. (1986). *Language and spatial cognition: An interdisciplinary study of the prepositions in English.* New York: Cambridge University Press.

Hesse, M. B. (1966). *Models and analogies in science.* Notre Dame, IN: University of Notre Dame Press.

Higgins, E. T. (1992). Achieving "shared reality" in the communication game: A social action that creates meaning. *Journal of Language and Social Psychology, 11*(3), 107–131.

Higgins, E. T. (1996). Knowledge activation: Accessibility, applicability and salience. In E. T. Higgins & A. W. Kruglanski (Eds.), *Social psychology: Handbook of basic principles* (pp. 133–168). New York: Guilford Press.

Hinton, G. E. (1979). Some demonstrations of the effects of structural descriptions in mental imagery. *Cognitive Science, 3,* 231–250.

Hintzman, D. L. (1986). "Schema abstraction" in a multiple trace memory model. *Psychological Review, 93*(4), 411–428.

Holland, J. H. (1992). *Adaptation in natural and artificial systems.* Cambridge, MA: MIT Press.

Holyoak, K. J., & Hummel. J. E. (in press). The proper treatement of symbols in a connectionist architecture. In E. Dietrich & A. B. Markman (Eds.), *Cognitive dynamics.* Cambridge, MA: MIT Press.

Holyoak, K. J., & Koh, K. (1987). Surface and structural similarity in analogical transfer. *Memory and Cognition, 15*(4), 332–340.

Holyoak, K. J., & Thagard, P. (1989). Analogical mapping by constraint satisfaction. *Cognitive Science, 13*(3), 295–355.

Holyoak, K. J., & Thagard, P. (1995). *Mental leaps: Analogy in creative thought.* Cambridge, MA: MIT Press.

Horn, B. K. P. (1973). *The Binford–Horn LINEFINDER* (No. Memo 285). Cambridge, MA: MIT Artificial Intelligence Laboratory.

Howard, I. P. (1978). Recognition and knowledge of the water-level principle. *Perception, 7,* 151–160.

Hubel, D. H., & Wiesel, T. N. (1965). Receptive fields and functional architecture in two nonstriate visual areas (18 and 19) of the cat. *Journal of Neurophysiology, 28,* 229–289.

Hubel, D. H., Wiesel, T. N., & LeVay, S. (1975). Functional architecture of area 17 in normal and monocularly deprived macaque monkeys. *Cold Spring Harbor Symposium on Quantitiative Biology, 40,* 581–589.

Hummel, J. E., & Biederman, I. (1992). Dynamic binding in a neural network for shape recognition. *Psychological Review, 99*(3), 480–517.

Hummel, J. E., & Holyoak, K. J. (1997). Distributed representations of structure: A theory of analogical access and mapping. *Psychological Review, 104*(3), 427–466.

Hutchins, E. (1983). Understanding Micronesian navigation. In D. Gentner & A. L. Stevens (Eds.), *Mental models* (pp. 191–225). Hillsdale, NJ: Lawrence Erlbaum Associates.

Hutchins, E. (1995). *Cognition in the wild.* Cambridge, MA: MIT Press.

Huttenlocher, D. P., & Ullman, S. (1990). Recognizing solid objects by alignment with an image. *International Journal of Computer Vision, 5*(2), 195–212.

Huttenlocher, J., & Lui, F. (1979). The semantic organization of some simple nouns and verbs. *Journal of Verbal Learning and Verbal Behavior, 18,* 141–162.

Imai, M., Gentner, D., & Uchida, N. (1994). Children's theories of word meaning: The role of shape similarity in early acquisition. *Cognitive Development, 9,* 45–75.

Jackendoff, R. (1987). On Beyond Zebra: The relation of linguistic and visual information. *Cognition, 26,* 89–114.

Jakobsen, R., Fant, G., & Halle, M. (1963). *Preliminaries to speech analysis.* Cambridge, MA: MIT Press.

James, W. (1989). *Psychology: The briefer course.* Notre Dame, IN: University of Notre Dame Press. (Original work published 1892)

Johnson-Laird, P. N. (1983). *Mental models.* New York: Cambridge University Press.

Johnson-Laird, P. N. (1988). *The computer and the mind.* Cambridge, MA: Harvard University Press.

Johnson-Laird, P. N., & Byrne, R. M. J. (1991). *Deduction.* Hillsdale, NJ: Lawrence Erlbaum Associates.

Johnson-Laird, P. N., Byrne, R. M., & Tabossi, P. (1989). Reasoning by model: The case of multiple quantification. *Psychological Review, 96*(4), 658–673.

Johnson-Laird, P. N., Hermann, D. J., & Chaffin, R. (1984). Only connections: A critique of semantic networks. *Psychological Bulletin, 96*(2), 292–315.

Johnson-Laird, P. N., Legrenzi, P., & Legrenzi, M. S. (1972). Reasoning and a sense of reality. *British Journal of Psychology, 63*(3), 395–400.

Johnson-Laird, P. N., & Savary, F. (1996). Illusory inferences about probabilities. *Acta Psychologica, 93,* 69–90.

Kaiser, M. K., Proffitt, D. R., & McCloskey, M. (1986). Development of intuitive theories of motion: Curvilinear motion in the absence of external forces. *Developmental Psychology, 22*(1), 67–71.

Karmiloff-Smith, A. (1990). Constraints on representational change: Evidence from children's drawing. *Cognition, 34,* 57–83.

Keane, M. T., Byrne, R. M., & Gentner, D. (1997). *Two views of mental models.* Unpublished manuscript.

Keane, M. T., Ledgeway, T., & Duff, S. (1994). Constraints on analogical mapping: A comparison of three models. *Cognitive Science, 18,* 387–438.

Kempton, W. (1986). Two theories of home heat control. *Cognitive Science, 10*(1), 75–90.

Keysar, B. (1994). The illusory transparency of intention: Linguistic perspective-taking in text. *Cognitive Psychology, 26,* 165–208.

Keysar, B., & Bly, B. (1995). Intuitions of the transparency of idioms: Can one keep a secret by spilling the beans? *Journal of Memory and Language, 34*(1), 89–109.

Kieras, D. (1978). Beyond pictures and words: Alternative information-processing models for imagery effects in verbal memory. *Psychological Bulletin, 85*(3), 532–554.

Kintsch, W., & Van Dijk, T. A. (1978). Toward a model of text comprehension and production. *Psychological Review, 85,* 363–394.

Knapp, A. G., & Anderson, J. A. (1984). Theory of categorization based on distributed memory storage. *Journal of Experimental Psychology: Learning, Memory, and Cognition, 10*(4), 616–637.

Kolodner, J. (1993). *Case-based reasoning.* San Mateo, CA: Morgan Kaufmann.

Kosslyn, S. M. (1994). *Image and brain.* Cambridge, MA: MIT Press.

Kosslyn, S. M., Ball, T. M., & Reiser, B. J. (1978). Visual images preserve metric spatial information: Evidence from studies of image scanning. *Journal of Experimental Psychology: Human Perception and Performance, 4,* 47–60.

Krauss, R. M., & Fussell, S. R. (1996). Social psychological models of interpersonal communication. In E. T. Higgins & A. Kruglanski (Eds.), *Social psychology: Handbook of basic principles* (pp. 655–701). New York: Guilford Press.

Krumhansl, C. L. (1978). Concerning the applicability of geometric models to similarity data: The interrelationship between similarity and spatial density. *Psychological Review, 85*(5), 445–463.

Kruschke, J. K. (1992). ALCOVE: An exemplar-based connectionist model of category learning. *Psychological Review, 99,* 22–44.

Kruskal, J. B., & Wish, M. (1978). *Multidimensional scaling.* Newbury Park, CA: Sage.

Kuipers, B. (1994). *Qualitative reasoning: Modeling and simulation with incomplete knowledge.* Cambridge, MA: MIT Press.

Lakoff, G. (1987). *Women, fire and dangerous things: What categories reveal about the mind.* Chicago, IL: University of Chicago Press.

Lakoff, G., & Johnson, M. (1980). *Metaphors we live by.* Chicago, IL: University of Chicago Press.

Landau, B., & Jackendoff, R. (1993). "What" and "where" in spatial language and spatial cognition. *Behavioral and Brain Sciences, 16*(2), 217–266.

Landau, B., Smith, L. B., & Jones, S. S. (1988). The importance of shape in early lexical learning. *Cognitive Development, 3,* 299–321.

Landauer, T. K., & Dumais, S. T. (1997). A solution to Plato's problem: The latent semantic analysis theory of acquisition, induction, and representation of knowledge. *Psychological Review, 104*(2), 211–240.

Landauer, T. K., & Dumais, S. T. (1996). How come you know so much? From practical problem solving to new memory theory. In D. Hermann (Ed.), *Basic and applied memory research.* Mahwah, NJ: Lawrence Erlbaum Associates.

Lassaline, M. E. (1996). Structural alignment in induction and similarity. *Journal of Experimental Psychology: Learning, Memory, and Cognition, 22*(3), 754–770.

Lenat, D. B., & Brown, J. S. (1984). Why AM and EURISKO appear to work. *Artificial Intelligence, 23*(3), 269–294.

Lenat, D., & Guha, R. V. (1990). *Building large knowledge-based systems.* San Francisco: Addison Wesley.

Leyton, M. (1992). *Symmetry causality mind.* Cambridge, MA: MIT Press.

Lindemann, P. G., & Markman, A. B. (1996). Alignability and attribute importance in choice. In G. Cottrell (Ed.), *Proceedings of the 18th annual meeting of the Cognitive Science Society* (pp. 358–363). Mahwah, NJ: Lawrence Erlbaum Associates.

Logan, G. D. (1988). Toward an instance theory of automaticity. *Psychological Review, 95,* 492–527.

Love, B. C. (1996). Mutability, conceptual transformation, and context. In G. W. Cottrell (Ed.), *Proceedings of the 18th annual meeting of the Cognitive Science Society* (pp. 459–463). Mahwah, NJ: Lawrence Erlbaum Associates.

Love, B. C., & Sloman, S. A. (1995). Mutability and the determinants of conceptual transformability. In J. D. Moore & J. F. Lehman (Eds.), *Proceedings of the 17th annual conference of the Cognitive Science Society* (pp. 654–659). Mahwah, NJ: Lawrence Erlbaum Associates.

Malt, B. C. (1995). Category coherence in cross-cultural perspective. *Cognitive Psychology, 29,* 85–148.

Mani, K., & Johnson-Laird, P. N. (1982). The mental representation of spatial descriptions. *Memory and Cognition, 10*(2), 181–187.

Markman, A. B. (1989). LMS rules and the inverse base-rate effect: Comment on Gluck and Bower (1988). *Journal of Experimental Psychology: General, 118*(4), 417–421.

Markman, A. B. (1997). Constraints on analogical inference. *Cognitive Science, 21*(4), 373–418.

Markman, A. B., & Dietrich, E. (1998). *In defense of representation.* Manuscript in preparation.

Markman, A. B., & Gentner, D. (1993a). Splitting the differences: A structural alignment view of similarity. *Journal of Memory and Language, 32*(4), 517–535.

Markman, A. B., & Gentner, D. (1993b). Structural alignment during similarity comparisons. *Cognitive Psychology, 25*(4), 431–467.

Markman, A. B., & Gentner, D. (1996). Commonalities and differences in similarity comparisons. *Memory and Cognition, 24*(2), 235–249.

Markman, A. B., & Gentner, D. (1997). The effects of alignability on memory. *Psychological Science, 8*(5), 363–367.

Markman, A. B., Gentner, D., & Wisniewski, E. J. (1998). *Implications of structural alignment for connectionist models.* Manuscript in preparation.

Markman, A. B., & Makin, V. S. (in press). Referential communication and category acquisition. *Journal of Experimental Psychology: General.*

Markman, A. B., & Medin, D. L. (1995). Similarity and alignment in choice. *Organizational Behavior and Human Decision Processes, 63*(2), 117–130.

Markman, A. B., & Wisniewski, E. J. (1997). Similar and different: The differentiation of basic level categories. *Journal of Experimental Psychology: Learning, Memory, and Cognition, 23*(1), 54–70.

Markman, A. B., Yamauchi, T., & Makin, V. S. (1997). The creation of new concepts: A multifaceted approach to category learning. In T. B. Ward, S. M. Smith, & J. Vaid (Eds.), *Creative thought: An investigation of conceptual structures and processes* (pp. 179–208). Washington, DC: American Psychological Association.

Markman, E. M., & Wachtel, G. F. (1988). Children's use of mutual exclusivity to constrain the meanings of words. *Cognitive Psychology, 20*(2), 121–157.

Marr, D. (1982). *Vision.* New York: W. H. Freeman.

McAfee, E. A., & Proffitt, D. R. (1991). Understanding the surface orientation of liquids. *Cognitive Psychology, 23,* 483–514.

McCarthy, J. (1968). Programs with common sense. In M. Minsky (Ed.), *Semantic information processing* (pp. 403–418). Cambridge, MA: MIT Press.

McClelland, J. L., & Rumelhart, D. E. (1981). An interactive activation model of context effects in letter perception: Part 1, An account of basic findings. *Psychological Review, 88,* 375–407.

McClelland, J. L., & Rumelhart, D. E. (1986). *Parallel distributed processing.* Cambridge, MA: MIT Press.

McCloskey, M. (1983). Intuitive physics. *Scientific American, 248*(4), 122–130.

McGurk, H., & MacDonald, J. (1976). Hearing lips and seeing voices. *Nature, 264,* 746–748.

McKoon, G., & Ratcliff, R. (1992). Inference during reading. *Psychological Review, 99*(3), 440–466.

Medin, D. L., Dewey, G. I., & Murphy, T. D. (1983). Relationships between item and category learning: Evidence that abstraction is not automatic. *Journal of Experimental Psychology: Learning, Memory, and Cognition, 9*(4), 607–625.

Medin, D. L., Goldstone, R. L., & Gentner, D. (1993). Respects for similarity. *Psychological Review, 100*(2), 254–278.

Medin, D. L., Lynch, E. B., Coley, J. D., & Atran, S. (1997). Categorization and reasoning among tree experts: Do all roads lead to Rome? *Cognitive Psychology, 32*(1), 49–96.

Medin, D. L., & Ross, B. H. (1989). The specific character of abstract thought: Categorization, problem solving and induction. In R. S. Sternberg (Ed.), *Advances in the psychology of human intelligence* (pp. 189–223). Hillsdale, NJ: Lawrence Erlbaum Associates.

Medin, D. L., & Schaffer, M. M. (1978). Context theory of classification. *Psychological Review, 85*(3), 207–238.

Medin, D. L., & Shoben, E. J. (1988). Context and structure in conceptual combination. *Cognitive Psychology, 20*(2), 158–190.

Metcalfe, J. (1991). Recognition failure and the composite memory trace in CHARM. *Psychological Review, 98*(4), 529–553.

Metcalfe, J. (1993). Novelty monitoring, metacognition, and control in a composite holographic associative recall model: Implications for Korsakoff amnesia. *Psychological Review, 100*(1), 3–22.

Metcalfe-Eich, J. M. (1982). A composite holographic associative recall model. *Psychological Review, 89*(6), 627–661.

Metzler, J., & Shepard, R. N. (1974). Transformational studies of the internal representation of three-dimensional objects. In R. Solso (Ed.), *Theories in cognitive psychology: The Loyola symposium* Hillsdale, NJ: Lawrence Erlbaum Associates.

Meyer, D. E., & Schvaneveldt, R. W. (1971). Facilitation in recognizing pairs of words: Evidence of a dependence between retrieval operations. *Journal of Experimental Psychology, 90*(2), 227–234.

Meyer, D. E., Schvaneveldt, R. W., & Ruddy, M. G. (1975). Loci of contextual effects on visual word recognition. In Rabbitt & Dornic (Eds.), *Attention and performance* (Vol. 5, pp. 98–118). New York: Academic Press.

Miller, G. A. (1956). The magical number seven plus or minus two: Some limits on our capacity for processing information. *Psychological Review, 63*, 81–97.

Miller, G. A., & Fellbaum, C. (1991). Semantic networks of English. *Cognition, 41*, 197–229.

Miller, G. A., & Johnson-Laird, P. N. (1976). *Language and perception.* Cambridge, MA: Harvard University Press.

Minsky, M. (1981). A framework for representing knowledge. In J. Haugeland (Ed.), *Mind design* (pp. 95–128). Cambridge, MA: MIT Press.

Mitchell, M. (1996). *An introduction to genetic algorithms.* Cambridge, MA: MIT Press.

Morris, M. W., & Murphy, G. L. (1990). Converging operations on a basic level in event taxonomies. *Memory and Cognition, 18*(4), 407–418.

Munro, A. (1975). Linguistic theory and the LNR structural representation. In D. A. Norman, & D. E. Rumelhart (Eds.), *Explorations in cognition* (pp. 88–114). San Francisco: W. H. Freeman.

Murphy, G. L. (1996). On metaphoric representation. *Cognition, 60*, 173–204.

Murphy, G. L. (1997). Reasons to doubt the present evidence for metaphoric representation. *Cognition, 62*, 99–108.

Murphy, G. L., & Wisniewski, E. J. (1989). Categorizing objects in isolation and in scenes: What a superordinate is good for. *Journal of Experimental Psychology: Learning, Memory, and Cognition, 15*, 572–586.

Neely, J. H. (1976). Semantic priming and retrieval from lexical memory: Evidence for facilitatory and inhibitory processes. *Memory and Cognition, 4*(5), 648–654.

Nelson, K. (1988). Constraints on word learning? *Cognitive Development, 3*, 221–246.

Nelson, K. (1996). *Language in cognitive development: Emergence of the mediated mind.* New York: Cambridge University Press.

Newell, A. (1990). *Unified theories of cognition.* Cambridge, MA: Harvard University Press.

Norman, D. A., & Rumelhart, D. E. (1975). *Explorations in cognition.* San Francisco: W. H. Freeman.

Nosofsky, R. M. (1986). Attention, similarity and the identification–categorization relationship. *Journal of Experimental Psychology: General, 115*(1), 39–57.

Nosofsky, R. M. (1987). Attention and learning processes in the identification and categorization of integral stimuli. *Journal of Experimental Psychology: Learning, Memory, and Cognition, 13*(1), 87–108.

Nosofsky, R. M., & Palmeri, T. J. (1997). An exemplar-based random walk model of speeded classification. *Psychological Review, 104*(2), 266–300.

Novick, L. R. (1988). Analogical transfer, problem similarity and expertise. *Journal of Experimental Psychology: Learning, Memory, and Cognition, 14*(3), 510–520.

Ohlsson, S. (1996). Learning from performance errors. *Psychological Review, 103*(2), 241–262.

O'Regan, J. K. (1992). Solving the "real" mysteries of visual perception: The world as an outside memory. *Canadian Journal of Psychology, 46*(3), 461–488.

Palmer, S. E. (1977). Hierarchical structure in perceptual representations. *Cognitive Psychology, 9*, 441–474.

Palmer, S. E. (1978a). Fundamental aspects of cognitive representation. In E. Rosch & B. B. Lloyd (Eds.), *Cognition and categorization* (pp. 259–303). Hillsdale, NJ: Lawrence Erlbaum Associates.

Palmer, S. E. (1978b). Structural aspects of visual similarity. *Memory and Cognition, 6*(2), 91–97.

Palmer, S. E. (1992). Common region: A new principle of perceptual grouping. *Cognitive Psychology, 9*(3), 441–474.

Palmeri, T. J. (1997). Exemplar similarity and the development of automaticity. *Journal of Experimental Psychology: Learning, Memory, and Cognition, 23*(2), 324–354.

Pavlicic, T., & Markman, A. B. (1997). The structure of the verb lexicon: Evidence from a structural alignment approach to similarity. In *Proceedings of the 19th annual conference of the Cognitive Science Society* (pp. 590–595). Stanford, CA: Lawrence Erlbaum Associates.

Perner, J. F. (1991). *Understanding the representational mind.* Cambridge, MA: MIT Press.

Piaget, J., & Inhelder, B. (1956). *The child's conception of space.* London: Routledge & Kegan Paul.

Pinker, S. (1991). *Learnability and cognition: The acquisition of argument structure.* Cambridge, MA: MIT Press.

Pinker, S., & Prince, A. (1988). On language and connectionism: Analysis of a parallel distributed processing model of language acquisition. *Cognition, 28*, 73–193.

Plate, T. A. (1991). *Holographic reduced representations: Convolution algebra for compositional distributed representations* (Technical Report No. CFG-TR-91-1). Toronto, Canada: University of Toronto.

Pollack, J. B. (1990). Recursive distributed representations. *Artificial Intelligence, 46*(1–2), 77–106.

Pollack, J. L. (1994). Justification and defeat. *Artificial Intelligence, 67*, 377–407.

Port, R. F., & Van Gelder, T. (Eds.). (1995). *Mind as motion.* Cambridge, MA: MIT Press.

Posner, M. I., Boies, S. J., Eichelman, W. H., & Taylor, R. L. (1969). Retention of visual and name codes of single letters. *Journal of Experimental Psychology, 79*(1, Part 2), 1–16.

Posner, M. I., & Keele, S. W. (1970). Retention of abstract ideas. *Journal of Experimental Psychology, 83*, 304–308.

Pylyshyn, Z. W. (1980). Computation and cognition: Issues in the foundations of cognitive science. *Behavioral and Brain Sciences, 3*(1), 111–169.

Pylyshyn, Z. W. (1981). The imagery debate: Analogue media versus tacit knowledge. *Psychological Review, 88*, 16–45.

Quillian, M. R. (1968). Semantic memory. In M. Minsky (Ed.), *Semantic information processing* (pp. 216–260). Cambridge, MA: MIT Press.

Raaijmakers, J. G., & Shiffrin, R. M. (1981). Search of associative memory. *Psychological Review, 88,* 93–134.

Ratcliff, R. (1988). Continuous versus discrete information processing: Modeling accumulation of partial information. *Psychological Review, 95*(2), 238–255.

Ratcliff, R., & McKoon, G. (1989). Similarity information versus relational information: Differences in the time course of retrieval. *Cognitive Psychology, 21*(2), 139–155.

Read, S. J., & Marcus-Newhall, A. (1993). Explanatory coherence in social explanations: A parallel distributed processing account. *Journal of Personality and Social Psychology, 65*(3), 429–447.

Read, S. J., & Miller, L. C. (1993). Rapist or "regular guy": Explanatory coherence in the construction of mental models of others. *Personality and Social Psychology Bulletin, 19*(5), 526–541.

Reed, S. K. (1972). Pattern recognition and categorization. *Cognitive Psychology, 3,* 382–407.

Reed, S. K. (1974). Structural descriptions and the limitations of visual images. *Memory and Cognition, 2,* 329–336.

Reed, S. K., & Bolstad, C. A. (1991). Use of examples and procedures in problem solving. *Journal of Experimental Psychology: Learning, Memory, and Cognition, 17*(4), 753–766.

Reed, S. K., Ernst, G. W., & Banerji, R. (1974). The role of analogy in transfer between similar problem states. *Cognitive Psychology, 6,* 436–450.

Reeves, L. M., & Weisberg, R. W. (1994). The role of content and abstract information in analogical transfer. *Psychological Bulletin, 115*(3), 381–400.

Regehr, G., & Brooks, L. R. (1993). Perceptual manifestations of an analytic structure: The priority of holistic individuation. *Journal of Experimental Psychology: General, 122,* 92–114.

Regier, T. (1996). *The human semantic potential.* Cambridge, MA: MIT Press.

Regier, T. (1997). Constraints on the learning of spatial terms: A computational investigation. In D. L. Medin, P. Schyns, & R. L. Goldstone (Eds.), *Psychology of learning and motivation: Vol. 36. Mechanisms of perceptual learning* (pp. 171–217). San Diego: Academic Press.

Rips, L. J. (1986). Mental muddles. In H. Brand & R. M. Harnish (Eds.), *The representation of knowledge and belief* (pp. 258–285). Tucson: University of Arizona Press.

Rips, L. J. (1994). *The psychology of proof: Deductive reasoning in human thinking.* Cambridge, MA: MIT Press.

Rips, L. J., & Conrad, F. G. (1989). Folk psychology of mental activities. *Psychological Review, 96*(2), 187–207.

Rips, L. J., Shoben, E. J., & Smith, E. E. (1973). Semantic distance and the verification of semantic relations. *Journal of Verbal Learning and Verbal Behavior, 12,* 1–20.

Rogoff, B. (1990). *Apprenticeship in thinking: Cognitive development in social context.* New York: Oxford University Press.

Rosch, E. (1975). Cognitive reference points. *Cognitive Psychology, 7,* 532–547.

Rosch, E., & Mervis, C. B. (1975). Family resemblances: Studies in the internal structure of categories. *Cognitive Psychology, 7,* 573–605.

Rosch, E., Mervis, C. B., Gray, W. D., Johnson, D. M., & Boyes-Braem, P. (1976). Basic objects in natural categories. *Cognitive Psychology, 8,* 382–439.

Ross, B. H. (1984). Remindings and their effects in learning a cognitive skill. *Cognitive Psychology, 16,* 371–416.

Ross, B. H. (1987). This is like that: The use of earlier problems and the separation of similarity effects. *Journal of Experimental Psychology: Learning, Memory, and Cognition, 13*(4), 629–639.

Ross, B. H. (1989). Distinguishing types of superficial similarities: Different effects on the access and use of earlier examples. *Journal of Experimental Psychology: Learning, Memory, and Cognition, 15*(3), 456–468.

Rothkopf, E. Z. (1957). A measure of stimulus similarity and errors in some paired-associate learning tasks. *Journal of Experimental Psychology, 53*(2), 94–101.

Rumelhart, D. E., & Abrahamson, A. A. (1973). A model for analogical reasoning. *Cognitive Psychology, 5*(1), 1–28.

Rumelhart, D. E., Hinton, G. E., & Williams, R. J. (1986). Learning internal representations by error propagation. In D. E. Rumelhart & J. L. McClelland (Eds.), *Parallel distributed processing: Explorations in the microstructure of cognition* (pp. 318–362). Cambridge, MA: MIT Press.

Rumelhart, D. E., & McClelland, J. L. (1986). On learning the past tenses of English verbs. In J. L. McClelland & D. E. Rumelhart (Eds.), *Parallel distributed processing: Explorations in the microstructure of cognition* (pp. 216–271). Cambridge, MA: MIT Press.

Sadler, D. D., & Shoben, E. J. (1993). Context effects on semantic domains as seen in analogy solution. *Journal of Experimental Psychology: Learning, Memory, and Cognition, 19*(1), 128–147.

Samarapungavan, A., Vosniadou, S., & Brewer, W. F. (1996). Mental models of the earth, sun, and moon: Indian children's cosmologies. *Cognitive Development, 11*, 491–521.

Schank, R. C. (1972). Conceptual dependency: A theory of natural language understanding. *Cognitive Psychology, 3*, 552–631.

Schank, R. C. (1975). *Conceptual information processing.* New York: Elsevier.

Schank, R. C. (1982). *Dynamic memory.* New York: Cambridge University Press.

Schank, R. C., & Abelson, R. (1977). *Scripts, plans, goals and understanding.* Hillsdale, NJ: Lawrence Erlbaum Associates.

Schank, R. C., Kass, A., & Riesbeck, C. K. (1994). *Inside case-based explanation.* Hillsdale, NJ: Lawrence Erlbaum Associates.

Schank, R. C., & Leake, D. B. (1989). Creativity and learning in a case-based explainer. *Artificial Intelligence, 40*, 353–385.

Schober, M. F. (1993). Spatial perspective-taking in conversation. *Cognition, 47*, 1–24.

Schober, M. F. (1995). Speakers, addressees, and frames of reference: Whose effort is minimized in conversations about locations? *Discourse Processes, 20*, 219–247.

Schooler, J. W., & Engstler-Schooler, T. Y. (1990). Verbal overshadowing of visual memories: Some things are better left unsaid. *Cognitive Psychology, 22*, 36–71.

Schwartz, D. L., & Black, J. B. (1996). Shuttling between depictive models and abstract rules: Induction and fallback. *Cognitive Science, 20*(4), 457–498.

Schyns, P. G., & Rodet, L. (1997). Categorization creates functional features. *Journal of Experimental Psychology: Learning, Memory, and Cognition, 23*(3), 681–696.

Searle, J. R. (1992). *Rediscovery of the mind.* Cambridge, MA: MIT Press.

Seifert, C. M. (1994). The role of goals in retrieving analogical cases. In J. A. Barnden & K. J. Holyoak (Eds.), *Advances in connectionist and neural computation theory: Vol. 3. Analogy, metaphor and reminding* (pp. 95–125). Norwood, NJ: Ablex.

Shafer, G. (1996). *The art of causal conjecture.* Cambridge, MA: MIT Press.

Shastri, L., & Ajjanagadde, V. (1993). From simple associations to systematic reasoning. *Behavioral and Brain Sciences, 16*(3), 417–494.

Shepard, R. N. (1962). The analysis of proximities: Multidimensional scaling with an unknown distance function, 1. *Psychometrika, 27*(2), 125–140.

Shepard, R. N., & Cooper, L. A. (Eds.). (1982). *Mental images and their transformations.* Cambridge, MA: MIT Press.

Sloman, S. A. (1996). The empirical case for two systems of reasoning. *Psychological Bulletin, 119*(1), 3–22.

Smith, E. E., & Medin, D. L. (1981). *Categories and concepts.* Cambridge, MA: Harvard University Press.

Smith, E. E., Shoben, E. J., & Rips, L. J. (1974). Structure and process in semantic memory: A featural model for semantic decisions. *Psychological Review, 81*, 214–241.

Smith, L. B., & Sera, M. D. (1992). A developmental analysis of the polar structure of dimensions. *Cognitive Psychology*, *24*(1), 99–142.

Smolensky, P. (1988). On the proper treatment of connectionism. *Behavioral and Brain Sciences*, *11*(1), 1–74.

Smolensky, P. (1990). Tensor product variable binding and the representation of symbolic structures in connectionist systems. *Artificial Intelligence*, *46*, 159–216.

Smolensky, P. (1991). Connectionism, constituency, and the language of thought. In B. Loewer & G. Rey (Eds.), *Meaning in mind: Fodor and his critics* (pp. 201–227). Cambridge, MA: Blackwell.

Spalding, T. L., & Ross, B. H. (1994). Comparison-based learning: Effects of comparing instances during category learning. *Journal of Experimental Psychology: Learning, Memory, and Cognition*, *20*(6), 1251–1263.

Spelke, E. S. (1990). Principles of object perception. *Cognitive Science*, *14*(1), 29–56.

Spellman, B. A., & Holyoak, K. J. (1996). Pragmatics in analogical mapping. *Cognitive Psychology*, *31*, 307–346.

Squire, L. R. (1987). *Memory and brain*. New York: Oxford University Press.

Sternberg, R. J., & Davidson, J. E. (Eds.). (1995). *The nature of insight*. Cambridge, MA: MIT Press.

Stich, S. P., & Warfield, T. A. (Eds.). (1994). *Mental representation*. Cambridge, MA: Blackwell.

Suchman, L. A. (1987). *Plans and situated actions: The problem of human–machine communication*. New York: Cambridge University Press.

Sulin, R. A., & Dooling, D. J. (1974). Intrusion of a thematic idea in retention of prose. *Journal of Experimental Psychology*, *103*(2), 255–262.

Swinney, D. A., & Hakes, D. T. (1976). Effects of prior context upon lexical access during sentence comprehension. *Journal of Verbal Learning and Verbal Behavior*, *15*, 681–689.

Talmy, L. (1975). Semantics and syntax of motion. In J. Kimball (Ed.), *Syntax and semantics*. New York: Academic Press.

Talmy, L. (1983). How language structures space. In H. L. Pick & L. P. Acredolo (Eds.), *Spatial orientation: Theory, research, and application* (pp. 225–282). New York: Plenum Press.

Tarr, M. J., & Pinker, S. (1989). Mental rotation and orientation-dependence in shape recognition. *Cognitive Psychology*, *21*, 233–282.

Taylor, H. A., & Tversky, B. (1992). Spatial mental models derived from survey and route descriptions. *Journal of Memory and Language*, *31*, 261–292.

Taylor, H. A., & Tversky, B. (1996). Perspective in spatial descriptions. *Journal of Memory and Language*, *35*(3), 371–391.

Thagard, P. (1989). Explanatory coherence. *Behavioral and Brain Sciences*, *12*, 435–502.

Thagard, P., Holyoak, K. J., Nelson, G., & Gochfeld, D. (1990). Analog retrieval by constraint satisfaction. *Artificial Intelligence*, *46*, 259–310.

Thelen, E. (1995). Time-scale dynamics and the development of an embodied cognition. In R. F. Port & T. van Gelder (Eds.), *Mind as motion* (pp. 69–100). Cambridge, MA: MIT Press.

Thelen, E., & Smith, L. B. (1994). *A dynamic systems approach to the development of cognition and action*. Cambridge, MA: MIT Press.

Tomasello, M. (1995). Pragmatic contexts for early verb learning. In M. Tomasello & W. E. Merriman (Eds.), *Beyond names for things* (pp. 115–146). Mahwah, NJ: Lawrence Erlbaum Associates.

Tourangeau, R., & Sternberg, R. J. (1981). Aptness in metaphor. *Cognitive Psychology*, *13*, 27–55.

Treisman, A., & Schmidt, H. (1982). Illusory conjunctions in the perception of objects. *Cognitive Psychology*, *14*, 107–141.

Tversky, A. (1977). Features of similarity. *Psychological Review*, *84*(4), 327–352.

Tversky, A., & Gati, I. (1982). Similarity, separability and the triangle inequality. *Psychological Review*, *89*(2), 123–154.

Tversky, A., & Kahneman, D. (1974). Judgment under uncertainty: Heuristics and biases. *Science, 185*, 1124–1131.

Tversky, B., & Hemenway, K. (1984). Objects, parts and categories. *Journal of Experimental Psychology: General, 113*(2), 169–191.

Tye, M. (1991). *The imagery debate.* Cambridge, MA: MIT Press.

Ullman, S. (1984). Visual routines. *Cognition, 18*, 97–159.

Ullman, S. (1996). *High-level vision.* Cambridge, MA: MIT Press.

Uttal, W. R. (1971). The psychobiological silly season—or—what happens when neurophysiological data become psychological theories. *Journal of General Psychology, 84*, 151–166.

Vandeloise, C. (1991). *Spatial prepositions: A case study from French* (A. R. K. Bosch, Trans.). Chicago: University of Chicago Press.

Van Gelder, T. (1992). *What might cognition be if not computation?* (Cognitive Science Research Report 75). Bloomington: Indiana University.

Van Gelder, T., & Port, R. F. (1995). It's about time: An overview of the dynamical approach to cognition. In R. F. Port & T. Van Gelder (Eds.), *Mind as motion.* Cambridge, MA: MIT Press.

Vosniadou, S., & Brewer, W. F. (1992). Mental models of the earth: A study of conceptual change in childhood. *Cognitive Psychology, 24*(4), 535–585.

Vygotsky, L. (1986). *Thought and language.* Cambridge, MA: MIT Press.

Ward, T. B. (1994). Structured imagination: The role of category structure in exemplar generation. *Cognitive Psychology, 27*(1), 1–40.

Ward, T. B. (1995). What's old about new ideas. In S. M. Smith, T. B. Ward, & R. A. Finke (Eds.), *The creative cognition approach* (pp. 157–178). Cambridge, MA: MIT Press.

Wason, P. C., & Johnson-Laird, P. N. (1972). *Psychology of reasoning: Structure and content.* Cambridge, MA: Harvard University Press.

Weisberg, R. W. (1995). Prolegomena to theories of insight in problem solving: A taxonomy of problems. In R. J. Sternberg & J. E. Davidson (Eds.), *The nature of insight* (pp. 157–196). Cambridge, MA: MIT Press.

Wellman, H. M. (1990). *The child's theory of mind.* Cambridge, MA: MIT Press.

Wertheimer, M. (1950). Laws of organization in perceptual forms. In W. D. Ellis (Ed.), *A source book of Gestalt psychology.* New York: Humanities Press. (Original work published 1923)

Wharton, C. M., Holyoak, K. J., Downing, P. E., Lange, T. E., Wickens, T. D., & Melz, E. R. (1994). Below the surface: Analogical similarity and retrieval competition in reminding. *Cognitive Psychology, 26*(1), 64–101.

White, B. Y., & Frederiksen, J. R. (1990). Causal model progressions as a foundation for intelligent learning environments. *Artificial Intelligence, 42*(1), 99–157.

Whitley, L. D. (Ed.). (1993). *Foundations of genetic algorithms* (Vol. 2). San Mateo, CA: Morgan Kaufmann.

Widrow, B., & Hoff, M. E. (1960). Adaptive switching circuits. In *IRE WESCON Convention Record* (pp. 96–104). New York: IRE.

Williams, M. D., Hollan, J. D., & Stevens, A. L. (1983). Human reasoning about a simple physical system. In D. Gentner & A. L. Stevens (Eds.), *Mental models* (pp. 131–153). Hillsdale, NJ: Lawrence Erlbaum Associates.

Wittgenstein, L. (1968). *Philosophical investigations* (G. E. M. Anscombe, Trans.). New York: Macmillan.

Woods, W. A. (1975). What's in a link: Foundations for semantic networks. In D. G. Bobrow & A. M. Collins (Eds.), *Representations and understanding: Studies in cognitive science* (pp. 35–82). New York: Academic Press.

Yamauchi, T., & Markman, A. B. (1998). *Category learning by inference and classification: The effect of multiple feature instantiations.* Manuscript in preparation.

Yu, A. C., & Margoliash, D. (1996). Temporal hierarchical control of singing in birds. *Science, 273*, 1871–1875.

Author Index

Subject Index